THE FUTURE OF ISLAMIC BANKING AND FINANC IN INDONESIA

Sharia compliance is the *raison d'etre* of Islamic banks. All of their instruments and activities should be based on *sharia* principles, which unfortunately exposes them to greater risks than their conventional counterparts, regulated under the dual banking system in Indonesia. These include inconsistencies between *fatwas*, unique reputational risks and inefficiencies in the regulatory framework governing Islamic banks.

The Future of Islamic Banking and Finance in Indonesia: Performance, Risk and Regulation critically examines the less-studied issue of developing an Islamic banking regulatory and supervisory framework that considers the risk pressures faced by Islamic banks operations in an Indonesian financial sector dominated by conventional banks. The book assesses the extent to which the global financial standards of the Basel Accords have been followed by Islamic banks in Indonesia, with respect to their regulation, supervision and risk management, to highlight the unresolved tensions in the multiple regulatory and supervisory institutions. The book proposes a middle-ground approach that accommodates modification of the existing financial regulatory and supervisory system in line with international best practice. The reforms proposed in this book offer a way for financial regulatory and supervisory agencies to further develop modern Islamic law and finance.

The book will be a valuable resource for scholars and policymakers interested in the dual banking system in Indonesia.

Romi Adetio Setiawan is a PhD graduate from Western Sydney University, Australia in the field of Islamic banking and finance law, and a lecturer of Islamic banking and finance at the State Islamic University of Bengkulu, Indonesia.

Islamic Business and Finance Series
Series Editor: Ishaq Bhatti

There is an increasing need for western politicians, financiers, bankers, and indeed the western business community in general to have access to high quality and authoritative texts on Islamic financial and business practices. Drawing on expertise from across the Islamic world, this new series will provide carefully chosen and focused monographs and collections, each authored/edited by an expert in their respective field all over the world.

The series will be pitched at a level to appeal to middle and senior management in both the western and the Islamic business communities. For the manager with a western background the series will provide detailed and up-to-date briefings on important topics; for the academics, postgraduates, business communities, manager with western and an Islamic background the series will provide a guide to best practice in business in Islamic communities around the world, including Muslim minorities in the west and majorities in the rest of the world.

The Informal Economy and Islamic Finance
The Case of Organization of Islamic Cooperation Countries
Shabeer Khan

Digital Transformation in Islamic Finance
A Critical and Analytical View
Edited by Yasushi Suzuki and Mohammad Dulal Miah

The Islamic Finance Industry
Issues and Challenges
Edited by Burak Çikiryel and Tawfik Azrak

Shariah Governance in Islamic Banking Institutions
Edited by Shafiullah Jan and Muhammad Ismail

The Future of Islamic Banking and Finance in Indonesia
Performance, Risk and Regulation
Romi Adetio Setiawan

For more information about this series, please visit: www.routledge.com/Islamic-Business-and-Finance-Series/book-series/ISLAMICFINANCE

The Future of Islamic Banking and Finance in Indonesia

Performance, Risk and Regulation

Romi Adetio Setiawan

Routledge
Taylor & Francis Group
LONDON AND NEW YORK

First published 2024
by Routledge
4 Park Square, Milton Park, Abingdon, Oxon OX14 4RN

and by Routledge
605 Third Avenue, New York, NY 10158

Routledge is an imprint of the Taylor & Francis Group, an informa business

British Library Cataloguing-in-Publication Data
A catalogue record for this book is available from the British Library

Library of Congress Cataloging-in-Publication Data
Names: Setiawan, Romi Adetio, author.
Title: The future of Islamic banking and finance in Indonesia : performance, risk and regulation / Romi Adetio Setiawan.
Description: New York : Routledge, 2023. | Includes bibliographical references and index.
Identifiers: LCCN 2023002821 (print) | LCCN 2023002822 (ebook) | ISBN 9781032494715 (hardback) | ISBN 9781032494777 (paperback) | ISBN 9781003393986 (ebook)
Subjects: LCSH: Banks and banking—Religious aspects—Islam. | Banking law—Indonesia. | Finance (Islamic law)—Indonesia.
Classification: LCC HG3368.A6 S485 2023 (print) | LCC HG3368.A6 (ebook) | DDC 332.109598—dc23/eng/20230510
LC record available at https://lccn.loc.gov/2023002821
LC ebook record available at https://lccn.loc.gov/2023002822

ISBN: 978-1-032-49471-5 (hbk)
ISBN: 978-1-032-49477-7 (pbk)
ISBN: 978-1-003-39398-6 (ebk)

DOI: 10.4324/9781003393986

Typeset in Bembo
by Apex CoVantage, LLC

This book is dedicated to my parents, my beloved wife, my kids and my brothers, without whose support I would not have been able to finish this book.

Contents

Glossary of Arabic and Indonesian Terms

Notes on terms used in the book

Both Arabic and Indonesian words have been italicised, except for proper names such as Qur'an and Majelis Ulama Indonesia.

The transcription of Arabic terms has usually been simplified by removing the diacritical marks that conventionally indicate pronunciation. For example, *sharī'ah* has been simplified to *sharia*: the *ī* (representing *yā'*) has been replaced with 'i', the phoneme ' (representing *'ayn*) has been suppressed and the *h* (representing *hā'*) has been suppressed.

When it comes to plural terms in Arabic, in some instances Indonesian conventions governing the use of Arabic words are followed (for example, *ulama* is used as both a plural and a singular noun), and in some instances English conventions are followed (for example, rather than *ahadith*, the term *hadith* is used as both a singular and a plural term).

After definitions of terms have been introduced (often in footnotes), there is periodic switching between Arabic, Indonesian and their English equivalents without notice. For example, sometimes *sharia* and sometimes 'Islamic law' is used.

'Urf tijari	common business
'Urf	customary practices or laws (synonymous with *adat*)
Adat	customary practices or laws (synonymous with *urf*)
Akad	contract, covenant
Al-'ahdu	agreement
Al-kharaj bi al dhaman	business transactions related to risks or liabilities
Al-kharaj bi al-ghonm	responsibility related to business transactions
Al-kutub al-mu'tabarah	the standard classical books which are used in *ijtihad*
Al-madhahib al-arba'ah	four Sunni schools of Islamic jurisprudence
Al-taysir al-manhaji	following a lenient opinion by the correct method of Islamic jurisprudence
Ba'i	sale, business activities
Ba'i al-inah	double sale used to circumvent the prohibition of lending with interest
Ba'i hukmi	a transaction is made based on meeting the formality condition

Ba'i ma'dhum	sale without possession
Ba'i mu'ajjal	a sale where the forward assets can be delivered later
Bathil	falsehood, void (legal)
Dalil	definitive proof, sign, indication
Darurah	necessity, need
Fatwa	legal opinion
Fiqh	Islamic jurisprudence
Fiqh muamalah	Islamic jurisprudence dealing with transactions
Fuqaha'	the experts in Islamic jurisprudence
Gharar	uncertainty or deceptive ambiguity
Hadith	narration of the words and deeds of the Prophet Muhammad
Hajj	pilgrimage
Halal	lawful, permissible
Hamish jiddiyah	security deposit held as collateral
Haram	unlawful, forbidden
Haramain	the two sacred places Medina and Mecca
Hilah	legal stratagem to achieve some desired outcome
Hukam-ul-asl	origin of law (also known as *asl*)
I'adah al-nazahar	review of the previous legal case
Ibadat	faith and worship (such as prayer and fasting)
Ibaha	permissibility (associated with the *fiqh* principle that anything is permitted as long it is not specifically prohibited)
Ijarah	lease
Ijarah wa iqtina	lease and ownership (also known as *ijarah muntahia bittamleek*)
Ijitihad	independent reasoning
Ijma'	consensus
Ijtihad jama'i	collective ijtihad
Ikhtilaf	difference of opinion
Illat	effective cause
Istidlal	looking to other arguments
Istihsan	juridical preference
Istinbath	conclusion
Istislah	public interest, collective good (synonymous with *maslahah mursalah*)
Istisna	a contract for the acquisition of goods by manufacture
Khatr	danger
Khud'ah	deception or cheating
Kitab	book
Kitab kuning	classical books of Islamic jurisprudence which are normally taught in Islamic boarding schools
Lil hajah	urgent need
Madhab	Islamic school of law (the four Sunni schools of law: Shafi'i, Maliki, Hanafi, and Hanbali)
Mafsadah	detrimental activities that cause market distortions

Manhaj	following the correct method from the four schools of Islamic jurisprudence
Maqasid al-sharia	the overarching purpose/objectives of Islamic law
Maqasid juz'i	a specific objective
Mas'alah furuiyyah	minor matters of branch issues
Mas'alah ushuliyah	fundamental principle
Maslahah mursalah	public interest, collective good (synonymous with *istislah*)
Maysir	gambling, speculation
Mu'allaq	to be linked or connected
Muamalah	commercial transactions
Mubah	permissible
Mudharabah	partnership investment contract (also known as *qiradh*)
Mudharib	fund manager
Mufti	jurist consult qualified to issue a *fatwa*
Mujazafat	speculative behaviour
Mujtahid	jurist
Muktamar	the highest level of meeting attended by representatives of each Islamic organisation
Murabahah	a sale with mark-up (profit)
Musharakah	contractual partnership; participation in investment
Musyabbah bih	the resemblance of original law to the already established case
Mutawatir	most authentic
Nash	original text from the Qur'an and *hadith*, also 'absolute truth'
Pancasila	the core philosophical principles of the Indonesian nation-state
Penghulu	headman of a region
Pesantren	Islamic boarding school
Qabdlu hukmi	a transaction made based on a legally agreed list of collective agreements
Qardh	loan
Qawaid fiqhiyah	Islamic legal maxims
Qiyas	analogical reasoning
Rabbul maal	property investor, capital owner (also known as *shahibul maal*)
Riba	usury or interest (interpretations are discussed in the text)
Ridha	willing to accept
Salaf	forward trade
Salam	a forward sale (fungible commodity)
Sharia	Islamic law (lit. 'the way')
Sukuk	Islamic securitisation
Sunnah	the living traditions based on the sayings and doings of the Prophet Muhammad

Sunni	a member of the largest branch of Islam who believes that the Caliph Abu Bakr was the rightful successor to Muhammad after his death; Sunni Muslims follow the traditions of the Prophet Muhammad and are guided by four schools of legal thought
Syubhat	doubt, obscurity (usually when there is no legal verdict on whether something is permitted or prohibited)
Ta'widh	the penalty if a debtor fails to repay borrowed money
Tabarru	making a donation, normally paid by a policy holder in Islamic insurance
Tahqiq al-manath	analysis of the determination of legal reasons
Takaful	Islamic insurance
Taqlid	conformity to the legal precedent of another without knowing the basis of that precedent
Tarjih	preference (usually when there are numerous principles and when judgement is not made due to an effective cause [*illat*] not being found)
Tawarruq	one of the Islamic derivative instruments
Tawarruq haqiqi	activity of Islamic hedging which is based on real transactions
Tawarruq Munazzam	complex hedging, organised Islamic hedging
Tijarah	trade-based contract
Ulama	Islamic jurists
Uqud al-murakkabah	combining two or more traditional contracts in one business activity
Urbun	earnest money; advance money used as the option in a sale contract
Usul al-Fiqh	the principles of jurisprudence or legal methodology (also known as *al-qawa'id al-ushuliyah*)
Wa'ad	a unilateral promise or undertaking which represents a contractual provision of all parties in the contract
Wadi'ah	deposit or deposit account
Wakkalah	agency, an investment contract in which agent represents investor
Zakah/Zakat	obligatory alms for Muslims
Zhulm	unjust acts of exploitation

Abbreviations and Acronyms

AAOIFI	Accounting and Auditing Organisations for Islamic Financial Institutions
BCBS	Basel Committee on Banking Supervision
BI	Bank Indonesia
BIS	Bank for International Settlements
BoD	Board of Directors
CAR	Capital Adequacy Ratio
FSA	Financial Service Authority
FSSA	Financial System Stability Assessment
GDP	Gross Domestic Product
GFC	Global Financial Crisis
IBRA	Indonesian Bank Restructuring Agency
ICAP	Impact and Consistency Assessment Program
IDIC	Indonesia Deposit Insurance Corporation
IFI	Islamic Financial Institution
IFSB	Islamic Financial Services Boards
IIFA	International Islamic Fiqh Academy
IIFM	International Islamic Financial Markets
IMB	*Ijarah Muntahia Bittamleek*
IMF	International Monetary Fund
IPF	Investor Protection Fund
IRR	Investment Risk Reserve
KPK	Komisi Pemberantasan Korupsi (Corruption Eradication Commission)
KSSK	Komite Stabilitas Sistem Keuangan (Financial System Stability Committee)
LCR	Liquidity Coverage Ratio
LIBOR	London Interbank Offered Rate
MENA	Middle East and North Africa
MPO	*Murabahah* Purchasing Order
MUI	Majelis Ulama Indonesia (the Indonesian Ulama Council)
NPF	Non-Performing Financing
NSB	National Sharia Board

NSB-MUI	National Sharia Board of Majelis Ulama Indonesia
NU	Nahdlatul Ulama
PBUH	Peace Be Upon Him (an honourific for Prophet Muhammad)
PER	Profit Equalisation Reserve
Persis	Persatuan Islam (an Islamic organisation in Indonesia)
PLS	Profit and Loss Sharing
PPKSK Law	Prevention and Resolution of Financial System Crisis Law
RWA	Risk Weighted Assets
SAC	Sharia Advisory Council
SSB	Sharia Supervisory Board
UNEP	United Nations Environment Programme

Tables and Figures

Tables

Figures

Acknowledgements

Romi Adetio Setiawan would like to acknowledge Routledge/Taylor & Francis for their guidance and continued support towards the publication of this book.

The author would like to express his highest gratitude to Dr Edward Mariyani-Squire and Dr Maria Bhatti for patiently devoting countless hours giving immense encouragement and outstanding support for this book project. He would also like to sincerely thank Professor Razeen Sappideen and Professor Carolyn Sappideen for their kindness, support, assistance and invaluable advice to successfully complete this book. He would also like to express his sincere gratitude to Tri Chamauliddah and our trio on Zi kids, for making his life more colourful and for everlasting love.

Lastly, the author would like to convey his heartiest gratitude and appreciation to all respected colleagues and institutions for their great help, inspiration and constant support in the publication of this book.

1 Introduction

1.1 Introduction

Modern Islamic banking, which emerged in Indonesia in the 1990s, faced several challenges from its inception. Chief among them was how Islamic banks would be regulated in a conventional banking environment. The Indonesian state responded to this challenge by creating what amounts to a dual banking system, with regulations governing both conventional and Islamic banks intended to be in line with global financial standards set by the Bank for International Settlements.[1] This book critically examines the pressures, constraints, and opportunities shaping the development of Islamic banking in Indonesia. It examines the unique, multifaceted regulatory framework that has been developed for Indonesian Islamic banks, which includes the Financial Service Authority (FSA), the National Sharia Board (NSB) of Majelis Ulama Indonesia (MUI), and individual banks' Sharia Supervisory Boards (SSB). This book raises questions about the effectiveness of this arrangement on the grounds of independency, accountability, and transparency. The book also explores some major challenges faced by Islamic banks relating to their operation in a highly competitive market environment dominated by conventional banks. In particular, it examines the risks faced by Islamic banks and how they have responded to the development of modern Islamic financial products which in some ways resemble conventional financial products while at the same time remaining compliant with the tenets of Islamic law (such as avoiding interest). It is argued that despite more flexible modern interpretations of *sharia*-compliant financial contracts, Islamic banks still face greater risks than conventional banks by virtue of their uniquely religious nature. However, it is further argued that through greater compliance with the international standards of the Basel Accords,[2] Islamic banks can improve their performance, especially via reforms to their supervisory and regulatory structures which harmonise with Islamic principles.

1.2 Scope of the Book

1.2.1 The Emergence of the Islamic Financial Industry

The modern Islamic financial industry is inspired and sustained by a classical commercial heritage. It is hard to exactly pinpoint when the first modern Islamic banking

DOI: 10.4324/9781003393986-1

activities took place; as Orsingher has noted: "[i]t is impossible with the documents discovered so far, whatever their kind, to determine when banking operations first took place or to provide a continuous uninterrupted account of their evolution".[3] However, in the modern era, most scholars believe that the pioneering experiment of reviving classical Islamic commercial law occurred in the 1960s in Egypt with the Islamic financial project of Mit Ghamr.[4] The establishment of the Islamic Development Bank in 1975 by the Organisation of Islamic Cooperation's member countries further encouraged member countries to strengthen the development of the Islamic banking sector.[5] The first modern full-fledged Islamic commercial bank, Dubai Islamic Bank, was set up in 1975.[6] Since then, the Islamic financial industry's growth trajectory has continued upward. Between 2009 and 2019, Islamic banking expanded at an average growth rate of 13.1%.[7] The total value of assets held by Islamic banks was estimated to be at US$2.733 trillion by the end of December 2019.[8] As such Islamic banking is now recognised globally as an alternative to conventional banking and has been successful in gaining general acceptance in Muslim and some non-Muslim countries, such as the United Kingdom, Luxembourg, South Africa, Australia, Austria, and Hong Kong.

Islamic banking is based on principles directed at reducing poverty and sharing prosperity, and has the potential to be a powerful force contributing to economic development.[9] Since *riba*[10] is categorically prohibited in classical Islamic law, but trading is permissible, modern Islamic banking is based on risk-sharing contracts: profit-and-loss-sharing partnerships (*musharakah* and *mudharabah*[11]), trade-based contracts (*tijarah*[12]) and fee-based contracts. Thus, all kind of interest-bearing contracts (for deposits and loans) which are risk-shifting are prohibited.[13]

An important aspect of Islamic banking is that it provides financing mostly for production, focusing on the need for working capital to enterprises in addition to their normal day-to-day retail banking.[14] It is important for many members of the Muslim community to use banking services which comply with the *sharia*.[15] Conventional banking transactions based on interest are thus rendered unacceptable to them. Further, it is impermissible for Muslims to invest in harmful activities, such as gambling and other activities/products considered harmful to society (especially the poor).[16] This also renders conventional banking unacceptable because in general it is a source of capital for businesses engaged in such activities.

Since the classical commercial heritage of Islam appears to contain limited scriptural and legal sources relating to an Islamic banking system, Islamic scholars, regulators, financial practitioners, and the general public consider the modern Islamic banking system to be an historic innovation. Yet despite its recent emergence in the last three decades, and despite the stereotype that Islamic law was 'set in stone' centuries ago, Islamic scholars have issued a number of *fatwas* sanctioning as '*sharia*-compliant' certain financial instruments that can be used by Islamic banks. Further, they have been continuously refining their judgements and conceptual apparatuses so as to improve the functionality and competitiveness of Islamic banks. However, there is still a need for uniformity of standards in Islamic banking because ambiguity on some matters exist. This is primarily due to different *fatwas* being issued within and across different nation-state jurisdictions. As Hassan and Mollah have noted, contemporary Islamic banking practices require the clarity of standardisation of Islamic financial instruments and professional training in the use of these instruments.[17] The differing opinions among Islamic scholars in the interpretation of the *sharia* and how it is evolving in the modern financial system is an issue that will repeatedly appear and be discussed throughout this book.

1.2.2 Challenges and Issues of Islamic Banking in Indonesia

During the recent global financial crisis, Islamic banking strategies of making low-risk investments due to risk-sharing, the avoidance of interest (*riba*), and the avoidance of complex derivatives involving speculation (*maysir*) and ambiguity (*gharar*),[18] appear to have had a protective effect and ensured their survival.[19] On the other hand, outside of such crisis situations, Islamic banks are severely disadvantaged in comparison to conventional banks in a number of ways. As with other financial institutions, bank profitability is influenced by the level of cost-efficiency, capital, and asset quality.[20] The cost of finance in Islamic banks is expensive for two reasons: first, because of their inability to use interest deductions to reduce their cost of capital (the use of debt), and secondly, by reason of the former, Islamic banks have to rely on equity capital (on which competitive dividends have to be paid) and on profit-sharing interest-free deposits.[21] In addition, Islamic banks can face the problem of adverse selection because profit-sharing contracts tend to attract riskier capital-poor entrepreneurs, and they also face a moral hazard problem because their profitability depends on the honest reporting by those entrepreneurs. Further, they are less able to mitigate risk by means of optimal portfolio diversification because of the legal prohibition on a range of products and activities. This cascades into another problem: since most depositors are risk-averse, and since Islamic banks are supposed to offer variable returns depending on the profitability of their investments, they can face liquidity risk if deposit returns fall below conventional market rates.[22]

It is arguable that these problems have inhibited the growth of Islamic banking in Indonesia. At the end of December 2020, the assets of Indonesian Islamic banks were estimated to be around 6.51% of bank assets for the market as a whole in contrast to 37% (end 2020) in neighbouring Malaysia.[23] According to a PWC survey, the growth of Islamic banking in Indonesia is estimated to reach up to 10% by 2025, which is well below the 2023 target of 15% set by Indonesia's FSA.[24] This has led to pressure for pragmatic compromises in Islamic banking practices. As Mariyani-Squire notes:

> [s]ome Muslim economists argue that in the real world of an increasingly global, competitive, and technologically advanced banking industry, it is simply not possible to maintain the standards embodied in the idealised theory of Islamic banking. Pragmatic compromises based on empirical realities need to be made in order for Islamic banking to exist at all. To remain viable private enterprises, Islamic banks must take into account and respond to the actual wants and needs of their potential clients. Since those clients do not themselves perfectly conform to the assumptions of theologically informed

> theory, to survive Islamic banks must modify their practices to take this fact into account.[25]

A central concern of this book, however, is that, aside from reduced profitability due to the prohibition on interest and the requirement of risk-sharing, Indonesian Islamic banks must also face the serious challenges of legal standardisation, supervisory frameworks, risk-management practices, product innovation, and jurisprudential disputes relating to the application of the prohibition of interest. Unsurprisingly, the last of these is the most controversial and is by no means restricted to Indonesia. As Bhatti notes:

> Although Islamic scholars unanimously agree that *riba* is prohibited under *Shari'a*, there is no consensus on the definition of *riba*. . . . How the prohibition against *riba* relates to contemporary finance is the subject of debate among Islamic scholars and in the world of Islamic banking and finance.[26]

1. *Regulatory and Supervisory Challenges*

Both Islamic banks and conventional banks are authorised to operate in Indonesia. The FSA is the main regulator for all these banks. The FSA adopts a risk-management approach based on international standards established under the Basel Accords. These international standards raise unique issues for Islamic banks.[27] Chapter 7 argues that the current regulatory and supervisory framework for Indonesian Islamic banks is not perfectly suited to them due to their *sharia*-specific risks, but that the Indonesian banking system, and Islamic banks in particular, should fully embrace the accountability and transparency principles of the Basel Accords so as to better integrate into the global financial market. It is noted in Chapter 8, however, that the application of these international standards may have the effect of requiring Islamic banks to have higher capital reserves to minimise their risks, which may reduce their profitability and make them less competitive than conventional banks.[28]

It is argued that there is a need for more systematic supervision of Islamic banking in Indonesia. Contentious issues include conflicts of interest between the management of Islamic banks and the Islamic banking supervisory bodies, especially in the form of '*fatwa* shopping';[29] the lack of transparency in banks' *sharia* compliance; and the high cost of achieving *sharia* compliance when SSB are overburdened with a complex and unpredictable approval process. A related problem is the limited number of Islamic scholars who have expertise in both finance and Islamic law and who are respected public figures in Indonesia. All of these issues, along with possible reforms informed by the Malaysian model of governance, will be discussed in Chapter 4.

2. *Risk Challenges*

Islamic banks in Indonesia are subject to the Basel rules because they share many common risk factors with conventional banks, but they also face additional challenges to their risk profiles due to *sharia* principles.[30] There are various ways of potentially managing risks. There is, first, the basic risk-sharing mechanisms of partnerships where all parties share profits and losses. Secondly, there are the risk-management principles under the Basel Accords. The Basel Accords provide international standards for risk management.[31] Thirdly, there is risk shifting (derivatives) and, finally, risk avoidance (hedging).[32]

As already mentioned, Islamic banks are principally aimed at promoting fairness via the profit-and-loss-sharing partnership model. Currently, however, this model is used in a quite limited fashion by Islamic banks because of the complexity inherent in projecting profit returns and the risk of losing capital holder investments. Islamic banks have been compelled to develop alternative financial instruments while simultaneously contending with the conflicting interpretations and opinions of scholars as to whether new kinds of financial instruments/products are acceptable in Islamic banking, or whether they too closely resemble conventional financial instruments. This issue will be critically examined by providing case studies with reference to how Islamic financial instruments are implemented in Indonesia and Malaysia to explore whether the risk-sharing principle hinders the efficiency and capital solvency of Islamic banks.

Risk shifting[33] and risk avoidance[34] are significant problems for Islamic banking because of the requirement that instruments be based on tangible assets and risk-sharing. This restricts the ability of Islamic banks to use some conventional strategies and instruments, such as hedging and derivatives. Islamic banks are less able than conventional banks to shift balance sheet risks and therefore are at increased risk of loss, which renders them less competitive both domestically and internationally.[35] The problem is exacerbated by the lack of innovation in Islamic banking instruments, as well as disputes among Islamic scholars on the permissibility of using these instruments. This may be in part due to the lack of knowledge and expertise in developing effective products in Islamic banking.[36] Consequently, one of the aims of this research is to provide guidance to policymakers and Islamic banking practitioners in relation to developing new Islamic financial instruments in keeping with global financial standards by examining the views of classical scholars and contemporary jurists.

Finally, in relation to risk management, it is argued that the regulatory bodies should realise that the existing national standards are unsatisfactory and that reforms are required in line with international standards whilst keeping in mind the constraint of *sharia* compliance.[37] It is a matter of ongoing debate as to how these international standards – which are technically not binding unless incorporated into domestic law – apply or can be adapted to Islamic banks, and to what extent these standards could assist the growth of Islamic banking.[38]

1.3 Methods and Sources

This book provides insights into how Islamic financial instruments and regulatory arrangements have evolved from the Indonesian perspective. It critically evaluates the risk-shifting and risk-avoidance strategies associated with the development of new Islamic banking products and argues that risks can be reduced through regulatory and supervisory reforms.

As such, one of the principal contributions of this book lies in its analysis of how *sharia* compliance contributes to unique risks to Islamic banks in Indonesia's dual banking system; how the banks have responded by engaging in somewhat contentious legal-financial innovations, which carry their own dangers (such as reputational risk); and the extent to which the existing Indonesian regulatory and supervisory frameworks diverge from international financial standards. Examining the regulatory framework for the dual banking system in Indonesia will enable the identification of unique sources of risk for Islamic banks that are not commonly discussed in the Islamic finance literature. It also points the way to possible regulatory/supervisory reforms compatible with both international standards and Islamic principles that would reduce risk and improve the performance of Islamic banks. The findings provide valuable insights for Islamic banks, especially with respect to the importance of standardisation, regulatory and supervisory reforms, and risk management in Indonesia so as to increase the competitiveness of Indonesian Islamic banking domestically and at the international level.

Three approaches to discursive analysis will be employed through the book. First, a standard doctrinal approach is used in the following areas:

- It examines classical and contemporary *sharia* of commercial law and whether there are indications as to how the *sharia* might be developing or evolving in the future.
- For comparative purposes, it locates other relevant sources, such as legislation and case law in Malaysia, the MENA region, and Australia, on Islamic banking.
- It conducts a doctrinal analysis pertaining to international financial standards (Basel Accords and Islamic Financial Services Board [IFSB][39]) to see the internal consistency of Islamic financial regulation and supervision.

Secondly, a comparative approach is used when examining Islamic financial regulations and supervisory arrangements across national jurisdictions in order to identify and critically assess the similarities and differences between them, including a detailed analysis on strengths or vulnerabilities. The book will also suggest potential reforms by comparing different Islamic finance laws and legal institutions.

Thirdly, it uses the comparative legal cultures approach to analyse the concept that *sharia* is an expression and development of the general culture of a society. This approach is premised on the belief that *sharia* as practised in Indonesia would not be clearly understood without understanding the concepts, beliefs, and politics of Indonesian society and culture.

In terms of source material, the book draws upon both primary and secondary literature. Primary sources of legislative law and case law materials from official bodies include:

- Laws passed by Dewan Perwakilan Rakyat (the house of representatives of the Republic of Indonesia) (e.g., *Law No 10 of 1998 on Banking* and *Law No 21 of 2008 on Islamic Banking*);

- FSA, BI, and Central Bank of Malaysia Regulations (e.g., *FSA Regulation No 24/POJK.03/2015 on the Products and Services of Islamic and Islamic Business Units, FSA Regulation No 18/POJK.03/2016 on the Risk Management Implementation for Commercial Bank, BI Regulation No 11/3/PBI/2009 on Islamic Bank, BI Regulation No 11/15/PBI/2009 on Converting the Conventional Bank into Islamic Bank, BI Regulation No 6/24/PBI/2004 on Banks Applying Islamic Principles, FSA Regulation No 65/POJK.03/2016 on Risk Management Practice for Islamic Bank and Islamic Business Units*, and *CBM Act, 2009 [Act 701], CBM Act, 1958 [Act 519]*);
- Decisions of Indonesian courts (e.g., *Bank BNI Syariah vs Darman Sugianto* [2019] 13/Pdt.G/2019/PTA.MU, 1–14 [Religious High Court of North Moluccas], and *CV Benua Enginering Consultant vs PT Bank Muamalat Syariah* [2012] 93/PUU-X/2012 1 [Constitutional Court of Indonesia], and *Syarifuddin Arsyad Temenggung [2019] 1555K/Pid.Sus/2019* [The Supreme Court of the Republic of Indonesia]);
- International banking standards of international regulators (e.g., The Basel Framework 2021, IFSB-17 Core Principles for Islamic Finance Regulation, AAOIFI 2012 on Governance and Auditing Standards);
- Standard operational procedures of Indonesian Islamic banking (e.g., Standard 5 of Islamic Banking for *Mudharabah* instrument); and
- *Fatwas* of the NSB of Indonesian Council of Ulama (e.g., Fatwa DSN MUI No.82/DSN-MUI/VIII/2011 on Commodity Trading Based on Sharia Principles on the Commodity Exchange) and the International Islamic Fiqh Academy (IIFA) on the use of organised *tawarruq* in its 19th meeting.

Secondary sources range from peer-reviewed publications, books, and media to unpublished works. Several legal case studies from Indonesian Islamic finance law are examined. The Malaysian cases is also analysed for comparative purposes, since Malaysia and Indonesia share many similarities, including history, culture, language, and religion. Case studies from the MENA region are also drawn upon because this region has a large Muslim population and is an Islamic jurisdiction.

1.4 Structure

The book consists of eight substantive chapters and a conclusion. In summary, the content of each chapter is as follows:

Chapter 2 lays out the primary and secondary sources of Islamic law, its jurisprudential theory, and the practice of *ijtihad* (independent reasoning) in Indonesia. This chapter suggests that in order to cope with an ever-changing world of contemporary banking issues, the dynamic methods of reasoning from Islamic jurisprudence can and should be applied to reduce tensions between Islamic scholars and avoid sectarian conflict in society. This serves as the necessary background to understanding potential conflicts between secular regulations and Islamic requirements for Islamic banking in Indonesia.

Chapter 3 discusses the capacity of Islamic law to adapt to the Indonesian regulatory and supervisory frameworks that govern its dual banking system of conventional and Islamic banks. It looks at the rationale, the objectives, and the impact of state-mandated regulation and supervision in Indonesian financial services. This chapter also seeks to demonstrate that there are weaknesses and challenges confronting Indonesia's dual banking system due to the secular state applying a framework premised on conventional banking, but which do not adhere with Islamic principles defining Islamic banks.

Chapter 4 further analyses the legal and institutional development of Islamic banking in Indonesia. Most importantly, it discusses the effectiveness of the relatively recently developed Islamic banking regulatory and supervisory framework. Particular attention is given to the intermediation between the FSA and the NSB-MUI, and to the independency, accountability, and transparency of banks' SSBs. This chapter also makes recommendations in relation to the reform of this supervisory system with respect to the Indonesian state financial authorities in order to ensure the stable functioning of Islamic banking and the overall Indonesian financial system.

In the chapters that follow, attention is focused on major challenges that are particular to Islamic banking in Indonesia. These include disputes over whether modern Islamic finance is 'truly' Islamic, including whether derivatives are permissible; whether Islamic banking is and can be compatible with Basel Accord directives; and whether Islamic banks face greater risks to their operations than conventional banking.

Chapter 5 explores the controversy in relation to Islamic finance's alleged mimicking of conventional financial practices which would thereby violate the substance of Islamic prohibitions of *riba*. As such, this chapter discusses the challenges of innovating and codifying *sharia*-compliant products. It examines how Islamic finance is attempting to evolve and keep up with dynamic changes in the banking sector whilst simultaneously trying to comply with *sharia* principles.

Chapter 6 examines the challenge of specific risks faced by Islamic banks, such as risk shifting and risk avoidance, by focusing on the controversy over the use of hedging and derivative instruments. It provides an analysis of the permissibility of *sharia*-compliant derivatives – *tawarruq* – from the *fatwas* of different countries and looks at controversial financial products to adjudicate the compatibility of *sharia* principles as compared to conventional banks' instruments regarding prudence and solvency.

After discussing the issue of inconsistency of the rulings of different *fatwa* bodies and the consequent problem of incorporating *sharia*-compliant financial products into regulation, Chapter 7 critically examines the contrasts between the regulatory and supervisory frameworks of Indonesian Islamic finance and the Basel Accords. It thus explores the challenges facing Islamic banking in implementing international standards in order to integrate into the modern global economy. It outlines how Islamic scholars have responded to this international financial standard from the perspective of *sharia* compliance. Chapter 7 argues that adherence to the Basel Accords would be beneficial to Islamic banks, as it would increase the transparency and accountability of the regulatory and supervisory process and address issues related to conflicting *fatwas*.

Following this discussion, Chapter 8 will provide an extensive analysis of whether the *sharia* imperatives impact upon Islamic banks' market profitability and liquidity, and whether they are exposed to greater risks than their conventional peers. As such, Chapters 7 and 8 both discuss the extent that international financial standards have been followed by Islamic banks in Indonesia when addressing risks. Chapter 7 discusses whether the reforms to financial regulation and supervision are needed to meet today's international best practice set by Basel, while Chapter 8 considers whether institutional reforms are required to who oversees Islamic banks' financial risk supervision in the Indonesian dual banking system in order to reduce the risk-management deficiencies and to increase harmonisation with respect to best international standard practice.

Chapter 9 concludes the book and summarises the themes and problems discussed throughout. It also briefly outlines proposals for the resolution of the problems identified, especially in relation to global financial standards. In this way, insight is offered into how to further develop modern Islamic finance in Indonesia based on these proposals. Finally, the chapter draws out the importance of future research on the regulation, supervision, and risk-management framework of Islamic banks to make them a truly viable alternative system of financing in keeping with international best practices.

Notes

1 The Bank for International Settlements (BIS) is an international financial institution owned by central banks that aims to foster global monetary and financial stability through international coordination. See Bank for International Settlements, 'About BIS' www.bis.org.

2 The Basel Accords are a set of international standards for banking regulations put forth by the Basel Committee on Bank and Supervision (BCBS). Since it was enacted in 1988, the regulation of bank capital requirements has been substantially upgraded from Basel I, II, and III. Basel III was fully implemented in 2019. While Basel IV has not been released by the Basel Committee, it is expected to be more stringent as well as an enhancement of the Basel III rules. See M. Magnus et al., 'Upgrading the Basel Standards: From Basel III to Basel IV?' (October 2017) PE 587 *Economic Governance Support Unit, European Parliament Briefing Paper.*

3 Orsingher Roger, *Les Banques Dans Le Monde* [Bank of the World] (D.S. Ault trans, Macmillan, 1967) vii.

4 Tariq Alrifai, *Islamic Finance and the New Financial System: An Ethical Approach to Preventing Future Financial Crises* (Wiley, 2015) 101–103.

5 Ibid.

6 Ibid.

7 Global Islamic Finance Report, 'Overview of the Global Islamic Financial Services Industry' Edbiz Consulting Limited, 43, www.gifr.net/publications/gifr2020/intro.pdf.

8 Ibid., 39.

9 Abayomi A. Alawode, 'Brief Islamic Finance' (Pt World Bank) (2015) *Understanding Poverty Financial Sector*, www.worldbank.org/en/topic/financialsector/brief/islamic-finance.

10 *Riba* is defined as a contracted 'return (or increase) on debt' in any transaction where money is exchanged for the same denomination of money. Any increase or decrease by one side in this transaction is known as *riba* and is prohibited in the *sharia*. Its prohibition is clearly indicated in the Qur'an (3:130).

11 *Musharakah* and *Mudharabah* are partnership-based contracts. *Musharakah* is a partnership between parties where each one contributes their financial capital and labour as shared inputs. The profit and loss that may occur in the business is distributed according to the

capital share of the partners or upon an agreed ratio. See Mufti Muhammad Taqi Usmani, *An Introduction to Islamic Finance* (IdaratulMa'arif, 1999), 16. *Mudharabah* is another type of profit-sharing where one partner provides financial capital to another for investing for commercial purposes. The money comes from the first partner, who is called the *rabb-ul-mal*, or the capital owner, while the work of management and responsibility is carried out by another partner, the *mudharib*. See Habib Ahmed, 'Islamic Banking and Shari'ah Compliance: A Product Development Perspective' (2014) 3(2) *Journal of Islamic Finance, IIUM Institute of Islamic Banking and Finance* 15, 17.

12 *Tijarah* refers to compensational contracts in all forms of transactions intended for profit.

13 Fatwa Majelis Ulama Indonesia (Indonesian Council of Ulama legal verdict) *Regulation 2015 No. 1 interest rate.*

14 Shakir Ullah and Kun-ho Lee, 'Do Customers Patronize Islamic Banks for Shari'a Compliance?' (Pt Palgrave Macmillan) (2012) 17(3) *Journal of Financial Services Marketing* 206.

15 Tina Harrison and Essam B. Ibrahim, *Islamic Finance: Principles, Performance and Prospects* (Springer International Publishing AG, 2016) 33.

16 Ibid., 68.

17 Hassan Abul and Mollah Sabur, *Islamic Finance: Ethical Underpinnings, Products, and Institutions* (Palgrave Macmillan, 2018) 214.

18 *Maysir* literally means 'gambling' and includes any business activity where the monetary gains are derived from intentional speculation. *Gharar* means uncertainty or deceptive ambiguity that might lead to risk or loss. See Akhter Md Uddin, 'Principles of Islamic Finance: Prohibition of Riba, Gharr and Maysir' (Pt University Library of Munich) (2015)(9) https://mpra.ub.uni-muenchen.de/67711/1/MPRA_paper_67711.pdf.

19 Maher Hasan and Jemma Dridi, 'The Effects of the Global Crisis on Islamic and Conventional Banks: A Comparative Study' (2011) 2(2) *Journal of International Commerce, Economics and Policy* 163, 187.

20 The result of a survey from 51 Islamic banks in the MENA region from 1994 to 2012 shows that Islamic banks should increase their level of capital to increase their profitability and they should not rely entirely on classical financing since it has less impact on their capital earnings. See Hajer Zarrouk, Khoutem Ben Jedidia and Mouna Moualhi, 'Is Islamic Bank Profitability Driven by Same Forces as Conventional Banks?' (2016) 9(1) *International Journal of Islamic and Middle Eastern Finance and Management; Bingley* 46, 47.

21 Alabbad Amal, 'Essays on the Performance, Disclosure, and Corporate Governance of Islamic Banks' (2015). https://doi.org/doi:10.7282/T3S46V07.

22 Edward Mariyani-Squire, 'Tensions in Islamic Economics' (2013) 12(1) *Trikonomika* 1, 5.

23 Otoritas Jasa Keuangan, 'Snapshot Perbankan Syariah Desember 2020 [Snapshot of Indonesian Islamic Banking December 2020]' *Otoritas Jasa Keuangan*, www.ojk.go.id/id/kanal/syariah/berita-dan-kegiatan/publikasi/Pages/-Snapshot-Perbankan-Syariah-Desember-2020.aspx; Fitch Ratings Singapore, 'Malaysia's Islamic Banking Sector Continues to Expand Despite Pandemic', *Fitch Ratings* (Singapore) www.fitchratings.com/research/banks/malaysia-islamic-banking-sector-continues-to-expand-despite-pandemic-28-02-2021.

24 Indonesian Banking Survey, 'Weathering the Rise in Credit Risk: What's Next for Banks in Indonesia?' (2017) *PWC* 10, www.pwc.com/id/en/publications/assets/financialservices/ibs-2017.pdf.

25 Mariyani-Squire, above n 22, 5.

26 Maria Bhatti, *Islamic Law and International Commercial Arbitration* (Routledge, 2018) 152–154.

27 The existence of various sects in Islam makes the issue of *fatwa* more complicated due to different perceptions and interpretations of *fiqh* among Islamic scholars. See Institute of Islamic Banking and Insurance, *Shari'ah Rulings and Finance*, 20 December 2017, www.islamic-banking.com/explore/islamic-finance/shariah-rulings.

28 Muhammad Shaukat Malik, Ali Malik and Waqas Mustafa, 'Controversies That Make Islamic Banking Controversial: An Analysis of Issues and Challenges' (2011) 2(1) *American Journal of Social and Management Sciences* 41, 45.
29 There are serious potential conflicts of interest in Islamic banking due to *fatwa* shopping in which Islamic scholars are captured by the bank to issue the controversial fatwa for the sake of personal interest. See ibid., 42.
30 Ghiath Shabsigh et al., 'Ensuring Financial Stability in Countries with Islamic Banking' (2017) 5 *International Monetary Fund* 10, www.imf.org/en/Publications/Policy-Papers/Issues/2017/02/21/PP-Ensuring-Financial-Stability-in-Countries-with-Islamic-Banking.
31 Luca Errico and Mitra Farahbaksh, *Islamic Banking: Issues in Prudential Regulations and Supervision*, IMF Working Paper No 98/30, International Monetary Fund (1998).
32 Some products of conventional derivatives are not permitted according to Islamic principles due to high speculation and uncertainty. However, derivatives are the powerful instrument for hedging, transfer, and managing risk. This tool is often used by conventional banks to optimize investment portfolios. In 2006, over-the-counter contracts worldwide were estimated at US$410 trillion, and they will continue to expand slowly, but massively. Razeen Sappideen, 'The Regulation of Hedgefunds' (2016)(7) *Journal of Business Law* 1; Inwon Song and Carel Oosthuizen, *Islamic Banking Regulation and Supervision: Survey Results and Challenges*, IMF Working Paper No 14/220, International Monetary Fund (2014) 7.
33 Risk shifting is the transfer of risk to another party, which is normally mitigated by the adoption of a risk-based deposit insurance assessment system or derivative instruments. José Almeida Brito and Kose John, 'Leverage and Growth Opportunities: Risk-Avoidance Induced by Risky Debt' (2002) *SSRN Electronic Journal* 1, 7.
34 Risk avoidance is the removal of hazards or exposures that can significantly affect the organisation's assets by not taking any exposure to a loan or financial asset which have higher risks or by hedging. See ibid.
35 Islamic banking relies heavily on their assets and focus on risk-sharing in their banking activities and investment banking operations, while conventional banks are characterised by risk transfer. See Zarrouk, Ben Jedidia and Moualhi, above n 20, 8.
36 Simon Kennedy, News, 'Fitch: Islamic Finance Standardisation Will Be Slow', *Reuters* (London), www.reuters.com/article/fitch-islamic-finance-standardisation-wi/fitch-islamic-finance-standardisation-will-be-slow-idUSFitb5gH0f.
37 Indonesia is one of the founding members of the Islamic Financial Service Board (IFSB) and is also a member of the Basel Committee on Banking Supervision (BCBS) and the International Organisation of Securities Commission (IOSCO). These international financial standards (in some respects) have been adopted into the regulation by the FSA and BI in supervising and monitoring the conventional and Islamic financial institutions such as banks, insurance companies, and in capital markets. See Tirta Segara, 'Bank Indonesia Tuan Rumah IFSB Annual Meeting [Bank Indonesia Hosts the IFSB Annual Meeting]' (Pt Bank Indonesia) (2015) *Siaran Pers*, www.bi.go.id/id/ruang-media/siaran-pers/Pages/sp_172415.aspx [tr author].
38 Alfred Kammer et al., IMF Staff Discussion Note, *Islamic Finance: Opportunities, Challenges, and Policy Options*, International Monetary Fund No SDN/15/05 (2015) 17.
39 IFSB is the Islamic Financial Services Board. It is the international standard-setting organisation that promotes the stability and soundness of Islamic banking by issuing global prudential standards and guiding principles that specifically relate to Islamic banking activities, www.ifsb.org.

2 Sources of Islamic Law in Indonesia

2.1 Introduction

Before one can examine of the regulation of Islamic banking and finance in Indonesia, as discussed in later chapters, one must first engage with the basics of Islamic law (*sharia*), especially as practised in Indonesia. As such, this chapter begins by investigating the sources of *sharia*. It elucidates the view that Islamic jurisprudence (*fiqh*) allows for an adaptive approach in which jurists (*mujtahid*) use a variety methods of reasoning to develop new rulings (*ijtihad*) derived from one or more of the four surviving Sunni schools of Islamic jurisprudence (*al-madhahib al-arba'ah*) – the Hanafi school, the Maliki school, the Shafi'i school, and the Hanbali school.[1] Such methodological pluralism can and does tend to result in differing scholarly opinions on a very wide range of issues between and within these schools. The chapter will then examine the approaches taken by Islamic scholars to deal with these differences of legal opinion as a means of ultimately producing legal consensus (*ijma'*). It is argued that Indonesian Islamic scholars apply the dynamic methods of reasoning from Islamic jurisprudence in order to cope with an ever-changing world and to serve the public interest (*maslahah*). This chapter will also provide some insight into the role of the Indonesian state in reducing tensions between Islamic scholars so as to avoid confusion and sectarian conflict.

In countries where the majority of the population are Muslims, as in Indonesia, the incentive to develop an interest-free financial system has facilitated the development and growth of Islamic banking institutions. With its emphasis on more equitable financing and non-derivative type transactions, Islamic finance is seen as a foundation for the inclusion of an explicitly moral dimension into economic life.[2] In Indonesia, 99% of Muslims are Sunni and mostly follow the jurisprudential school initiated by Imam Muhammad b. Idris Shafi'i, initiated in the 8th century CE.[3] This chapter will not discuss the methodological intricacies of the four Sunni jurisprudential schools, but rather will outline the primary and secondary sources of the *sharia* in general and indicate how the *sharia* is capable of being adapted to the requirements of contemporary Indonesian Muslims.[4] It will also be shown, particularly in the Indonesian context, how disagreements between jurists can and do emerge in the process of adaptation.

DOI: 10.4324/9781003393986-2

In any discussion of the *sharia* in the Indonesian context, it should be borne in mind that, in contrast to several Muslim-majority countries, the Indonesian state is not a theocracy. Indeed, due to its Dutch colonial past, the Republic's Constitution and legal system is heavily inspired by the Roman-Dutch civil law system. Yet rather than describing Indonesia as a secular state in the sense of, for example, the French state which explicitly prohibits religious doctrines from informing or characterising public institutions and policies, the Indonesian state could more accurately be classified as a religiously pluralist one; that is, its state ideology, the *Pancasila*, enshrines religious equality for all major religions of the archipelago.[5] It has thus been uniquely labelled by some scholars a '*Pancasila* state'.[6] As such, although *sharia* rulings are not mandated under the constitution, nor can they override state law, elements of the *sharia* are not constitutionally prohibited from being *incorporated* within state laws.[7] (A further discussion on the role of the Indonesian government in developing Islamic finance will be discussed in Chapters 3 and 4.) Although the interaction of state law and the *sharia* is central to this book, it should be acknowledged that local customary law, which pre-dates modern legal structures and economic relations, have also played an important role across the Indonesian archipelago, especially at the local level. Even before any complex financial system existed, and even where specific knowledge about the Islamic prohibition on interest was lacking, it appears likely that the basic concept of profit-sharing – not just between individuals, but at a communal level – was well understood and practised in civil society. This is discussed further in the next section.

2.2 Sources of *Sharia*

Since the majority of Muslims in Indonesia are Sunni,[8] this book will be focused throughout on the Sunni approach to interpreting and extending *sharia*. Islam is a juridical religion – that is, it is not just a religion of belief, but also a religion of law. Indeed, all Muslims should be aware of and adhere to the *sharia*, which encompasses all aspects of their daily lives. Islamic law is regarded as being derived from divine revelation – for Muslims, absolute truth (*nash*) – but it also involves a human dimension in providing shape and detail in the application of divine commands. To understand how the *sharia* is (and can be) further developed in the light of Islamic jurisprudence (*fiqh*), it is thus important to be clear about the nature of the sources of the *sharia*. In Islam every action is required to cohere with the main Islamic tenets, which are based on the Qur'an and the *hadith* that constitute the wellspring of Islamic jurisprudence, and from which the secondary sources of the *sharia* are derived by means of analogical reasoning (*qiyas*) and scholarly consensus (*ijma'*). *Ijtihad* is the independent reasoning of Islamic jurists relating to the validity of certain *sharia* rules in cases that are not mentioned in the Qur'an and the *hadith*.[9]

2.2.1 Primary Sources of Sharia

The first and most sacred source of legal and moral guidance is the Qur'an – the book of revelation from God which was transmitted through the Prophet Muhammad

PBUH.[10] Broadly speaking, although the Qur'an is primarily focused on theological or metaphysical themes, it also teaches how people should conduct themselves in their private and public affairs, ranging from acts of worship, family relations, property rights, commercial transactions, taxation, and more. Unlike most secular legal systems that presuppose a doctrine of legal positivism, the Qur'an does not differentiate between law and morality, but rather sees the two as intimately linked and interdependent.[11]

That said, when it comes to commercial dealings, the Qur'an itself contains relatively few technical legal verses which can be readily applied to the growing number of issues and problems facing Muslims today.[12] Although the messages of the Qur'an are necessarily subject to interpretation – something which can and does give rise to disagreement as to the meanings of various words, phrases, and verses – the general rule adhered to by all scholars is that the Qur'anic message is a source of knowledge that cannot be superseded or abrogated by any other source.[13]

Hadith are the second primary source of the *sharia*. *Hadith* are the recorded sayings, habitual actions, and behaviours of the Prophet Muhammad PBUH, presented in the form of narratives recalled and reported by the early Muslim community soon after the Prophet's death.[14] These *hadith* were eventually compiled into collections, the best known and most utilised being Sahih al-Bukhari and Sahih Muslim.[15] *Hadith* are endowed with a unique legitimacy because they provide valuable details about exemplary prophetic behaviour relating to issues of human conduct that the Qur'an is silent on. They thus became an indispensable resource for jurists who were required to formulate law relating to new matters in a manner that conformed to the religion as practised by the Prophet Muhammad PBUH.[16] The prophetic *hadith* also provide insight to jurists with respect to the basis for constructing a comprehensive body of constructed Islamic law called *fiqh*.[17] When it comes to commercial matters not directly related to matters of faith or theology, such as property ownership rights, sale-purchase agreements, lease contracts, lending, borrowing, etc., these fall under the sub-category of Islamic commercial law or *fiqh muamalah*.[18] (*Muamalah* literally means 'transactions' or 'dealings'.[19]) So when it comes to the development of Islamic finance in the modern period, it is normatively based on the already established criteria of *fiqh muamalah*.

2.2.2 Secondary Sources of Sharia

Ijtihad is the secondary source of the *sharia*. It refers to the juristic process for deriving a legal ruling on a particular issue.[20] The objective is to deliver juristic interpretation and should be open to all jurists who have a creative imagination and training in matters of *fiqh*. The derivation of rules based on legal reasoning may be based on consensus (*ijma'*), analogy (*qiyas*), preference (*istihsan*), or public interest (*istislah*, or *maslahah mursalah*) following the methodology characterising a recognised jurisprudential school.

Ijma' refers to the agreement by Islamic jurists across all four schools on a specific matter after canvassing different legal views and opinions (including individual opinions or *fatwa*) of jurists based on the Qur'an and *hadith*.[21] *Ijma'* is considered the third source of law in Islam after the Qur'an and *hadith* because it is held that if there is agreement by all ranks of qualified jurists (*mujtahid*)[22] on any given matter, the likelihood of all scholars being simultaneously in error is vanishingly small.[23]

Consensus in relation to fundamental principles or 'root' issues (*mas'alah ushuliyyah*) requires the agreement of all Islamic jurists generally in that particular period of time. In relation to relatively less important matters or 'branch' issues (*mas'alah furuiyyah*), universal consensus is not required because branch issues are usually relatively minor matters of implementation in a particular time and place.[24] Where there is legal consensus, it is applicable to all Muslims, and once consensus is agreed by *mujtahid* on a particular matter, it is thereafter treated as if it were divine law and cannot be cast aside in the future.[25] It should be noted that this particular convention has long functioned as a means of maintaining cultural and religious uniformity and constancy in Islamic societies. It has also been utilised at times by leaders and scholars as a political tool to silence dissident religious voices and opponents.[26] Indeed, many significant scholars throughout Islamic history have claimed unanimous consensus on a number of legal and theological theories and have endeavoured to sort out which claims can be taken to be genuinely so, rather than being artefacts of temporal politics.[27] *Ijma'* can be used by the future Islamic jurist as a foundation in constructing a solution of new legal cases.[28] Whether political interests play a role in the use of *ijma'* in Indonesia will be discussed in the following section.

The next source of Islamic law is analogy or *qiyas*. This is a form of logical reasoning that seeks to establish a ruling on a novel case by drawing an analogy with an already established case, based on there being some essential feature common to the novel and the established case. The degree of commonality between the new and the already established case determines the degree of certainty that the ruling over the new case applies.[29] Exclusive reliance on analogy as a source of law is controversial. Most controversy about the use of analogy stems from the disputes over the interpretation of the original law (*hukam-ul-asl*, generally known as *asl*) either in terms of the meaning of a text (Qur'an or *hadith*) or a disputed understanding of material facts.[30] In this case, the *Shafi'i* school holds that *Asl* in the analogy must be supported by references to the primary sources of the Qur'an and/or *hadith*. So, the rulings which are drawn from analogy cannot be used as guideline in *Asl*, as *qiyas* cannot be obtained from *qiyas*.[31] Despite controversies over the use of analogical reasoning, this source has nonetheless proved to be indispensable in developing Islamic law, since the modern world has given rise to innumerable new cases thanks to both advances in technology and the development of all sorts of new cultural practices. Without the tool of *qiyas*, it would be impossible for Islamic jurists to produce legislation to address problems for which there were no clear pre-existing legal rulings.

Preference or *istihsan* is to consider something good. Jurists use *istihsan* to express their preference for judgements in Islamic law over other possibilities.[32] *Istihsan* can be defined as leaving the analogy while adopting a more suitable outcome that meets the public interest. Some say *istihsan* allows for greater latitude in formulating laws in connection with matters encountered in society.[33] The use of *istihsan* as the source of law is disputed by some jurists as lacking any textual authority.[34] *Istihsan* sometimes separates the ruling on a specific matter from the ruling of similar cases due to textual evidence, which requires giving a different ruling to it, particularly in a matter where the textual evidence would lead to hardship for the believer. *Istihsan* is used by modernist jurists as a principle for reforming Islamic law.[35] Thus, to some extent *istihsan* can be legitimate in the *sharia* as long as it does not contradict the Qur'an and *hadith*.

Public interest or *istislah* (also known as *maslahah mursalah*) means considerations of public interest. The public interest is considered a legitimate goal in Islamic law if it is logical, is of benefit to the general public, does not harm others, and does not contradict the established rulings of the *sharia*.[36] The position of *istislah* as a source of law is accepted by Islamic scholars where there is no objection to this legal reasoning in the Qur'an and *hadith*.[37]

Of course, the *sharia* does not exist in a legal vacuum in Indonesia (or anywhere else). Thanks to the rich history of pre-colonial customary law (*adat*) and Islamic law implemented in different ways across the archipelago, as well as the Dutch colonists' legal system imposed at the beginning of the 19th century, Indonesia's legal environment has always been complex and varying combination.[38] The next section will discuss the ways in which it is possible for the *sharia* to adapt to the contemporary state legal system in Indonesia, including how the *ulama* respond to local customary and commercial activities, as well as whether there are points of conflict between the *sharia* and other legal systems.

2.3 *Sharia* in Conjunction With Indonesian Legal Systems

Although the popular pejorative image of the *sharia* in predominantly Western media is one of rigidity and exclusion,[39] the fact is that the *sharia* evolves and adapts to meet changing social, economic, and cultural conditions and in different locations. In this regard, the work of *ijtihad* should not be restricted in efforts to reconcile the *sharia* with the greatly divergent practice in the secular state legal systems.

Evidence that the *sharia* can be adapted and applied in the context of Indonesia can be seen by how the *sharia* is able to accommodate local traditions and norms. Certainly in the pre-colonial period, and even throughout the colonial period to some extent, the practices of customary laws by the 'headman' of a region (*Penghulu*) for the civil and family law (such as inheritance law and marriage law), were initially in conflict with Islamic law. However, later *Penghulu* came to accept that both systems of law could be quite adaptable to each other. The Islamic jurists (*ulama*) of that time were able to provide suitable solutions to the problems that could arise out of conflicting traditional cultural customs and Islamic teachings.[40] Communities in Indonesia realised that customary law can actually be balanced with Islamic law as long as the practices of the former do not directly conflict with Islamic teachings. During the Dutch colonial period, for the most part, the colonial administration allowed 'local' inheritance and marriage laws to prevail, but imposed Dutch criminal and tort law.[41] In the independence period, despite much debate over the incorporation of the *sharia* into the Republic's Constitution, according to M.B. Hooker, "the status of sharı'ah in the Indonesian legal system was as much as the Dutch had left it",[42] and the same went for customary law. That said, the *Constitution of 1945* itself did reflect religious themes. *Undang-Undang Dasar (UUD) Tahun 1945* Chapter 28 Article 1 states: "Every citizen is given the freedom to choose and practice his belief", "freedom to worship, according to his religion or belief",[43] and that "every citizen must respect other's people right" to practise their religion.[44] Thus believers of each of the constitutionally recognised religions are permitted by the state to use their own marriage and inheritance laws in accordance to their respective teachings.[45] This religious impartiality on the part of the state maintains religious and cultural pluralism in the nation.[46]

2.3.1 The Place of Local Custom in Islamic Law

That the spirit of the *sharia* is to be adaptive and to meet the needs and comforts of believers is summed up in the Qur'anic declaration "He has not placed any hardship for you in religion".[47] When it comes to matters related to commerce and transactions between people, the *sharia* is adaptive so as to ensure its ethical goals are fulfilled: fair dealing, economic justice, and the prevention of disputes and oppression. On this view, therefore, everything that ensures human happiness within the spirit of divine ethical guidance is permitted in the *sharia*. This forms a basis for the Islamic permissibility of customary practices that did not have their origin in divine revelation. Furthermore, during the time of Prophet Muhammad PBUH, many cases have been reported in which rulings were based on the pre-Islamic customs of the Arab people.[48] This provided further grounds for the consideration of allowing pre- and non-Islamic customary laws and traditions by Islamic legal scholars. The term in Islamic law and jurisprudence is, in Arabic, *'adah*, or in Indonesian, *adat*, which means a custom or habit of an individual or group that is recognised by a community as morally acceptable behaviour.[49] Another word used in Arabic to denote custom is *'urf*[50] (meaning 'to know'), but this refers to the norms of a community as a whole (rather than individuals), and in that sense is more limited in its scope than *'adah*.[51] Both *'adah* and *'urf* are thus an important means of resolving cases that arise with respect to the implementation of Islamic law.

The *sharia* rules, which are based on juristic opinion, have often been formulated on the basis of prevailing customs. When those customs change due to the evolving needs of the people, the corresponding *sharia* rules can change along with them to avoid causing hardship in people's lives.[52] Take, for example, the trading of goods. The acceptable time interval between an offer being made by a buyer and its acceptance by a seller is not stipulated by the Qur'an or the *Sunnah*. Thus, Shafi'i scholars stipulate that the period of the interval should be determined by what is customary for the people in a given community or region. In this way, *'urf* is incorporated directly into the *sharia*. Following from this, if the customary time interval were to shorten from decade to decade, the religiously mandated time interval would correspondingly shorten. So, any existing customary tradition may be accepted in Islamic law as long as it does not contradict basic moral values or obligatory rulings embedded in Islamic law. For example, for commercial transactions, it is the clarity of agreement (*Al-'ahdu*) and the contract (*akad*) that is essential.[53] A customary tradition which forbade clear contracts would itself be prohibited by the *sharia*. Thus,

Islamic jurists tend to view acceptable existing customary traditions as a reasonable method of achieving development and maintaining harmony in society. It also opens the doors of creativity and innovation for Muslims to develop their economy with the guidance of Islamic principles.[54]

2.4 Difference of Opinion in Islamic Law (*ikhtilaf*)

The next section will discuss the principles used by Indonesian Islamic jurists in solving *sharia* issues in Indonesia, potential conflicts of interest that can arise in conducting *ijtihad*, and why conflicting opinions arise between jurists in *ijtihad*. Some may argue that the gates of *ijtihad* have been closed because the only acceptable *mujtahid* are those with qualifications comparable to the pious companions Prophet Muhammad PBUH. Such a restriction would effectively exclude virtually all recent Islamic scholars from being qualified to engage in *ijtihad*.[55] However, many contemporary Islamic scholars are against the contention that the *mujtahid* are extinct and that the gate of *ijtihad* is closed.[56] They argue that the *de facto* prohibition on *ijtihad* is not true in theory or in practice, and that *ijtihad* is an option for all jurists who have innovative ideas that do not violate basic principles that are universally agreed upon by all scholars.[57]

As discussed previously, the *mujtahid* apply the jurisprudential methodology of *Usul al-Fiqh*[58] and the legal maxims (*Qawaid Fiqhiyah*)[59] in *ijtihad*. *Fiqh* includes law which is not mentioned explicitly in the Qur'an and requires further explanation via the use of *hadith* and, if the case is still not clear, can be resolved through *ijtihad*.[60] The jurists use legal maxims as guidelines for a particular ruling or decision in deducing various cases that come under the common rulings.[61]

Unlike most other Muslim-majority countries, Indonesia does not have a grand *mufti*[62] who would use *ijtihad* to make *fatwa* for all Muslims in the country. This is likely due to historical reasons: The Indonesian archipelago was never ruled by a single Muslim Sultan, but rather by numerous Sultanates with their own *ulama*, devolving right down to the village level. Further, and in the post-independence period, the state eschewed a single religious authority, instead allowing the proliferation of several mass-based Islamic organisations in Indonesian civil society with their own political trajectories (although they were not political parties). These organisations have their own *ulama* but do not generally have a single preeminent scholar, and so will deliberate upon new matters by means of collective *ijtihad* (*ijtihad jama'i*). Although *fatwa* issued by these organisations are not invested with the power of the state, they do elicit considerable respect from and influence over their followers.[63]

This section will focus on three major Islamic organisations that dominate the religious landscape of Indonesia: MUI, Muhammadiyah, and Nahdlatul Ulama (NU). All three bodies offer their own *fiqh* rulings on both old and new matters that come to public attention; 75% of Indonesian Muslims identify themselves with either Nahdlatul Ulama or Muhammadiyah.[64] Although the *ulama* of these two organisations identify themselves as followers of the Shafi'i school of *fiqh*, the majority of Indonesian Muslims themselves do not really know about the Shafi'i school even though they follow it; however, they often align with one of these organisations (or take teachings from both).[65]

2.4.1 Ijtihad *by Majelis Ulama Indonesia*

The MUI was instituted by the Suharto government in 1975 with the aim of creating a national council of *ulama* that could represent all Indonesian Muslims, from traditionalists to modernists.[66] The establishment of MUI itself is also supported by the other major civil society Islamic organisations, including NU, Muhammadiyah, Persatuan Islam ('Persis'), and other unaffiliated *ulama*. As Hosen has argued, to this day the MUI includes a wide spectrum of groups representing *ulama* from many different backgrounds as the premise that the MUI's *fatwa* could be accepted for all Muslim organisations.[67] Because it provides a meeting forum for *ulama* from various organisations in discussing Islamic matters, the government has always favoured the MUI's *fatwa* on religious issues despite it not being a governmental institution. Due to this special relationship between MUI and the government, the MUI tends to issue *fatwa* that support government objectives,[68] although after the fall of the Suharto regime in 1998, the MUI has sometimes struck out against the implicit arrangement[69] (see Chapter 4 for further discussion).

In 1986, the MUI stated that it used *ijtihad jama'I* (collective *ijtihad*) in adjudicating new problems. Yet only a year later, the MUI announced that various methods would be used in issuing *fatwa*.[70] MUI does not strictly follow one Islamic school in issuing *fatwa*, and it does not fully explain how the *ulama* perform *tarjih*.[71] The MUI has thus been able to employ a wider range of methods than any single school of *fiqh* and has thus proved more flexible in its judgements on new issues. As Hosen said: "[i]n the Indonesian context, the MUI's attempts to open its mind by considering all methods of all schools can be seen as a 'reformation' of the *fiqh* approach".[72]

It is not easy to understand the methods used by MUI. K.H. Ma'ruf Amin,[73] the general chairman of MUI, stated that there are at least four methods for reaching a conclusion (*istinbath*) to issue *fatwa*: (1) Choosing the easiest already established opinion which is in line with *manhaj*[74] (*al-taysir al-manhaji*), (2) A state of distinction between *halal* and *haram* (*at-tafriq baina al-halal wal haram*), (3) Analysis of the determination of legal reasons (*tahqiq al-manath*), and (4) Review (*i'adah al-nazhar*).[75]

An Indonesian Professor in Islamic Law, Jaih Mubarok, who is also a member of the MUI, has stated that the procedure for determining a *fatwa* in MUI is as follows.[76] First, the proposed issue is discussed at a commission meeting to determine the nature and substance of the problem. Second, the commission issues a summons to a member who clearly understands the nature of the problem. Third, after all relevant information has been gathered, the *ulama* conducts research into the opinions of the four Sunni Islamic schools and the relevant *fiqh* experts (*fuqaha'*). If the Qur'an, *hadith*, *ijma'*, and *qiyas* do not yield answers, then the *ulama* will look to other arguments through the prism of what is in the public interest (*istidlal*). When the opinion of the *ulama* is uniform or a definitive proof (*dalil*) is discovered, then the *ulama* can use that proof to issue a *fatwa*. If, however, the *ulama* find contradictory arguments based on traditional sources of evidence, the *ulama* will perform *tarjih*[77] and choose the strongest opinion. If *tarjih* is unsuccessful for some reason, the members of *ulama* can perform *ilhaq al-masa'il bi naza'iriha*, which technically means connecting a new case to an older case from classical works (such as *Al-Kutub Al-Mu'tabarah*[78]) by setting aside the discrepancy between them. Sixth, the next method to use is *ijtihad jama'i* (collective *ijtihad*), where the group of jurists deliberating together in the meeting solve the problem by referring to the origin of matters using the theorisation of Islamic legal methodology (*al-qawa'id al-ushuliyah*)[79] and Islamic legal maxims (*al-qawaid al-fiqhiyah*).

Thus, the MUI jurists have relied extensively on the methods of *ijtihad* and *istidlal* in issuing *fatwa* in order to reduce the challenge of dependence on the methodology of the classical period (which draws extensively on medieval traditions) by considering all methods from all schools.[80] It should be noted that the MUI *mujtahid* is not required to reveal the methods of *ijtihad* unless the intended recipients are also *mujtahid*. This practice is used to avoid tensions at the grass-roots level because the MUI holds that a *fatwa* should be based on what is deemed the strongest opinion from a *fiqh* school, but common people may be unfamiliar with such an opinion, or it may contradict traditional teachings, especially in rural areas.[81] Nonetheless, in the post-Suharto era, the MUI has sometimes drawn heavy criticism from other Islamic organisations and scholars. For example, in 2009 the former MUI leader and president of Indonesia, Kyai Haji Abdurrahman Wahid, somewhat hyperbolically argued that:

> This quasi-governmental organization [i.e. MUI], which was established by Suharto's New Order regime in order to control Indonesia's Muslim community, has largely fallen into the grip of radicals, and is now dictating to, and in many ways controlling, the actions of government. Thus it is not surprising that fatwas originating with the MUI are counter-productive and provoke controversy, such as those banning secularism, pluralism and liberalism, and branding as deviant certain groups within society, thus provoking violent actions in the name of Islam.[82]

Insofar as even a moderated version of this point of view holds currency among some Indonesians, it implies that the MUI's *fatwas* are unlikely to be universally accepted as valid and so can contribute to *ikhtilaf* in Indonesian Muslim society.

2.4.2 **Ijtihad** ***by Nahdlatul Ulama***

NU was founded by Kyai Haji Hasjim Asy'ari in 1926 largely in response to what he saw as new puritanical movements, most shockingly exemplified by the Wahhabi conquest of Mecca and Medina.[83] NU must be included in any discussion of *ijtihad* in Indonesia for two reasons. First, NU is the single largest grass-roots Islamic organisation in Indonesia (and the world) with between 35 and 40 million members residing largely in rural areas of the country. Second, NU's *ulama* have sometimes issued *fatwas* that have variance with most other jurists in Indonesia.

The source of the variance in some of NU's *fatwas* lies in NU's professed mission as a defender of 'traditional' Islam,[84] indigenous Indonesian Islamic practices, and religious pluralism. With respect to its 'traditionalist' approach to *fiqh*, it affirms the practice of *taqlid* (that is, the obligation to follow the opinions of great *ulama* of the past) and strict adherence to one of the four classical schools of *fiqh* – that is, the Shafi'i, Hanafi, Maliki, and Hanbali schools.[85] The vast majority of NU's *ulama* follow the Shafi'i school,[86] as exemplified in the books used in their Islamic boarding schools (*pesantren*), such as *Waraqat*, *Hujjah al-Wushul*, *Lam'u al-jawami'*, *al-Mushtasyfa*, and *al-Asybah wan al-Nazha'ir*. However, recently, with the rise of new issues in its community, the NU's younger *ulama* have been motivated to reduce their reliance on the classical books of *fiqh* (*Kitab Kuning*) and appear to be more willing to criticise the works of classical scholars.[87] The NU has a unit devoted to *ijtihad* known as Lajnah Bahtsul Masail. This unit is composed of *kyai*[88] and *ulama* who collectively issue *fatwa* using their own group methods.

Critics of NU, such as its historical rival Muhammadiyah, claim that NU is 'exclusivist' because it does not invite jurists from other Islamic groups to participate in its *fatwa* decision-making process. Indeed, some Muhammadiyah clerics have gone so far as to allege that the *fatwas* issued by the Lajnah Bahtsul Masail only consider the interests of their own group and dismiss out-of-hand the opinions of those who are not affiliated to them.[89]

2.4.3 **Ijtihad** ***by Majelis Tarjih Muhammadiyah***

Muhammadiyah, formed in 1912, is identified as the major 'modernist' (*tajdid*) Islamic organisation in Indonesia and is one of the oldest surviving Indonesian Islamic organisations from that period. It was created by the reformist missionary K.H. Ahmad Dahlan, who was influenced by the late 19th-century revivalist movement identified with Muhammad Abduh and Rashid Rida. Dahlan saw religious conformity to pre-modern traditions and local 'superstitions' as preventing Malays from developing intellectually, politically, economically, and culturally.[90] Muhammadiyah remains largely guided by this vision, and thus has often been at odds with NU.[91] Although it does not have as many members as NU, its membership nonetheless runs into the millions, largely drawn from urban areas.

The *ijtihad* committee of Muhammadiyah is known as Lajnah Tarjih (formerly known as Majelis Tarjih).[92] There are three steps in the method of *ijtihad* of Lajnah Tarjih: (1) *Bayani*, which means interpreting the meaning of verses in the Qur'an and *hadiths*; (2) *Qiyasi* is the effort analogy of novel issue in corresponding to existing law; and (3) *Istishlahi*, which is based on the *maslahah* and expanded into five types: *istihsan*, *saddu al-dzari'ah*, *istishlah*, *'urf*, and *ijtihad kauniyyah*.[93]

The variety of understandings of the principal methodology of *fiqh* (*istinbath al-hukmi*) is the root cause of Muhammadiyah dissent from NU. The differences occur in the way they investigate the matters which lead to different end results. For example, in Muhammadiyah's Lajnah Tarjih, all *fatwas* should directly refer to the Qur'an and *Sunnah*, and then to the point of view of a Sunni *madhab*.[94] While in NU's Lajnah Bahtsul Masail, the process should firstly refer to the positions taken by

Imams of the four Sunni *madhahib* in the classical books. In addition, about 91% of NU *ulama* use reference texts from Imam Shafi'i and his school, whereas Muhammadiyah's Lajnah Tarjih is more open and not limiting references to just the Shafi'i *madhab*.[95] Another difference is that Lajnah Tarjih is inspired by the concept of Islamic reformism and modernism inspired by Ahmad bin Hanbal, Ibn Taimiyyah, Jamaluddin al-Afghani, and Muhammad Abduh. NU's Lajnah Bahtsul Masail on the other hand, is often affiliated with the *ulama* of Mecca and Medina (*haramain*), and Abu al-Hasan al-Ash'ari and Abu Mansur Al-Maturidi, Abu Hamed Al-Ghazali, Syaikh Ahmad bin Zaini Dahlan, Syeikh Nawawi al-Bantani, and Syekh Mahfudz al-Tirmasy.[96] However, it should be noted that their disagreements are best thought of as 'family disputes' since NU and Muhammadiyah both adhere to the essentials of the Sunni tradition and have overlapping religious missions of providing religious education and Islamic teaching.[97]

Much like NU, Muhammadiyah has been criticised for its 'exclusivism' when it comes to formulating *fatwa*. As Rajafi has noted, although Lajnah Tarjih's internal rules state that jurists from other Islamic organisations should be invited to assist in the determination of *fatwa*, in fact this only ever happened once in 1986 during the Muktamar Tarjih Muhammadiyah in Malang, East Java.[98] Like NU, it does not seriously consider the validity of positions offered by scholars outside its own organisational structure. Thus, given its particular *fiqh* methods and its exclusivism, it is unsurprising that this sometimes contributes to *ikhtilaf* in Indonesian Muslim society.

2.4.4 Bank Interest in the View of MUI, NU, and Muhammadiyah

Disagreements between MUI, NU, and Muhammadiyah have arisen over issues of Islamic finance, such as the 'correct' *sharia* position to take with respect to interest rates. For example, MUI and Muhammadiyah agreed that bank interest is prohibited and considered *riba*. By contrast, NU stated that the interest on money from a bank is similar to the fee from pawnshop loans.[99] NU classified bank interest on deposits into three categories: (1) It can be *haram* if the debtor is taking benefit out of the money owed to the borrowers. (2) It can be *halal* if there is no agreement in the beginning of a transaction, and this type of activity is considered as *'urf*, which commonly occurs in the society, where society in general knows that if money is put in the bank interest will automatically be taken out of it. (3) It can be in between *haram* and *halal* or *syubhat*, as this is still debatable, but the Muktamar of Lajnah Bahtsul Masail announced that people should prefer the first view (*haram*) and to be wary of interest.[100]

Disputes of this nature between *fatwas* of major Islamic organisations have given rise to confusion and scepticism about Islamic financial law in Muslim nation-states, and as such it is important to understand that the *sharia* as it is understood in Indonesia can be different from that which is implemented in other Muslim-majority states. It has to be recognised that Islamic scholars (not just in Indonesia) may come with different interpretations of the *sharia* compliance of Islamic banking products. It is by virtue of this fact that a conceptual space is opened up for considering the modernisation of Islamic finance by means of the evolving nature of *ijtihad*. It is this 'opening' that will be utilised in the course of this book.

2.5 Concluding Remarks

The practice of *ijtihad* had a history of frequent recourse to theological and juristic debates which gave rise to secondary sources of Islamic law: consensus (*ijma'*), analogy (*qiyas*), preference (*istihsan*), and public interest (*istislah*, or *maslahah mursalah*). Needless to say, the theorisation of Islamic legal methodology (*ushul fiqh*) and Islamic legal maxims (*qawa'id al-fiqhiyyah*), although being strict in their textual hermeneutics, also offered room for normative guidance and growth via the jurists in their interpretation of the law.

As discussed in Sections 2.2 and 2.3, the *fatwa* bodies such as MUI, Lajnah Tarjih, and Lajnah Bahtsul Masa'il do not currently work cooperatively on issuing *fatwas* which are accepted by the Muslim general public. There is thus a need to reconstruct the way *ijtihad* is conducted in Indonesia so that it does not erode public confidence in these large mass organisations as a source of mainstream Islamic guidance. At the same time, the application of *ijtihad* by the jurists should also embrace other rationalising legal tools that enable the adaption and extension of the *sharia* to accommodate today's changed (and changing) conditions of life, morality, and public acceptance.

When it comes to the legal character of the nation-state, the Indonesian Republic is not easily classified on the secular–religious spectrum. The national ideology of *Pancasila*, by design, is sufficiently vague as to allow a multiplicity of religious 'ways of life', uninhibited by detailed state regulation; in principle, the state would only intervene or interfere with religio-legal provisions of any self-identified community – whether those provisions arise out of Islamic law, Catholic canon law, or local customary law – only as a last resort to protect the national interest (for example, to prevent sectarian civil unrest). It is widely accepted in Indonesian society that the state has the authority to implement national laws that are recognised as being in the public interest, irrespective of the source or inspiration for those laws. The fact that a national law may have its historical origins in colonial Dutch law, or the *sharia*, or customary law (*adat*), is not what 'characterises' the state. The state retains its autonomy, in principle at least, by virtue of its consideration of the aims and intended outcomes of the laws it implements, not by the origins or motives behind those laws. Thus, for example, if Islamic law is used as a source of or inspiration for positive law in Indonesia, it does not follow that the Indonesian state is theocratic. Likewise, if a customary law is used as a basis in constructing a national law, it does not follow that Indonesia is somehow, in its essence, a 'traditional customary' state.

As will be argued in the next chapter, since Indonesia is not an Islamic theocracy, its financial regulatory framework does not require the state to act as the arbiter of Islamic legal provisions vis-à-vis financial products and institutions. Rather, its general mandate is to prioritise the furtherance of social and economic justice for the society as a whole. The following discussion of the regulatory frameworks of banking and financial services in Indonesia will demonstrate how the state seeks to find a balance between its non-partisan objectives and the sanctioning of explicitly religiously regulated financial institutions.

Notes

1 *Al-madhahib* is the plural world of *madhab* (school). Although there were a number of other jurists who were also popular during their own times, only these four major schools of thought are now recognised by the vast majority of Sunni Muslims as defining normative Islam.

2 Lena Rethel, 'Whose Legitimacy? Islamic Finance and the Global Financial Order' (Pt Routledge) (2011) 18(1) *Review of International Political Economy* 75.

3 *Madhab* could be translated as 'school or doctrine of legal methodology and substantive ruling'. After the demise of the Prophet Muhammad PBUH in 632 BCE, there was a major crisis for the Muslim world in the question of succession which divided the Muslim community into two distinct religio-political communities of interpretation, designated subsequently as Sunnism and Shiism. Both these sects can be divided into subcategories of interpretation; there are different branches of Sunni Islam just as there are different branches in *Shia* Islam. Imam Shafi'i (767–820 CE) was one of the four great Sunni Imams and was a prominent scholar and the first contributor to the principles of Islamic jurisprudence; his legacy on juridical matters and teaching eventually led to the Shafi'i school of *fiqh* (*Madhab*). The Shafi'i school of thought is the second largest followed by Muslims worldwide. See Toni Johnson and Lauren Vriens, 'Islam: Governing Under Sharia' (2014) 25 *Council on Foreign Relations*.

4 This research will focus on Islamic matters which deal with the contemporary Muslim condition in Indonesia and does not specifically place emphasis on the Shafi'i *madhab*. It is useful knowing that every Muslim who has a little knowledge of Islam must follow the *fatwa* from Ulama and has to follow a *madhab* (*taqlid*). But *Mujtahid* who are competent of Qur'anic and *hadith* knowledge and Arabic must not follow any Ulama, they must do *ijtihad* and find the evidence which does not contradict with al-Nash (Qur'an and *Sunnah*). See Wahbah Zuhayli, *Fiqh al-Islami wa-Adilatuhu* [Islamic Jurisprudence and Its Proofs] (Dar al-fikr, 2001) 45 [tr author].

5 Agung Vazza, 'Indonesia, Country with High Tolerance', *Republika* (Jakarta), 14 June 2017, www.republika.co.id/berita/en/speak-out/17/06/14/orhxaq413-indonesia-country-with-high-tolerance. The major religions recognised in the Indonesian Constitution are Islam, Protestantism, Catholicism, Hinduism, Buddhism, and Confucianism. There is ongoing debate over the constitutional validity and protection of other minority and micro religions that are not explicitly mentioned in the Constitution but which are in fact practised in Indonesia. A 2017 ruling of Indonesia's Constitutional Court seems to have affirmed the validity of these other religions.

6 *Pancasila* is the core political ideology of Indonesia; it is derived from the Sanskrit language *panca*, meaning 'five', and *sila*, meaning 'principles'. *Pancasila* consists of belief in God, Indonesian nationalism, humanitarianism or just and civilized humanity, democracy, and social justice. The *Pancasila* was formulated during the era of President Soekarno (one of the founding fathers of the Republic of Indonesia in 1945). See J.M. Muslimin, 'Islamic Law in the Pancasila State' (2012) 12(1) *Journal Ahkam* 15.

7 Ibid.

8 *Sunni* and *Shia* are the two main sub-groups in Islam. Worldwide, *Sunnis* comprise 87–90% of Muslims, while *Shia* make up 10–13% of Muslims. Pew Research Center, *Mapping the Global Muslim Population*, October 2009, www.pewforum.org/2009/10/07/mapping-the-global-muslim-population/.

9 Rafat Y. Alwazna, 'Islamic Law: Its Sources, Interpretation and the Translation of It into Laws Written in English' (2016) 29(2) *International Journal for the Semiotics of Law-Revue Internationale de Semiotique Juridique* 251, 252.
10 Abdullah Saeed, *The Qur'an: An Introduction* (Routledge, 2008) 23.
11 L Ali Khan, 'The Qur'an and the Constitution' (2010) 85(161) *Tulane Law Review* 161, 169.
12 Saeed, above n 10.
13 The translation of the Qur'an from Arabic into other languages may differ depending on the language and its interpreters, but the Arabic version that exists today is essentially the same as when it was first compiled in the 7th century CE. The divine scheme of Qur'anic preservation, not only the words but also the sequence of presentation, was carried out primarily through the process of memorising the text by the first generation of Muslims who immediately heard and committed to memory the Qur'an revealed to Prophet Muhammad PBUH. Many later generations of Muslims followed their predecessors in memorising the entire Qur'an, which is termed as *Huffaz*/those who memorize the entire Qur'an and the servants of the Qur'an. See ibid., 86.
14 Alwazna, above n 9, 252.
15 Jonathan Brown, *The Canonization of al-Bukhārī and Muslim: The Formation and Function of the Sunnī Ḥadīth Canon* (Brill, 2007).
16 Nasruddin Yusuf, 'Hadis Sebagai Sumber Hukum Islam [Hadith as the Source of Islamic Law]' (2015) 13(1) *Journal Al-Syir'ah Ilmiah* 21, 21 [tr author].
17 *Fiqh* literally means 'deep understanding'. It usually refers to the large body of Islamic law constructed by learned jurists on the basis of the teachings of the Qur'an and the *hadith*. *Sharia* covers global aspects in human life, including obedience in worship and building good relations between human beings. So, *fiqh* is a part of *Sharia*. See H. Chad Hillier, 'Muhammad Iqbal on Al-Fiqh: Towards a Natural Law Jurisprudence' (2010) 12(3) *Journal of Islamic Law and Culture* 258, 267.
18 Islamic jurists categorised Islamic jurisprudence into seven fields (*Fiqh*): (1) *Fiqh Ibadah*, in relation to all aspect of human obedience to God, such as prayer, fasting in Ramadhan, pilgrimage (*hajj*), and ritual purity in Islam (*Thaharah*); (2) *Al-Ahwal Syakshiyah*, related to family matters, such as marriage, divorce, heredity, *nafkah*, and children's obligation to parents; (3) *Fiqh Muamalah*, covers all matters related to rights of ownership as well as resolution of disputes, such as sale and purchase agreements, leases, debt, pawning, and grants; (4) *Al-Ahkam As-Sulthaniyah*, related to constitutional law; (5) *Fiqh Al-Jinayat*, related to criminal law; (6) *As-Siyar*, covers matters related to international relations, including war and peace; and (7) *Fiqh Al-Adab*, dealing with character, propriety, good manners, and reconciling with those who disagree. See Gemala Dewi et al., *Hukum Perikatan Islam Indonesia* [Islamic Commercial Law in Indonesia] (Kencana, 2005) 27 [tr author].
19 Mohammad Taqiuddin Mohamad et al., 'The Historical Development of Modern Islamic Banking: A Study in South-East Asia Countries' (2013) 1(1) *African Journal of Business Management* 1.
20 Where legal reasoning (*ijtihad*) is used, this can result in a diversity of opinions by scholars. However, the differences mostly occur in branch issues (*Mas'alah furu'iyyah*), such as in determining how much a person should pay for alms (*zakah*) each month. But on issues of principle (*Mas'alah ushuliyyah*), such as the command to perform prayer (*shalah*) and fasting (*Shoum*), it is clearly mentioned in the Qur'an and the *hadith*. See Abdul Ghoni, *Islamic Wisdom* (Elex Media Komputindo, 2018).
21 Islamic jurists can be from different backgrounds of *madhab* on the *ijma'*, since these four schools recognise each other's validity even though they interacted in legal debate over the centuries. Wael B. Hallaq, *Shari'a: Theory, Practice, Transformations* (Cambridge University Press, 2009) 100.
22 *Mujtahid* literally means 'Islamic jurist'; it is a person who is qualified to exercise legal reasoning. Islamic jurists, or *Mujtahid*, could be classified into four levels: the first and

highest level are the Independent Jurists (*Mujtahid Mutlaq Mustaqil*) – a level often reserved Imam Abu Hanifa, Imam Maliki, Imam al-Shafi'I, and Imam Ahmad – because of their ability to set the fundamental principles of *fiqh* independently derived from their knowledge of the Qur'an and the *hadith*. The second category is Absolute Jurists (*Mujtahid Mutlaq Muntasib*). These are jurists who follow the methodology of well-known schools in producing new solutions for new legal cases. The third category is the school's jurists (*Mujtahid fil Madhab*). These are jurists who are eligible to analogise new legal cases when an unequivocal judgement by the Imam cannot be found. These jurists undertake legal reasoning using the principles of *fiqh* and the judgement of the Imam. The fourth and final category is the *fatwa's* jurist (*Mujtahid fi al Fatwa*). This is a jurist who has a profound knowledge of a particular school and is capable to prefer the most adequate from one verdict to the other, but still following the previous methodologies of the Imam. This level of Islamic jurist is based on the Sunni sect of Islam, while the *shia* sect has its own degrees of jurisprudence. See Zuhayli, above n 4.

23 The Islamic jurists must possess all the conditions of *mujtahid*, such as having good knowledge of the Qur'an and *hadith*, a very good command of Arabic, knowledge of previous *ijma'* issues, being proficient in the entire range of procedures of inferential reasoning, and strong knowledge of *fiqh*. See ibid., 45.

24 Sakirman, 'Epistimologi Ushul Fiqh dalam Konstruk Historis [The Epistimology of Islamic Jurisprudence in Islamic History]' (1 January 2016) 25(1) *Jurnal Emprisima* 1, 9 [tr author].

25 The result of consensus could be valid for the whole period and authoritative as long as it does not oppose clear statements in the Qur'an and the *hadith*. See Andrew C. Worthington and Alsadek H. Gait, *A Primer on Islamic Finance: Definitions, Sources, Principles and Methods*, Discussion Papers in Finance finance:200909, Griffith University, Department of Accounting, Finance and Economics (2009), 4.

26 Abdullah bin Hamid Ali, 'Scholarly Consensus: Ijma: Between Use and Misuse' (2010) 12(2) *Journal of Islamic Law & Culture* 92. There is also some disagreement between the *madhabs* themselves over the proper scope of *ijma'*. For example, following Imam Malik Ibn Anas, the Maliki *madhab* never agreed with the *ijma'* of the scholars. In Malik's view, *ijma'* was restricted to that of the companions of Prophet Muhammad PBUH and the direct successors of those companions in the city of medina is binding.

27 Ibid.

28 Maimun Maimun, 'Rekonstruksi Konsep Ijmak dalam Berijtihad di Era Modern [Reconstructing the Concept of Concensus in Legal Reasoning at the Modern Period]' (2018) 10(2) *Journal of Law and Economics, ASAS* 1, 46, [tr author].

29 For example, the unambiguous and certain prohibition on the consumption of wine as found in the Qur'an and *hadith* can be applied by analogy to the consumption of vodka, about which the Qur'an and *hadith* are silent, on the basis that there is certain knowledge that both wine and vodka possess the common essential property of being capable of causing intoxication, which by *ijma'*, is the underlying reason for the divine prohibition on wine. The certainty of the prohibition on the consumption of alcohol *as a general category* can similarly be further derived.

30 *Asl* refers to the original law or already established case that is used as a basis for making determinations about the new case (*musyabbah bih*). Some scholars, such as Ibnu Ishaq al-Syairazi and Ibnu al-Sam'ani, are of the view that *asl* can be derived from the case which was established based on *ijma'*, while others argue against this. Al-Syaukani, the well-known reformist jurist, affirmed that the opinion of al-Syairazi and al-Sam'ani are the most valid, and said that the ruling obtained from *ijma'* is definitive (*qat'i*) because the source of *ijma'* itself is *nash* (Qur'an and *hadith*). See Ahmad Masfuful Fuad, 'Qiyas Sebagai Salah Satu Metode Istinbat al-Hukm [Qiyas as One of the Way of Inference]' (2016) 15(1) *Jurnal Penelitian Hukum Islam Mazahib* 42, 46.

31 Alwazna, above n 9, 253.

32 Ibid.

33 Ahmad Hasan, 'The Principle of Istihsan in Islamic Jurisprudence' (Pt Islamic Research Institute, International Islamic University, Islamabad) (1977) 16(4) *Islamic Studies* 347.

34 Imam Al-Shafi'i never accepted *istihsan* and argued that the evidence (*dalil*) should be based on *al-nash* in order to avoid the proliferation of opinions that would arise out of mere subjective judgement. Although it is accepted in Hanafi *fiqh*, the use of *istihsan* was highly restricted in the Maliki and Hanbali *madhabs*. See Hallaq, above n 21, 324. See also Mohammad Hashim Kamali, 'Istiḥsān and the Renewal of Islamic Law' (2004) 43(Winter 2004) *Islamic Studies* 561.

35 For example, bank interest (*riba*) is prohibited. Taking late fees is also traditionally considered *riba*. But some jurists allow the use of money from *riba* to be allocated, for example, to assist the poor or for public purposes (such as public toilets, schools, and hospitals). It is preferable, as it helps others rather than just leaving interest obtained unused. See Nurhadi Nurhadi, 'Bunga Bank Antara Halal dan Haram [The Bank Interest Rates: Between *Halal* and *Haram*]' (October 2017) 4(2) *Journal of Education and Social Religious Study, Nur El-Islam* 30, 49.[tr author].

36 Alwazna, above n 9, 254.

37 Ahmad Chairul Hadi, 'Problematika Pembiayaan Mudharabah di Perbankan Syariah Indonesia [The Problems of Mudharabah Contracts in Indonesian Islamic Banking]' (2011) 3(2) *Al-Iqtishad: Jurnal Ilmu Ekonomi Syariah* 193. [tr author].

38 See, for example, M.A. Jaspan, 'In Quest of New Law: The Perplexity of Legal Syncretism in Indonesia' (April 1965) 7(3) *Comparative Studies in Society and History* 252–266, and Kurnia Warman, Saldi Isra and Hilaire Tegnan, 'Enhancing Legal Pluralism: The Role of Adat and Islamic Laws Within the Indonesian Legal System' (2018) 21(3) *Journal of Legal, Ethical and Regulatory Issues* 1–9.

39 Mohamad Abdalla, 'Islamic Australia? What Place Is There for Sacred Law in a Secular Land?', *Religion & Ethics, ABC,* www.abc.net.au/religion/islamic-australia-what-place-is-there-for-sacred-law-in-a-secula/10099858.

40 For example, in Kampung Naga in West Java, the inhabitants are all Muslims; however, in the marriage procession they must agree and read the *Jatukrami* pledge, which does not permit divorce and polygyny within the village on the basis that it could cause *fitnah* and social disunity. This is an *adat* rule which they say does not contradict the particular *sharia* rules of marriage for two reasons. First, this *adat* is categorised as *Al-urf as-shahih*, which should be maintained because divorce is something that God hates, and the men *are* freely permitted to marry another wife outside the village, *but* they are no longer permitted to live in the village if they make this choice. And second, the interests of the village (*maslahah*) overrides the personal desires of any individual. See Neng Eri Sofiana, 'Ikrar Jatukrami: Ikrar Pernikahan Konteks Sunda [Jatukrami Pledge: The Wedding Vows in Sundanese Context]' (2019) 4(1) *Jurnal AQLAM-Journal of Islam and Plurality* 80, [tr author].

41 Muhammad Hisyam, *Caught between Three Fires: The Javanese Pangulu under the Dutch Colonial Administration, 1882–1942* (Universiteit Leiden, 2001) vol. 37.

42 M.B. Hooker, *Indonesian Islam: Social Change Through Contemporary Fatwa* (University of Hawaii Press, 2003), 20.

43 *Undang-Undang Dasar Negara Republik Indonesia 1945* [The Constitution of the Republic of Indonesia 1945] ch 28 art 1 [tr Asian Human Rights Commission], www.unesco.org/education/edurights/media/docs/b1ba8608010ce0c48966911957392ea8cda405d8.pdf

44 Arskal Salim, *Contemporary Islamic Law in Indonesia* (Edinburgh University Press, 2015) 59.

45 Ibid.

46 "Unity in Diversity" or "*Bhinneka Tunggal Ika*", which is mentioned in the Indonesian Constitution (Article 36A), is a foundation stone for Indonesian society and is a national motto to unite the society from different religious backgrounds, such as Muslims, Hindus, Christians (Protestantism and Catholicism), Buddhists, and Confucians. In

a country that upholds tolerance, diverse cultural and social cultures, consisting of 17,508 islands and 1,128 ethnic groups, the spirit of tolerance is wrapped up with a cultivated sense of nationalism and love of the motherland. Agung Vazza, 'Indonesia, Country with High Tolerance', *Republika* (Jakarta), 14 June 2017, www.republika.co.id/berita/en/speak-out/17/06/14/orhxaq413-indonesia-country-with-high-tolerance.

47 Habib Ahmed, 'Islamic Law, Adaptability and Financial Development' (2006) 13(2) *Islamic Economic Studies* 79, 85. Also see Qur'an 22:78.

48 Luqman Zakariyah, 'Custom and Society in Islamic Criminal Law: A Critical Appraisal of the Maxim 'al-ʿĀdah Muḥakkamah' (Custom Is Authoritative) and Its Sisters in Islamic Legal Procedures' (2012) 26(1) *Arab Law Quarterly* 75, 76.

49 Ibid., 77.

50 Scholars divided '*urf* into two categories: (1) A valid custom (*'urf shahih*), which is practised by a community, does not contravene the interest of the people, is reasonable, and does not contradict the text in the Qur'an and *hadith*. An example of *'urf shahih* is the custom of trading in rice, wheat, and sugar by using small milk cans rather than scales as a measuring device. This custom can be changed using kilo scales at a later time. (2) An invalid custom (*'urf fasid*) that is practised by the people but there is evidence to show that it contradicts *sharia* principles, is not reasonable, encourages corruption, or is against the interests of people. For example, the practice of gambling with money. Although it is common among many people, this act is clearly contrary to the text of the Qur'an and *hadith*. Therefore, such practice is invalid and must be discarded. See Ansari Yamamah, 'The Existence of Al-Urf (Social Tradition) in Islamic Law Theory' [43] (December 2016) 21(12) *IOSR Journal of Humanities and Social Science (IOSR-JHSS)* 43.

51 Zakariyah, above n 48.

52 Yamamah, above n 50.

53 Nurfaizal, '*Prinsip-Prinsip Muamalah dan Implementasinya Dalam Hukum Perbankan Indonesia* [The Foundation of Islamic Commercial Law and Its Implementation in Indonesian Banking]' (2013) 13(1) *Jurnal Hukum Islam* 14, 192. [tr author]

54 Mashur Malaka, 'Praktek Monopoli dan Persaingan Usaha [The Monopoly Market and Business Competition]' (July 2014) 7(2) *Jurnal Al-'Adl* 14, 39, 43.

55 Wael B. Hallaq, 'Was the Gate of Ijtihad Closed?' (1984) 16(1) *International Journal of Middle East Studies* 3, 5.

56 Ibid., 17.

57 Ibid., 18.

58 *Usul al-fiqh* literally means 'roots of deep understanding'. It can be classified into the two following parts: (1) *Ushul* literally means 'sources, original rule, or foundation', and (2) *Fiqh* means 'legal rules'. *Ushul fiqh* represents the theory and legal methodology that the *mujtahid* abides by for the purpose of deducing or extracting the legal rules for any problem issues.

59 The Independent jurists (*Mujtahid Mutlaq mustaqil*) established the Islamic legal maxims (*Qawaid Fiqhiyah*) of Islamic law, which are also the general rules of *fiqh* that portray the goals and objectives of *sharia*. There are five leading Islamic legal maxims in *fiqh*, such as (1) 'matters are determined according to intentions', (2) 'certainty is not overruled by doubt', (3) 'hardship begets facility', (4) 'harm must be eliminated', and (5) 'custom is a basis for judgement'. See Buerhan Saiti and Adam Abdullah, 'The Legal Maxims of Islamic Law (Excluding Five Leading Legal Maxims) and Their Applications in Islamic Finance' (1 November 2017) (2016) 29(2) *Journal of King Abdulaziz University: Islamic Economics*.; Zuhayli, above n 4 [tr author].

60 Akhyar Ari Gayo, '*Dinamika Legislasi Hukum Islam: Analisa Atas Upaya Pembentukan Hukum Perikatan Syariah* [Islamic Law Legislation Dynamic: Analysis on the Means of Forming Sharia Law of Obligations]' (2015) 4(3) *Jurnal Rechtsvinding* 15, 485. [tr author].

61 Saiti and Abdullah, above n 59.

62 A *mufti* (jurist consult) is a renowned qualified scholar capable of issuing a *fatwa* to a community. A *mufti* is normally chosen by the State or a 'peak' religious body and is thereafter recognised by the State. The *fatwa* of a *mufti* is generally treated as authoritative for the Muslims of the region and is viewed as a reliable reference in a sharia court by the *Qadi* (judge). See John L. Esposito and Natana J. DeLong-Bas, *Shariah: What Everyone Needs to Know* (Oxford University Press, 2018) 72.

63 Nadirsyah Hosen, 'Behind the Scenes: Fatwas of Majelis Ulama Indonesia (1975–1998)' (2004) 15(2) *Journal of Islamic Studies* 147. 67.

64 Saiful Mujani and R. William Lidle, 'Politics, Islam, and Public Opinion' (2004) 15(1) *Journal of Democracy* 109.

65 Hosen, above n 63.

66 Petrik Matanasi, 'Majelis Ulama Indonesia: Cara daripada Soeharto Mengatur Islam [Indonesian Ulama Council: How the Soeharto's Regime Managed Islam]', *Politik, Tirto* (Jakarta), https://tirto.id/majelis-ulama-indonesia-cara-daripada-soeharto-mengatur-islam-fQRG.[tr author].

67 Hosen, above n 63, 153.

68 M.B. Hooker states that during the 1975–1990s regime, the MUI's function was to support the programs and policies of the government rather than to exercise independent judgement on what it deemed to be in the public interest. M.B. Hooker, 'Islam and Medical Science: Evidence from Malaysian and Indonesian Fatawa, 1960–1995' (1997) 4(4) *Studia Islamika* 1.

69 P. Gillespie, 'Current Issues in Indonesian Islam: Analysing the 2005 Council of Indonesian Ulama Fatwa N0. 7' (2007) 18(2) *Journal of Islamic Studies* 202–240.

70 Majelis Ulama Indonesia, *Himpunan Keputusan dan Fatwa Majelis Ulama Indonesia* [The Compilation of Fatwas of Majelis Ulama Indonesia (MUI)] (Sekretariat MUI, Masjid Istiqlal, 1995).

71 *Tarjih* is one of the *fiqh* methods offered by al-Syatibi which literally means 'outweighing'. For example, if the *ulama* found proof from one *hadith* and or *madhab* which contradicts another, the *ulama* can choose the position that they judge to be stronger and may also make judgements about what is in the public interest. Muhammad Amin Al-husaini Al-kharsani, *Taysiir at-Tahriir 'ala Kitaabi at-Tahriir fi Ushul al-Fiqh al-Jaami' bayna Isytilahii al-Hanafiyah wa al-Syafi'iyyah* [Facilitating the Refinement of the Book al-Tahriir that Combines the Hanafi and Shafi'i Terms] (Dar Al Kotob Al Ilmiyah, 2017) 153 [tr author].

72 Hosen, above n 63, 160.

73 KH stands for 'Kyai Haji', Kyai means an Islamic scholar or religious leader or master who has a dominant role as a religious leader and people's guide in society, and *Haji* means a person who has taken the *hajj* pilgrimage. In Indonesian society a person who has returned from the *hajj* obtains the title *Haji*. This title is given to someone who has fulfilled the fifth Islamic pillar. Rachmad Hidayat, '*Santri, Kyai, and Ulama: Framing Masculinities within Indonesian Religious Elites*' (Paper presented at the International Workshop on Masculinities in Asia, Singapore), www.researchgate.net/publication/313644523_Santri_Kyaiand_Ulama_Framing_Masculinities_within_Indonesian_Religius_Elites.

74 *Manhaj* means to follow the teaching of *madhab* through the rules and the way of thinking which was compiled by the four Imams. Jaih Mubarok, *Metodologi Ijtihad Hukum Islam* [The Methods of Ijtihad in Sharia Law] (UII Press, 2002) 230 [tr author].

75 Ma'ruf Amin, '*Solusi Hukum Islam (Makharij Fiqhiyah) Sebagai Pendorong Arus Baru Ekonomi Syariah di Indonesia* [Islamic Legal Solutions *(Makharij Fiqhiyah)* as a Driving Force for the New Flow of Sharia Economy in Indonesia]' (Scientific Oration State Islamic University of Maulana Malik Ibrahim, 2017).[tr author].

76 Mubarok, above n 74, 170–171.

77 Al-kharsani, above n 71.

78 *Al-Kutub Al-Mu'tabarah* refers to the standard classical books which are used in the *ijtihad* by NU *ulama*. The NU confine their literature only to the books which are popular among them. The aim is to maintain NU's scientific repertoire and only use books which are truly authentic. Mz Shofiyullah, 'Al-Kutub Al-Mu'tabarah: Kajian atas Sumber Rujukan dalam Beristinbat Menurut NU, Muhammadiyah, dan Persis [*Al-Kutub Al-Mu'tabarah*: The Analysis of Source of Reference in *Istinbath* according to NU, Muhammadiyah and Persis]' (2008) 42(1) *Jurnal Asy-Syir'ah* 37, 42 [tr author].

79 *al-qawa'id al-ushuliyah* or *Ushul Fiqh* is the general Islamic theory in *fiqh* which is used by *Mujtahid* in order to arrive at rulings from the proofs. Dar Al-Ifta Al-Misriyyah, 'Islamic Legal Theory (Ushul al-fiqh)' (Pt Dar al-Iftaa Al-Missriyyah) (2020), www.dar-alifta.org/Foreign/ViewArticle.aspx?ID=110&CategoryID=3.

80 Hosen, above n 63, 160.

81 Muhammad Khalid Masud, Brinkley Messick and David S. Powers, *Muftis, Fatwas and Islamic Legal Interpretation* (Harvard University Press, 1996) 69, 25.

82 Abdurrahman Wahid, *Ilusi negara Islam: Ekspansi gerakan Islam transnasional di Indonesia* [The Illusion of an Islamic State: Expansion of the Transnational Islamic Movement in Indonesia] (Wahid Institute, 2009) 18. Also see Mun'im Sirry, 'Fatwas and Their Controversy: The Case of the Council of Indonesian Ulama (MUI)' (February 2013) 44(1) *Journal of Southeast Asian Studies* 100–117.

83 Carool Kersten, *A History of Islam in Indonesia: Unity in Diversity* (Edinburgh University Press, 2017). Also see Faisal Ismail 'The Nahdlatul Ulama: Its Early History and Contribution to the Establishment of Indonesian State' (2011) 5(2) *Journal of Indonesian Islam* 247–282.

84 In the context of NU's narrative, 'traditional' refers to the approach to theology, jurisprudence, and spirituality that pre-dates the various modernist movements that came to prominence in Egypt, British India, and Arabia in the late 19th century CE. Ibid.

85 Greg Fealy and Robin Bush, 'The Political Decline of Traditional Ulama in Indonesia: The State, Umma and Nahdlatul Ulama' (2014) 42(5) *Asian Journal of Social Science* 536, 541.

86 Mubarok, above n 74.

87 NU clerical figures who have proved influential in Indonesia include K.H. Sahal Mahudz, K.H. Hasyim Muzadi, K.H. Salahuddin Wahid, K.H. Said Aqil Sirodj, KH. Masdar Farid Mas'udi. Their idea of moderate modernism has inspired a million Muslims in Indonesia. See Hilmy Masdar, 'Quo-vadis Islam Moderat Indonesia? Menimbang Kembali Modernisme Nahdlatul Ulama dan Muhammadiyah [Quo-vadis Moderate Islam Indonesia? Reconsidering the NU and Muhammadiyah Modernism]' (2012) 36(2) *Jurnal Miqot* 271 [tr author].

88 *Kyai* are religious teachers and spiritual leaders.

89 Hosen, above n 63, 151; Ahmad Rajafi, 'Ijtihad Eklusif, Telaah atas Pola Ijtihad 3 Ormas Islam di Indonesia [Exclusivism of *Ijtihad*, a Review of Form of *Ijtihad* on Three Large Islamic Organisations in Indonesia]' (2016) *Jurnal Ilmiah Al-Syirah* 8 [tr author].

90 Carool Kersten, *History of Islam in Indonesia: Unity in Diversity* (Ediburgh University Press, 2017) 109.

91 Muhammadiyah's focus is to eliminate some superstitious rituals of Indonesian Muslims (*Tahayul, Bid'ah dan Churafat* or "TBC") on the grounds that these three customs are responsible for the stagnation of Muslim society. See Hosen, above n 63, 151, and see A'an Ardianto, 'TBC Sebagai Seteru Abadi Muhammadiyah [TBC as the Eternal Enemy of Muhammadiyah]', *News, UMM Malang* (Malang), 1 February 2020, www.umm.ac.id/id/muhammadiyah/18352.html.

92 Rajafi, above n 89, 9.

93 Abdul Munir Mulkhan, *Masalah-masalah Teologi dan Fiqh dalam Tarjih Muhammadiyah* [Questions about Theology and Fiqh in Tarjih Muhammadiyah] (SIPRESS, 2005) vol. 1, 101 [tr author].

94 Mulyono Jamal and Muhammad Abdul Aziz, 'Metodologi Istinbath Muhammadiyah dan NU: (Kajian Perbandingan Majelis Tarjih dan Lajnah Bahtsul Masail) [Methodology of *Istinbath* in Muhammadiyah and NU: The Comparative Analysis between *Majlis Tarjih* and *Lajnah Bahtsul Masail*]' (2013) 7(2) *Jurnal hukum dan Ekonomi Islam* [tr author].
95 Ibid.
96 Ibid.
97 Ibid.
98 Rajafi, above n 89.
99 Muhammad Ghafur W., 'Pengaruh Fatwa MUI Tentang Keharaman Bunga/Interest Terhadap Perkembangan Perbankan Syariah di Indonesia [The Influence of MUI Fatwa on the Prohibition of Banking Interest in the Development of Islamic Banking in Indonesia]' (2008) 17(2) *Jurnal Penelitian Agama* 355, 359 [tr author].
100 Ibid.

3 The Regulation of the Banking System in Indonesia

3.1 Introduction

This chapter argues that flexible legal systems are vital to the development of regulatory frameworks in financial institutions operating under a dual Islamic and conventional banking system. This is particularly important when financial institutions are dealing with complex *sharia*-related issues, as opposed to relying on 'one law for all'. This is because conflicts may arise between national law on the one hand, which generally assumes a framework which is not *sharia* compliant, and the *sharia* on the other. This chapter sets the table for exploring such conflicts by examining the Indonesian state's dual banking system regulatory framework.

The Indonesian government has amended the financial regulatory and supervisory framework which entails multi-authorities separated from the Central Bank of Indonesia (Bank Indonesia, or BI) and has emphasised that effective regulation of the banking sector encourages competition and banking system stability. In the chapters that follow, attention will be focused on the implementation of Indonesia's multiple regulatory and supervisory strategy in keeping with national and international objectives, and what legal and economic challenges and vulnerabilities arise therefrom.

The recent trend of economic development in Indonesia has been spurred on by the growth of the financial services industry. As of 2021, a report from the Indonesia Banking statistic shows that bank assets account for 79.8% of total assets, as compared to other financial institutions (insurance companies 10.5% and pension fund companies 6.4%).[1] The main challenge for Indonesia is to effectively regulate and supervise the banking sectors, since the major banks underpin Indonesia's economic stability. As for improving the financial system in Indonesia, in 2011 the FSA was established as a separate entity to supervise and regulate the financial sector and oversee crisis management.[2]

It is well understood that inefficient institutions are incompatible with increasing financial competition and thus, over time, are liable to fail.[3] Further, static financial regulations in a changing financial environment, combined with lagardly regulatory reforms, will contribute to banking instability.[4] Further, bankers may not be fully aware of the consequences of regulatory inaction and may ultimately take excessive risks to benefit from the open market. With this concern in mind, this chapter

DOI: 10.4324/9781003393986-3

examines the financial regulatory and supervisory system, whether the Indonesian government's objectives inadvertently erect barriers to banks in dealing with the ongoing changes in the global banking environment, and whether there is scope for regulatory reforms to Indonesia's dual banking system.

This chapter begins at an elementary point by examining banking functions and a discussion of the bank as a special company in stabilizing the economy. From there it gives an account of the transformation of the regulatory frameworks of the Indonesian banking system. Issues relating to the power of, and the relationships between, the multiple regulatory and supervisory authorities will also be discussed. Finally, the chapter examines the inequality in the regulatory framework governing the dual system of Indonesian financial institutions.

3.2 Banking Functions and Shift of Strategic Focus

Many observers have noted how banking institutions have evolved and their functions have shifted from merely facilitating commercial transactions to more complex non-traditional roles.[5] For the purpose of this chapter, it is important to know the main functions of banks in Indonesia. *Law No 10 of 1998 on Banking* states that, "Banks are to manage demand deposits and originate loans, which in turn supports the national economic growth, stability and increases general welfare".[6] Other types of institutions, such as finance companies, do not originate loans, and money market mutual funds do not offer demandable deposits.[7]

As illustrated in Figure 3.1, traditionally, as the financial intermediary, a bank acts as a collector of funds from the community (the 'source of funds'). The bank has to assure the safety of investors' and depositors' funds, managing their funds and providing interest ('cost') to clients. Banks also originate loans to those who are capital-poor and need funds ('use of funds'), through credit or bank loans, where the bank will charge interest to borrowers ('revenue'). Thus, the bank provides funds to a number of types of borrowers: households who wish to purchase assets or consumer goods; businesses that wish to acquire physical capital to expand their operations; and farmers who wish to purchase physical capital, fertilizers, and seeds. Thus, banks indirectly help to increase national economic growth both through the facilitation of consumption and investment expenditure. In this context, the role of banks is to minimise the cost of financial transactions, facilitate risk-sharing to gain benefit from the use of funds, and to minimise asymmetric information.

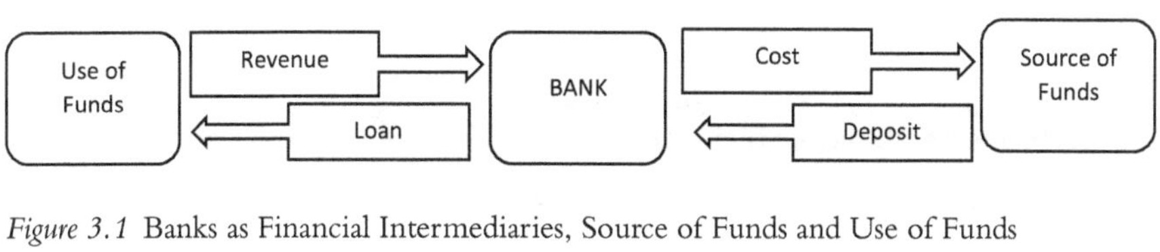

Figure 3.1 Banks as Financial Intermediaries, Source of Funds and Use of Funds

Source: Original notes are adapted from the Indonesian Financial Service Authority[8]

Apart from the main functions just discussed, the government of Indonesia has approved other 'side' functions for banks to meet national and international market demand.[9] These include the following:

1. *Provide a payment system in banking.* The bank facilitates money transfers from one person to another by which the payer discharges the payment obligations to the beneficiary.[10]
2. *Provide an international payment system.* Geographical distance, culture, and currencies which create hurdles for international transactions could be solved by a bank, through the advent of technology, such as an electronic payment system facilitating a payment made from one bank account to another.[11] This modern payment system substitutes the traditional payment of using cash and forgoing the direct intervention of bank employees, such as debit cards, credit cards, internet banking, and an e-commerce payment system.
3. *Money creation.* Money is created through the fractional reserve banking system in the form of new bank deposits when a bank issues a loan. Demand deposits are used as a means of payment through a clearing mechanism.[12] The circulation of money creation is regulated by BI to prevent excessive circulation of money.
4. *Bank as a means of investment.* The bank serves as a middleman between a company and investors when the company wants to issue stock or bonds at the initial public offering. The bank acts as a proxy for the company and sells the shares on the market to the investors.[13]
5. *Bank as a place to store valuables.* The bank provides safe deposit boxes or lockers where customers can store valuable items.[14]

With the recent growth of the global economy, the banking functions in financial systems have developed markedly towards fee-based income and dealer-derivative transactions.[15] Banks are becoming more aggressive in offering multiple types of products to meet the needs of market competition. More and more banks are deciding to put their capital at risk with the aim of benefiting from the interest rate return out of their different activities, thereby providing higher returns to their shareholders.[16] The ever-growing complexity of global banking and the unique role of banks means that the fortunes of banks have a greater impact on national economies than ever before. Although later core chapters focus on Islamic banking with an interest-free system, this chapter attends to conventional banking and issues relating to interest rate activities. Such issues are important to examine in order to assess which prudential standards the Indonesian government applies to Islamic banks as an alternative system of banking.

3.3 The Regulatory Frameworks of the Indonesian Banking System

As banks' competitive strategies change in response to trends in the financial marketplace, so too will their organisational architecture. Banks may be unaware of the applicable law, as the law itself is less flexible in meeting the needs of banking expansion, or that the regulation is outdated and unable to adjust with recent market developments. As a result, Hamdaoui and Maktouf state that the effectiveness of regulation diminishes over time in banking business activities where the domestic regulations have become outdated.[17] Similarly, Scherer further explains:

> When it [i.e., bank regulations] works well, it lubricates the functioning of every other industry and thereby contribute to economic growth. But when it functions badly, the consequences can be grave. And grave they were in the first decade of the 21st Century. The actions of banking industry firms, combined with default by their regulators and imprudence by their customers, were key precipitating factors of "great recession" commencing in 2008, leading inter alia to substantial unemployment and under-employment.[18]

As will be discussed in this section, banks are the key to economic success in the country. Having such an important functional role in the economy, banks and other financial institutions are strictly regulated by the financial authorities in Indonesia. The primary challenge for regulators is not only to balance the regulatory framework which nurtures innovation in the financial market, but also to oversee customer protection. The Indonesian government directed that the bank should ensure that they comply with the principal regulation for banks, based on *Law No 7 of 1992* concerning banking as amended by *Law No 10 of 1998* and its implementing regulations as well as the *Law of the Republic Indonesia Number 3 of 2004 Concerning Amendment to Act of the Republic of Indonesia Number 23 of 1999 Concerning Bank Indonesia.*[19]

It is important to understand the historical evidence of financial regulatory and supervisory frameworks in Indonesia in order to address whether the government has been too strict or too lenient with respect to controlling banking operations in the context of a dynamic competitive market.

3.3.1 The Forces of Change

For the sake of gaining a better overview on the evolution of the regulatory and supervisory frameworks, the period can be split into three phases before the Islamic interest-free banking system was born.

1. *First Period (1970–1983)*

This was a period of an oil and gas boom, which greatly benefited the Indonesian economy. The government was able to manage this revenue and allocate the budget to control inflationary pressures, impose credit ceilings, and subsidise interest rates.[20] BI also provided incentives to state banks and several private banks to support their operation and mobilise public funds.[21] Banking in Indonesia was governed by the *Basic Banking Law 1967* and by several regulations and decrees.[22] Foreign banks were licensed to operate in Indonesia by opening representative offices and branch offices; however, foreigners could not establish a 100% foreign-owned locally incorporated bank or savings bank even through joint ventures. There were also restrictions on the rate of interest which could be charged by non-domestic banks. Foreign banks were not supposed to earn interest rates on loans greater than domestic banks. However, in practice, as Hornick observes, "these interest rate restrictions are not always observed and foreign banks do sometimes charge higher rates than their domestic counterparts".[23]

2. *Second Period (1983–1988)*

The second phase was initiated by the fall in oil prices in the early 1980s. BI no longer subsidised interest rates. Instead, the government announced discount window facilities known as Bank Indonesia Certificates (SBI), which were designed to absorb banks' excess liquidity, and also introduced an instrument for money market operations and liquidity management named Money Market Commercial Paper (SBPU).[24] SBI, or discount windows, were aimed at providing the facility for banks to borrow funds from BI in case of a liquidity mismatch, but due to lack of expertise, many banks relied on financing their loans from funds obtained in the money market, which caused their profits to be sensitive to the volatility of interest rates.[25]

3. *Third Period (1988–1997)*

In 1988–1997, the government introduced a series of reform packages to improve banking stability. These packages aimed at the liberalisation of banking to reduce the gap between state banks and private banks, by promoting prudent regulation, such as by adopting the Basel Capital Accords of 1988, improving the effectiveness of money market instruments, and formulating a more floating interest and exchange rate.[26] As a result of these reforms, the government restricted the banking industry in mobilising their deposits and reduced their reliance on the government.

The reform package, as illustrated in Figure 3.2, provides four types of banks under *Law No 7 of 1992*:

1 BI, as the central bank, acts as the regulator and supervisor of all other banks.
2 Commercial banks provide payment transfers from one bank account to another and mobility of business transactions.
3 Rural banks provide savings in terms of fixed deposits and saving accounts. They focus on the provision of loans to small- and medium-sized enterprises and are not permitted to provide payment transfer services, to do business in foreign currencies, or to do any type of share investment.[27]
4 Foreign banks are representative offices of a bank whose head office is domiciled overseas and may only be established pursuant to a licence granted by the Chairmen of BI.[28]

With the regulatory reforms, more types of banks could now operate in Indonesia. The increasing numbers of banks and branches were not fully anticipated by

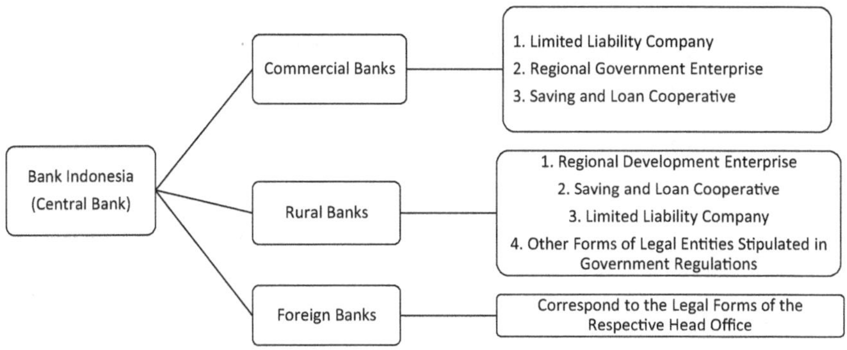

Figure 3.2 The Indonesian Bank System under *Law No 7 of 1992*

Source: Original notes are adopted from *Law No 7 of 1992* on banking[29]

the supervisory authority, and the supervision of these banks shifted from having relatively fixed rates to more floating interest and exchange rates. These reforms also led to state-owned banks becoming less prevalent in the country, and as more private banks were approved by the government to operate in Indonesia, they became aggressively competitive in issuing loans by sometimes forgoing sound credit analysis. This led to a high level of non-performing loans.[30] According to Abdullah and Santoso, these reforms led to Indonesian banks becoming more prone to interest rate risk and foreign exchange risk exposure, and a clear danger emerged of banks failing to pay their costs due to their inability to cover those risks with capital requirements.[31]

In mid-1997, a banking crisis occurred in Indonesia following the persistent depreciation of the Indonesian rupiah. The crisis forced BI to bail out several systemically important banks to restore the stability and solvency of the banking system and restructure the program in 1998.[32] This crisis hit the Indonesian economy very badly, requiring a longer period for economic recovery compared to its neighbouring countries in south-east Asia, particularly Singapore, Malaysia, Brunei, and Thailand.[33]

During this period, the government's response was to restructure and recapitalise only viable banks. This led to many other banks being frozen out of operations or closed in 1998–1999 to prevent further disruption.[34] The number of banks in Indonesia fell from 239 to 153, and comprised 5 state banks, 38 private national foreign exchange banks, 45 private national non-foreign exchange banks, 26 regional banks, 29 joint banks, and 10 foreign banks.[35] Swandayani and Kusumaningtias note that Bank Muamalat Indonesia (established in 1992), which was the only Islamic bank that existed at that time, was more resilient during the 1998 crisis and even made a profit of over Rp 300 billion (AUD 30 million).[36]

This evidence shows the lack of prudential regulations, the lack of law enforcement, and the need for bringing the supervisory and regulatory practices closer to international standards. As argued by Abdullah and Santoso:

> The deregulation packages in the 1980s and 1990s might have contributed to the fragility of the banking sector in Indonesia due to lack of prudential regulation, good governance, market discipline and law enforcement. . . . It is therefore necessary to bring regulatory and supervisory approaches closer to international standards.[37]

In summary, there is evidence of a lack of adherence to international financial standards by Indonesian banks before and during the 1990s monetary crisis due to the lack of credit analysis on the one hand and banks' profit sensitivity to interest rate fluctuations on the other. Therefore, the idea of prudential regulation of banks in keeping with the international regulatory and supervisory standards will be further discussed throughout the book.

3.3.2 Initial Attention to **Sharia**

The impact of the 1990s financial crisis devastated the Indonesian economic recovery process. For this reason, the Indonesian government sought an alternative banking system. After prolonged study of neighbouring countries, the government agreed to incorporate an interest-free profit-sharing system, thereby initiating a new 'dual' banking system. (The term 'dual banking system', where the conventional banking and Islamic banking systems operate side by side, appeared in Indonesia after the passing of *Law No 10 of 1998*, which amends *Law No 7 of 1992 on Banking.*[38])

Under *Law No 10 of 1998 on Banking*, the system of banking is classified into two categories: conventional banks and banks with profit and loss sharing. At this stage, the term 'Islamic bank' is not specifically mentioned in this law, but additional types of banking products and services with profit-and-loss-sharing systems based on *sharia* principles are introduced for commercial banks.[39] (Curiously, the use of the term 'Islamic bank' was not countenanced by the government, but the term '*Sharia* bank' was deemed acceptable. The latter is now the commonly used term in Indonesia, whereas 'Islamic bank' is virtually unheard of.[40])

As discussed earlier, although the Indonesian government provided reform packages to increase banking competitiveness in the global market and controlled interest rates to safeguard financial market stability, it has proved difficult for BI as a single authority to supervise all these banks (both interest-based and interest-free). The following section will discuss the challenges of the current supervisory and regulatory authorities and how these bodies interlink.

3.4 Present Regulatory and Supervisory Authorities System in Indonesia

Effective banking supervision is essential in order to monitor the management of banking risk exposure to protect depositors, provide a government safety net, and ensure economic stability. Ineffective banking supervision and 'light' regulation may lead private institutions to act in their own interests, including even taking aggressive legal action against supervisory authorities.[41] Unfortunately (as explained next), as yet there is no consensus about what would count as the 'best' form of banking supervision in the contemporary financial system. For example, there is still much debate over how much power should be given to bank supervisors by government regulations, and whether giving them additional power could be misused for political ends.[42]

It is the task of the supervisory authority to monitor the behaviour of banks, to improve their corporate governance, and to ensure the security and risk sensitivity of their capital requirements. However, giving greater power to a governmental supervisory authority can give rise to the possibility of self-interested politicians interfering with the supervisory authority for their own personal benefit; relatedly, it could also result in the central bank's authority to issue a decision being undermined due to the involvement of state firms and politically well-connected firms.[43] For example, the 1990s monetary and banking crisis and then economic crisis in Indonesia resulted chiefly from political instability, corrupt banks and political leaders, and the institutional instability of the central monetary authority itself, which hamstrung its efforts to prevent the continual currency decline in 1997.[44] Sato comments,

> President Soeharto's sudden dismissal of the central bank governor in February 1998, due to his opposition to the planned pegging of the Indonesian currency in the U.S. dollar, left a strong impression that the president would intervene politically in the central bank.[45]

There are two alternate views on forms of supervisory authority. One is the independent supervision perspective, where supervisory authorities with statutory independence are created by the government. Such supervisory authorities have the power to oversee and administer credit allocation behaviour in the financial system by private and state banks, free from government interference. Such an approach also minimises information asymmetry and administration by centralising supervisory functions.[46] Another approach is a private empowerment view, where the supervisory agency's powers are limited, but the supervisory agency has sufficient power to provide accurate disclosures of bank information so that all private agents can monitor bank conditions and provide incentives for optimal bank management.[47]

With regard to banking supervisory authority, the Basel Committee released the second pillar of the Accords focusing explicitly on the supervisory practice of banks to overcome the shortcomings in supervisory practice in many countries and to ensure bank resilience during the crisis.[48] The Basel view is that supervision is not only about overcoming the banking crisis problem, it should also consider the relationship between bank supervision and its impact on macroeconomics. Beck, Demirguc-Kunt, and Levine argue that bestowing all power to a supervisory authority may give rise to acts of undue self-interest on the part of an authority's personnel, which would obviously have a negative influence on bank development and social welfare.[49] They also argue that if the supervisory authority applies policies that are too strict and rigid with respect to, for example, limitations on foreign ownership of financial institutions, then such a regime will weaken the scale of international networks.[50] On the other hand, banks with supervisory practices favouring public transparency tend to be more developed and vigilant.[51] In countries where the corruption amongst politicians and government officials is rampant, the uppermost concern should be with ensuring that a supervisory authority is not captured and utilized for political purposes, or for the personal benefit of politicians and bureaucrats.[52]

A related issue is whether there should be a separate supervisory authority for monetary and banking supervision, and whether all these tasks should only be in the hands of a central bank or dispersed among multiple agencies. As Davis and Obasi argue,

> Central Banks already have the key responsibility of monetary policy and that adding the extra job of bank supervision may risk overstretch. There is also the concern that if central banks also supervise bank activities, there could develop a conflict of interest between the execution of both jobs, especially during a downturn where the central bank may adopt an overly loose monetary policy to contain adverse effect on bank credit quality and profitability.[53]

Davis and Obasi conclude ambivalently that, "up to now, there is no way to decide which type of agency structure is better . . . whether to have a single supervisory authority or to have multiple authorities for the finance service sector".[54]

It is clear that models of supervisory authorities indeed vary, with each country deciding on a model which caters for the wide scope of business activities carried out by their financial institutions. In the context of Indonesia, it is now the case that the financial authorities are independent bodies, and it is intended that they be free from any interference. Policymakers decided to split the job of supervision by creating a special agency, the Financial Service Authority, independent of BI, whose duty is to supervise banks and other markets institutions. These supervisory agencies will be discussed further next, using the Indonesian context as a case study.

3.4.1 Bank Indonesia and the Political Capture View

The view that central banks can be and have been 'captured' by politicians, and thus operate according to the interests of politicans rather than the general public, has been a hot topic among scholars for some time now.[55] This section will briefly discuss whether the independence of financial authorities can compromised due to the influence of politicians, and whether the separation of financial agencies could lead to contested or ambiguous overlapping of responsibilities and information asymmetry.

Before 2013, BI had the functions of maintaining monetary policy and financial policy. However, on 31 December 2013, the financial regulatory and supervisory function was transferred to the Financial Service Authority (FSA, in Indonesian, Otoritas Jasa Keuangan). BI retained responsibility for monetary policy and external stability.[56] In particular: (1) maintaining the stability of prices of goods and services reflected in the development of the inflation rate; and (2) maintaining the stability of the rupiah exchange rate against foreign currencies.[57]

The separation of BI and the FSA was intended to reduce the duties of the central bank. The FSA *Law No 21 of 2011* vests the authority with the role of the financial services sector regulator and supervisor. The FSA is an independent body of the Indonesian Government Agency, it has the authority to regulate, supervise, inspect, and investigate financial institutions without interference from any party.[58] The FSA is not, however, the Lender of the Last Resort when a bank has a liquidity crisis. This function remains with BI. The demand and supply of money is monitored and regulated by BI.[59] BI also functions to facilitate the payment system and authorises the creation of cash money (paper money and coins) and non-cash, such as cheques, demand deposits, and money orders, as well as forms of payment that rely on technology, such as credit cards and debit cards.[60] BI also conducts clearing between banks in the form of rupiah and foreign currencies.

Simply put, the FSA of Indonesia is responsible at the micro level for all financial services, whereas BI operates at the macro level and is responsible for ensuring monetary stability as well as financial system stability.[61]

The issue of separation between financial authorities has been discussed at length by academicians in the context of how well versed these financial authorities are in their overlapping activities. Beck, Demirguc-Kunt, and Levine argue that supervision should not only focus on criteria relating to banking crises, but the supervisory authority also needs to emphasise the relationship between bank supervision and the macro economy.[62] This will be discussed next.

Furthermore, BI is a fully autonomous and independent body of the Indonesian government, which means it is free from interference by external parties and has the right to refuse or disregard any attempt by any political party in performing its functions.[63] Again, questions may be raised about how much independence it actually possesses: although BI is regulated by statute and has the authority to issue its own policy rules and regulations, in fact its operations cannot be entirely be divorced from politics. The Deputy Governor of BI is nominated by the House of Representatives (Dewan Perwakilan Rakyat). Arguably, the nominated Deputy Governor is vulnerable to political influence (both reward and retribution) and can thus become a quasi-political figure when appointed.[64]

This political influence on BI's supervisory authority became evident in the case of the disbursement of BI's liquidity support scheme in 1997 (in Indonesian, Bantuan Likuiditas Bank Indonesia, or BLBI). The total scheme was Rp 147.7 trillion (AUD 147.7 billion) and was disbursed to 48 banks. In fact, 95% of BLBI funds were misused by the recipients, and there were indications of irregularities in the distribution process.[65] Although several bankers' names were linked to this misuse, they were never seriously pursued or prosecuted, as the government issued a letter of termination of the investigation of the case (in Indonesian, Surat Pemberhentian Penyidikan Perkara [SP3]).[66]

In September 2008, the Corruption Eradication Commission (KPK, or Komisi Pemberantasan Korupsi) said it was willing to investigate this huge corruption case, following the cancellation of several SP3s by the Attorney General's Office.[67] In April 2013, the former Head of the Indonesian Bank Restructuring Agency (IBRA), Syafruddin Arsyad, was charged and tried in the corruption court.[68] IBRA was one of a series of reforms taken by the Indonesian government, in agreement with the International Monetary Fund, in January 1998, in response to the banking and economic crisis which emerged following the monetary crisis of mid-1997.[69] Arsyad was convicted and sentenced to 13 years in prison in 2018.[70] But with his attorney, Arsyad took legal action to a higher level by filing an appeal with Indonesia's Supreme Court. In July 2019, Arsyad was officially released from detention following the Supreme Court's decision to grant his appeal in the alleged corruption of the BLBI case. This was done on the grounds that, in the opinion of the Cassation Counsel, the legal stipulation against Arsyad was not in accordance with procedures, because the defendant should not have been convicted of a criminal act of corruption, but rather should have entered the category of civil law or administrative law.[71]

Arguably, this case illustrates the fact that although the supervisory authority is by statute an independent body, this body is still subject to political influence and lacks the power to fend off political capture. This is in line with Quintyn and Taylor's theoretical argument that politicians do not maximise social welfare and rather induce banks to channel their funds to politically connected firms, particularly in countries where the diffraction of government power is seen as a direct challenge to parliamentary sovereignty or to the principle of authority separation.[72] Similarly, in relation to banking, Davis and Obasi argue that,

> Since most countries do not have the proper institutional framework that induces politicians and government official to act in the best interest of their citizens, the heavy handed supervision of banks may become a form of abuse of power that will simply divert the flow of credit to the leaders and their associates.[73]

It should be noted, however, that wherever there is a potential for disputes between the regulatory authority and other government agencies, BI can, in principle, disentangle itself from political influence by relying upon international standards as a means of legally asserting its independence and is also the relevant authority for adopting and implementing the Basel Accords based on the commitment of the G20 leaders' summit.[74]

3.4.2 The Financial Service Authority of Indonesia

The Financial Service Authority (FSA) has the functions of maintaining an integrated regulatory and supervisory system for all activities in the financial services industry and maintaining the stability of the Indonesian financial system. This includes banking supervision and non-banking supervision, such as capital markets, insurance, pension funds, and other financial services.

More specifically, the FSA has authority to regulate and supervise banking and non-banking institutions, including licensing for the establishment of bank and financial institutions and business activities of banks. The FSA is also authorised to regulate and supervise banks' and non-banks' solvency rating, prudential aspects, and conduct supervision.[75]

The FSA retains the authority to take preventative measures for consumers and the public, which includes providing information and education to the public on the characteristics of the financial services sector, services, and products; requesting financial institutions to halt their activities if they have the potential to harm the community; and other actions deemed necessary in accordance with statutory provisions in the financial services sector.[76] In addition to taking preventative actions, the FSA also provides consumer complaints services and is authorised to conduct legal defences, such as ordering or taking certain actions against financial institutions to settle with consumers who have been disadvantaged and filing lawsuits to recover the assets of the parties involved to obtain compensation from the party that caused losses to harmed parties as a result of violations of the laws and regulations of the financial services sector.[77]

For example, in 2011, Bank Mega was found to be in breach of the *BI Regulation No 5/8/PBI/2003* as superseded by the *Regulation No 11/25/PBI/2009 on the application of risk management by commercial banks.*[78] Bank Mega was sanctioned in a civil case law related to misconduct which caused the loss of Elnusa's deposit funds. The decision of the South Jakarta District Court dated 22 March 2012 was that Bank Mega immediately disburse Elnusa's deposit and interest with the total of Rp 111 billion (AUD 111 million).[79] Following the court's decision on 24 May 2011, the Board of Governors of BI imposed a number of restrictions on Bank Mega, including a prohibition on opening new branch offices for one year and on soliciting new customers for on-call deposits or extending existing on-call deposits to customers.[80]

The Board of Commissioners (Dewan Komisioner) of the FSA consist of nine members and are collective and collegial in nature; the chief executives are the members of the Board of Commissioners in charge of leading the implementation of the supervision of financial services activities and reporting the performance of its duties to the Board of Commissioners. The composition of the FSA Board of Commissioners is shown in Figure 3.3.

All nine members of this Board have the same voting rights. The first seven members are elected by the parliament (Dewan Perwakilan Rakyat) based on candidates proposed by the president of Indonesia. These seven Commissioners each has a term of office of five years and can be reappointed only once.[81] The eighth and ninth Commissioners are appointed by the president based on candidates proposed by the Governor of BI and the Ministry of Finance.[82] These two Commissioners end their terms if they no longer serve on the Board of Governors of BI or as top officials of the Ministry of Finance.[83]

The Board of Commissioners are prohibited from having an interest in the financial institutions that they supervise. Thus, the Board of Commissioners are restricted from being involved in the management of the financial institutions under FSA supervision or being a member of any political party.[84] The reason for the inclusion of the Governor of BI on the Board of Commissioners in the FSA ex officio is to facilitate coordination and sharing of information between the FSA and BI. However, about

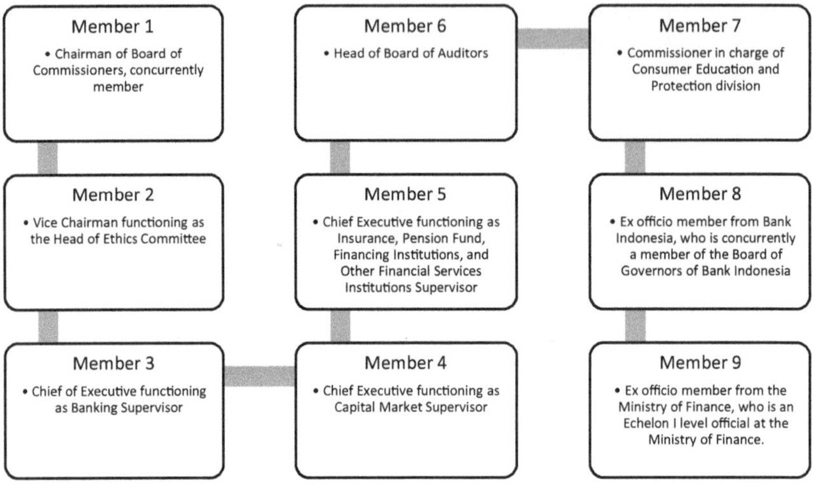

Figure 3.3 Organisation Structure of the Board of Commissioners

Source: Original notes are adapted from *Law No 21 of 2011* on FSA art 44(1)

one-third of the supervisors in the FSA are from BI, which raises the challenge of capacity building and other legacy issues associated with the potential overlap of supervisory authorities between the FSA, BI, and the Indonesia Deposit Insurance Corporation (IDIC, in Indonesian, Lembaga Penjamin Simpanan).[85] As described by the IMF–World Bank joint mission on Indonesian Financial Sector Assessment, this is "an ineffective use of resources and could adversely affect accountability and information sharing. Additional clarity on mandates and closer cooperation between BI and OJK [i.e., the FSA] regarding macroprudential oversight is needed".[86]

The Financial System Stability Committee (Komite Stabilitas Sistem Keuangan, widely known as KSSK) was formed as a coordinating body to maintain the stability of the national financial system and is a forum that monitors the overlapping authorities that are fragmented across multiple agencies. Its members consist of the Minister of Finance as the coordinator, the Governor of BI, the Chairman of the FSA Board of Commissioners, and the Chairperson of the Board of Commissioners of the Indonesian Deposit Insurance Corporation.[87] Decision-making in this forum is based on deliberation to reach consensus.[88] If consensus is not reached, then decisions are made based on majority voting.[89] The task of this forum is to monitor and evaluate financial system stability, conduct meetings at least once in three months, make recommendations to each member to take action on, and make policies in order to maintain financial system stability.[90] The forum also establishes and implements policies needed to prevent and handle crises in the financial system in accordance with their respective authorities. The forum's decisions related to the settlement and award of a failed bank which is suspected to have a systemic effect is binding on the Deposit Insurance Corporation and required to be submitted to the House of Representatives for approval.[91]

3.4.3 The Indonesian Deposit Insurance Corporation

As of 2004, International Standard and Poor's (S&P) has classified the Indonesian Banking Industry as 'high risk'. This poor ranking was given due to the unstable condition of the Indonesian economy and the poor management of the banking system in Indonesia.[92] Thus, the Indonesian Deposit Insurance Corporation (IDIC, in Indonesian, Lembaga Penjamin Simpanan) was created to restore public confidence in the banking system after the financial crisis of 1998. The IDIC functions to guarantee bank customer deposits and participate actively in maintaining the stability of the banking system according to its authority.[93] As of 31 June 2019, IDIC Deposit Statistics show that approximately 98% of saving accounts contain Rp 100 million (AUD 10,000) or less.[94] In 2008, the government issued *Regulation No. 66 of 2008 concerning Amendments to Law No 24 of 2004* on the Deposit Insurance Corporation, which changed the value of deposits guaranteed by IDIC to Rp 2 billion (AUD 2 million). This regulation can be adjusted according to macroeconomic conditions.

3.5 Conflicting Views on Regulatory Frameworks

This section looks at the legal and regulatory framework for Indonesian financial institutions in achieving their objectives. Although the government of Indonesia has enacted the required laws and policies to regulate Islamic financial institutions (as will be discussed in the next chapter), the issue arises as to whether this will create tensions in the regulatory frameworks. This is because the laws designed for conventional banks may not be able to regulate the Islamic financial institutions effectively.[95] In fact, the issue of whether Islamic financial institutions should be governed either solely by provisions based on *sharia* law or the existing state law has been a much debated matter. Whilst mainly Muslim countries, such as Iran and Pakistan, have fully adopted Islamic laws, others, such as Indonesia and Malaysia, have implemented dual systems, whereas common law countries such as the UK are generally pragmatic 'neutral' systems.[96]

In their evaluation of different legal systems, Grassa and Gazdar note that although Muslim-dominant countries who incorporate the *sharia* in their jurisdictions show a significant development in the performance of Islamic banking, countries with the British common law traditions tend to support financial development to a much greater degree than countries that have inherited the French civil law tradition.[97] Grassa and Gazdar further argue that those countries which adopted a mixed legal system based on common law and *sharia* law are more flexible and better able to make changes to their regulatory arrangements in response to changing socio-economic conditions, whereas those countries that are based on civil law and *sharia* law are less flexible in terms of making changes to their existing laws.[98] Proponents of Islamic finance argue that the dynamism and flexibility of changing the legal system to meet the need for financial growth can foster the development of the Islamic financial system.[99] For example, the introduction of taxation reforms in the UK based on the *Finance Act 2003* ended the multiple payment of Stamp Duty Land Tax on Islamic mortgages. This position is consistent with the view of scholars who have argued that the legal rules matter a great deal to the development of financial institutions and that these rules should be endogenously adjusted to new economic realities.[100]

Although Islamic banking systems have some differences from their conventional counterparts in terms of their philosophy and economic roles, in fact Islamic banks in Indonesia cannot be entirely separated from conventional banks. Indeed, it may be argued that both Islamic and conventional banks operate in essentially the same way at the grass-roots level; as Hanif notes: "Evidences suggest Islamic banking is very much practiced like modern conventional banking".[101] But then, the issue arises as to whether dual authorities (a *sharia*-compliant Supervisory Authority and Financial Supervisory Authority) are required in the dual banking system, and whether there is a conflict if both Islamic and conventional banking rules are fundamentally reconciled within the same regulatory framework.

As discussed previously in Chapter 2, Indonesia upholds a unique form of legal pluralism that includes customary law, secular law derived from the Dutch colonial period, and the *sharia*. Because this pluralism is deeply ingrained in the society, it is arguable that legal centralism could not be effectively applied in Indonesia, as it would entail abolishing other legal systems, such as religious law and other types of self-regulation, and could thereby cause civil and political instability. As Hoebel stated more generally:

> We must have a look at society and culture at large in order to find the place of law within the total structure. We must have some idea of how society works before we can have a full conception of what law is and how it works.[102]

Therefore, as discussed previously, the law should be a dynamic and fluid institution with the ability to adapt to societal changes, bearing in mind the cultural particularities and constraints of the nation. Hence, financial regulation should be flexible enough to meet the needs of the marketplace nationally and internationally. The need for Islamic banks originates with Indonesian Muslims who want a financial institution that meets their faith; however, since Indonesia is not an Islamic state, there is ambiguity as to whether the *sharia* can be harmonised (or compromised) with the other law. This depends on whether banking and financial institutions find it acceptable for conventional banks to open Islamic windows to effectively create more players in the market. The immediate question to be faced is the legal difficulties arising from how Islamic principles of Islamic banking can be ensured.[103] (This will be further discussed in Chapters 4 and 5.)

Commentators have suggested several solutions to regulate *sharia* and non-*sharia* financial institutions. Mansyur, for example, argues that separate state-sanctioned laws for Islamic finance should exist to facilitate justice and provide legal clarity and certainty for the regulatory and supervisory authority.[104] The dilemma here is how the Islamic banking system would interact with the conventional banking system if they are each bound by entirely different legal structures. Syarif purposes that the government may adopt a combinatorial regulatory framework for Islamic finance by drawing upon both the *sharia* sources *(fatwas) and* international Islamic financial standards promulgated by IFSB, the Basel Accords, and other international standard-setting bodies.[105] The problem here is that if the regulatory authority relied exclusively on international standards to dictate domestic law, it is likely that some of these standards will be incompatible and inappropriate for national institutional and cultural particularities.[106] As will be discussed in the following chapter, another attempted solution is to specify a separate entity who should have authority to supervise Islamic banking. Karim and Archer propose that a separate entity should supervise Islamic banks and that the sensible regulation is significant to Islamic banks in order to maintain confidence and a sound regulatory environment.[107] This authority is more important than the rules themselves, as there are dissenting opinions among scholars in interpreting Islamic law. In what follows, it is argued that rather than seeking to impose a unitary legal system, the flexibility in national legal systems should be taken advantage of to facilitate the development of financial institutions in a dual system regulatory framework.

3.6 Concluding Remarks

Drastic reform to the Indonesian banking sector took place in the post-1998 crisis period, where Indonesia was hit by a sudden collapse of confidence as footloose international short-term capital took flight. Part of this reform included taking initiatives to improve the Islamic finance market players. However, further improvements are required for the legal framework to effectively regulate the banking and financial system in the Indonesian dual system of regulatory framework; however, this has arguably given rise to challenges for Islamic banking because the state generally applies a framework which is not *sharia* compliant. The following chapters are motivated by this concern. An analysis will be provided of the legal and regulatory framework of Islamic banking in Indonesia in order to assess whether the current Islamic banking practice is effective and able to achieve global market demand.

Notes

1 Otoritas Jasa Keuangan, *Statistik Perbankan Indonesia Desember 2021* (Indonesia Banking Statistics December 2021) 14.

2 Otoritas Jasa Keuangan, *Latar Belakang Pembentukan OJK* [The Background of the Establishment of the FSA], [tr author], www.ojk.go.id/id/Pages/FAQ-Otoritas-Jasa-Keuangan.aspx.

3 John H. Boyd, Gianni De Nicolo, and Bruce D. Smith, 'Crises in Competitive Versus Monopolistic Banking Systems' (2004) 36(3) *Journal of Money, Credit, and Banking* 487.

4 Mekki Hamdaoui and Samir Maktouf, 'Financial Reforms and Banking System Vulnerability: The Role of Regulatory Frameworks' (2020) 52 *Structural Change and Economic Dynamics* 184.

5 Christopher James and Joel Houston, 'Evolution or Extinction: Where Are Banks Headed?' (1996) 9(2) *Journal of Applied Corporate Finance* 8.

6 Undang-Undang Republik Indonesia Nomor 10 Tahun 1998 Tentang Perbankan *[Law No 10 of 1998 on Banking*] (Indonesia) art 2(4) [tr author].

7 Raghuram G. Rajan, 'Do We Still Need Commercial Banks?', *The National Bureau of Economic Research*, www.nber.org/reporter/fall98/rajan_fall98.html.

8 Otoritas Jasa Keuangan, 'Bank Umum [Banking]' (2017), [tr author], www.ojk.go.id/id/kanal/perbankan/Pages/Bank-Umum.aspx#:~:text=Bank%20umum%20adalah%20bank%20yang,jasa%20dalam%20lalu%20lintas%20pembayaran.

9 Undang-Undang Republik Indonesia Nomor 10 Tahun 1998 Tentang Perbankan [*Law No. 10 of 1998 on Banking*] (Indonesia) art 1(1) [tr author].

10 Undang-Undang Republik Indonesia Nomor 7 Tahun 1992 Tentang Perbankan [*Law No. 7 of 1992 on Banking*] (Indonesia) art 1(1) [tr author].

11 Ibid.

12 Ibid.

13 Ibid.

14 Ibid., art 3(5).

15 HR Machiraju, *Modern Commercial Banking* (New Age International, 2008) 1–2.

16 James and Houston, above n 5.

17 Hamdaoui and Maktouf, above n 4.

18 F.M. Scherer, *The Banking Industry*, Faculty Research Working Paper Series RWP 14-042, Harvard Kennedy School (2014) 2.

19 Further reading on Bank Indonesia Acts can be downloaded from this link www.bi.go.id/en/tentang-bi/uu-bi/Contents/Default.aspx.

20 Burhanuddin Abdullah and Wimboh Santoso, 'The Indonesian Banking Industry: Competition, Consolidation, and Systemic Stability' (BIS Paper 4, Bank for International Settlements, 2001).

21 Ibid.

22 Undang-Undang Republik Indonesia Nomor 16 tahun 1967 Tentang Pokok-Pokok Perbankan [*Law No. 14 of 1967 on Basic Banking Law*]. Peraturan Kementerian Keuangan No 034/MK/IV/2/68 February 20, 1968, Tentang Tempat dan Bidang Usaha Serta Prosedur Perizinan Bank Asing [Ministry of Finance Decree No 034/MK/IV/2/68 February 20, 1968, on the Statement of Policy Regarding Foreign Banks].

23 Robert N. Hornick, 'Foreign Banking in Indonesia' (1984) 6(3) *Northwestern Journal of International Law & Business* 760, 767.

24 Abdullah and Santoso, above n 20, 81.

25 Ibid.

26 Ibid.

27 Undang-Undang Republik Indonesia Nomor 7 Tahun 1992 Tentang Perbankan [*Law No. 7 of 1992 on Banking*] (Indonesia) [tr author].

28 *Law No. 10 of 1998 Concerning Banking* stated that the Islamic Rural Bank is a bank which based its activities on conventional or *sharia* principles, and in so doing shall not provide any service in money transfer or payment transactions.

29 Under *Regulation No. 56/POJK.03/2016 concerning maximum ownership of foreigner in a commercial bank*, a commercial bank can be established jointly by Indonesian and foreigner investors with the maximum foreign participation of 99% of the total issued and paid-up capital. A single owner cannot control an Indonesian bank. *The Regulation of Indonesian Financial Services Authority No. 39/POJK.03/2017 concerning single ownership in Indonesian Banking.*

30 According to Abdullah and Santoso, above n 20, the problem of loans had increased gradually from 6% in 1990 to 17% in 1992, which became the trigger for the Asian financial crisis in the 1990s.

31 Abdullah and Santoso, above n 20, 82.

32 Ibid., 80.

33 Abdul Ghofur Anshori, *Perbankan Syariah di Indonesia* [Islamic Banking in Indonesia] (Gadjah Mada University Press, 2018) 1 [tr author].

34 Mohammad Sadli, *The Indonesian Crisis* (Institute of Southeast Asian Studies, 1999).

35 Abdullah and Santoso, above n 20, 84.

36 Desi Marilin Swandayani and Rohmawati Kusumaningtias, 'Pengaruh Inflasi, Suku Bunga, Nilai Tukar Valas dan Jumlah Uang Beredar Terhadap Profitabilitas pada

Perbankan Syariah di Indonesia Periode 2005–2009 [The Effect of Inflation, Interest Rates, Foreign Exchange Rates, and Money Supply to the Profitability of Islamic Banking in the Indonesia Period 2005–2009]' (2012) 3(2) *AKRUAL: Jurnal Akuntansi* 147, 148 [tr author].

37 Abdullah and Santoso, above n 20, 82.

38 Siti Fatimah Zahra, Ascarya and Nurul Huda, 'Stability Measurement of Dual Banking System in Indonesia: Markov Switching Approach' (2018) 10(1) *Al-Iqtishad: Jurnal Ilmu Ekonomi Syariah (Journal of Islamic Economics)* 25, 26.

39 *Law No. 10 of 1998 Concerning Banking*, Chapter 22 stated that a commercial bank is a bank which based its activities on conventional and/or *sharia* principles, and in doing so provides any service in payment.

40 Zakaria Bahari, Zahri Hamat and Mutiara Dwi Sari, 'History of Islamic Bank in Indonesia: Issues Behind Its Establishment' (2016) 2(5) *International Journal of Finance and Banking Research* 178, 182.

41 James R. Barth, Gerard Caprio and Ross Levine, 'The Regulation and Supervision of Banks around the World: A New Database' World Bank, 1 https://openknowledge.worldbank.org/handle/10986/19664.

42 Felix Dalimartha and Faisal Santiago, 'Banking Legislation Renewal as a Preventive Effort of Banking Corruption Crime' (Proceedings of the 1st International Conference on Law, Social Science, Economics, and Education, ICLSSEE 2021, Jakarta, Indonesia, 6 March 2021). Also see Ratna Nurhayati and Seno Wibowo Gumbira, 'Countermeasures Criminal Action of Corruption in Banking in the Lending of Credits' (2021) 27(3) *Journal of Contemporary Issues in Business and Government* 1278.

43 Marc Quintyn and Michael W. Taylor, *Regulatory and Supervisory Independence and Financial Stability*, IMF Working Paper No WP/02/46, International Monetary Fund (2002) 7.

44 Yuri Sato, 'Bank Restructuring and Financial Institution Reform in Indonesia' (2004) 3(1) *The Developing Economies* 91, 102.

45 Ibid., 108.

46 Barth, Caprio and Levine, above n 41, 33.

47 E Philip Davis and Ugochi Obasi, *The Effectiveness of Banking Supervision*, Working Paper No. 09-27, Department of Economics and Finance, Brunel University (2009).

48 Basel Committee on Banking Supervision, *Overview of Pillar 2 Supervisory Review Practices and Approaches* (Bank For International Settlements, June 2019).

49 Thorsten Beck, Asli Demirguc-Kunt and Ross Levine, 'Bank Supervision and Corporate Finance', *World Bank* 8, http://citeseerx.ist.psu.edu/viewdoc/download?doi=10.1.1.508.2262&rep=rep1&type=pdf.

50 Ibid.

51 Quintyn and Taylor, above n 43, 20.

52 Beck, Demirguc-Kunt and Levine, above n 49, 18.

53 Davis and Obasi, above n 47, 5.

54 Ibid.

55 Theory of regulatory capture of supervisory and regulatory financial agencies has been expressed by several authors. For more information, see, e.g., James D. Hamilton and Charles H. Whiteman, 'The Observable Implications of Self-Fulfilling Expectations' (1985) 16(3) *Journal of Monetary Economics* 353.; Jean-Jacques Laffont, and Jean Tirole, 'The Politics of Government Decision Making: Regulatory Institutions' (1990) 6(1) *Journal of Law, Economics and Organization* 1; David Epstein and Sharyn O'Halloran, *Delegating Powers: A Transaction Cost Politics Approach to Policy Making Under Separate Powers* (Cambridge University Press, 1999).

56 Bank Indonesia, *Status and Position of Bank Indonesia*, www.bi.go.id/en/tentang-bi/fungsi-bi/status/Contents/Default.aspx.

57 Ibid.

58 Undang-Undang Republik Indonesia Nomor 21 Tahun 2011 Tentang Otoritas Jasa Keuangan [Law No 21 of 2011 on Financial Services Authority] (Indonesia) ch 1, art 1 [tr author].
59 Ibid.
60 Krisna Wijaya, *Analisis Kebijakan Perbankan Nasional [Analysis of National Banking Policy]* (Elex Media Komputindo, 2013) [tr author].
61 The code of ethics for Indonesian bankers can be found at *Law No 10 of 1998* in Article 49, a member of the board of commissioners, board of directors, or bank employee, who knowingly and wilfully creates falsified or causes fraud, requests or accepts permits or a remuneration, gratuity, for personal gain or for the benefit of his family in return of his efforts to obtain in favour of another person shall be imprisoned for a minimum of three years and a maximum of eight years, and fined to a minimum of Rp 5 billion and maximum of Rp 100 billion. See Bank Indonesia, Code of Ethics and Code of Conduct, 2013, www.bi.go.id/en/tentang-bi/governance/commitment/kode-etik/Contents/Default.aspx.
62 Beck, Demirguc-Kunt and Levine, above n 49.
63 Bank Indonesia, *Bank Indonesia Function: Status and Position of Bank Indonesia* www.bi.go.id/en/tentang-bi/fungsi-bi/status/Contents/Default.aspx.
64 Hamdani, Articles, 'Independensi, Bank Indonesia Harus Bebas dari Tekanan Politik [Bank Indonesia Independence, BI Must be Free From Political Interference]', *Economics*, *Kompasiana* (Jakarta), 11 May 2018, [tr author], www.kompasiana.com/cangkoiburong/5af4e3d7ab12ae5cc5443992/independensi-bank-indonesia-harus-bebas-dari-tekanan-politik#.
65 Mehulika Sitepu, 'Yang Perlu Anda Ketahui dari Kasus BLBI Terbaru [What You Need to Know about the Latest BLBI Case]', *BBC Indonesia* (Jakarta), 27 April 2017, [tr author], www.bbc.com/indonesia/indonesia-39724323.
66 Ibid.
67 Budi Utomo, 'Perjalanan Kasus BLBI 1998 Hingga 2019 [The Journey of the 1998 BLBI Case to 2019]', *Tagar* (Jakarta), [tr author], www.tagar.id/perjalanan-kasus-blbi-1998-hingga-2019.
68 *Syafruddin Arsyad Temenggung* (2019) 1555 K/Pid.Sus/2019, 1–122 (The Supreme Court of the Republic of Indonesia).[tr author].
69 IBRA was established based by Presidential Decree No. 27 of 1998. The objectives were to administer the government's blanket guarantee program and to supervise, manage, and restructure distressed banks. IBRA allowed the establishment of a bad bank financial vehicle and segregate the bad debts away from established banks in order to promote the overall recovery of Indonesia's financial system. The agency was finally terminated in 2004, as it had a troubled record, the agency being criticised for being slow in its restructuring task, lack of transparency, and alleged irregularities, based on the Presidential Decree No. 15 of 2004.
70 *Syafruddin Arsyad Temenggung* (2019) 1555 K/Pid.Sus/2019 (The Supreme Court of the Republic of Indonesia).
71 Ibid.
72 Quintyn and Taylor, above n 43, 29.
73 Davis and Obasi, above n 47, 9.
74 Bank Indonesia, *Financial System Stability: The Roles of Bank Indonesia*, www.bi.go.id/en/perbankan/ssk/peran-bi/peran/Contents/Default.aspx.
75 Ibid.
76 Undang-Undang Republik Indonesia Nomor 21 Tahun 2011 Tentang Otoritas Jasa Keuangan [*Law No. 21 of 2011 on Financial Services Authority*] (Indonesia) art 9.
77 Ibid., ch 6, art 29–30.
78 *Bank Indonesia Regulation No. 5/8/PBI/2003 as amended by the Bank Indonesia Regulation No. 11/25/PBI/2009 on the Application of Risk Management by Commercial Banks.*
79 *PT. Elnusa, Tbk Vs PT. Bank Mega, Tbk* (2011) 284/Pdt.G/2011/PN.Jak.Sel, 1–142 (South Jakarta District Court).[tr author].

80 Johansyah Difi, 'Bank Indonesia Imposes Sanctions on Bank Mega' (Pt Bank Indonesia) (2011), www.bi.go.id/en/ruang-media/siaran-pers/Pages/sp_131811.aspx.
81 Undang-Undang Republik Indonesia Nomor 21 Tahun 2011 Tentang Otoritas Jasa Keuangan [*Law No. 21 of 2011 on Financial Services Authority*] (Indonesia) art 14(3).
82 Ibid., ch 4 art 10.
83 Ibid., art 17(1).
84 Ibid., art 22.
85 See Section 3.3.3 for the details about the functions and duty of IDIC.
86 International Monetary Fund and World Bank, 'Republic of Indonesia Financial Sector Assessment' (World Bank, 2017).
87 Peraturan Kementerian Keuangan No 92/PMK.01/2017 Tentang Organisasi dan Tata Kerja Sekretariat Komite Stabilitas Sistem Keuangan [*Ministry of Finance Regulation No 92/PMK.01/2017 on Organisation and Working Instructions of the Secretariat for the Financial System Stability Comittee*] (Indonesia). [tr author].
The Indonesian Deposit Insurance Corporation, or Lembaga Penjamin Simpanan, is an independent state institution that functions to guarantee the savings of banking customers in Indonesia. This body was formed based on Law of the Republic of Indonesia No. 24 concerning the Deposit Insurance Agency which was established on 22 September 2004. This law came into force 12 months from the enactment so that the establishment and operation of the IDIC began on 22 September 2005.
88 Otoritas Jasa Keuangan, *Financial System Stability Forum*, Otoritas Jasa Keuangan, www.ojk.go.id/en/kanal/perbankan/stabilitas-sistem-keuangan/Pages/Forum-SSK.aspx.
89 Ibid.
90 Ibid.
91 Ibid.
92 Lavinda, '*S&P Pertahankan Rating Indonesia Tetap BBB-* [S&P Maintain the Indonesian Ranking at BBB-]', *Makro News, CNN Indonesia* (Jakarta), [tr author] www.cnnindonesia.com/ekonomi/20180531200039-532-302651/sp-pertahankan-rating-indonesia-tetap-bbb-.
93 Bank Indonesia, *Deposit Insurance Company* (2013), www.bi.go.id/en/tentang-bi/manajemen-krisis/lembaga-penjamin-simpanan/Contents/Default.aspx.
94 The Indonesian Deposit Insurance Corporation, 'Distribusi Simpanan Bank Umum Periode Juni 2019 [Distribution of Commercial Banks Deposit June 2019]', *Lembaga Penjamin Simpanan* [tr author], www.lps.go.id/documents/10157/197446/distribusi+simpanan+juni+2019+pdf/00cda988-dcc0-49f3-bc2b-1a6a259e6c7d.
95 Rihab Grassa and Kouthar Gazdar, 'Law and Islamic Finance: How Legal Origins Affect Islamic Finance Development?' (2014) 14(3) *Borsa Istanbul Review* 158, 159.
96 Fazlurrahman Syarif, 'Regulatory Framework for Islamic Financial Institutions: Lesson Learnt between Malaysia and Indonesia' (2019) 2(2) *Journal of Halal Product and Research* 79, 80.
97 Grassa and Gazdar, above n 96, 163.
98 Ibid., 96, 163.
99 Habib Ahmed, 'Islamic Law, Adaptability and Financial Development' (2006) 13(2) *Islamic Economic Studies* 79, 80.
100 Rafael La Porta et al., 'Law and Finance' (1998) 106(6) *Journal of Political Economy* 1113, 1126.
101 Hanif Muhammad, 'Differences and Similarities in Islamic and Conventional Banking' (2011) 2(2) *International Journal of Business and Social Science* 166.
102 E. Adamson Hoebel, *The Law of Primitive Man: A Study in Comparative Legal Dynamics* (Harvard University Press, 2009) 5.
103 Uzaimah Ibrahim, Aishath Muneeza and Rusni Hassan, 'Conflicts Facing Islamic Banking in Malaysia: Dual Banking System Versus Dual Legal System' (2012) 6(11) *Australian Journal of Basic and Applied Sciences* 246, 250.

104 H.M. Ali Mansyur, 'Aspek Hukum Perbankan Syariah dan Implementasinya di Indonesia [Legal Aspect of Islamic Banking and Its Implementation in Indonesia]' (2011) 11 *Jurnal Dinamika Hukum* 67, 74 [tr author].

105 Syarif, above n 97, 10.

106 This would be analogous to the World Bank's imposition of the 'Washington Consensus' on less developed countries, irrespective of national differences. See Joseph Stiglitz, *Globalisation and Its Discontents* (W.W. Norton & Company, 2002).

107 Rifaat Ahmed Abdel Karim and Simon Archer, *Islamic Finance: The Regulatory Challenge* (Wiley, 2011) 255.

4 Islamic Banking Regulation and Supervision

4.1 Introduction

Although the regulatory and legal challenges faced by Islamic banking might be multidimensional, they originate from one source – namely, the application of Islamic law to modern profit-oriented business behaviour – which some see as an attempt to mix two ostensibly incompatible institutions.[1] In Indonesia, however, regulators are not faced with a simple binary opposition between the *sharia* and secular law that would require privileging of one over the other. The real challenge facing regulators is how to minimise the difficulty that may be created by an imbalance in the integration of Islam and modern banking.

Indonesian Islamic banking legislation now constitutes an important component of overall banking legislation, of which the production of *fatwas* and bank supervision play a central role. The supervision of the dual banking system in Indonesia consists of two types of entities: government supervisory bodies, BI and the FSA, and non-governmental supervisory bodies, the National Sharia Board of Majelis Ulama Indonesia (NSB-MUI) and individual banks' Sharia Supervisory Boards (SSBs). In terms of the history of Indonesian finance, Islamic banking has only recently been legislatively recognised. As such, there is still much room for development and improvement. One of the most important issues that needs to be dealt with is the public perception of Islamic banks relating to their supervision and *sharia* compliance, and whether that supervision should be performed by the state or by non-state bodies.

After discussing the Indonesian regulatory framework's objective in regulating financial institutions, this chapter examines the emergence of the currently existing laws relating to the regulation and supervision of Islamic banking. This chapter will raise an important concern and criticism of the structure – namely, that there are potential conflicts of interest built into *fatwa* production and bank supervision institutional arrangements. This defect can undermine public trust in Islamic banking and is not beneficial to the state's prudential management of Indonesia's financial system. The chapter ends by outlining a reform to the supervisory institutional arrangements, inspired by the Malaysian model, that would at least reduce such conflicts of interest.

DOI: 10.4324/9781003393986-4

4.2 Islamic Banking: Institutional and Religious Consciousness

As financial intermediaries, Islamic banks collect funds from depositors and invest those funds into *sharia*-compliant activities. Islamic banks must strictly adhere to *sharia* requirements to counter any immoral incentives arising from moral hazards and unethical business behaviour. For this reason, individual Islamic banks have an additional layer of corporate governance, namely, SSBs which ensure their transactions adhere to Islamic principles.

Islamic banking has certain unique characteristics and requirements. Islamic law imposes a set of ethics that prohibit exploitation and avoids involvement in activities that are deemed morally undesirable, such as drugs, alcohol, prostitution, and gambling. The SSBs are responsible for ensuring that banking activities are *sharia* compliant. In short, Islamic banks have a non-financial (religious) responsibility to comply with Islamic law and ensure their Islamic *bona fides* to the public, in addition to their financial responsibility of achieving a competitive financial return and compliance with the legal authorities.[2] Yet despite these unique characteristics, Islamic banking is still accused of mirroring the interest costs of conventional banks. For instance, the *murabaha* financial product structure[3] has a similar risk profile to a conventional bank loan and creates *sharia*-compliant replicas of debt[4] (this is discussed in Chapter 5). Another major problem is that although Islamic banking products are supervised by the SSBs, the independence of the SSBs can be compromised by virtue of the fact that SSB members draw their incomes and social status from their association with the banks that they supervise (discussed in Section 4.4.2).

4.3 Dual Supervisory Bodies in the Dual Banking System

As described before, Indonesia has adopted a dual banking system with dual supervisory bodies: namely, governmental bodies (BI and FSA) and a non-governmental organisation (NSB-MUI) for the *sharia* issues. Since Islamic and conventional banking are prescribed by BI and the FSA, in order to control the banks, some general regulations can be applied for both types of banks, with certain exceptions with regard to Islamic-specific regulations and supervision.

BI and the FSA have to ensure that Islamic banks comply with general regulations governing all banks in order to maintain macro financial stability. In addition to this, Islamic banks must be *sharia* compliant in all their activities. The enforcement of this *sharia* compliance is in the hands of regulators, as mentioned in Chapter viii Art 51 of the *Law of Republic of Indonesia No. 21 of 2008 on Islamic Banking*, which states that "Islamic Banks and Islamic Business Units are obligated to maintain the compliance with Islamic principles and Islamic management principles which is governed by BI regulations". However, the actual day-to-day *sharia* supervision process is delegated to banks' own SSBs which have been approved by the MUI, which is thereby ultimately responsible for supervising the *sharia* compliance of Islamic banking activities. (The discourse over the policy issues and effectiveness of these non-governmental bodies will be discussed in Section 4.4.)

Other regulatory bodies that are also involved in Islamic finance include the Ministry of Finance of Indonesia and the Indonesia Deposit Insurance Corporation, which are the responsible authorities to protect consumers of financial institutions.[5] Furthermore, the religious courts and the National Sharia Arbitration Body are responsible for dealing with Islamic finance disputes.[6] In October 1993, the National Sharia Arbitration Body in Indonesia (Badan Arbitrase Syariah Nasional), was established by the MUI to handle legal disputes in Islamic banking activities outside the courts.[7] Based on the issuance of *Constitutional Court Decision No. 93/PUU-X/2012 related to Judicial Review* Art 55 para (2) and (3) *Law No. 21 of 2008 concerning Islamic Banking*, for the disputes on Islamic banking that are not resolvable by arbitration, a religious court is appointed to settle legal-religious matters, including Islamic banking disputes.[8] However, in the event of an appeal, disputes on Islamic financial matters may be heard by the High Court of Indonesia as the final court of appeal.

In relation to stability and liquidity requirements for Islamic banks, such as Capital Adequacy Ratios (CAR), Non-Performing Financing (NPF) under the Basel Accords,[9] these requirements are mandated by BI and the FSA and apply to all banks in Indonesia. Indonesia also participates in the establishment of the International Islamic standard-setting, such as the IFSB, which provides global prudential standards and guiding principles for the soundness and stability of the Islamic financial industry.[10] Indonesia is also a member of the Accounting and Auditing Organisation for Islamic Financial Institutions (AAOIFI), which sets best practices for handling the financial reporting requirements of Islamic financial institutions. These international Islamic finance standards are, at most, advisory, and their guidelines and standards are not binding.[11] Although many national regulators participate in IFSB committees, only Malaysia has incorporated many of the IFSB standards into their regulations. On the other hand, Saudi Arabia and Qatar, as active IFSB members, have not adopted IFSB standards related to Islamic finance and *sharia* governance.[12] This may be because it is unclear what impact IFSB standards may have on the practices of the Islamic finance industry.[13] The FSA of Indonesia supports the efforts to increase the adoption of IFSB standards, one of which is through the Impact and Consistency Assessment Program (ICAP),[14] which is based on the results of self-assessment and is designed to assess the consistency of regulations in adopting the IFSB standards.[15]

The Investor Protection Fund (IPF) is another institution which is supervised by the FSA to provide insurance for investors in the capital market and overcome disputes in investments caused by fraud.[16] As for the deposit guarantee in Islamic and conventional banks, insurance is provided by the Indonesia Deposit Insurance Corporation, which is an independent institution that functions to insure depositor's funds, as mandated by the president of the Republic of Indonesia based on Indonesia *Law Number 24 of 2004 concerning Indonesia Deposit Insurance Corporation*.[17]

4.4 Islamic Banking Law: Emergence and Problems

The idea of establishing an Islamic banking industry was initiated during the Suharto regime in 1983, when the government issued its December package, allowing the bank to provide financing with zero interest. When Indonesia's first official Islamic bank, Bank Muamalat Indonesia, was established in 1991, there was still ambiguity in the regulation of Islamic banking, as no banking regulations were in place to explicitly support it. At that time banking legislation defined the bank's revenue as that derived from interest. This was remedied in 1992 when *Government Regulation No. 72 of 1992 on banks* provided details on applying profit-sharing principles and defined the bank's profit-sharing, but without explicitly mentioning the words 'Islamic' or '*Sharia*' in it.[18] Further, *Law No. 7 of 1992 on Banks* was issued to support the first Islamic bank in Indonesia. Six years later, in 1998, the dual banking system was recognized in Indonesia after the *Law No. 10 of 1998 on Banks* was amended. This opened up the opportunity for conventional banks to operate Islamic Business Units and contribute to the growth of Islamic banking in Indonesia. Thereafter, *Law No. 23 of 1999 on Bank Indonesia* was issued to provide monetary supervision for Islamic banks.

In efforts to further develop Islamic banking in Indonesia, in 2004 BI introduced an initial Islamic monetary instrument known as the *Wadi'ah* Certificate[19] under the auspices of BI's *Regulation No. 6/7/PBI/2004 on Bank Indonesia Wadi'ah Certificate.* This enabled Islamic banks with excess liquidity to deposit their funds with BI based on the *wadi'ah* contract. In 2000, BI instituted an Islamic interbank money market under the regulation of *Bank Indonesia No 2/8/PBI/2000 on Sharia Interbank Money Markets.* This allowed banks to conduct short-term interbank financial transactions based on Islamic principles.

The regulation of Islamic Business Units for conventional banks that wish to offer Islamic banking products was carried out in 2002 by BI.[20] In 2006, the office channelling system was introduced by BI, allowing conventional banks to establish an Islamic Business Unit without building new infrastructure, thereby saving on infrastructure, staffing, and equipment costs for banks.[21] Islamic banking products were formulated with reference to the NSB-MUI under the regulation of *Bank Indonesia No. 7/46/PBI/2005 on Fund Mobilisation and Financing Agreements for Bank Conducting Business Based on Sharia Principles.*

On 16 July 2008, the House of Representatives passed a new *Law No. 21 of 2008 on Islamic Banking.*[22] As a representative of a wide range of Islamic organisations in Indonesia, there is no doubt that MUI played an important role in pushing the Islamic banking law to be passed by the House of Representatives.[23] This law separated the regulation of Islamic banks from conventional banks in Indonesia.[24] When this law came into effect, it did not radically alter the existing regulatory framework for Islamic banking – BI maintained its pre-eminent role in the supervision and regulation of Islamic banking.[25] This can further be seen from *The Constitution of the Republic of Indonesia 1945*, as stated in Chapter xi Art 29 para (1,2) that: First, the state is obliged to make laws or regulations or conduct policies for the implementation of a sense of faith to God Almighty from a group of followers of religion who need it. Second, the state is obliged to make laws and regulations to prohibit anyone from harassing religious teaching without any interference.[26] This paragraph has been interpreted as meaning the government is obliged to accommodate the implementation of religious institutions by making laws for those who need it – including laws relating to the religious financial obligations of Indonesian citizens – in order to achieve harmony between religious communities. Hence, the state also must respect the existence of other religions and is prohibited from radically altering the existing regulations or law such that they would infringe on religious freedom.

Obviously Islamic banks have to comply with the regulations of BI and the FSA, but as already noted, Islamic banks are also required to follow Islamic principles in their transactions based on the *fatwas* issued by the NSB-MUI. The products of Islamic banks are declared *sharia* compliant after obtaining *fatwa* recognition from the NSB-MUI and approval from BI. Art 2 of the *Regulation of Bank Indonesia PBI No 10/16/PBI/2008 concerning implementation of Islamic principles on Islamic financial transactions* states that Islamic bank activities should follow *fatwas* which are issued by an authorised institution in accordance with the principles of justice, balance, mutual benefit, and universalism, and must not contain *gharar*, *maysir*, *riba*, *zhulm*, or entail trade in *haram* products or services. In addition to this, Art 5 of the same regulation says that the BI is authorised to impose sanctions on those banks which breach these obligations, including administrative sanctions under Art 58 of the *Law No. 21 of 2008 on Islamic Banking*, and fines of up to Rp 200 billion (AUD 20 million).[27]

It should also be noted that although the FSA has the authority to impose sanctions, the process of determining whether an Islamic bank has actually breached Islamic principles is in the hands of the NSB-MUI, not the FSA, because the former is the only body authorised by BI to supervise *sharia*-compliant supervision as well as to issue *fatwas* about Islamic financial products. The key issues discussed in the following sections include the transparency of the process of supervision by the NSB-MUI and the process via which the FSA influences the *sharia* supervision of Islamic banks.

4.4.1 **Sharia** *and the State Regulatory System*

With reference to *sharia* compliance, Islamic doctrines are not a constitutive part of the state regulatory system. The only significant exception is the granting to *ulama* of a role in doctrinal supervision through the internal SSB system and the NSB.[28] This system is overseen by the MUI under state auspices and is endorsed by the state as a source of policy advice on Islamic issues.[29]

The NSB is an integral part of the MUI. It is responsible for overseeing all Islamic financial matters, providing *fatwas* in Islamic finance, and maintaining the harmonisation of *sharia* views among SSBs' members. The plan to form the NSB was initiated by banking practitioners and Islamic scholars recommending that the government facilitate the establishment of banks based on *sharia* principles. The NSB was expected to play a role as supervisor, to provide a guide to *sharia* values and the implementation of Islamic teachings in economic life, and to coordinate the responses of the *ulama* to issues related to Islamic finance.[30]

The NSB is an autonomous private body, not a state agency, and it operates under the auspices of the MUI. The NSB was established by the MUI in 1999 based on the board decree of MUI No. Kep-754/MUI/II/99 on the formation of the NSB.[31] Its purpose is to formulate, analyse, and verify products and services for Islamic financial institutions and provide guidelines for the financial business activities. As an integral part of the MUI, the NSB has as its priority the development of Islamic finance and economics. It also conducts research on Islamic products and services and issues *fatwas*.[32] The NSB-MUI is the highest private authority in Indonesia capable of issuing *fatwas* relating to Islamic finance, banking, and economic issues.[33]

There are always advantages and disadvantages resulting from the separation of the NSB-MUI from the government. The advantage is that the NSB-MUI is free from government intervention in the sense that the state should not seek to influence the *ulama* in passing *fatwas*. The disadvantage is that the independence of this body still needs to be questioned, because members of this board are also working as SSB members in Islamic banks and receive salaries and facilities from them, which could constitute a conflict of interest that undermines the full independence of the NSB-MUI from the banks problematic.[34] This in turn could reduce the effectiveness of the FSA because it cannot sanction an Islamic bank for breaching *sharia* principles until and unless it is deemed to be so by the NSB-MUI.

Another disadvantage is related to the pace of the transformation of *fatwas* into positive regulations. This explains the limited range of Islamic financial products, because the process for approval of new Islamic financial products is slow and cumbersome. It requires approval of both the FSA and the NSB-MUI.[35] In 2017, the FSA received eight requests for new Islamic bank products. Two requests were rejected, one application was returned because it did not meet the applicable conditions, and five requests were being processed.[36]

During 2017, the FSA issued five regulations for Islamic banking and Islamic capital markets which were based from *fatwas* and eight circular letters regulating the Islamic financial services sector. In making the regulations or circulars concerning Islamic institutions, the FSA considers applicable regulations, *fatwas*, and the security and safety of customers in approving new products proposed by Islamic banks. This can be seen from several copies of the FSA regulations, such as the FSA *Regulation on the Implementation of the Pension Program Based on Sharia Principles, No. 33/POJK.05/2016* in the section of Consideration (c) that the "implementation of Islamic pension programs must always meet the principles of the *sharia*, including *fatwa* stipulated by the NSB of Indonesian Ulama Council".

The use of *fatwas* as a basis for making regulations in Indonesia is normally not debated by Indonesian legal experts because it is widely understood that the *fatwas* are religious advice given by the *ulama* regarding issues experienced in society. Therefore, they are not constructed based on extreme views so as to not contravene or challenge state law.[37] *Fatwa* advice can rather be conceptualised as a bridge bringing together two perspectives, namely the religious and state legal frameworks. It should be noted, however, that limiting the source of *fatwas* to only the MUI may cause distrust among other Islamic scholars in society and could impede the development of new Islamic financial products by limiting alternative viewpoints.

4.4.2 Institutions of **Fatwa** *Production*

The NSB-MUI implements the decisions of MUI in supervising Islamic financial institutions. The NSB also works with the MUI to explore and formulate Islamic values and principles (including traditional aspects) in the form of *fatwas* relating to products and transactions at Islamic financial institutions, which should be followed by any bank engaging in Islamic business transactions.[38] Generally, where an Islamic financial institution makes a submission to the NSB-MUI in order to determine compliance with *sharia*, the NSB-MUI formulates a *fatwa* relating to the relevant products and transactions an institution wishes to introduce.[39]

The procedure for determining a *fatwa* by the NSB-MUI is carried out in plenary deliberations attended by all NSB-MUI members, BI personnel, representatives from banking institutions, as well as other financial institutions operating in insurance and capital markets.[40] The *fatwa* is discussed in the plenary meeting, and in the final stage a draft of the *fatwa* can be amended entirely or may be rejected. Mostly, however, the draft *fatwa* is accepted with critical notes from the members of the plenary.[41] It can be said that the NSB-MUI is responsible for *sharia* supervision at the national level and provides *fatwas* for new financial products based on proposals from Islamic banks, while the banks' own SSBs are responsible for *sharia* supervision at the level of individual banks.

Based on the *Indonesian Financial Services Authority Regulation No. 24/POJK.03/2015 concerning the products and activities of Islamic Banks and Islamic Business Units*, Chapter 4 Para 1 states that "all newly proposed financial products should receive an NSB-MUI *fatwa*, and must obtain the approval from the FSA". This proposal of new financial products must be submitted to the FSA at least 30 days before receiving the *fatwa* from the NSB-MUI.[42] In 2015, there were 32 Islamic banking products that had been approved by the FSA, comprising eight aspects of banking activities in the fields of collecting funds; financing; trade finance; treasury; temporary deposit investment; partnership and cooperation; payment system and electronic banking; and other activities, such as safe deposit boxes, traveller's cheques, payroll, virtual accounts, cash pick-up and delivery, escrow agents, and bank's guarantee.[43]

An SSB is, in theory, independent of a bank's management and is an internal authoritative body.[44] SSBs are important to the Islamic financial industry in that they are charged with ensuring that their financial institutions consistently comply with *sharia* rulings.[45] The membership of SSBs are drawn from scholars with substantial knowledge of the *sharia*. Its members are elected at a general meeting of shareholders, and the proposed SSB members are then submitted to the NSB-MUI for verification. The verified names are then submitted to BI for approval.[46] SSBs act as ex officio members of the NSB-MUI to supervise the *sharia* compliance of banks.[47] The appointment and dismissal of an SSB is regulated by BI No. 11/3/PBI/2009 on *Islamic Commercial Bank* and Circular Letter No 12/13/DPbS/2010 on *The implementation of Good Corporate Governance for Islamic Commercial Banks and Islamic Business Units*.

In Indonesia, an SSB is proposed by the general meeting of a bank and is required to gain approval from the NSB-MUI. The SSBs supervise at the bank level, while the NSB-MUI operates at the national level and covers a wide range of Islamic financial institutions, including the approval and dismissal of SSB members.[48] In other words, the *sharia* supervision of Islamic banks could be classified into two levels. At the macro level, the NSB-MUI has responsibility for financial stability issues on *fatwa* matters, such as *fatwa* harmonisation and standardisation, and is the state level of advice and supervision of Islamic financial institutions. At the micro level, the SSBs are the ex officio of the NSB-MUI that have responsibility for *sharia* supervision for the individual banks to which they are attached.

As explained earlier, although SSB acts as the ex officio of an NSB-MUI and the members of SSB are approved and dismissed by the NSB-MUI, it is well known that an SSB works for and is salaried by an Islamic bank. It is also noted in the Regulation of *FSA No 65/POJK.03 of 2016 on Risk Management Practice for Islamic Bank and Islamic Business Units* where "Islamic Banks bear the costs associated with operational activities undertaken by SSBs including the salary of SSB members".[49] This provision has added more costs for Islamic banks, as Mardian said:

> Since the position of SSB is only available in Islamic financial institutions, there is a controversy regarding the fees payable to SSB and NSB-MUI, which in fact increases costs for Islamic financial institutions to achieve this sharia compliance objectives, whereas in conventional financial institutions this additional entity is not required.[50]

On the other hand, SSB members have responded to this criticism by arguing that compliance with Islamic principles, due to the work of SSBs, has increased the competitiveness and profitability of Islamic financial institutions due to their approval of innovative Islamic products and services.[51] This profitability, they assert, demonstrates that the cost of employing SSB members is more than covered by the higher revenue generated.[52] It should be noted, however, that this is arguably only true for large Islamic financial institutions. Small institutions with limited operating budgets have tended to appoint SSB members from their own existing internal staff to save on the costs associated with maintaining a mandatory SSB.[53]

The previously outlined procedures have been designed to ensure that both *fatwa* production and the supervision of compliance with approved *fatwas* are free from conflicts of interest. However, in practice, conflicts of interest in the making of *fatwas* cannot be avoided. This is because the SSB members are mostly also members of the NSB-MUI. Ideally, the Islamic bank should consult with their SSB to propose a *fatwa* for new products, this proposal should then be submitted to the NSB-MUI, which will make an independent determination on a *fatwa*. However, since the members of both SSB and the NSB-MUI are often the same people, there is no truly independent deliberation in the procedure of *fatwa* making.[54] This conflict can be clearly seen in the Indonesian *Law No. 21 of 2008 concerning Islamic Banking*, Chapter 26 (2) which states that "a minimum of two and maximum of five SSB members are required for each Islamic bank and SSB members are allowed to supervise other financial institutions (a maximum of two Islamic banks and two non-Islamic banks)". In this case, as noted by Amin Suma, one member of an SSB sometimes supervises more than three financial institutions, which could impact the effectiveness of an SSB; however, a bank cannot stop its SSB member from working as a supervisor of other rival banks, as it is permitted in law.[55]

It is appropriate to compare the situation in Indonesia with its nearest neighbour, Malaysia, which has a burgeoning Islamic banking sector. Like Indonesia, Malaysia's national Sharia Advisory Council – the highest body responsible for the supervision of *sharia*-compliance supervision and for validation of all Islamic financial products – is attached to the Central Bank of Malaysia (Bank Negara Malaysia). This entity stands at arm's length from all banks' SSBs – that is, there is no overlapping membership between them. Further, based on the Malaysian Sharia Governance Framework 2010, a minimum of five SSB members are required in an Islamic financial institution. Malaysian SSB membership may include different nationalities (where appropriate), and this committee is not allowed to supervise another Islamic financial institution.[56] Nor does the appointment of SSB members require the approval from Malaysia's National Sharia Advisory Council of the Central Bank. Instead, SSB members are generally appointed by the shareholders of the banks, and their remuneration is proposed by the management and approved by the banks' Boards of Directors.[57] The institutional arrangements in Malaysia thus prevent the conflict-of-interest problems that have been identified in Indonesia. Thus, it is reasonable to propose that Indonesia should follow Malaysia's lead in this regard by unambiguously separating the membership and functions of the NSB-MUI from the SSBs of individual banks that they are supposed to be supervising.

4.4.3 The Mandate of the Sharia Supervisory Boards

As indicated, there is a conflict of interest built into the system of *fatwa* production within Islamic banking in Indonesia. However, the extent of the problem does not end there. The SSBs are a principal source of essential information about banks' *sharia* compliance. Neither the FSA nor BI play any supervisory or auditing role in this regard.

In Indonesia, the current mechanism for the direct supervision of each Islamic bank is that each SSB must report twice yearly on *sharia* compliance to BI, the NSB-MUI, as well as to the bank's Board of Commissioners and Managing Director (to which an SSB is attached), as stipulated in Art 27 Chapter IV on *Regulation of Bank Indonesia No. 6/24/PBI/2004 on Banks Applying Islamic Principles*. Based on the external circular letter number 5/SEOJK.05/2018, concerning *The Report of Sharia Supervisory Board on Pension Fund Based on Islamic Principles* issued by the FSA, the content of each SSB's report should comprise five aspects: (1) the contract agreements into which the bank has entered; (2) how the funds are managed; (3) where the funds are invested; (4) how the invested funds are beneficial for developing the economy or harmful for society; and (5) other activities.

With respect to (1), the SSB must state whether the supervised banking activities are *sharia* compliant or not, and the SSB must also elaborate the reasons for recommendations (such as explaining why Islamic principles were not met for certain contracts) and explain how its recommendations are likely to result in improvements (such as changes in the contract agreements so that they would better conform with Islamic principles). As to (2), the SSB must oversee adherence to standards and procedures of banking fund management, where the funds of conventional and

Islamic banking activities should not be combined. With respect to (3), the SSB must explain the methods of portfolio choice in the bank that determine how funds are distributed for investment, administration, and management. For (4), the SSB has to oversee the practice of system and procedure to assess the benefits to the bank's customers, such as analysing whether customers receive benefits from the funds and whether customers are engaged in *sharia*-compliant activities with bank funds. For (5), the SSB has to oversee the system and procedure of fund management of non-investments (such as *zakat*, *infaq*, and *sadaqah* funds).

It is clear that all of the *sharia*-compliance aspects of bank supervision fall under the purview of the SSBs and are at no stage checked independently by the FSA or BI despite the fact that Islamic banks are a growing sub-sector of the Indonesian financial system. Although these state authorities do receive SSB reports, there is no mechanism for independent authentication of their contents. Essentially, the FSA must accept their contents 'on faith'. Given that SSBs are employees of the banks they supervise, one could argue that the relation of asymmetric information here gives rise to a potential principal–agent problem: SSB members (agents) may have a financial incentive to misreport, not fully disclose, or subjectively reinterpret ostensibly 'un-Islamic' practices in their reports to FSA (the principal). One might argue that this overstates the problem because the SSBs must also provide their reports to the NSB-MUI, and the latter is better equipped to evaluate the contents of these reports, thereby undermining the incentive to misreport. This argument, however, is weak. As was noted, since SSB members are often also members of the NSB-MUI, this fact could implicate the NSB-MUI itself in the possible sanctioning of misreporting: if, hypothetically, an SSB were to present a dubious report, it could then be 'evaluated' by the very members of the NSB-MUI who wrote it. The key issue of concern here is not whether the conflicts of interest identified here are manifested in actual misbehaviour. Rather, the issue of concern is first and foremost one of perception. If conflicts of interest are perceived to exist by financial market participants, it undermines trust in the honesty and authenticity of not just individual banks, but the entire financial system. This very point is made by Shayan, CEO and Board Member of Barakat Foundation, Tehran: "the biggest risk facing the global financial system is not a fall in its earning power but most importantly a loss of faith and credibility on how it works".[58] This is particularly important to Islamic banks because they specifically trade on their reputations for adhering to religious-ethical principles. If faith in this reputation is eroded by perceived conflicts of interest, the potential future growth of Islamic banks in the marketplace is thereby undermined. It is thus important to consider institutional regulatory reforms that would enhance the perceived probity of Islamic banks, and thus the dual banking system.

4.4.4 A Model of Sharia Supervision

Unfortunately, there is lack of evidence about which type of supervisory approach best suits Islamic banking. Whether a single type of regulatory authority or separated regulatory authority is appropriate depends upon several factors in its jurisdiction.[59] Some implement a single type of supervisory authority for both Islamic and conventional banks (e.g., Saudi Arabia, Ethiopia, Kazakhstan, Kenya, Kuwait, Qatar, Tunisa, Turkey, the UAE, and the UK). Others have separate supervisory units that technically fall under a single supervisory authority (e.g., Bahrain, Indonesia, Jordan, Lebanon, Pakistan, and Syria).[60]

The primary factors relevant to *sharia*-compliant supervision are associated to the cost and issues of coordination, communication, and sharing among the separate agencies. Indonesia adheres to a centralised Sharia Board system, which is efficient in terms of communications within their members, but the issues of coordination with governmental supervisory body persist. To recap, the NSB-MUI is the central board responsible for producing and harmonising *fatwa* and ensuring the consistency of published *fatwas*. The NSB-MUI also manages the SSBs who do the onsite *sharia*-compliance supervision. As argued earlier, problems of conflict of interest exist in this set of arrangements, and this can potentially negatively affect the public's perception of Islamic finance. It could also result in the mis-selling of Islamic financial products by those who have a conflict of interest in giving the *fatwas*.[61]

The key issue for Indonesia in considering institutional regulatory reform of the supervision of *sharia* compliance of Islamic banking is thus whether a relationship should be established between the FSA (or BI) and SSBs through the NSB-MUI. At present, no such relationship exists. If we look at Malaysia by way of contrast, a national Sharia Advisory Council is incorporated within Malaysia's central bank – Bank Negara Malaysia[62] – which rules on the conformity of products and activities of all the Islamic banks.[63] Islamic financial institutions are thus legally required to follow the *sharia* standards laid down by the central bank's own Council. Further, in the case of conflicting opinions or disagreements among *sharia* advisors, disputes are referred to the central bank's council for adjudication. In short, every aspect of bank supervision – including Islamic banks – is ultimately held by Malaysia's central bank. This serves to greatly diminish perceptions of conflict of interest in Malaysian Islamic banking.

Indonesia could and should consider reforms along similar lines to achieve this same goal. The supervisory functions of the NSB-MUI and its SSBs could be incorporated into the FSA's own structure so as to provide authoritative, independent state supervision of Islamic banking practices. Further, a temporal prohibition on employment with Islamic banks for former staff of the FSA could also be implemented. The NSB-MUI function of laying down the parameters for all Islamic financial contract-products and transactions would thus reside with the FSA itself, and the SSB functions could be transferred to FSA sub-committees which would independently supervise, audit, and report on individual Islamic banks and conventional banks with Islamic banking windows. Because the former functionaries of the NSB-MUI and its SSBs would no longer be dependent on private banks for employment and salaries, nor could they expect remuneration after leaving the FSA, the perception – and the actuality – of conflict of interest would be greatly reduced, if not eliminated entirely. Furthermore, such an institutional regulatory reform would provide greater assurance of *sharia* compliance of purported Islamic financial activities; would promote, in the long term, the consistency of *fatwas* and interpretations between banks and regions; would give a state imprimatur to Islamic banks on a par with conventional banks; and would streamline the overall supervisory apparatus enabling BI and the FSA to be better informed about all Indonesian financial entities, thereby better enabling them to manage and ensure the stable functioning of the Indonesian financial system as a whole.

4.5 Concluding Remarks

This chapter has outlined the emergence of legislation designed to incorporate Islamic banking practice and products into the broader financial system of Indonesia. It has also explained the institutional structure of financial *fatwa* production/deliberation and bank supervision that is now in place for Islamic banks (and conventional with Islamic banking windows) in Indonesia. As explained, *fatwa* production is delegated to the NSB-MUI, which formally stands outside the state bodies of BI and the FSA; and bank supervision is monitored by individual SSBs, which in turn fall under the auspices of the NSB-MUI.

Although it cannot be said that this institutional arrangement is dysfunctional, there is nonetheless considerable room for improvement. This is because, as has been argued here, there are substantive conflicts of interest embedded within the system. Chief among these are, first, that members of SSB are employees of (and thus to some extent financially dependent on) the individual banks that they supervise and report on; and second, there is considerable overlap in the membership of these individual SSBs and the NSB to which they report.

Following the lead of Malaysia, it has been argued in this chapter that a reform to these institutional arrangements could be made to increase the integrity of Islamic banking supervision in Indonesia. That reform would basically be to take supervisory responsibilities and influence out of the hands of banks themselves, and instead centralise financial *fatwa* production/deliberation and bank supervision within the official monetary authorities of the state – in Indonesia's case specifically, the FSA. This would greatly reduce the conflict of interest problem and would also streamline the currently more cumbersome process of producing, implementing, and monitoring compliance with *fatwas* related to all manner of Islamic banking practices in Indonesia. This last concern with regulatory efficiency is of vital importance now and into the future because of the increasing innovation in the development of Islamic financial instruments in Indonesia, which is the topic of the next chapter.

Notes

1 There have been many discussions regarding the incompatibility of *sharia* and modern banking and finance. Most importantly, scholars point out that the essence of modern Islamic banking and finance is the generation of returns based on earned profit (rather than unearned *riba*), but that profit making is constrained by the axioms of *ihsan* (beneficence) and *'adalah* (social justice), which constitute the 'spiritual substance' of the *sharia*. For a detailed criticism of modern 'Islamic' banking on the grounds that, in practice, it has abandoned the 'substantive' purposes of Islamic law, see Mehmet Asutay, 'Conceptualising and locating the social failure of Islamic finance: Aspirations of Islamic moral economy vs. the realities of Islamic finance' (2012) 11(2) *Asian and African Aria Studies*

Journal 93; Masudul Alam Choudhury, 'Islamic Economics and Finance: A Fiasco' (2008) 20(1) *The Middle East Business and Economic Review* 38; Asyraf Wajdi Dusuki and Abdulazeem Abozaid, 'A Critical Appraisal on the Challenges of Realizing Maqasid al-Shari'ah in Islamic Banking and Finance' (2007) 15(2) *IIUM Journal of Economics and Management* 143; Abdullah Saeed, 'Idealism and Pragmatism in Islamic Banking: The Application of Sharī'ah Principles and Adjustments' (1998) 4(2) *Journal of Arabic, Islamic and Middle Eastern Studies* 89; Asad Zaman, 'Crisis in Islamic Economics: Diagnosis and Prescriptions' (2011) 25(1) *JKAU: Islamic Econ* 147–169.

2 Inwon Song and Carel Oosthuizen, *Islamic Banking Regulation and Supervision: Survey Results and Challenges* (International Monetary Fund, 2014).

3 *Murabaha* is a product in Islamic finance in which one party buys a good for cash and then sells it to a second party with additional cost for deferred payments. See Farlex Financial Dictionary, S.v. "Murabaha" (2019) Farlex, https://financial-dictionary.thefreedictionary.com/Murabaha.

4 Saad Azmat et al., 'Why Interest Free Islamic Banking Is Not Free from Interest?' (Pt Deakin University, Australia) (2015), www.deakin.edu.au/__data/assets/pdf_file/0003/392295/islamic-banking-not-free-from-interest-Azmat-Azad-Ghaffar-and-Bhatti.pdf.

5 Undang-Undang Republik Indonesia Nomor 21 Tahun 2011 Tentang Otoritas Jasa Keuangan [*Law No. 21 of 2011* on Financial Services Authority] (Indonesia) Ch 43 [tr author].

6 The religious courts (*Pengadilan agama*) are established under the decree of the president. The National Shariah Arbitration Body (*Badan Arbitrasi Syariah Nasional*) was formerly known as the Indonesian Muamalat Arbitration Body (*Badan Arbitrase Muamalat Indonesia*).

7 Art 1 para 1, *Law No. 30 of 1999* concerning arbitration and alternative dispute resolution to settle legal disputes outside the courts is based on the upfront agreement by the parties in the dispute. *Badan Syariah Arbitrase Nasional* was previously named the Board of Muamalat Indonesia Arbitrage/*Badan Arbitrase Muamalat Indonesia*.

8 Art 49 para 1 of *Law No. 3/2006* on religious courts states that the religious court is authorised to examine, decide upon, and resolve disputes in the field of *Sharia* economics.

9 Basel Accords are set by the Basel Committee on Bank Supervision (BCBS); the Accords are used as consultative papers for central banks across the world in regard to banking supervision rules, including minimum capital requirements and market disclosure.

10 Financial Service Authority of Indonesia, *Islamic Banking in Indonesia in Brief* (2019), www.ojk.go.id/en/kanal/syariah/tentang-syariah/Pages/Perbankan-Syariah.aspx.

11 Bank Indonesia, *Islamic Banking in Indonesia in Brief* (2019), www.bi.go.id/en/perbankan/syariah/Contents/Default.aspx.

12 Ahmad A. Alkhamees, *A Critique of Creative Shari'ah Compliance in the Islamic Finance Industry* (Brill | Nijhoff, 2017) 226.

13 Ibid.

14 The purpose of ICAP was to assess the impact and consistency of IFSB standard in member countries, to identify the gaps that might have a serious impact on the financial sector in member jurisdictions, and it also extended the capacity of IFSB to redeem gaps in order to ensure effective implementation of standards in member countries. See Islamic Financial Services Board, *Impact and Consistency Assessment Program (ICAP)* (2019), www.ifsb.org/implementation.php?content=5.

15 Anto Prabowo, '*OJK dukung upaya peningkatan adopsi standar IFSB*/The FSA Supports the Effort of IFSB Standard Adoption' (2018), www.ojk.go.id/id/berita-dan-kegiatan/siaran-pers/Pages/Siaran-Pers-OJK-Dukung-Upaya-Peningkatan-Adopsi-Standar-IFSB.aspx.

16 There is also Indonesia Sharia Stock Index (ISSI), which is a composite index of Islamic stocks listed on the Indonesia Stock Exchange.

17 Indonesia Deposit Insurance Corporation, *The History of IDIC* (2019), www.lps.go.id/web/guest/sejarah.

18 Peraturan Pemerintah No 72 Tahun 1992 Tentang Bank Berdasarkan Prinsip Bagi Hasil [*Government Regulation No 72 of 1992 on Banks Applying Profit Sharing Principles*] (Indonesia) [tr author].
19 Bank Indonesia *Wadi'ah* Certificate (BIWC) is issued by the Bank Indonesia, the Islamic banks deposit their funds to Bank Indonesia for a certain period based on the agreement and decree of Bank Indonesia, and it cannot be used by Bank Indonesia, as the contract is based on the *wadiah* principle. See Darsono et al., 'Dynamics of Financing Products and Contracts' in Muhammad Syafii Antonio (ed), *Dynamics of Islamic Finance Products and Contracts in Indonesia* (Tazkia Publishing, 2012) 1–477, 332.
20 *Bank Indonesia Regulation No. 4/1/PBI (2002) on Changes to the Business Activities of Conventional Commercial Banks into Commercial Banks based on Sharia Principles and the Opening of Offices of the Bank based on Sharia Principles of Conventional Commercial Banks.*
21 *Bank Indonesia Regulation No. 8/3/PBI/2006 on the Changes of Conventional Bank into Bank that Provides the Islamic Business Activities based on Sharia Principle, and the Opening of New Bank Office that Provides the Islamic Business Activities by the Conventional Bank.*
22 The law was based on three draft bills submitted by Bank Indonesia, the Indonesian Syariah Banking Association (in Indonesia, *Asosiasi Perbankan Syariah Indonesia*), and the Association of Indonesian Muslim Intellectuals (in Indonesia, *Ikatan Cendikiawan Muslim Indonesia*). The three drafts were similar in content, but the draft from Bank Indonesia had the most influence on the final form of the law.
23 See Ahyar A. Gayo, *Laporan Akhir Penelitian Hukum tentang Kedudukan Fatwa MUI dalam Upaya Mendorong Pelaksanan Ekonomi Syariah* [The Final Report on the Status of Fatwa MUI in Support of Islamic Financial Activities], Ministry of Law and Human Right Republic of Indonesia No 4 (2011).
24 In the past, it was still regulated jointly through conventional banking law. The first Islamic bank in Indonesia (Bank Muamalat Indonesia) was established in 1991 but began operations in 1992, based on the regulations stipulated in *Law No 7 of 1992 Concerning Banking*, by referring to the term "bank based on the profit sharing principle".
25 Tim Lindsey, 'Between Piety and Prudence: State Syariah and the Regulation of Islamic Banking in Indonesia' (2012) 34(1) *The Sydney Law Review* 107.
26 *Undang-Undang Dasar Republik Indonesia 1945* [Constitution of the Republic of Indonesia 1945].
27 The evidence of enforcement of the sanctions can be seen from the ruling of the court, where in 2019 the former General Manager of Bank Syariah Mandiri in Medan was sentenced to 1 year, 4 months with a fine of Rp 1 billion (AUD 1 million) in two months' subsider, the panel of judges charged the defendant according to Art 63 para (1) *Law No. 21 of 2008* concerning Islamic banking, the defendant intentionally made or caused a false recording in the books or reports, documents or reports of business activities, and/or transaction reports or account of an Islamic bank and committed a loss to the Bank Syariah Mandiri of Rp 7.9 billion (AUD 7.9 million). See *Rudi Purwanto* (2017) No. 16/PID.SUS-TPK/2017/PT.MDN (High Court Medan). [tr author].
28 Peraturan Bank Indonesia No 11/15/PBI/2009 Tentang Perubahan Kegiatan Usaha Bank Konvensional Menjadi Bank Syariah [*The Regulation of Bank Indonesia* No 11/15/PBI/2009 on Converting the Conventional Bank into Islamic Bank] Art 14(c) [tr author].
29 Lindsey, above n 25, 114.
30 Gayo, Akhyar Ari, *Laporan Akhir Penelitian Hukum tentang Kedudukan Fatwa MUI dalam Upaya Mendorong Pelaksanan Ekonomi Syariah* [The Final Report on the Status of Fatwa MUI in Support of Islamic Financial Activities], Ministry of Law and Human Right Republic of Indonesia No. 4 (2011) 43.
31 Ibid., 45.
32 Ibid.
33 Ibid.
34 Dini Rosdini and Nanda Putri Ghassani Fildzah, 'Comparison of Conservatism in Islamic and Conventional Banks in Indonesia and Malaysia' (2019) 23(2) *Jurnal Manajemen* 239.

35 Based on the *Financial Service Authority Regulation No. 24/POJK. 3/2015*, Art 4 para 7, all new products of an Islamic bank can only be issued after obtaining approval from the FSA. Although the products may be verified as Islamic by NSB-ICU, the bank has to obtain approval from the FSA, which requires at least three months to proceed.
36 Otoritas Jasa Keuangan, *Laporan Perkembangan Keuangan Syariah Indonesia 2017* [The Report on the Development of Islamic Finance in Indonesia 2017], Financial Service Authority of Indonesia No (2017) 105 [tr author].
37 Aini Silvy Arofa, 'Regulasi Terkait Pengawasan Terhadap Penerapan Prinsip-prinsip Syariah pada Lembaga Keuangan Syariah [Regulations on Sharia-compliant Supervision in Islamic Financial Institutions]' (2014) 6(2) *Jurnal Hukum Islam dan Bisnis* 229, [tr author].
38 Dewan Syariah Nasional – Majelis Ulama Indonesia, *Sekilas tentang DSN MUI – Sejarah Berdirinya* [A Brief About DSN MUI – The History of Establishment] (2018), https://dsnmui.or.id/kami/sekilas/.
39 Ibid.
40 Gayo, above n 30.
41 Ibid.
42 Peraturan Otoritas Jasa Keuangan No 24/POJK.03/2015 Tentang Produk dan Aktivitas Bank Syariah dan Unit Usaha Syariah [*Financial Service Authority Regulation No 24/POJK.03/2015 on The Products and Services of Islamic Banks and Islamic Business Units*] Indonesia [tr author].
43 Financial Service Authority, *Products and Activities for Banks and Islamic Business Units Who Provide Islamic business transactions* (2015), www.ojk.go.id/id/kanal/perbankan/regulasi/surat-edaran-ojk/Pages/-SEOJK-Nomor-36032015-tentang-Produk-dan-Aktivitas-bus-uus.aspx.
44 The Indonesian title is *Dewan Pengawas Syariah* (DPS). See Yoyo Sudaryo and Aditya Yudanegara, *Investasi Bank dan Lembaga Keuangan* [Financial Institutions and Banks' Investment] (Penerbit Andi, 2017) 37.
45 Gayo, above n 30.
46 Peraturan Bank Indonesia No 11/3/PBI/2009 Tentang Bank Syariah [Regulation of Bank Indonesia, No. 11/3/PBI/2009 on Islamic Bank] Ch I, Art 3.
47 The SSB is a representative from the National Sharia Board of Indonesian Council of Ulama and has the responsibility to provide a report to the NSB-MUI. See Majelis Ulama Indonesia, *sekilas tentang DSN-MUI [NSB-MUI in Breif]*, https://dsnmui.or.id/kami/sekilas/.
48 Ali Rama, 'Analisis Kerangka Regulasi Model Syariah Governance Lembaga Keuangan Syariah di Indonesia [Analysis of the Concept of Regulation for Islamic Governance Model in Islamic Financial Institution in Indonesia]' (2015) 1(1) *Journal of Islamic Economics LARIBA*, [tr author].
49 See, Peraturan Otoritas Jasa Keuangan No 65/POJK.03/2016 Tentang Penerapan Manajemen Resiko Bagi Bank Umum Syariah dan Unit Usaha Syariah [*The Regulation of Financial Service Authority of Indonesia* No 65/POJK.03 of 2016 on Risk Management Practice for Islamic Bank and Islamic Business Units] Ch 4 [tr author].
50 The financial returns of IBs are disrupted due to the financial cost involved in achieving *Maqasid al-Shari'ah* objectives. Salah Alhammadi, Khaled Alotaibi and Dzikri F. Hakam, 'Analysing Islamic Banking Ethical Performance from Maqasid al-Shari'ah Perspective: Evidence from Indonesia' (2020) *Journal of Sustainable Finance and Investment* 1, 18; Sepky Mardian, 'Tingkat Kepatuhan Syariah di Lembaga Keuangan Syariah [The Level of Sharia Compliance in Islamic Financial Institutions]' (2015) 3(1) *Jurnal Akuntansi dan Keuangan Islam* 57, 61 [tr author].
51 See, Muhammad Amin Suma, *Asuransi Syariah dan Asuransi Konvensional: Sistem, Konsep, Aplikasi dan Pemasaran* [Islamic Insurance and Conventional Insurance: System, Concept, Application and Marketing] (Kholam Publishing, 2006) 43 [tr author].
52 Ibid.

53 A study case at the Islamic Financial Cooperation in Bojonegoro shows that, hiring SSB members externally caused this small institution to pay double salary for SSB members and have to provide office facilities for them. Due to budget constraints, this institution pays relatively less salary and does not provide office facilities for SSB members, and as a result their SSB members do not work optimally. Itsna Nur Farikhah, *Implementasi Peran dan Fungsi Dewan Pengawas Syariah (DPS) pada Koperasi Simpan Pinjam Pembiayaan Syariah (KSPSS) (Study Kasus di Forum Koperasi Syariah Bojonegoro)* [The Implementation of Role and Functions of Sharia Supervisory Board at Islamic Financial Cooperation, Case Study at Bojonegoro] Universitas Islam Negeri Walisongo, 2018) 87 [tr author], http://eprints.walisongo.ac.id/8161/1/132311074.pdf.
54 Mardian, above n 50.
55 Suma, above n 51, 41.
56 *Guidelines on Shariah Governance Framework for Islamic Financial Institutions 2010 s II (2) 2.3*, www.bnm.gov.my/index.php?ch=en_announcement&pg=en_announcement&ac=287&lang=en.
57 Naji Mansour Nomran, Razali Haron and Rusni Hassan, 'Bank Performance and Shari'ah Supervisory Board Attributes by Islamic Banks: Does Bank Size Matter?' (2017) 6(Special) *Journal of Islamic Finance* 174, 183.
58 Siti Amaroh and Masturin, 'The Determinants of Maqasid Shariah Based Performance of Islamic Banks in Indonesia' (2018) 11(1) *Jurnal Iqtishadia Kajian Ekonomi dan Bisnis Islam* 354, 362.
59 Jose Vinals and Jonathan Fiechter, *The Making of Good Supervision: Learning to Say 'No'* (International Monetary Fund, 2010) 16.
60 Song and Oosthuizen, above n 2, 21.
61 Hichem Hamza, 'Sharia Governance in Islamic Banks: Effectiveness and Supervision Model' (2013) 6(3) *International Journal of Islamic and Middle Eastern Finance and Management* 226, 233.
62 Bank Negara Malaysia is the Malaysian Central Bank.
63 Hamza, above n 61.

5 Islamic Financial Instruments in Indonesia

5.1 Introduction

This chapter investigates the case for Islamic financial products and services offered by Indonesian Islamic banks and Islamic Business Units. It is argued that Indonesian Islamic financial scholars produce financial instruments that are almost identical to conventional finance and frequently cost roughly the same as conventional bank products. The main difference being (as discussed later) that they are technically satisfying an Islamic principle that prohibits interest. The issue here is whether Islamic banks can co-opt the Islamic groups that criticise Islamic finance for violating the pure intent (or 'substance') of Islamic bans against *riba*; and whether they can remain competitive if the products offered are limited to the early theoretical risk-sharing models of Islamic banking. The chapter also discusses whether these theoretically ideal products could provide value for banks' shareholders and customers and meet the modern needs of businesses and the community.

This chapter begins with an analysis of the principles of Islamic financial instruments and the rationale behind the interest rate prohibition. It then examines the linkage of conventional bank interest rates with the returns on the various Islamic financial instruments used by Indonesian banks. It will also investigate the gaps between the Islamic principles governing contracts in the classical period and the practice of Islamic financial contracts today. Finally, it examines the consequences if Islamic banks do not benchmark against interest rates.

5.2 Disagreement of Scholars' Interpretations of Islamic Financial Principles

5.2.1 Pecuniary Motives and Islamic Principles

It is an elementary tenet of all major schools of economic thought that unless regulated, capitalist enterprises, including banks, are driven in all their actions by the profit motive. Different economic paradigms have their own preferred principles that would guide the regulation of enterprises. In the case of Islamic economics and finance, the self-interest of banking enterprises is curtailed and regulated by the *sharia*: the moral and legal validity of financial products and banking practices in all respects[1] depends on supporting evidence from the Qur'an, *hadith*, and *ijma*.[2] Islamic

DOI: 10.4324/9781003393986-5

products must be made in good faith, and the objects must meet the requirements of Islamic law.

Islamic finance has unique features which distinguish it from conventional finance. Each contract must follow Islamic financial principles – namely, free of interest (*riba*), free from excessive uncertainty and (potentially deceptive) ambiguity (*gharar*), free from speculation and gambling (*maysir*), and free from falsehood (*bathil*).[3] The purpose of these prohibitions is referenced in the Qur'anic verse "And if someone is in hardship, then [let there be] postponement until [a time of] eases. But if you give [from your right as] charity, then it is better for you, if you only knew".[4] This verse is directed to certain virtues that should be inherent in trade and contracts, such as avoiding exploitation which could result in unnecessary hardship that violates the spirit of tolerance and wisdom.

Under the principles of Islamic finance, business and trade activities should be accompanied by an underlying genuine trade and business-related activity – that is, said activities must involve actually existing physical goods or services. In fact, this is the most important feature of Islamic finance: financial transactions must be asset-backed or -based.[5] Thus, there should be close links between financial and productive flows, and the funds must be channelled into real financial business activities. (This will be of specific importance to the discussion of derivatives in Chapter 6.)

The transfers of credit and risk are also acknowledged in Islamic finance; indeed, these two notions cannot be separated from the economic system. However, these two characteristics should be used judiciously to avoid speculative behaviour. In this respect, Islamic jurisprudence allows the use of transferring credit and risk to achieve economic ends and not for the purpose of protecting individuals from their own greed.[6] As was discussed earlier in Chapter 3, the issue of whether modern Islamic banking practices are 'truly Islamic' has been the subject of much debate, and whilst one may argue that some of today's Islamic products resembles those of conventional instruments, these Islamic products technically comply with the *sharia* and satisfy Islamic principles.[7] The following sections look more specifically at these key principles of Islamic finance.

5.2.2 Riba

Although scholars universally agree that *riba* is prohibited, as it is clearly mentioned in the Qur'anic verses 2:275–280, there are differences of opinion on the issue of interest in the modern banking system.[8] The key issue is whether interest in the modern system of banking can be treated as equivalent to that of *riba* activities in the prophetic and the classical Islamic periods (roughly, the 7th century and the 8th–13th centuries).

Riba in Arabic literally means 'elevation' or 'increase'. In monetary terms, it is a financial gain that is *not* due to the fair sale, lease, or hiring of a product or resource. Although this arguably includes making a profit on the sale of an asset in an unfair or exploitative fashion (such as price gouging in a shortage), its most common and primary reference is to making a financial gain by charging a fee purely for access to money.[9] The pre-modern exemplar is the practice of the moneylender, and the modern exemplar is conventional financial transactions involving the payment of interest on loans for such things as real estate, cars, and investment in capital goods. This includes interest paid on savings and fixed deposit accounts.

Much like the classical Greek view of Aristotle, Islamic principles regard money purely as a medium of exchange that possesses no value in itself. Money 'created out of' money is deemed duplicitous and 'unnatural', and is prohibited. Thus, interest cannot be paid or be payable for deposits or loans.[10] Islamic scholars consider money as capital when it is invested in a business, but when the money is advanced to a business in the form of a loan to be repaid, it is considered as debt. That debt does not entitle the lender to interest, however, and the debtor should only repay the debt at similar value, irrespective of the passage of time. Similarly, an investment return should not merely be a function of the passage of time, but rather should be linked to shared risk-taking.[11] This was the majority view of Islamic scholars from the classical period. However, Islamic scholars today hold varying opinions over the permissibility of interest in the modern banking system.[12] In Indonesia, some NU scholars who are in favour of 'modern' interest have argued that bank interest in the modern banking system is not in the form of loans (*qardh*) but in the form of partnership investment (*qiradh*).[13] For example, when a customer deposits their money into the bank as savings, the bank then forwards this money into real economic activities through investment loans (*qiradh*) to generate income. In return, the bank earns a profit and divides this profit in the form of interest based on the conventional time value of money calculation to their customers who put their money in the bank.[14] Other scholars who are against the taking of 'modern' interest say that this rate of interest may be far less or far more than the actual proportion of profits that the financier might have deserved because there is no direct relationship between what a bank is paid by a borrower-enterprise and the profits made (if any) by the enterprise. Although both parties have agreed to the contract and regard it as fair, the fact is that, as in the theory of opportunity cost, one could earn more than profit-return from the bank if the owned resource is fully utilised in business activities. This activity is categorised as *zhulm* (usury or unjust acts of exploitation).[15]

Prominent Islamic scholars in the Muslim World League (Majma' al-Fiqh al-Islami) and MUI who are against modern bank interest argue that there is no guarantee as to whether or not the income earned from interest comes from legitimate business activities which comply with Islamic values.[16] This is also the argument used by Muhammadiyah scholars to prohibit bank interest, where the *illat* (cause) of *riba* is the existence of exploitation or acquisition of additional money by denying rights to another. However, an implication of this position is that if no such exploitation occurred in the financial transaction, then the bank interest is not considered *riba* even if there is an additional gain from the principal amount of money.[17]

Meanwhile, the MUI has taken a more conservative view than both NU and Muhammadiah scholars. It has defined *riba* as simply where the lender of money earns additional money out of the principal amount of a loan. This harkens back to the classical objection that money is only a medium of exchange, and it would be 'unnatural' and *prima facie* unjust to exchange a given amount of money for a larger amount. To support its position, the MUI refers to a well-known passage in the

Qur'an which states: "But if you repent, then you shall be entitled to [the return of] your principal: you will do no wrong, and neither will you be wronged".[18] Based on this, the MUI has stated that any additional money coming from a loan (*qardh*) which is calculated from the principal amount is considered *riba.*[19]

5.2.3 Gharar

A second feature that is prohibited in Islamic finance is *gharar* in contracts and transactions. There have been many discussions among the Muslim scholars over the exact meaning of *gharar*. For Arab lexicographers, *gharar* means *khatr* (danger) and *khud'ah* (deception or cheating). Faruq and Hassan defined it as "a transaction in which the object of the contract or the commodity is not yet determined for both or either parties".[20] Bellalah and Masood said that this includes ambiguity about the nature, quality, and specification of the subject matter of the contract, including the rights and obligations of the parties, as well as tenure and delivery of the item of exchange, and the 'end result' of a contract.[21] Al-Zuhayli has his own definition: "*bay' ma la yu'lam wujuduh wa 'adamuh aw la tu'lam qillatuh wa kathratuh aw la yaqdir 'ala taslimih*", which means "the sale of a thing about which it is unclear as to whether it is obtainable and actually exists, can be quantified and measured, or can be delivered".[22]

There have been many claims that the element of uncertainty had become a problematic one in the conventional banking business contract.[23] There is no doubt the prohibition of *gharar* should not exist in an Islamic business contract, but there are few people who have a clear idea about the extent of *gharar* in the business contract of a modern banking system. The aforementioned definitions on the prohibition of *gharar* promote business ethics; enforce transparency among participants' dealings; and limit speculation, deception, and asymmetry of information. The definitions are also in line with the views of classical jurists, such as Imam Malik bin Anas in his work *al-Muwatta'*, which gives the examples of prohibitions on the sale of an unborn baby animal, as this transaction would contain a necessary element of *gharar.*[24]

In the modern banking system, the problem of asymmetry of information can result in unfairness to one of the parties, such as in the case where a company does not specify the serious financial problems to potential investors who could lose their investment if the company collapses.[25] With respect to banking in particular, asymmetrical information can arise out of asymmetries built into loan contract conditions, such as giving a lender the right to change the terms of a contract without notice or to end a contract without consultation with the borrower.[26] Such practices contribute to the deterioration of trust and the moral values of honestry and fair dealing and are intended to be avoided in Islamic contracts.

However, this does not mean Islamic law prohibits all types of uncertainty. For example, Bellalah and Masood note that risk and uncertainty are normal, even inevitable, features of business: there is never complete certainty as to whether a business will gain a profit or incur a loss.[27] This is particularly relevant to what is called *salam*-based financing in Indonesia, which allows the non-existent object of sale at a price based on previous experience and market conditions.[28] In Indonesia, the practice of *salam* has been used widely and been accepted in society, especially in farming (where there is a delay between demand-orders and supply) and in online transactions (such as selling goods via social media where there is a delay in supply). It can be viewed as an economic necessity, where major grocery chains all depend on future contracts for perishables. This has been corroborated in the *fatwa* of MUI No 05/DSN-MUI/IV/2000 on *salam* trading. In fact, scholars distinguish between excessive uncertainty that invalidates contracts and minor uncertainty, which is tolerated.[29] The example of this can be seen at the prepaid forward sale (*salam* and *istisna*) contract in Islamic finance (discussed in Sections 5.5.2 and 5.5.3), where the commodity sale is not yet determined at the inception of the contract. Since the financing of agricultural and industrial activities is impossible otherwise, it is allowed despite the necessary presence of *gharar*.

5.2.4 Maysir

Maysir literally means 'gambling'. It refers to acquiring money by depriving another by means of 'chance'.[30] The rationale behind the prohibition of *maysir* (speculation or gambling) has two grounds. First, it contains the element of *gharar* (especially where a gambler stands to win or lose large sums of money). Second, the act of *maysir* in financial transactions creates unearned wealth for some and losses for others, instead of being due to a productive or trade activity (which benefits all parties). *Maysir* is explicitly explained as the game of hazard in the Qur'an: "O you who have believed, indeed, intoxicants, gambling (sacrificing on) stone altars (to other than Allah), and divining arrows are but defilement from the work of Satan, so avoid it that you may be successful".[31]

Maysir can occur in any form of business activity where monetary gains are derived from mere chance or speculation, where at least one or more of the parties would lose their assets or investments, and where the gambler gets wealth without effort.[32] In Islamic jurisprudence, any transactions that are based on making gains from gambling under conditions of uncertainty, such as speculative share trading, put options, and conventional insurance contracts, are considered explicit forms of gambling.[33]

In particular, insurance has proved to be an important point of debate for modern Islamic scholars. About 200 scholars participating in an international conference on Islamic economics in 1976 in Makkah concluded that insurance practised in conventional insurance companies is against the *sharia*. The basis for this view was that the premiums which are paid by policy holders are invested by insurance companies in non-*sharia*-compliant investment areas, and the profit-earning from these investments were retained in the insurance company rather than being distributed among policy holders (only being disbursed when insurance claims are paid).[34] As the alternative to this, Islamic scholars have developed and advocated an alternative Islamic form of insurance – *takaful* – which is based on risk-sharing, common benefit, and mutual solidarity. In order to avoid a contract involving 'money for money' (a premium for compensation), the policy holder makes a donation (*tabarru*).[35] The issues of uncertainty and speculation are avoided by making policy holders *mutual* insurers such that all policy holders bear the risks and receive the benefits of pooled premiums and permissible investments from those premiums.[36] Unlike in conventional insurance where policy holders have no interests or rights to the underwriting surplus, *takaful* policy holders are, in theory, entitled to surpluses from the underwriting fund and income from invested premiums based on a mutual insurance model.[37]

5.3 Criticisms of Islamic Financial Instruments in Indonesia

The major criticism of innovative Islamic financial products is that they have the appearance of conventional products. For example, Abdullah Saeed asserts that the current practice of Islamic banking is not completely free from bank interest because so-called 'Islamic' financial products are in fact interest-bearing and are merely renamed as 'profit' or 'rent' to fulfil the Islamic injunction against the collection of interest.[38] The same contention was also made by Dusuki and Abozaid, and Choudury and Khan, who argue that modern Islamic finance has strayed too far from the main purposes/objectives of the *sharia* (the *maqasid al-sharia*), and that its products are only 'Islamic' in name, not in substance.[39] For example, Islamic banks are exposed to conventional interest-based transactions when the bank comes to mark-up transactions, profit return calculations, and the transfer of risk to customers in *mudharabah* contracts (discussed in the next section).

Although these claims may be true in certain respects, these innovated products still retain some distinctively Islamic features that are intended to instantiate certain Islamic values. Islamic scholars have extended the classical law of contracts beyond what was imagined possible in the classical period itself. Some scholars regard such modern extensions of the law as being supported by traditional legal stratagems (*hilah*) which enable them to bridge the gap between today's Islamic financial contracts and the original trading contracts in classical *muamalah fiqh* books.[40] Some scholars have also found ways to construct new kinds of contracts by marrying two or more traditional contracts in one business activity (known as *uqud al-murakkabah*).[41] Although the practice of using bank interest in modern Islamic finance has raised many debates, the Indonesian Islamic financial scholars have used these as *hilah* as a way to circumvent a broad interpretation of the *riba* prohibition.[42] This section will examine certain similarities between conventional instruments and Indonesian Islamic financial products.

5.3.1 Types of Equity Deposits

In conventional banks, depositors are debtholders, which compels the bank to ensure sufficient liquidity, especially where funds are on call.[43] By contrast, the 'standard' form of account in Islamic banks is based on profit-and-loss-sharing, whereby the bank and depositors are equity holders, but this type of account concerns many Islamic bankers, as the bank generally has to guarantee stable profit returns to its depositors. There are two basic types of saving accounts: saving accounts (*wadi'ah*) and investment accounts (*mudharabah*), as summarized in Table 5.1.

Table 5.1 Type of Deposit Accounts in Islamic Banks

Modes of finance	*Types of account*	*Monthly fees*	*Minimum balance*	*Profit share*	*Bonus*	*Capital is guaranteed*	*Use in practice*
Islamic	Saving account (*wadi'ah*)	No	Yes	No	Yes, but theoretically not required	Yes	Widely used
	Saving account (*Mudha-rabah*)	Yes	Yes	Yes	No	Theoretically no, but practically guaranteed by IDIC[44]	Widely used
Conven-tional	Saving account	Yes	Yes	Interest is calculated based on daily balance	Discounts are given for shopping at popular merchants	Both capital and interest are guaranteed	Widely used

Source: Author

The table shows the difference between conventional and Islamic banking deposit accounts

5.3.2 Saving/Current Accounts Using **Wadi'ah** *Contracts*

Wadi'ah is an Arabic word meaning 'safekeeping' and entails keeping another's property safe and returning it on demand.[45] This is the usual basis for current accounts and saving accounts in Islamic banks. There are small differences between saving accounts and current accounts. In relation to saving accounts, the bank is deemed to utilise the funds at its own risk and may voluntarily choose to share the profits obtained with depositors (but is under no obligation to do so). For current accounts, the bank acts as custodian of deposits and commits to returning deposits on demand, with no profit (or loss) to be disbursed to this account.[46] The difference between the two (savings and current accounts) lies in the utilisation of deposited funds to generate profit. Under the former, banks are allowed to use these funds at their own risk, and in the latter, banks are prohibited from using the deposited money but are permitted to take deposit fees.[47] In any case, the bank needs to assure depositors that the money will be available on demand to depositors.

This type of contract is comparable to conventional banks' current/saving accounts and is in wide use by Islamic banks. Under this type of account, the bank is entitled to utilise the deposited money for trading in the short term and for liquidity purposes, with any profit going to the bank, and the bank guarantees depositors against any loss in this account. Generally, these accounts do not involve charges on the account, nor charges for withdrawing funds using cheques (the bank only charges for the use of ATM cards service).[48] Although no profit is provided to the customer, Islamic banks still voluntarily provide a 'bonus' for depositors to make the account attractive to customers. However, the Indonesian depositors are sensitive to changes in interest rates, and the existence of this profit motive in depositors could have the implication them shifting their funds to conventional banks if the latter offer higher returns. Kasri and Kassim stated in their findings based on evidence from Indonesia that, "[t]he customers of Islamic banks are 'rational' depositors who are driven largely by the return that they get from saving".[49] This is why Islamic banks need to prove a 'bonus' that is competitive with the conventional banks' deposit interest rates. This is also the reason why to some extent Islamic banks need to 'mimic' conventional banks – if they don't, they will have difficulty surviving in a competitive market (due to insufficient customer growth and/or fluctuations in customers which could cause a liquidity crisis for the Islamic banks).

5.3.3 Saving/Current Accounts in the Form of Mudharabah

Although it may be alleged that these products are mirroring conventional saving or current accounts, Islamic banks in practice have separated the *mudharabah* and *wadi'ah* accounts. Whereas there is no return to depositors in *wadi'ah* accounts, in *mudharabah* accounts the customer is liable to earn a profit. The depositors act as asset investors (*rabbul maal*), and the bank acts as a fund manager on behalf of depositors (*mudharib*). The money is then invested by the bank as a fund manager in various profitable *halal* activities. The profits earned are distributed between the depositors and the bank in accordance with a mutually pre-agreed profit-sharing ratio. (This ratio must be disclosed to a depositor prior to opening an account.) The bank, as fund manager, is not entitled to a guarantee against financial loss of the capital that has been deposited. However, the bank would be liable for this loss if proven negligent or if the bank were in breach of the contract.[50] In practice, the deposited capital of all types of saving accounts (including *mudharabah*- and *wadi'ah*-based saving accounts) are guaranteed, because depositors' funds are insured up to Rp 2 billion (AUD 200,000) by the Indonesia Deposit Insurance Corporation.[51] Under *mudharabah*-based saving, customers can withdraw their money at any time, at call. The bank provides monthly returns by calculating the average customer balances per month. (Depositors can withdraw amounts above RP 100 million [AUD 10,000] with only one day's notice.)[52]

Mudharabah accounts are frequently used in Indonesian Islamic banks as compared to *wadi'ah* saving accounts; it is reported that the total third-party funds for *mudharabah* saving accounts were increased from Rp 3.17 trillion (AUD 327.5 billion) in 2014 to the total of Rp 3.72 trillion (AUD 371.8 billion) in 2018.[53] The significant difference between a *mudharabah* contract and a *wadi'ah* saving account is that the former does not guarantee capital return, but the latter effectively does. The differences between *wadi'ah*, *qardh*, and *mudharabah* saving accounts is illustrated in Table 5.2.

5.3.4 Penalty and Profit Return: Between Interest and Need

1. Penalty on Late Payment of Financial Obligations

Conventional banks can obtain some revenue via the imposition of fees or penalties when customers withdraw their funds from investment accounts before some

Table 5.2 Islamic Bank Deposits

	Mudharabah *saving*	Wadi'ah *saving*	Qardh *saving*
Type of funds	Investment funds	Deposit with guarantee	Benevolent loan
Withdrawal	Restrictions on withdrawal	No restrictions on withdrawal, at call	No restrictions on withdrawal, at call
Benefits	Profit-and-loss-sharing	Profit voluntarily given (optional); no admin fees	No admin fees
Capital return	No warranty; the capital will be returned (in practice, the risks are borne by the bank)	Warranty of 100% capital return	Warranty of 100% capital return

Source: Bank Indonesia, 2005

The table shows the types of deposits in Islamic banking

agreed-upon time or fail to pay contracted instalments on a loan of some kind. However, in the case of Islamic banks, penalties should only be imposed in the service of 'social needs', because most Islamic scholars deem the imposition of a fee for the use of money, or the failure to repay borrowed money, as a prohibited form of *riba*.[54] This puts Islamic banks at a serious disadvantage because without any penalty for violation of a contract, these banks face the problem of greater liquidity risk and losses of profit. For this reason, Muhammadiyah and MUI scholars in Indonesia have sanctioned another type of penalty known as *ta'widh*, which can be applied to debtors who default without any valid excuse.[55] The nominal amount of *ta'widh* going to the bank should be based on the real losses suffered by the bank.[56] However, if the debtor is facing serious financial difficulty (*in extremis* destitution), then a 'virtuous solution' should be made according to the contract agreement.[57]

The practice of Islamic banks imposing penalties has proved to be a topic of some controversy among Indonesian scholars. The key issue is whether the penalty should be in the form of money or in the form of some other valuable asset. NU scholars prohibit a late fee penalty in the form of money, as there are no textual references in the classical books of *fiqh* that interpret the penalty in monetary form.[58] Most *fiqh* books relied upon by NU scholars are based on the Shafi'i school, whereas *ta'widh* in the form of money is textually prescribed only by the Maliki school – and this opinion is based on an appeal to the public interest (*maslahah*) in order to prevent the debtor from taking advantage of the creditor.[59]

2. *Controversies Over Rate of Profit Returns to Depositors*

In a country where both the conventional and Islamic system of banks are operating, Islamic banks face the paradoxical struggle of attempting to follow the strictures of the *sharia* and at the same time compete in the market against banks that are not so constrained. This, in turn, causes the majority of Islamic deposit practices to resemble conventional bank deposits (that is, Islamic bank deposits attract a profit rate that closely reflects conventional interest rates). Payment by Islamic banks of the profit return in *mudharabah* deposit contracts is determined based on *realised* profit from business investments, not projected returns. At the commencement of the contract, Islamic banks and customers can only agree on the profit-sharing *ratio*, not a predetermined fixed amount as realised profit will not be known *ex ante*. How then is the ratio determined? In Indonesia, this has been settled by and standardised by regulation. The FSA in 2005 issued a circular mandating that all Islamic banks use the interest rate benchmark to determine their profit-sharing ratio in their long-term securities, including term deposits.[60]

More specifically, the profit-sharing calculation uses two methods: profit-sharing and net revenue sharing. The FSA has issued a method for calculating Islamic deposit account returns, but it is not the only method that is followed for all Islamic banks, because each bank has a different method of calculation. The FSA does not interfere with the *mudharabah* calculation methodology determined by the bank's policy.[61] There are four calculations of the ratio for Islamic deposits which are given by the FSA, and all of them clearly show the use of an Expectation Bank Rate (EBR) as a benchmark.[62] For example, a customer enters into a *mudharabah* financing contract for 12 months with total principal amount of Rp 400 million. The bank applies a stress test for projected income: Rp 3.6 billion/annum, with an EBR at 17% per year. The ratio for bank profit is 1.89%, and the ratio for the customer is 100% – 1.89% = 98.11%. The formula for calculation is given here:

Projected profit instalment = balance of principal instalment × EBR

Therefore, the projected profit instalment would be: Rp 400 million/17% = Rp 68 million, and the total instalment fee that should be paid by the customer would be Rp 400 million + Rp 68 million, which comes to Rp 468 million.

In Malaysia, Islamic scholars have attempted to address this problem by means of a provision to cover the lower returns on capital invested by depositors in Islamic banks by seeking to eliminate the incentive to customers to move their funds to a bank with a fixed interest rate. Islamic banks in Malaysia use a Profit Equalisation Reserve (PER) and an Investment Risk Reserve (IRR) with the condition that the maximum PER is not more than 30% of the shareholders' capital. The maximum PER transfer per month must not exceed 15% of gross profit before the distribution of profit-sharing.[63] If the bank's net profit decreases, customers of Islamic banks may get smaller returns than customers receiving interest on their deposits from conventional banks. To retain customers and remain competitive, Malaysian Islamic banks use the PER to increase the profit-sharing ratio for customers, which is added to the reserve amount that they have deducted from the previous profit-sharing.

This Malaysian innovation, however, has not been well received in Indonesia by the FSA. This is because the complicated management of PER and IRR raises issues of liquidity for the bank, as this reserve fund can create idle money in the bank, which cannot be used for productive capacities.[64] Although the practice of PER is not recommended by the FSA, the use of PER is accepted by the MUI, which has issued *fatwa* No 87/DSN-MUI/XII/2012 on the Method of Profit Equalisation (Income Smoothing) for Third Parties.[65] Agustianto, a member of MUI, stated that the permissibility of using PER is based on *maslahah* to maintain the loyalty of customers in an Islamic bank, but PER is not to be used universally. The use should be limited to certain conditions and certain customers which are potentially sensitive to interest rates.[66]

Given customers' predominant demand for fixed-rate return deposits, Malaysian Islamic financial scholars also innovatively developed what has been called a *murabahah* deposit (also known as *tawarruq* deposits).[67] This attracts a rate of return that is comparable to the fixed-interest rate offered by conventional banks.[68] By this type of contract, both the customer and bank benefit from profit investments in the following way. The customer purchases a *sharia*-compliant commodity which they then immediately re-sell to the bank at an agreed market price.[69] In this way, the bank profits out of the investment and the customer profits when the fixed deposit matures.[70] The introduction of the commodity *murabahah* deposit emerged in Malaysia as a result of regulations by the Bank Negara Malaysia under *Islamic Financial Service Authority (IFSA) 2013 Act* 759, s 28.[71]

In Indonesia, the *murabahah* deposit product proved to be highly controversial. Its rejection by most Indonesian scholars meant that this product does not have a place in the Indonesian Islamic banking system. This rejection by Indonesian scholars occurred despite the fact that both the AAOIFI and the IFSB issued standards for the use of *murabahah*-based deposit products in Islamic finance.[72] Again, although the Indonesian scholars acknowledged that Islamic banks need to develop modern products that can provide relatively certain returns to depositors who would otherwise be attracted by better returns from conventional banks, this fixed rate of return on the *murabahah* deposit product is nonetheless widely regarded by Indonesian Islamic scholars as essentially being a disguised interest rate. It is thus perceived by some as 'the thin edge of the wedge' that could ultimately normalise interest-taking within all Islamic banking contracts.[73] (The use of *tawarruq* in Indonesia is discussed in Chapter 6.)

5.4 Islamic Credit Contracts and Their Relation to Interest-Based Contracts

As noted, in practice, the calculated profit rates and service charges are often very similar to (or at least very closely aligned) to interest rates offered by conventional financial institutions. This is one of the main reasons for the periodic accusation that Islamic credit contracts are only 'superficially Islamic' – that in 'substance' they are functionally conventional loan contracts.[74] As Zaman puts it, "It appears that no matter how the transactions are structured by the IBFI [Islamic Banking and Financial Institutions], as long as these are made into 'contract' documents, these are termed as Islamic".[75] Khan confirms this serious problem and argues that "The predominance of interest-based financing is still the norm in Islamic Banks, the

Table 5.3 Loans and Advance Contracts

PLS mode	1. Partnership (*Mudharabah*) 2. Corporation (*Musharakah*)	
Non-PLS mode	Sales contracts	1. Cost-plus sale (*Murabahah*) 2. Advance fee (*Salam*) 3. Ordered item (*Istishna*)
	Lease contracts	1. Lease (*ijarah*) 2. Lease and ownership (*ijarah wa iqtina'*)

Source: Bank Indonesia, 2005

The table shows the types of PLS mode contracts in Islamic banks

main difference being that now it is no longer explicitly identified as interest-based finance and that the business is no longer dominated by non-Muslims".[76]

Briefly, there are three types of loan contracts offered by Islamic financial institutions that formally avoid charging interest, as summarised in Table 5.3: (1) profit-loss sharing (PLS) contracts, which can take the form of a partnership (*mudharabah*) or a corporation (*musharakah*); (2) sales (or trade) based contracts, which can take the form of a cost-plus transaction (*murabahah*), an advance fee contract (*salam*), or an ordered item contract (*istishna*); and (3) leasing-based contracts, which can take the form of a lease (*ijarah*) or a lease-and-ownership (*ijarah wa iqtina*) arrangement.[77]

5.4.1 Controversies in Mudharabah*-Based Financing*

It appears that *mudharabah*, or profit-and-loss-sharing financing, is the primary distinctive feature of Islamic finance, yet it is a subject of intense controversy. Boudjellal provides an excellent exposé on the evolution of Islamic banking from the mid-1970s onwards:

> The *leitmotiv* of Muslim economists was the compliance to the principle of profit and loss sharing (PLS) instead of the interest-bearing practices of conventional banking. . . . However, after nearly three decades of Islamic banking practices, . . . Islamic banks failed to comply with an alternative solution to interest-bearing practices.[78]

In the 1970s, it was hoped that PLS contracts would be the 'jewel in the crown' of Islamic banking in the Muslim world, because in its purist form it perfectly encapsulated the Islamic economic ideals of cooperative sharing of profits and risk, and thus an equitable, non-predatory relationship between capital-rich and capital-poor business partners.[79] It was widely believed that this type of contract, when used as the basis of banking, could entirely eliminate any hint of *riba* from the financial transactions of Muslims. However, as time passed, the optimism about PLS contracts waned. In practice, the contract was not overly popular with customers and did not prove to be as profitable for the banks as was hoped. In response, Islamic banks began to modify the traditional PLS contract to make it a more financially viable product, and it was these innovative efforts that has sparked controversy over the contract.

There have been criticisms that in practice of *mudharabah* contracts may not be *sharia* compliant. The key claim is that *mudharabah* credit had been misused to develop a fixed deposit product where the rate of return is offered to customers up front and where the bank asks the fund manager (borrowing customer) for guarantees (normally in the form of collateral such as assets) – all of which breach the profit-sharing principle that is supposed to define it as 'Islamic'.

As mentioned earlier, *mudharabah* is partnership financing where a bank becomes a joint owner (*shahibul maal*) of a *prima facie halal* business venture by virtue of the fact that it provides the necessary capital. The entrepreneur (*mudharib*) contributes knowledge, skill, and effort to run the business venture. The profit will be shared according to a mutual agreement set out in the contract; however, if there is a loss, the total loss is borne by the Islamic bank. The entrepreneur's/manager's only loss is deemed to be the wasted time and effort they expended in running the business (assuming the manager is not in breach of the agreement and not negligent).[80] There are several issues in implementing the *mudharabah*-based financing contract in Indonesia, covering the *sharia* issues, legal issues, and operational issues.

According to MUI scholars, it is permissible for the bank to ask a customer for collateral for the *maslahah* purpose and for risk protection.[81] This practice is supported by the regulation of BI No. 7/46/PBI/2005 on *The Deposit and Financing of Funds for Banks Conducting Business Based on Sharia Principles*, and the MUI's *Fatwa MUI No. 7/DSN-MUI/IV/2000 on Mudharabah Financing*.[82] However, this issue has given rise to controversy among Indonesian scholars who have argued that the application of taking a guarantee from the entrepreneur/fund manager renders invalid the profit-sharing agreement because the investor (the bank) should bear the risk associated with losses in the business, and thus the bank is not entitled to take a guarantee; if the guarantee were to be demanded, then the form of contract would be similar to that of a pawnbroker (where the pawned asset should be returned after the full amount is received), which substantively deviates from the risk-sharing nature of a *mudharabah*-based contract.[83] The implication of this criticism is that *mudharabah* contracts should remain 'pure' as per the classical conception. The problem with this criticism, however, is that no bank – be it Islamic or conventional – will ever accept the risk of losses without the security of collateral. Indeed, in reality, Islamic banks all over the world always ask for collateral for *mudharabah* financing to reduce risk. Without this security, it is argued, Islamic banks are much less likely to be viable at all in a competitive market environment, or in other words, to demand that Islamic banks use only 'pure' classical contacts is equivalent to inadvertently demanding that Islamic banks be driven from the market in the long run.

Another contentious issue with modern *mudharabah* contracts relates to the predetermined return (repayment) of the capital by the *mudharib* to the bank in instalments irrespective of whether a loss occurs in the business due to the *mudharib*'s negligence. According to FSA standards, all parties' shares should be based on the profit ratio. The recognition of *mudharabah* business income can be determined based on the profit-sharing report from the fund manager, and it is not allowed to recognise income based on projected value.[84] However, in practice the fund manager (customer) has to pay back the profit return more than its owned ratio.[85] This normally occurrs because the bank assumes the fund manager did not properly calculate the profit share monthly or did not tell the truth about their real income and tweaked the report so that the instalment payments were small. The bank then determines the amount of fixed return up front in the agreement, though the real business profit return has not been calculated.[86] This practice also contradicts the MUI's *Fatwa MUI No. 7/DSN-MUI/IV/2000 on Mudharabah Financing* where the profit-sharing ratio should not be linked (*mu'allaq*) with a future prediction. Since a contract may be written where the repayment of defined instalments must be made on a regular basis to the bank, it has been argued that in substantive terms this is almost identical to a conventional interest-based loan agreement. In other words, when the Islamic terminology is stripped away, the modern *mudharabah* contract is virtually indistinguishable from a conventional loan contract.[87]

All these issues make the *mudharabah* contract less competitive and more inefficient for financing arrangements.[88] The FSA regulations concerning *mudharabah* financing does not fully regulate the substance of the agreement between the bank and the customer.[89] In this way, it can be argued that the practice of *mudharabah* agreements in Indonesia have been modified in such a way as to be partially similar to the mechanism of loan agreements in conventional banks; the only difference is that it 'technically' maintains the special kind of partnership agreement and thereby satisfies the *sharia* principles.

5.4.2 *The Criticism of* Murabahah-*Based Financing and Interest*

The *murabahah* type of contract is based on a sales contract with mark-up or cost-plus arrangements. The price or rate of return (the price of the goods plus profit) is fixed and predetermined at the beginning of the contract.[90] The buyer agrees to pay the price of the goods plus the mark-up price as the profit to the bank. The implementation of this contract can be illustrated in the following diagram:

First, the customer agrees to take the loan for purchasing goods from the Islamic bank. The bank then buys the goods required by the customer and immediately sells

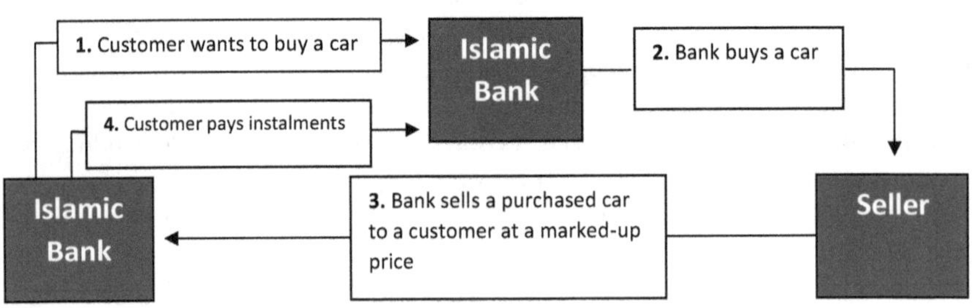

Figure 5.1 Illustration of the Murabahah Scheme

Source: Author

those goods to the customer, adding a profit mark-up.[91] The customer repays the total amount by some future date as a lump sum or in instalments over time. In this way, the payment of interest is avoided, and the mark-up price is charged instead. However, *murabahah* contracts are akin to lines of credit in conventional banks. The main point that differentiates this contract from a conventional bank's facility is that the ownership of commodity (ownership certificate or outright ownership) is held by the bank until the debt has been paid.

Murabahah is the most widely used mode of financing by Islamic banks which constitutes up to 80% of the total Islamic global financing volume.[92] Most banks use *murabahah* for debt financing instead of PLS financing, as the bank risks are transferrable to the client via this instrument.[93] The *murabahah* type of contract has been criticised by some Indonesian scholars, such as Azhar and Sjahdeini, as the mark-up rate mimics an interest rate since the mark-up is fixed and agreed to prior to the sale.[94] In practice, the bank marks up their profit-plus price in *murabahah* contracts before the bank owns the goods (*ba'i ma'dhum*) and may sell the asset without possessing it, which is also prohibited based on a *hadith* narrated by Hakim bin Hizam.[95] Further, Islamic banks use conventional market interest rates to benchmark their mark-up rates, which gives the distinct impression that the former dictates the latter.

MUI scholars defend *murabahah*-based financing by arguing that it does not in fact entail interest because the transactions (and the associated profit) arises out of trading; it would only be *riba* if the bank's return were purely based on a contracted act of lending money.[96] This is also the argument made by Prihantono, who asserts that whereas an interest rate is a monetary surplus generated purely by the exchange of money, by contrast, in a *murabahah* contract, a monetary surplus is gained via the trade in real goods and is (theoretically) not time dependent.[97] The fact that there happens to be little risk to the bank in each trade is an incidental or contingent feature of the trade which has no bearing on the matter. So although *murabahah* contracts do *resemble* conventional interest rate loans, it is going too far to claim that Islamic banks carry out *ba'i ma'dum* and *hilah* to take *riba*. The *murabahah* contract is thus *sharia* compliant, as it has been combined with other contracts (*al-uqud al-murakkabah*) where there are three *halal* contracts (*murabahah, wa'ad*, and *wakkalah*).[98]

5.4.3 What Is the Harm in Using Conventional Interest Rates as a Benchmark?

As explained earlier, although interest-based products (deposits and loans) are prohibited, and although the products offered by Islamic banks technically comply with the *sharia* as interpreted by the MUI, it seems clear that profit rates (and lease rates) are empirically closely related to conventional bank interest rates (they 'track' as if pegged). For example, in a cost-plus (*murabahah*) transaction, since the bank sells the commodity to a customer at the current price plus the mark-up cost, if the market price of commodities fluctuates over time, the Islamic bank is exposed to price risk. Under Islamic law there can be no change to the pre-determined price once it is fixed.[99] The bank is also prohibited from charging more to the client in the transaction due to commodity price fluctuation. While for the majority of Islamic finance scholars it would be highly desirable to have 'pure' financial products that are unrelated to interest rates, in the real world of a competitive financial system that is dominated by conventional banking, it appears that perfect adherence to the ideal versions of Islamic financial products is not practically possible. Some scholars take the view that Islamic banks can use a conventional interest rate benchmark as a guide to *murabahah*-based financing.[100] There are a number of related reasons for this.

First, on the liability (deposit) side of the ledger, customers – both Muslims and non-Muslims – appear to be driven by strong pecuniary motives. Many depositors look for the best rate of return offered in the market. In Indonesia, for example, where conventional and Islamic financial systems co-exist, almost 50% of their Islamic banking customers are less than satisfied with the value of profit return, indicating their awareness of and sensitivity to alternative (conventional) returns available. Thus, Islamic banks' profit shares need to be competitive relative to the interest paid by the conventional banks.[101] This is important, as depositors may withdraw funds and shift them to other banks to increase profits or to minimize their losses, because under PLS-based instruments deposit holders share losses on returns. Many depositors are also looking for security for their deposits and stability in returns that maintains the purchasing power of their savings. If an Islamic bank cannot satisfy these demands relative to conventional banks, they will suffer from periodic liquidity crises and ultimately will be driven out of the market (or at best remain niche institutions). Thus, Islamic banks are compelled to offer competitive and stable rates of return to depositors via innovative products that are comparable and competitive with conventional deposit accounts.

Second, on the asset (investment) side of the ledger, Islamic banks face a number of challenges. One is the problem of adverse selection: riskier ventures will be attracted to PLS contracts. This is compounded by the problem of moral hazard (entrepreneurs may be encouraged to engage in even riskier trading behaviour knowing that they will not bear the entire risk). These problems combined would substantially increase the risk profile of Islamic banks specialising in PLS contracts compared to their conventional competitors (which do not offer PLS contracts).[102] For these reasons, in order to survive in the banking sector, Islamic banks have had to shift away from the ideal PLS contract and develop a 'modern' PLS contract that mitigates the additional risks they would otherwise face. Further, they have been forced to develop other kinds of contracts – especially the 'modern' cost-plus, lease, and lease-and-ownership contracts as substitutes for the PLS contract because these contracts are inherently less risky for Islamic banks.

Finally, one of the most important 'macro' reasons why Islamic banks are 'forced' to take into account money market interest rates is that they exist in a financial system regulated by a secular monetary authority – that is, BI – which is itself integrated into a global financial system. Without imposing the use of interest calculation on Islamic banks, the central role in the transmission of monetary policy would be unclear.[103] Relative interest rates between Indonesia and other countries has a significant impact on capital inflows to Indonesia, which in turn has an impact on the currency exchange rate as well as on net exports and thus inflation and unemployment. Since BI is partly responsible for inflation targeting and external stability, it cannot 'afford' to ignore interest rate levels and movements in the rest of the world relative to domestic bank interest rates. And since Islamic banks are integrated within the Indonesian monetary system as financial intermediaries, their profit rates and leasing rates must be subject to a degree of regulation just as conventional domestic interest rates are.[104] Even if all the banks in Indonesia were Islamic banks that used 'profit rates' and 'leasing rates' (instead of 'interest rates'), BI would still need to regulate profit rates and leasing rates in a way that took into account – and were thus implicitly 'pegged' – to interest rates in other economically significant economies in North America, Asia, and Europe.

In sum, Islamic banks must walk a fine line between the Islamic ideals of offering perfectly fair, equitable, and non-exploitative *riba*-free contracts on the one hand and the real-world pressures that demand that they 'match' their conventional *riba*-based competitors in increasingly globalised financial markets on the other. Like other Islamic banks all over the world, Indonesian Islamic banks have been forced to walk this line. As to whether they can retain their Islamic identity as time passes is uncertain – nothing is a forgone conclusion. What is clear, however, is that it will not just depend on 'competitive forces'. It will also depend on future possible shifts in religious preferences and commitments of customers – both households and enterprises – as well as on possible changes in the regulatory environment, both nationally and internationally, in which Islamic banks operate.

5.5 Concluding Remarks

The differences between Indonesian scholars on the question of whether the taking and receiving of interest on 'modern' loan contracts is permissible is unlikely to be resolved any time soon. In contemporary Islamic finance, certain Islamic financial products can be – and often are – seen as mimicking conventional bank products. This perception is based largely on the conspicuous fact that in practice interest rates are used as a benchmark for determining competing profit and lease rates. For some Muslims, both scholars and laypeople, it is puzzling that this practice has been deemed *sharia* compliant by leading scholars despite the fact that it is also acknowledged that, in some respects, these products might 'contain' *riba* – something that was widely condemned and prohibited in the classical *fiqh* literature.

Although there has been a preoccupation with the *riba* question, especially in academic circles, it should also be recognised that there is at least universal agreement that Islamic banks should not charge *usurious* interest rates under any circumstances whatsoever, even if permissible under secular law (which is not something that can be said for conventional banks or small moneylenders). Furthermore, actual (not just 'theoretical') Islamic financial contracts are in fact characterised by other essential features that play no *defining* role in conventional financial contracts (except when contingently constrained by secular law). Chief among these are that contracts must ultimately be based on the sale/purchase of actually existing (or soon-to-exist) goods; that the base goods should be *halal* in nature; that the contract should not be essentially dependent on acts that are akin to gambling; and that the essential terms and conditions of a contract must be transparent and unambiguous. In these respects, the innovated financial products of Islamic banks in Indonesia (and elsewhere) do retain a distinctively 'Islamic' character.

All that said, Islamic financial instruments are still at an early phase of evolution. Many significant problems and challenges remain. For example, the legitimacy of innovated Islamic financial instruments is still a subject of dispute, and there is ongoing debate about what kinds of innovations are religiously permissible or forbidden. Finally, the regulation of Islamic banks still differs considerably from one country to the next.

Certainly, critiques of Islamic finance by educated sceptics are not to be dismissed out of hand. Rather, they should be taken as constructively critical. There should be careful examination of all the other factors affecting Muslims with an eye to developing institutions that enhance financial stability and economic development. The future growth of the Islamic financial system in line with these goals will largely depend on innovations in Islamic financial instruments so as to meet market demand and customers' preferences, enhance liquidity, develop interbank and secondary markets, and risk management, while at the same time ensuring that these innovations honour the spirit of the *sharia*.

In the following chapter, the challenges associated with the development and application of new Islamic derivative instruments in the market and is also concerned with examining the application and suitability of the Basel Accords to the operations of Indonesian Islamic bank products.

Notes

1 This includes how lent money is likely to be spent. For example, a loan that known to be for the purpose of producing or trading in forbidden products (such as pork, alcohol, or prostitution) would itself be prohibited.

2 Sunna is a rule inferred from the sayings or actions of the Prophet Muhammad PBUH, either in a specific pronouncement or action or in his approval of an action or practice of someone else, as recorded in the prophetic tradition (transmitted by the *hadith*). *Ijma'* is a consensus of Islamic jurists. *See* Hesham M. Sharawy, 'Understanding the Islamic Prohibition of Interest: A Guide to Aid Economic Cooperation between the Islamic and Western Worlds' (2000) 29 *Georgia Journal of International and Comparative Law* 153, 154.

3 Mahmoud A. El-Gamal, *Islamic Finance: Law, Economics, and Practice* (Cambridge University Press, 2006) 46; Ibrahim Warde, *Islamic Finance in the Global Economy* (Edinburgh University Press, 2010) 52; Akhter Md Uddin, 'Principles of Islamic Finance: Prohibition of Riba, Gharr and Maysir' (Pt University Library of Munich) (2015)(9) https://mpra.ub.uni-muenchen.de/67711/1/MPRA_paper_67711.pdf.

4 Qur'an 2:280.

5 Mondher Bellalah and Omar Masood, *Islamic Banking and Finance* (Cambridge Scholars Publisher, 2013) 15.

6 Ibid., 16.

7 Abdullah Saeed, *Islamic Banking and Interest: A Study of the Prohibition of Riba and Its Contemporary Interpretation* (E.J. Brill, 2nd edition, 1999) 95. Also see Frank E. Vogel, *Islamic Law and Finance: Religion, Risk, and Return* (Kluwer Law International, 1998).

8 Ibid.

9 International Monetary Fund, *An Overview of Islamic Finance*, IMF Working Paper No. WP/15/120, International Monetary Fund (2015), www.imf.org/external/pubs/ft/wp/2015/wp15120.pdf, 7.

10 Abu Umar Faruq Ahmad and M. Kabir Hassan, 'The Time Value of the Money Concept in Islamic Finance' (2006) 23(1) *American Journal of Islamic Social Sciences* 66, 73.

11 International Monetary Fund, *An Overview of Islamic Finance*, IMF Working Paper No. WP/15/120, International Monetary Fund (2015), www.imf.org/external/pubs/ft/wp/2015/wp15120.pdf, 7.

12 Muhammad Yasir Yusuf, 'Dinamika Fatwa Bunga Bank di Indonesia: Kajian Terhadap Fatwa MUI, Muhammadiyah dan Nahdlatul Ulama [The Variety of Fatawa on Bank Interest in Indonesia: The Analysis of Fatwa MUI, Muhammadiyah and Nahdlatul Ulama]' 14(2) *Media Syariah* 151. See also Abdul Salam, 'Bunga Bank Dalam Perspektif Islam (Studi Pendapat Nahdlatul Ulama dan Muhammadiyah) [Interest Rate in Islamic Perspective (Study of the Opinion of Nahdlatul Ulama and Muhammadiyah)]' (2013) 3(1) *Jurnal Ekonomi Syariah Indonesia*; Nurhadi Nurhadi, 'Bunga Bank Antara Halal dan Haram [The Bank Interest Rates: Between *Halal* and *Haram*]' (October 2017) 4(2) *Journal of Education and Social Religious Study, Nur El-Islam* 30, 49.

13 There are various interpretations of 'modern'; for example, Zaman explains the ulama opinion on the distinction between the modernists and the Islamists, where the modernist's view is sometimes too far from the Islamists, while the Islamists are too restrictive. Other scholars, such as Brohi, express that to understand modernism one must begin from modern knowledge – scientific, historical, and cultural knowledge – so that they are not totally at a loss to know what to do. However, for the purpose of this research, by 'modern' I mean that the effort to rethink Islamic norms in ways that are compatible with the conditions which are imperatives of modernity, without neglecting the true spirit of Islam. See Qasim Muhammad Zaman, 'Religious Discourse and the Public Sphere in Contemporary Pakistan' (2008) 123 *Revue des mondes musulmans et de la Méditerranée* 55. Also see Muhammad Qasim Zaman, *The Ulama in Contemporary Islam: Custodians of Change* (Princeton University Press, 2002); Wael B. Hallaq, 'Was the Gate of Ijtihad Closed?' (1984) 16(1) *International Journal of Middle East Studies* 3.

14 Some Indonesian scholars who are in favour of bank interest from Nahdlatul Ulama include K.H. Maimoen Zubair, K.H. Abdurrahman Wahid (GusDur), Gus Muwafiq, and Gus Baha. See Raudhatul Qur'an Wal Hadits, 'Haramkah Bank?? Ulama NU Menjawab (Is Bank Interest Haram? The Answer from NU Scholars) (YouTube, 3 November 2019), 00:00:00–16:57:00, www.youtube.com/watch?v=qHkhkVbIp_U.

15 Muhammadiah Scholars argued that *riba* is defined as usury, and that *riba* occurred if there is an unjust exploitation in the activity related to bank interest. Fathurrahman Djamil, *Metode Ijtihad Majlis Tarjih Muhammadiyah* [The Method of Ijtihad of Majlis Tarjih Muhammadiyah] (Logos, 1995). This argument is in line with Mondher Bellalah and Omar Masood. See Mondher Bellalah and Omar Masood, *Islamic Banking and Finance* (Cambridge Scholars Publisher, 2013) 16.

16 Some prominent Islamic scholars, such as Bellalah and Masood, El-Gamal, Obaidullah, and Ahmad, stated that the prohibition of *riba* is also associated with the excessive speculation and the occurrence of a zero-sum game in which one gains at the expense of another. See Uddin, above n 3, 6; Ausaf Ahmad, 'Contemporary Practices of Islamic Financing Techniques' (1994) 2(1) *Islamic Economic Studies*; Mondher Bellalah and Omar Masood, *Islamic Banking and Finance* (Cambridge Scholars Publisher, 2013); Mahmoud A El-Gamal, 'Interest and the Paradox of Contemporary Islamic Law and Finance' (2003) 27 *Fordham International Law Journal* 108.

17 Yusuf, above n 12, 156.

18 Qur'an 2:279.

19 Yusuf, above n 12, 156 [tr author].

20 Abu Umar Faruq Ahmad and M Kabir Hassan, 'The Time Value of Money Concept in Islamic Finance' (2006) 23(1) *American Journal of Islamic Social Sciences* 66, 88.

21 Mondher Bellalah and Omar Masood, *Islamic Banking and Finance* (Cambridge Scholars Publisher, 2013) 20.

22 Wahbah Zuhayli, *Fiqh al-Islami wa-Adilatuhu* [Islamic Jurisprudence and its Proofs] (Dar al-fikr, Beirut, 2001) vol. 5, 3411.[tr author].

23 In May 2020, Justice Gleeson noted that the Australian Securities and Investments Commission (ASIC) reported that there were unfair contract terms done by big four banks to their small business loans, where ASIC found that the banks varied the terms and conditions of the contract without giving the borrower prior notice and an opportunity to exit from the contract without penalty. See Australian Securities & Investments Comission, '20-123MR Court Declares Bendigo and Adelaide Bank Contract Terms Unfair' (Pt ASIC) (2020), https://asic.gov.au/about-asic/news-centre/find-a-media-release/2020-releases/20-123mr-court-declares-bendigo-and-adelaide-bank-contract-terms-unfair/.

24 Malik ibn Anas, *Al-Muwatta' of Imam Malik ibn Anas* (Aisha Abdurrahman Bewley trans, Diwan Press, 2014).

25 Gara Afonso, Anna Kovner and Antoinette Schoar, 'What Happened to US Interbank Lending in the Financial Crisis?', *VOX CEPR Policy Portal* (London), https://voxeu.org/article/what-happened-us-interbank-lending-financial-crisis; Larry McDonald and Patrick Robinson, *A Colossal Failure of Common Sense: The Incredible Inside Story of the Collapse of Lehman Brothers* (Random House, 2009).

26 Australian Securities & Investments Comission, above n 23.

27 Mondher Bellalah and Omar Masood, *Islamic Banking and Finance* (Cambridge Scholars Publisher, 2013) 20.

28 Ibid.

29 Ibid.

30 Hans Visser, *Islamic Finance: Principles and Practice* (Edward Elgar Publishing, 2013) 52.

31 Qur'an 5:90.

32 Hans Visser, *Islamic Finance: Principles and Practice* (Edward Elgar Publishing, 2013) 52.

33 Syeikh Mustafa Al-Zarqa argues that conventional insurance is permissible provided funds are not invested contrary to *Sharia* prohibitions. See Mustafa Al-Zarqa, *Nizam al-Ta'min: haqiqatuh, wa al-ra'y al-shar'i fih* [*System of Insurance: Its Nature and the Sharia Perspective*] (Mu'assasat Al-Risalah, 1994) 703.

34 Mubbsher Munawar Khan et al., 'Comparative Analysis of Islamic and Prevailing Insurance Practices' (2011) 2(10) *International Journal of Business and Social Science* 282, 283.

35 Zaitun Abdullah, Barkah and Rifkiyati Bachri, 'Hybrid Contract on *Sharia* Life Insurance in Indonesia' (Paper presented at the IOP Conference, Jakarta), https://iopscience.iop.org/article/10.1088/1755-1315/175/1/012129/pdf.

36 Ibid.

37 Mondher Bellalah and Omar Masood, *Islamic Banking and Finance* (Cambridge Scholars Publisher, 2013) 21.

38 Saeed, above n 7, 2–3.

39 Masudul Alam Choudhury, 'Islamic Economics and Finance: A Fiasco' (2008) 20(1) *The Middle East Business and Economic Review* 38; Asyraf Wajdi Dusuki and Abdulazeem Abozaid, 'A Critical Appraisal on the Challenges of Realizing Maqasid al-Shari'ah in Islamic Banking and Finance' (2007) 15(2) *IIUM Journal of Economics and Management* 143; Feisal Khan, 'How 'Islamic' Is Islamic Banking?' (2010) 76(3) *Journal of Economic Behaviour & Organization* 805.

40 Saeed, above n 7, 2–3.

41 Muhammad Maksum, 'The Sharia Compliance of Islamic Multi Contract in Islamic Banking' (2017) 162 *Social Science, Education and Humanities Research* 154, 155.

42 Ibid., 154.

43 Ibid.

44 IDIC refers to the Indonesia Deposit Insurance Corporation, which is an independent government body. See Chapter 4 for details.

45 Issa Qaed Mansour Qaed, 'The Concept of Wadiah and Its Application in Islamic Banking' (2014) 2(11) *Journal of Research in Humanities and Social Science* 70, 71.

46 Ascarya and Diana Yumanita, *Bank Syariah* (Pusat Pendidikan dan Studi Kebanksentralan 2005) 17 [tr author].

47 Saving account in Islamic terms is *wadi'ah yad dhomanah*, and current account in Islamic terms is *wadi'ah yad amanah*. See ibid.

48 Bank Muamalat Indonesia, '*Tabunganku* [My deposit]', PT Bank Muamalat Tbk, www.bankmuamalat.co.id/tabungan-consumer/tabunganku.

49 Rahmatina A. Kasri and Salina H. Kassim, 'Empirical Determinants of Saving in the Islamic Banks: Evidence from Indonesia' (2009) 22(2) *J.KAU: Islamic Economics* 3, 16.

50 In the model of *mudharabah*, the risk of capital is borne by the capital owner while the manager loses his reputation and time, unless the loss is due to negligence on the part of the manager. Ascarya and Yumanita, above n 46, 73.

51 Indonesia Deposit Insurance Corporation, *Insurance Deposit* (2018), www.lps.go.id/simpanan-yang-dijamin.

52 'The Standard Book for *Mudharabah* Instruments for Islamic Banking 5/Buku Standar produk Mudharabah seri standar produk perbankan syariah 5', *(Jakarta)* [2019] *Financial Services Authority of Indonesia* No 1, 1–292, 21 February 2019.

53 1 AUD is equal to Rp 10,000. See Financial Services Authority of Indonesia, *Sharia Banking Statistic December 2018*, Financial Services Authority of Indonesia (2018) 9.

54 Habib Ahmed, 'Maqasid al-Shari'ah and Islamic Financial Products: A Framework for Assessment' (2011) 3(1) *ISRA International Journal of Islamic Finance* 149.

55 Fariz As, *Tinjauan Hukum Islam Terhadap Praktik Denda Keterlambatan di Perbankan Syariah (Studi Murabahah di Bank Syariah Mandiri Semarang)* [The Practice of Penalty Fee in Islamic Banking Based on Islamic Law (Case Study of Murabahah Business Contract at Bank Syariah Mandiri Semarang)] (Universitas Negeri Semarang, 2018); *Fatwa* No. 43/DSN-MUI/VIII/2004 concerning penalty (*ta'widh*).

56 *Fatwa* No. 43/DSN-MUI/VIII/2004 concerning penalty (*ta'widh*).

57 This could be in the form of rescheduling or roll over, based on the *Fatwa* No. 47/DSN-MUI/II/2005.

58 As, above n 55, 88, [tr author].

59 Mamat Norazlina and Ahmad Ridzwan, '*Maslahah* Approach Towards Imposition of *Ta'widh* in Islamic Banking' (2019) 39 *Global Journal Al Thaqafah* 39, 41.

60 Peraturan Otoritas Jasa Keuangan No 21/POJK.03/2014 Tentang Kewajiban Penyediaan Modal Minimum Bank Umum Syariah [Regulation of Financial Service Authority No 21/POJK.03/2014 on Minimum Capital Requirement for Islamic Commercial Banks] (Indonesia) ch 4, art 31(1); Surat Edaran OJK Nomor SEOJK.03/2005 Tentang Perhitungan Aset Tertimbang Menurut Resiko Untuk Resiko Pasar Dengan Menggunakan Metode Standar Bagi Bank Umum Syariah [Circular Letter Number SEOJK.03/205 on Calculation of Risk Weighted Assets for Market Risk Using the Standard Method for Islamic Commercial Banks], [tr author].

61 The Standard Book for *Mudharabah* Instrument for Islamic Banking 5/Buku Standar produk Mudharabah seri standar produk perbankan syariah 5', *(Jakarta)* [2019] *Financial Services Authority of Indonesia* No 1, 1–292, 21 Februari 2019, 256.

62 Ibid., 271.

63 Simon Archer and Rifaat Ahmed Abdel Karim, 'Profit-Sharing Investment Accounts in Islamic Banks: Regulatory Problems and Possible Solutions' (9 September 2009) 10(4) *Journal of Banking Regulation* 300.

64 FSA stated that the system of PER and IRR calculation is difficult to adopt in the Indonesian banking system and has the potential to cause a huge amount of idle money and would be difficult to maintain. See Nasirwan and Muhamad Irfan Sukarna, *Laporan Perkembangan Keuangan Syariah Tahun* 2013 [The Report on the Development of Islamic Finance Year 2013] (Financial Services Authority of Indonesia, 2013) 135 [tr author].

65 National Syariah Board, Fatwa MUI No. 87/DSN-MUI/XII/2012 tentang Metode Perataan Penghasilan (Income Smoothing) Dana Pihak Ketiga [The Method of Profit

Equalisation (Income Smoothing) for Third Party], (National Sharia Board – Indonesian Council of Ulama, 2012).

66 Wahyudi Hidayat, 'Profit Equalisation Reserve (PER) dan Investment Risk Reserve (IRR) dan (Idealisme) Ber Bank Syariah [Profit Equalisation Reserve (PER) and Investment Risk Reserve (IRR) and Idealism in Islamic Banking]', *Kompasiana* (Jakarta), [tr author], www.kompasiana.com/liwaganteng/550f6a00a33311af35ba7ea5/profit-equalization-reserve-per-dan-investment-risk-reserve-irr-dan-idealisme-ber-bank-syariah.

67 Commodity *Murabahah* deposit is also known as *Tawarruq*; the product provides a facility for capital guarantee and fixing of returns on capital. See Islamic Financial Services Board, *Islamic Financial Services Industry: Stability Report* (2017), www.ifsb.org/docs/IFSB%20IFSI%20Stability%20Report%202017.pdf, 1.

68 Andika Aldi and Dimas, 'Dinamika Tawarruq Sebagai Inovasi Produk Perbankan Syariah [The Dynamic of Tawarruq as an Innovative Islamic Banking Product]', *Komite Nasional Ekonomi dan Keuangan Syariah* (Jakarta), https://knks.go.id/berita/298/dinamika-tawarruq-sebagai-inovasi-produk-perbankan-syariah?category=1.

69 Ismail Abdul Ghafar, 'Tawarruq Time Deposit with Wakalah Principle: An Option That Triggers New Issues' (2016) 9(3) *International Journal of Islamic and Middle Eastern Finance and Management* 388.

70 Ibid.

71 Ibid.

72 M. Kabir Hassan et al., 'A Survey on Islamic Finance and Accounting Standards' (2019) 19 *Borsa Istanbul Review* S1; Fathullah Asni and Jasni Sulong, 'Non-Ethical Elements in Tawarruq Munazzam Product for Islamic Housing Financing in Malaysia' (2018) 8(12) *International Journal of Academic Research in Business and Social Sciences* 1013; Salman H. Khan, 'Why Tawarruq Needs to Go: AOIFI and the OIC Fiqh Academy: Divergence or Agreement?', *New Horizon Islamic Banking*, www.newhorizonislamicbanking.com/index.cfm; Ahmad A. Alkhamees, *A Critique of Creative Shari'ah Compliance in the Islamic Finance Industry* (Brill | Nijhoff, 2017); Ellida Fauziah Ahmad et al., 'The Acceptability of Tawarruq as a Product for Financing Within the Islamic Banking System' (2017) 1 *International Journal of Management and Applied Research* 31; Abdul Ghafar, above n 69.

73 Aldi, Andika and Dimas, above n 68.

74 M. Choudhury, 'Islamic Economics and Finance: A Fiasco' (2008) 20(1) *Middle East Business and Economic Review* 38–51; A. Dusuki and A. Abozaid, 'A Critical Appraisal on the Challenges of Realizing Maqasid al-Shari'ah in Islamic Banking and Finance' (2007) 15(2) *IIUM Journal of Economics and Management* 143–165; F. Khan 'How "Islamic" Is Islamic Banking?' (2010) 76 *Journal of Economic Behavior & Organization* 805–820.

75 M. Raquibuz Zaman, 'Usury (Riba) and the Place of Bank Interest in Islamic Banking and Finance' (2008) 6(1) *International Journal of Banking and Finance* 1, 10.

76 Khan, above n 39, 811.

77 Ascarya and Diana Yuminita, 'Bank Syariah: Gambaran Umum' '(Islamic Bank: General Overview)', (2005) Pusat Pendidikan dan Studi Kebanksentralan (Centre of Central Bank Education), Bank Indonesia Jakarta, www.bi.go.id/id/publikasi/seri-kebanksentralan/Documents/14.%20Bank%20Syariah%20Gambaran%20Umum.pdf, 25.

78 Mohammed Boudjellal, 'Three Decades of Experimentation: Rethinking the Theory of Islamic Banking' (2006) 10(1) *Review of Islamic Economics* 23, 23.

79 Ibid.

80 According to Islamic principles, if a business's loss is due to negligence of the manager, the total loss of capital will be the responsibility of the manager, but if the loss occurs naturally due to unavoidable falls in the market, the total loss is borne by the capital owner and the manager loses his time for investing his skill in the business. It is also wise to say that the loss is not always money but could also be the time which is spent in managing the business. See Anjum Siddiqui, 'Financial Contracts, Risk and Performance of Islamic Banking' (2008) 34(10) *Managerial Finance* 680, 683.

81 'The standard book for *Mudharabah* instrument for Islamic banking 5/Buku Standar produk Mudharabah seri standar produk perbankan syariah 5', *(Jakarta)* [2019] Financial Services Authority of Indonesia No 1, 1–292, 21 February 2019, 74.

82 Peraturan Bank Indonesia Nomor 7/46/PBI/2005 Tentang Akad Penghimpunan dan Penyaluran Dana Bagi Bank yang Melaksanakan Kegiatan Usaha Berdasarkan Prinsip Syariah [Regulation of Bank Indonesia No 7/46/PBI/2005 on the Deposit and Financing of Funds for Banks Conducting Business Based on Sharia Principles] (Indonesia); Dewan Syariah Nasional, *Fatwa No. 7/DSN-MUI/IV/2000 on Mudharabah Financing* (Majelis Ulama Indonesia, 2000).

83 Among the Indonesian scholars who are against the taking of collateral in *mudharabah* is Dr Erwandi Tarmidzi Azhar, 'Mudharabah Bank Syariah, Berbagi Riba Berkedok Syariah [Mudharah in Islamic Bank, Sharing *Riba* under the Guise of Sharia]', *Majalah Pengusaha Muslim* (Jakarta), [tr author], https://pengusahamuslim.com/2780-mudharabah-bank-syariah-1476.html.

84 Financial Services Authority of Indonesia, *Buku Standar produk Mudharabah seri standar produk perbankan syariah* 5 [The Standard Book for Mudharabah Instrument for Islamic Banking 5] (Financial Services Authority of Indonesia, 2019) 93 [tr author]. Also see 'Pernyataan Standard Akuntansi Keuangan [Statement of Financial Accounting Standards]', *Akuntansi Mudharabah (Jakarta)* [2007] Ikatan Akuntan Indonesia, 105, 1–42, para 22.

85 In the case of the Islamic Financial Cooperation (Baitul Maal Wat-tamwil – BMT) Nahdlatul Ulama, Bondowoso shows that in practice *mudharabah* financing makes calculations based on the average gross income of the customer and not based on real income, which is against the standard of the FSA. In Fadilatul Imamah, 'Penentuan Nisbah Bagi Hasil Pada Pembiayaan Mudharabah dan Perlakuan Akuntansinya (Studi Kasus pada KSPPS BMT NU Cabang Wringin Kabupaten Bondowoso) [The determinant of Profit Sharing Ratio on Mudharabah Financing and Its Accounting Treatment (Case Study at KSPPS BMT NU Branch Wringin, Bondowoso Regency)]' (2019) 8(2) *E-Jurnal Ekonomi dan Bisnis Universitas Udayana* 199, 218 [tr author].

86 Ibid.

87 Muhammad Arifin Badri, 'Mencari Solusi Bank Syariah [Finding the Solution for Islamic Banks]', *Majalah As-Sunnah* (Surakarta), [tr author]; Azhar, above n 83.

88 Total *mudharabah* financing only accounted for 17.3% of the total financing in 2017. See 'The standard book for *Mudharabah* Instruments for Islamic Banking 5/Buku Standar produk Mudharabah seri standar produk perbankan syariah 5', *(Jakarta)* [2019] Financial Services Authority of Indonesia No 1, 1–292, 21 February 2019, 74.

89 As stated in the FSA standard book under the *mudharabah* scheme, a bank (investor) can ask a fund manager (customer) to sign a debt acknowledgement letter if the profit return is not paid on a scheduled time and/or breach the contract. This means *mudharabah* contracts are considered as a debt and not as a partnership scheme which is against the idea behind *mudharabah*. 'The standard book for *Mudharabah* instrument for Islamic banking 5/Buku Standar produk Mudharabah seri standar produk perbankan syariah 5', *(Jakarta)* [2019] Financial Services Authority of Indonesia No 1, 1–292, 21 Februari 2019, 216.

90 Ascarya and Diana Yuminita, 'Bank Syariah: Gambaran Umum' '(Islamic Bank: General Overview)', (2005) Pusat Pendidikan dan Studi Kebanksentralan (Centre of Central Bank Education), Bank Indonesia Jakarta, www.bi.go.id/id/publikasi/seri-kebanksentralan/Documents/14.%20Bank%20Syariah%20Gambaran%20Umum.pdf, 24.

91 Usually, the bank does not purchase the goods required by customers since this can be time consuming for a bank to manage the purchasing of the goods. The bank thus contacts both the buyer and seller and they meet up at the bank, the money then being transferred by the bank to the customer's account after the agreement is signed. In other words, the customer becomes a bank representative to buy the goods. Syamsun Nahar, News, '*Murabahah* Based Financing/Pembiayaan Jual-beli

murabahah', *finance, Okezone* (Jakarta), 14 March 2012, https://economy.okezone.com/read/2012/03/14/316/593050/pembiayaan-jual-beli-murabahah.

92 Abdelrahman Yousri Ahmad, 'Does Islamic Banking Help in Economic Development of Muslim Countries' (2016) 6(2) *Journal of Islamic Business and Management* 19, 12.

93 Tarek Zaher and Kabir Hassan, 'A Comparative Literature Survey of Islamic Finance and Banking' (2001) 10(4) *Finacial Markets, Institutions and Instruments* 155, 157.

94 Sutan Remy Sjahdeini, *Perbankan Islam dan Kedudukannya dalam Tata Hukum Perbankan Indonesia* [Islamic Banking and Its Position in the Indonesian Banking Law System] (Pustaka Utama Grafiti, 1999) 117, [tr author]. Erwandi Tarmidzi Azhar, 'Panduan Murabahah yang Sesuai Syariah [Guideline for Sharia-Compliant Murabahah]', *Majalah Pengusaha Muslim* (Jakarta), https://pengusahamuslim.com/5473-panduan-murabahah-yang-sesuai-syariah-bagian-1.html; Aminah Lubis, 'Aplikasi Murabahah Dalam Perbankan Syariah [The Application of Murabahah in Islamic Banking]' (2016) 2(2) *Jurnal Kajian Ilmu-ilmu Keislaman* 181.

95 Azhar, 'Panduan Murabahah yang Sesuai Syariah [Guideline for Sharia-Compliant Murabahah]' and n 83. Also see Sunan Abi Dawud No 3503, https://sunnah.com/abudawud:3503.

96 See the *fatwa* of the National Sharia Board of Indonesian Ulama Council Number: 04/DSN-MUI/IV/2000 on *Murabahah* Contract https://dsnmui.or.id/category/fatwa/page/12/.

97 Prihantono, 'Akad Murabahah dan Permasalahannya dalam Penerapan di Lembaga Keuangan Syariah [Murabahah Conctract and Its Issues in Implementation in Islamic Financial Institutions]' (2018) 14(2) *Jurnal Al-Maslahah Ilmu Syariah* 219, 233 [tr author].

98 Otoritas Jasa Keuangan, *Standar Produk Perbankan Syariah: Murabahah* [Standard for Islamic Banking Products: Murabahah] (Otoritas Jasa Keuangan, 2016) 22; Rida Ahroum, Othmane Touri and Boujemaa Achchab, 'Murabaha and Musharakah Moutanaquissah Pricing: An Interest-Free Approach' (2020) 11(1) *Journal of Islamic Accounting and Business Research* 201.

99 Muhammad Taqi Usmani, *An Introduction to Islamic Finance* (Idaratul Ma'arif, 1998).

100 The use of conventional benchmarks such as the London Inter-Bank Offered Rate (LIBOR) is allowed by some Islamic scholars, including El Gamal. While in Indonesia this is termed as JIBOR (Jakarta Inter-Bank Offered Rates), JIBOR could be used to determine the rate of profit in *murabahah* and leasing products in an Islamic bank, this benchmark being based on money supply and demand and not based on the real price of commodities/assets. See Trisiladi Supriyanto, 'The Concept of Rate of Profit and Stability in Islamic Bank/*Konsep rate of profit dan stabilitas ekonomi perbankan syariah*' (2015) 14(2) *Etikonomi* 175, 178 [tr author].

101 The customers of Bank Syariah Mandiri in Indonesia have the highest potential to switch to another bank; 40.55% of its customers in Bogor were not satisfied with the value of return on profit. See Mukhamad Najib, 'Analysis on the Customer's Brand-switcher at Islamic Bank and Conventional Bank (case Study at Region of Darmaga Bogor)/*Analisis Konsumen Berpindah Merek (Brandswitcher) pada Bank Syariah dan Bank Konvensional (studi kasus pada nasabah di wilayah Darmaga Bogor)*' (July 2009) 4(1) *Islamic Finance and Business Review* 1, 17 [tr author].

102 Kuran Timur, 'Islamic Economics and the Islamic Subeconomy' (1995) 9(4) *Journal of Economic and Prespectives* 155; Muhammad Akhyar Adnan and Muhamad Muhamad, 'Agency Problems in Mudarabah Financing: The Case of Sharia (Rural) Banks, Indonesia' (2007) 15(2) *IIUM International Journal of Economics, Management and Accounting* 219.

103 Thomas B. Pepinsky, 'Islamic Finance in Multicultural Indonesia' (Paper presented at the Yale Indonesia Forum Internation Conference, Yogyakarta) 4.

104 Thomas B. Pepinsky, 'Development, Social Change, and Islamic Finance in Contemporary Indonesia, World Development' (2013) 41 *Journal of World Development* 157, 161; Kasri and Kassim, above n 49.

6 Islamic Derivatives in Indonesia

Debate and Legal Challenges

6.1 Introduction

In an effort to be competitive in national and international financial markets, Islamic banks have, with the imprimatur of religious scholars, developed new kinds of financial products resembling conventional banking products while at the same time conforming, as much as practicable, to the principles of the *sharia*. As discussed in this chapter, there have been some debates amongst Islamic scholars about the validity of these Islamic products. Arguably, the most controversial innovation in the field of Islamic finance is 'Islamic derivatives' or 'derivative-like' products. The controversy stems first from conflicting scholarly opinions about whether derivatives are acceptable in *sharia* terms, and second from the fact that the construction and trade in these complex hedging instruments is permitted in some Muslim jurisdictions but is prohibited in others. For example, Indonesian scholars at the MUI do not accept certain kinds of derivative transactions, such as the *tawaruq* derivative instrument due to its similarity with interest-based financing, and argue that it is speculative and may entail an element of 'fictitious' trade.[1] *Tawaruq* derivatives were also prohibited by the IIFA of the Organisation of Islamic Cooperation in its 19th meeting in Jeddah in 2009.[2] Yet scholars in Malaysia and at the International Islamic Financial Markets (IIFM) approve the use of such derivatives, stating that they are an essential element of sound risk management in the Islamic financial market, and they should be deemed permissible on the grounds of eliminating opportunity costs and serving the public interest (*maslahah*).[3]

This chapter first examines the controversial use of derivative instruments from an Islamic perspective and discusses those hedging instruments which are deemed *sharia* compliant in Indonesia. It then analyses their usage in Islamic finance and the issues and challenges that arise. It finally examines the legal challenges associated with recognising derivatives and considers the prospect of harmonising the Islamic standards for a worldwide constituency.

6.2 Three Legal Positions on Derivatives

6.2.1 Derivatives and Their Functions

This section will explain conventional derivatives and their intended functions before examining the controversy in relation to derivative contracts and *sharia*-compliant

DOI: 10.4324/9781003393986-6

alternatives. Derivatives are financial instruments where the value of a trade is based on an underlying asset, such as commodities, currencies, or securities.[4] Derivatives can be categorised as follows:

1 *Commodity derivatives*, where the underlying assets are based on commodities such as oil, energy, crude palm oil, gold, etc.
2 *Financial derivatives*, where the value of transactions depends on the financial assets attached to it, such as currencies, stocks, securities, and interest rate.[5]

Some critics blame derivatives for the collapse of important companies such as Lehman Brothers and the American International Group in 2008. While acknowledging this, others argue that derivatives can still bring substantial economic benefit if managed and properly handled in a regulated market.[6] The main function of derivatives is that they allow users to transfer the risk to another party in the form of forwards, futures, options, and swaps.[7] Derivative instruments such as futures and options can be used to hedge risk against adverse movements in the underlying asset's price; for example, it can be used to protect producers from the adverse price declining on stocks or agricultural commodities.[8]

The users of derivatives markets are often classified into two broad categories: those engaged in risk-hedging and those engaged in non-hedging (non-speculative) transactions. The former enters a derivative contract to protect against the risk of losses due to fluctuation in the interest rates, currencies, stocks, and commodities. The latter activities are inherently more risky and should be properly monitored by financial regulators, as the speculators attempt to gain profit out of deferred prices through the market timing, such as by buying derivatives in one market and selling them simultaneously in another for a profit based on differences in the market price.[9]

6.2.2 Controversies Over Derivatives in Islamic Finance

The question of the permissibility of the use of derivatives in Islamic finance is hotly debated by *sharia* scholars. This is in large part because derivatives are entirely new instruments in modern Islamic finance and thus have no precedent in classical *fiqh* literature.[10] In Islamic law, it is held that business transactions should always duly consider both risk and responsibility (*al-kharaj bil al-daman wal kharaj bil al-ghonm*).[11] Since the intended function of derivatives is to hedge against risk, thereby making the overall returns of financial institutions more stable over time, *fiqh* considerations of derivatives must necessarily be concerned not only whether they entail *riba*, *gharar*, and/or *maysir*, but also whether their use in risk management is in the public interest (*maslahah*).[12]

There are three different scholarly positions on derivatives in Islamic finance. First, there are those who are in favour of the use of derivatives even if they seemingly violate some 'pre-modern' prohibitions on *gharar*. They highlight the necessity of derivatives as a tool in managing the risk of loss arising from market volatility and argue for this on the basis of public interest (*maslahah*) and *'urf tijari* (common business). This is the view of the Sharia Advisory Council of Securities

Commission Malaysia and the IIFM.[13] The rationale behind their opinion is that futures trading can be traced to the time of the Prophet Muhammad PBUH, which can be seen from some elements such as the condition, and the underlying asset in the trading.[14] For example, it is narrated that the Prophet PBUH said whomever wished to make *a salaf* (forward trade) should do that for a specific weight, specific quantity, and for a specific period of time.[15] These elements also exist in present-day futures trading; however, in the modern period, such derivative products are extremely complex, numerous, and highly diversified across stock and investment markets.[16]

A second position completely prohibits the use of derivatives. This judgement is made by the IIFA of the Organisation of Islamic Cooperation and supported by European Council for Fatwa and Research.[17] This position is motivated by a precautionary principle because it focuses on the concern that permitting derivatives could lead to excessive speculation by opportunists – instead of genuine hedging using "real" transactions – where the derivative markets serve large traders at the expense of small traders by way of market manipulation, which can contribute to market crashes. Aside from this empirical concern, this position also holds that derivatives contain the element of *gharar*, where there is a deferment of both actual asset delivery and final payment, thereby rendering such transactions impermissible. Since those who oppose derivatives take the view that in the context of derivative instruments, purchases or sales cannot be affected for a future date, they deem every type of future and forward contract invalid.[18] Secondly, in most cases of future transactions, the seller does not possess the commodities and does not have a capacity to guarantee the delivery, and thus this type of transaction is not intended for genuine hedging or investment but for speculation. The speculators buy the asset in the market not to be owned, and the asset is directly sold back to the market in order to get profit from price changes in the market.[19] On this view, therefore, the *sharia* prohibits all forward and futures contracts intended to gain profit through the difference in price only but permits derivatives for real investment purposes in the expectation of some benefit in the future.[20]

The third position holds that if certain conditions set down by the *sharia* are met, futures derivatives are permissible; where those conditions cannot be secured, then such derivatives are impermissible. On this view, all derivatives must be for genuine hedging purposes, traded 'hand-to-hand' on spot markets, and must be guaranteed by a clearinghouse which is able to ensure the elimination of *gharar* resulting from counterparties' risks and guarantee the delivery of underlying assets.[21] This opinion is mostly adopted in those countries where transactions heavily depend on agricultural-based economies and market volatility, such as Bangladesh, Pakistan, Indonesia, Egypt, and Malaysia.[22]

6.2.3 Debatable Activities in the 'Grey Areas' of Derivatives

All types of modern derivatives (entailing short positioning) have been treated with suspicion by informed Muslims. This is probably precipitated by some high-profile cases of financial disaster attributable to financial market players using derivatives to continually pass on risk to other players, thereby resulting in a seemingly unending 'greater fool' spiral of risk transferral.[23] One example of this spiral of risky speculation is the story of Black Wednesday that 'broke the pound' in just one day. On 16 September 1992, George Soros made an enormous bet against the pound sterling by short selling in one day, and pocketed US$1 billion from this one trade, thereby cementing his reputation as the world's premier currency speculator. A more recent example is the global financial crisis that began in the United States in 2007, which as Donald Johnston notes, "was not a direct product of an asset bubble but rather the impact on lenders who had bet on such derivatives for better rates of return during a period of very low interest yields on conservative debt instruments".[24]

When it comes to the *ulama*, however, there is not total unanimity on the question of short positioning (or short selling). As noted, *ulama* from different jurisdictions and different institutions hold conflicting views. This section will argue that a moderate middle-ground position can be sustained by plausible argumentation against the 'precautionary' position on one side (a position that would rule out derivatives altogether) and against extreme liberalism on the other (which would effectively allow almost any derivative product to be deemed 'Islamic'). The moderate position advocated here is not an unheard of innovation. This position is rooted in the classical *fiqh* tradition by relying on the established maxims of *al-aslu fi al-ashya' al-ibaha* – a maxim of presumptive permissibility – postulating that unless there is unequivocal evidence that something (such as a new kind of commercial transaction) is forbidden in the *sharia*, it is permitted (*halal*).[25]

Imam Malik ibn Anas approved uncertainty under certain conditions in Islamic contracts, with the rationale being that economic activities cannot be entirely separated from uncertainties.[26] In practice, as per the transactions agreement in the financial derivatives, the values of the underlying assets are predetermined for the purpose of hedging the price of the asset, and if the price increases then the party who loses will have to pay the difference.[27] Thus, in derivatives it is not the underlying asset alone that should be the subject matter, but also the uncertainty about the movement of price of that asset. For example, in short selling, the investor borrows shares (original shares) from a broker (or institution) at a certain interest rate and agrees to return the shares to the broker in the future or at the broker's request.[28] The usual practice is to sell the equivalent number of shares for delivery at a future date. This is done in anticipation that the share price will drop prior to the date for delivery where the investor buys the same number of shares at a lower price. This allows a profit margin based on the sale at a higher price with delayed date of delivery. The original shares are then returned to the broker/institution. The process of short selling can be illustrated in Figure 6.1.[29]

Short selling is risky but is deemed worthwhile if an investor is sure that a stock's value will drop in the short term. Iqbal and Mirakhor state that *gharar* occurs in short selling, as it is a case of selling an item that is not in the seller's possession (*ba'i*

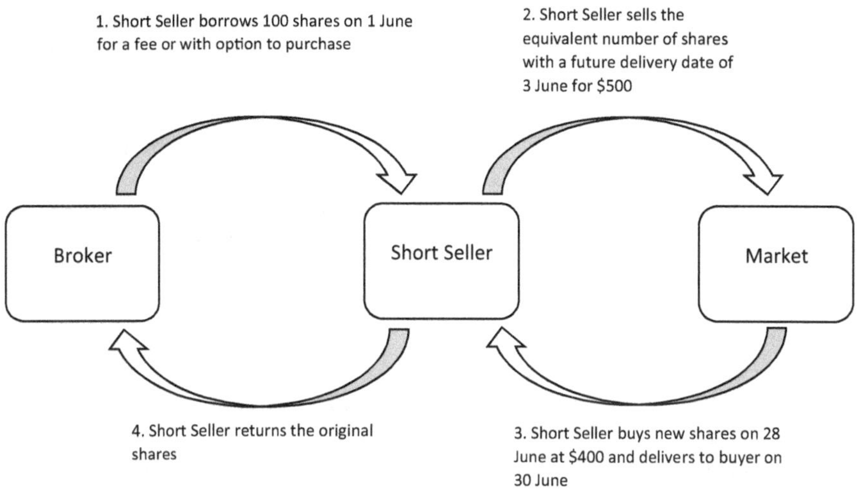

Figure 6.1 The Illustration of Short Selling
Source: Author

al-ma'dum).[30] This is because the seller cannot guarantee delivery of the item to the buyer, and there is no real intention to sell or to buy, but rather only the intention to make a return by speculating (gambling) on the difference from market fluctuation with borrowed money.[31] In addition to this, the broker lends the shares to the investor at interest, and the short seller has to bear the interest risk for the period of holding the borrowed shares. The short seller also has to bear the risk of a sudden request by the broker to return the shares, which generally happens when the broker wishes to sell the borrowed shares, especially when the price of the shares goes up.[32] The investor has to bear the risk of buying back the shares at unfavourable conditions and thus bear a loss.

Nonetheless, given that derivatives are one of the most important tools for hedging against price fluctuations in the market, they can, if utilised prudently, bring substantial economic benefits and improve the management of market risk and investment risk.[33] However, Islamic financial engineers must be wary of the fact that derivatives can be (and are) used for speculative purposes, and as such must be well regulated.[34] It could be argued that by prohibiting genuine Islamic investors from using derivative instruments, *ulama* would be imposing undue hardship (*darurah*) on investors by leaving them exposed to greater risk of loss and bankruptcy than non-Islamic investors. Such a prohibition would also render Islamic investors, which include Islamic banks, less competitive relative to their conventional rivals who would not be so constrained.

Furthermore, it may be inappropriate to make an analogical link between short selling and selling an item not in the seller's possession (*ba'i al-ma'dum*). It is arguable that the prohibition on short selling by Indonesian scholars may actually be simply due to a misunderstanding about what short selling means. The misunderstanding arises because the Indonesian Stock Exchange defines short selling as "the transaction in which the seller does not own the shares at the time the transaction is conducted".[35] However, this definition is incomplete; according to the US Securities and Exchange Commission, short selling can *also* be a sale which is consummated by the delivery of a stock borrowed by, or for the account of, the investor.[36] This means the investor has the right to sell the borrowed shares and has agreed to buy prior to the delivery date and to return the borrowed security to the stock lender to satisfy the contract (even if at a higher price). Thus, short selling does not necessarily take the form of *ba'i al-ma'dum* and thus need not be judged impermissible.

Another argument about derivatives is offered by Dusuki, Smolo, and Injadat and is related to opportunistic investors who use derivatives exclusively to make a profit from a speculation (*mujazafat*) about a security's price change, rather than engaging in genuine hedging.[37] A counterargument to this, however, is that so-called speculators are simply making a profit based on the accuracy of their predictions about what will occur in the future.[38] Insofar as their predictions are based on information or knowledge that would render their predictions superior to mere chance guesses, their behaviour does not necessarily take the form of gambling. Rather, the behaviour would simply be a somewhat risky trading endeavour, like so many activities that are acceptable in the *sharia*.[39]

6.2.4 Derivatives Enable Hedging Against Risk

When it comes to core tenets of faith and worship (*'ibadat*), the virtual prohibition on legal innovation is regarded as a desirable, essential feature of the religion by all classical and modern mainstream Islamic scholars. However, when it comes to worldly matters of commercial transactions (*muamalah*), a strict conservative view on the prohibition of hedging instruments could place Islamic businesses (including banks) into a severely disadvantaged position relative to their conventional counterparts.[40]

This argument has been advanced most stridently by Malaysian *ulama*, and it has also gained some traction among Indonesian *ulama*.[41] With the growing number of Indonesian Islamic banking transactions in international and domestic Islamic markets – including foreign remittances, trade flows, and, importantly, the financing of the Indonesian pilgrimage to Mecca – hedging instruments are urgently required to mitigate the risk exposures arising from exchange rate fluctuations. In response, the Indonesian Islamic Banking Working Group (Working Group Perbankan Syariah) asked the MUI to provide a *fatwa* allowing hedging on foreign currencies.[42] Based on this request the MUI issued several derivatives based on urgent need (*lil hajah*), public need (*maslahah*), and permissibility (*ibahah*). The MUI realised that such derivatives are not permitted in *sharia*, but stated that the result of avoiding them may lead to detriment in economic activities (*mafsadah*).[43] Furthermore, the IFSB in 2005 stated that the contemporary Islamic financial industry worldwide was exposed to market risks in almost all of its financial instruments, including *sukuk*, *salam*, and *murabahah* assets.[44] This market risk occurs due to the fluctuations in interest rates, exchange rates, and market prices. The occurrence of interest risk would be more common at Islamic banks in a country where the customers treat conventional and Islamic banks as substitutes.[45]

Islamic banks are also subject to rate mismatch risks in foreign exchange, where differences occur in the levels of benchmarking between foreign and locally denominated assets. For example, foreign parties are normally valued using the foreign benchmark LIBOR (London Interbank Offered Rate) and the local party priced using the local benchmark JIBOR (Jakarta Interbank Offered Rate).[46] In this regard, IFSB scholars suggested that there should be a *sharia*-compliant mechanism to minimise this inevitable risk exposure from price and rate volatility.[47]

The rationale for using derivatives is that Islamic banks could ensure the sufficiency of internal funds by minimising the impact of unnecessary cash flows while simultaneously increasing their competitiveness within the global market by reducing their cost barriers to market entry through stable and competitive pricing of Islamic financial products.[48] For example, in the contract between crude palm oil producers and margarine manufacturers, both parties signed a forward contract to avoid the risk of uncertain market price volatility and the risk of supply scarcity. Margarine manufacturers need palm oil for the next six months and crude palm oil would be produced in the next six months. Over the six-month period, the crude palm oil producer would have been exposed to the risk of insufficient demand and a falling price, whereas the margarine manufacturer would have been exposed to the risk of a palm oil shortage and rising prices.[49] The forward contract benefits both parties by hedging against price fluctuations and thereby providing greater certainty to their business activities and plans. Greater certainty in turn provides a foundation for further productive investment, employment, and production in the future.

Disregarding the use of derivatives in the matter of risk management would arguably contradict *maqasid al-shariah* and the protection of assets from undesirable risks.[50] As the great 12th-century scholar Imam Al-Ghazali said, the purpose of *maqasid al-shariah* is to give special attention to religion (*din*), life (*nafs*), dignity (*nasl*), intellect (*aql*), and wealth (*mal*).[51] These five elements are essential for human beings, and the inability to protect one of the elements would harm humanity.[52] For example, while it is important for Islamic banking to hedge risks in order to protect their assets from the volatility of market prices, it is also important to ensure these risk-hedging activities are conducted in an ethical manner, the Islamic rationale behind this being that a lack of restraint over human desires leads to disastrous ends, including greed, exploiting others, and striving for zero-sum gains.[53] According to Yazid et al., also supported by Wijaya and Ismail, each Islamic financial contract must have its specific objectives, or *maqasid juz'i*, which Islamic scholars have referred to as the ultimate aim for that specific rule to fulfil human needs in many matters and bring benefits to the public interest.[54] Thus, when the *maqasid al-shariah* is applied to derivatives, the *maqasid* of such transactions is as a means to hedge risks against adverse movements in the underlying asset's price, which can bring substantial economic benefit when they are well regulated and properly handled in a fair market.

6.3 Criticism of the Existing Derivatives in Indonesian Islamic Finance

Although some popular types of derivative instruments, such as forwards, options, swaps, and futures, have been recognised as permissible by the NSB-MUI in Indonesia, the attempts to make other derivative instruments permissible have been much debated by Indonesian scholars. This section will exclusively focus on the use of *tawarruq* in Indonesia and the criticisms thereof.

Some derivatives contracts in Islamic finance do not fully meet the conditions of *sharia* compliance, such as forward contracts using *ba'I salam*, where the delivery of an asset can be altered based on the schedule as well as delayed payment.[55] In *ba'i mu'ajjal*, the payment of agricultural commodities on the forward assets can be delivered later.[56] Similarly, in the *istishna* contract, the purchase or order of not-yet-existent manufacturing goods can be paid in instalments or based on the agreement of the borrower promise to deliver according to the term and contractual specification.[57] Other derivatives are *urbun* and *wa'ad*. In *urbun*, the buyer offers an advance payment as an option on the conclusion of a sale contract, whereas *wa'ad* is a unilateral promise or undertaking and also represents a contractual provision of both parties.[58]

As shown in Table 6.1, although there are several types of derivative financing which are approved by the MUI, some other types of derivatives have been deemed Islamically unacceptable and are still mired in legal controversy among Indonesian Islamic scholars. Most of the MUI's approved derivatives are adapted from standard forms of Islamic contracts that were codified in the classical period, rather than being developed specifically for modern business institutions and transactions.[59] To some extent, the MUI follows the IIFA and will endorse the latter's *fatwas*, but on other occasions, the MUI will issue *fatwas* that contradict the IIFA's position. The inconsistency between the two bodies can be quite confusing, and only contributes to uncertainty in Indonesian financial markets because, as it turns out, the *fatwas* of the IIFA are an unreliable guide to the *fatwas* of the MUI.

Table 6.1 Islamic Version of Hedging Contracts in Indonesia by MUI

Type of derivatives	*Permissible*	*Impermissible*
Forward	*Salam*,[60] *Istishna*,[61] *Ba'i Mu'ajjal*[62]	*Ba'i al-inah*
Option	*Urbun*,[63] *Wa'ad*[64]	*Ba'i al-ma'dum*
Swap	*Wa'ad*,[65] currency swap[66]	*Tawarruq Munazzam* (complex hedging)
Futures	Commodity future,[67] *al-istishna'*	-

Source: Author

The table shows the types of hedging contracts in Indonesia.

Evidence of this can be seen in the position of MUI on *tawarruq*, which is the most controversial form of derivative in Islamic finance.[68] In contemporary Islamic finance, *tawarruq* means seeking cash by way of buying an item on credit, selling it to a third party at a price cheaper than the original price, and then pocketing the difference.[69] According to Salman, the practice of *tawarruq* in Islamic finance can be categorised into two mechanisms: First is *tawarruq hakiki* (real *tawarruq*), where a customer who needs cash buys an item on an instalment plan over a predetermined period and then sells that item to a third party without the knowledge of the first party at a lower cost to pocket the difference. Second is *tawarruq munazzam* ('organised *tawarruq*'), where a customer approaches the bank to borrow money, and the bank refuses but instead offers to sell goods to the customer, who then sells them back to the bank via a third party at a lower or higher price, so that a bank can pocket the difference.[70] The main differences between these two are that, on the one hand, *tawarruq munazzam* is not based on real transactions, as in practice the customer is not receiving the goods in reality, but simply based on the agreement where it mentions that the bank will order a third party to sell the goods to a customer.[71] On the other hand, with *tawarruq haqiqi* the transaction is real, as the customer will directly receive the goods and has an option to own the goods and also to sell it to a third party.[72]

In Indonesia, the NSB-MUI's prohibition on using *tawarruq munazzam* in an Islamic bank are based on the decision from 19th Jeddah IIFA Conference in 2009.[73] Three reasons were given for the prohibition. Firstly, the *tawarruq* contract is basically intended to gain cash and is not based on a real transaction. The trading of goods is merely a device to make the contract permissible despite no actual trade occurring. Secondly, there is no transparency and the contract also contains an element of uncertainty (*gharar*). Thirdly, *tawarruq* has more *mafsadah* (bad causes) compared to the *maslahat* (benefits).[74] This is also the contention of NU scholars, such as Syamsuddin, who prohibit *tawarruq* on the grounds of *mafsadah* based on the legal maxim "avoiding harm takes precedence over bringing about benefit", and say that banks are supposed to leave this, as the detriment may increase if we allow it.[75] Similarly, Prabowo also commented that it is well known that in practice the contracting parties in a *tawarruq* are simply aiming to acquire more liquidity through the purchase of an unreal commodity (or through identifying the value of a commodity based on historical price behaviour), which is similar to *ba'i al-inah* and is prohibited by prophetic tradition.[76]

At the global level, apart from the international *ulama* in the Islamic Fiqh Academy, there are renowned scholars like Nejatullah Siddiqi and Abbas Mirakhor, who argue that *tawarruq* is prohibited in Islamic law because it is a fictitious transaction, consists of *gharar*, and is considered to be 'selling money'.[77] This is supported by AAOIFI Standard No. 30, which states that the application of commodities in *tawarruq* should not be fictitious and should avoid *ba'I al-inah*, it should be based on a real transaction and purchase to own.[78] However, commentators who are in favour of *tawarruq*, such as Asni and Sulong, and Salman, argued that fictitious transactions in *tawarruq* could be eliminated if it is well regulated by implementing a dual agency whereby an Islamic bank has been appointed to conduct all transactions on the customer's behalf by way of multiple agency appointments.[79] In line with this, Asyraf also argues that the permissibility of using *tawarruq* is based on the justifications from the Qur'an 2:275, "Allah has permitted trading" and the legal maxim which states "*mu'amalah* is permissible, except when there is a provision prohibiting it".[80] There is also a middle position between the opposing poles on the question of the permissibility of *tawarruq*. Contemporary scholars, such as Dr Rafi Yunus Al-Misri, point out that the permissibility over the use of *tawarruq* can vary, depending on the conditions and need – viz., it is considered a sin if the transaction is intended for obtaining cash instead of real trading, but *tawarruq* can be permissible in case of *darurah*, where there is no other choice of transaction that could be used in getting a cash.[81]

Regardless, in the contemporary world, the use of *tawarruq* as a derivative instrument in Islamic banking is undeniably necessary for obtaining liquidity in order to survive through tough competition with its conventional bank counterparts. In Malaysia and the Middle East, the use of *tawarruq* is even showing considerable progress in its use, and there are many Islamic banks which are relying on this contract to accommodate their large customers' need for liquidity.[82] As the Malaysian *ulama* have done, Indonesian scholars should consider reviewing the use of *tawarruq* as a new product that would enable Indonesian Islamic banks to obtain more liquidity just as many Malaysian and Middle Eastern banks have done. Otherwise, investors will be confused about this innovative product, especially in light of the fact that financial market participates are not bound by nationality, but rather regularly engage in cross-border transactions where *tawarruq* is permitted in neighbouring jurisdictions but is prohibited in Indonesia.

6.4 The Challenge of Legal Uncertainty

As mentioned in Chapter 4, Indonesia has adopted two separate supervisory bodies – governmental and non-governmental – to oversee Islamic finance in the country. This section argues that the key to providing both legitimacy and legal certainty to the question of derivatives in Indonesian Islamic finance is the harmonisation of the positions taken by these supervisory bodies and then the transformation of MUI *fatwas* into legally binding rules for Islamic financial transactions. This section also examines the current challenges associated with incorporating MUI *fatwas* about derivatives into legally binding rules in the context of Indonesia's dual financial system.

Legal uncertainty related to the consistent assessment of *sharia* compliance and standardisation of *fatwas* into commonly binding principles and rules is still the greatest constraint on Indonesian Islamic finance. This is because the background knowledge and education of Indonesian Islamic jurists differs from one scholar to another.[83] For example, Indonesian jurists who have completed their Islamic education in Saudi Arabia may be influenced by Wahhabism or Salafism. Although not all scholars who are trained in Saudi Arabia may hold this thought, the influence of Wahhabism and Salafism has been growing in Indonesia since the late 1980s with the increase in the number of Indonesian graduates from Islamic universities in Saudi Arabia and Yemen.[84] Meanwhile, scholars who completed their studies at

Al-Azhar University in Cairo may not belong to one particular school of thought, as the 'Azhar' approach tends to encourage an ecumenical mainstream pluralism with respect to theology and jurisprudence.[85] Furthermore, scholars who have acquired Islamic knowledge from traditional NU and Salafi Islamic schools (*pesantren salaf*) generally apply their thinking solely based on classical Islamic books (*kitab kuning*), which are mainly influenced by Imam Shafi'i's doctrines.[86] On the other hand, Islamic jurists who have studied at modern Islamic boarding schools (*pesantren modern*) may not limit themselves to one school of thought or one particular Islamic organisation. In addition to this, the Islamic background of legal experts is also influenced by their embedded religious organisations, such as Muhammadiyah, NU, and Persis.[87] Because of all these differences it would appear that it is almost impossible for the major Islamic civil society organisations of Muhammadiyah, NU, and Persis (to say nothing of the many other smaller organisations) to institutionally unify their efforts to come to a consensus on *fatwa* rulings. Indeed, it is this organisational sectarianism that is the major source of *ikhtilaf* among the MUI scholars themselves.[88]

At several meetings, the MUI has discussed the issue of the commodity *murabahah* products in *tawarruq* contracts. According to the chairman of the MUI, K.H. Ma'ruf Amin, although *tawarruq* contracts have been much studied and discussed, a *fatwa* authorising *tawarruq* contracts has not yet been issued.[89] This is because a number of scholars have strongly argued that this contract appears to entail *riba* in substance, even though the surface form of the contract has the appearance of legal validity.[90] By way of contrast, as discussed in Chapter 4, Malaysian financial institutions do not face the same kind of legal uncertainty because the regulatory framework is more streamlined there. In Malaysia, the transformation of *fatwas* into binding state rules is processed and performed by the Shariah Advisory Council at Central Bank of Malaysia as one entity. As such, there is no legal conflict or slippage between *fatwas* and secular regulations.[91]

In Indonesia, Islamic banking requires the approval of the FSA to incorporate *fatwas* into their business transactions as per *Law No. 21 of 2008 on Islamic Banking*.[92] As was mentioned in Chapter 4, Indonesian regulators only take direction about Islamic financial instruments from the *fatwas* issued by the MUI and are less concerned with *fatwas* issued by Islamic financial institutions in Malaysia or Middle Eastern countries. The rationale behind this is that it may not be socially prudent or appropriate to utilise non-MUI *fatwas*, as it may lead to conflicts among scholars from various Islamic mass organisations. Referring to MUI's *fatwa* would at least reduce such tension, since MUI is now regarded as Indonesia's most authoritative clerical body due to drawing upon *ulama* from the major Islamic organisations and having the backing of the state.

However, the problem of the inconsistency of *fatwas* from the Indonesian *fatwa* council is obvious. The MUI's argument over the denial of *tawarruq* in Islamic banks is contested by their own opinion, as in 2011 when the MUI issued a *fatwa* allowing the use of *tawarruq* in the Islamic money market, *contra* the rulings of the IIFA.[93] In response to many requests from investors to use *tawarruq* for risk management of their liabilities, and global market pressure where companies need to obtain liquidity to compete, the MUI issued *Fatwa No. 82 of 2011 on Commodity Trading Based on Sharia Principles on the Commodity Exchange*, that declared it permissible to engage in commodity *murabahah* contracts using the *tawarruq* form in the capital and money market.[94] Syamsuddin, who is also a NU scholar, argues that the MUI *fatwa* over the use of *tawarruq* in capital markets is based on need (*lil hajah*) for liquidity, even though the MUI acknowledged that the *tawarruq* is 'technically' not *sharia* compliant due their fictitious nature, where the transaction (*ba'i hukmi*) is simply a formality and no actual goods are delivered (*qabdlu hukmi*).[95] Again, this issue is genuine and is a contentious one, because on the one hand the MUI permits the use of *tawarruq* in capital markets, contradicting the *fatwa* of the IIFA, but at the same time the MUI also prohibits its use in other markets. Furthermore, the benefits of using *tawarruq* in Islamic financial markets are undeniable. As noted by Samsuri, as a result of the MUI *fatwa* granting permission to use *tawarruq* in the Indonesian Islamic capital market, small corporations are able to meet their liquidity needs and are thus more efficient and as competitive as their conventional rivals.[96] This is another reason why the MUI should probably review its opinion on *tawarruq* to perhaps give greater latitude to its use in Indonesian Islamic banking.

Recently, attempts have been made to develop legal standards and uniform market practices for Islamic derivatives. For example, there is an existing platform for *sharia* international standardisation, the IIFM where Indonesia, Malaysia, Brunei Darussalam, and several other countries are members and co-founders.[97] This *sharia* harmonisation perhaps could be done through government intervention such as FSA and Bank Negara Malaysia, particularly in ASEAN where these sub-continents have a long history of mutual business dealings and mutual ancestors.[98] Ercanbrak argues that 'legal differences can act as a barrier to trade because contracting parties are less inclined to enter into a transaction when it is governed by the law of another state".[99] Therefore, an internationally agreed set of rules or standards is significant in freeing up the flow of trade and can be achieved by regulatory and supervisory authorities across jurisdictions.[100] However, it is likely to be counterproductive if harmonisation of international *sharia* standards were to be delegated to a non-governmental supervisory entity such as the MUI. This is because it would most likely trigger *ikhtilaf* problems. For example, non-governmental organisations from different countries are likely to hold different opinions on what is permissible or not; the greater the number of organisations, the greater the likelihood of *ikhtilaf*. Furthermore, even if the harmonisation can be carried out, there will be no law that can be enforced that can protect the agreements that bind them. Thus, the regulator would need fill this gap and facilitate further development of *sharia* harmonisation across jurisdictions, like what the Sharia Advisory Council of the Central Bank of Malaysia has done in incorporating an international *fatwa* into their local laws.

The Indonesian financial markets also face the challenge of public perception and legitimacy. According to Adiwarman, many Indonesian investors and households are uncertain about the status and viability of Islamic financial services, and are thus liable to avoid Islamic finance due to the confusing array of different opinions over new products.[101] This problem of conflicting legal opinions by *ulama* is also the reason why BI and the FSA of Indonesia are yet to issue a regulation pertaining to the application of complex hedging, based on the *tawarruq* commodity *murabahah* in Islamic finance.[102] Further, the lack of clarity by secular authorities also contributes to the somewhat negative perception that the general public (including private investors) have about Islamic finance in Indonesia.[103] This type of *sharia* risk associated with the instrument is a challenge for Indonesian authorities in putting it into standard practice.

The lack of coherent *fatwas* and secular laws relating to the use of Islamic financial products such as *murabahah* products is not just a theoretical matter. It has given rise to legal disputes in the courts over their validity. For example, in the case of *PT Bank BNI Syariah vs Daman Sugianto*,[104] an Islamic financial contract was suspected of containing an element of *riba* in the *murabahah* transaction.[105] On 19 September 2019 the Labuha Religious Court agreed to a provision to postpone the execution of the plaintiff's collateral project by PT Bank BNI Syariah until the decision was legally binding on account of the fact that there is no clarity over the *murabahah* transaction.[106] On 2 October 2019, PT Bank BNI Syariah submitted a memorandum of appeal that the Labuha Religious Court's decision was not in accordance with civil procedural law, because the provisional decision should only have been carried out during the process and not until it was legally binding.[107]

In the principal case, the reason for alleging the *murabahah* contract was not *sharia* compliant was that the customer should receive goods instead of money in the *murabahah* transaction. Since PT Bank BNI Syariah only offered money instead of goods, it was argued that the practice resembled *riba*.[108] The customer in this case contended on appeal that the *murabahah* contract be declared invalid. However, in the course of proceedings the customer had admitted to having received Rp 200 million (AUD 20,000) and accepted (*ridha*) the contents of the *murabahah* contract. The customer also paid instalments to the bank three times, but subsequently defaulted.[109] Warning letters (summons) had been sent by the bank three times, and according to the law, if there were no reply the third time, the bank had the right to auction off collateral if the debtor failed to fulfil his obligation.[110]

Fortunately, there is a compilation of Islamic economic law in Indonesia (*Kompilasi Hukum Ekonomi Syariah* or KHES) which has been established in accordance with *Supreme Court Regulation No. 2 of 2008 concerning the Compilation of Sharia Economic Law*. Hence, the customer's claim which states that the *murabahah* agreement is not in accordance with the terms of Islamic *fiqh* of *muamalah* cannot be justified, because the *murabahah* contract has been followed by a *wakalah* contract.[111] In Article 119 of KHES, the customer in this case becomes the representative of the Islamic bank to purchase goods according to the legally agreed list of the collective agreement (*qabd al-hukmi*).[112] The Religious High Court finally found in favour of PT Bank BNI Syariah and expressly reserved the right to resume the auction of the plaintiff's collateral projects, as well as requiring the plaintiff pay court costs.[113]

6.5 Concluding Remarks

This chapter began by analysing the controversy over the use of derivatives in contemporary Islamic finance. It is argued that the lack of clarity in the use of derivatives in Islamic finance arises out of the fact that the new kinds of financial products do not exist in the classical *fiqh* literature, and is further complicated by the inconsistency of the *fatwas* issued by various Islamic institutions and *ulama*.

Law No. 21 of 2008 on Islamic Banking was also analysed in this chapter in relation to how to incorporate *fatwa* (peculiarly related to derivatives) into legally binding rules. The *fatwas* that have been issued by various institutions and *ulama* do not constitute a uniform body of codified law. Further, the *fatwas* produced by non-Indonesian bodies do not have great purchase in Indonesia because they often do not take into consideration the particularities of the Indonesian context. To accommodate local conditions, Indonesian scholars of MUI, along with financial authorities, have established the *Kompilasi Hukum Ekonomi Syariah* which has been approved by the Supreme Court of Indonesia. The rationale behind this is if the application of an Islamic financial contract is found to contain *gharar* and/or *riba*, then the contract should be judged in terms of the *Kompilasi*.

From the *fiqh* perspective, most Indonesian *ulama* hold that every financial transaction should be viewed in the light of public benefit (*maslahah*) and the maxim of permissibility (*ibaha*) – viz. that any given type of transaction is permitted as long as it is not prohibited by the Qur'an or a *mutawatir hadith*. Insofar as *tarwarruq* derivatives are based on the trade in real goods, they do not strictly entail trade in money and so avoid *riba*; and insofar as they entail knowledgeable avoidance of losses and do not in themselves cause losses for others, they do not entail *gharar* or *maysir*. As such, they avoid those characteristics which would be prohibited, and thus based on *ibaha* should be permissible. Further, derivatives are one of the most important aspects in business transactions, where all prices of commodities fluctuate due to currency movements, interest rates, and unforeseen circumstances. Using *tawarruq* could be the tool to control such risks and mitigate the volatility of financial markets. It is on this basis that it can be argued that it also passes the *maslahah* test and is why *tawarruq* products have been deemed permissible in Malaysia and the Middle East. However, confusion is created for transnational investors by the MUI's contrary view that *tawarruq* products are impermissible. This contributes to legal uncertainty and undermines confidence in Indonesia's Islamic finance industry.

It is based on this reasoning that we suggest that Indonesian Islamic scholars should re-evaluate the permissibility of using derivatives such as *tawarruq*. While the revision of reasoning is important, it is not sufficient. As indicated in this chapter (and in Chapter 4), the dual supervisory system for Islamic finance also needs to be considered: without an efficient institutional mechanism for implementing correct legal reasoning, the latter is moot. As such, proposals for reform will be further discussed in Chapter 8 in relation to whether the existing dual entity of supervisory bodies in Islamic finance should be reformed to address the issues outlined in this chapter and Chapter 4, and whether a new *sharia* model of supervision should be developed for Indonesia.

Indeed, Islamic banks are still in their early stages compared to conventional banks and the practice of Islamic banking faces many challenges when handling risk. This can be observed from two categories of risk: *common risk*, which is similar to the risk faced by conventional banks, and *Islamic-specific risk*, which only occurs in Islamic banks due to their specificities and the method of operation. The high level of non-performing products in Indonesian Islamic banks highlights the difficulties in risk management within Islamic banks. This requires exploration of policies and tools that can help Islamic banks overcome these risks. The following chapter will investigate the risks inherent in Islamic banking considering the Basel Accords and analyse these from international standard perspectives where these will be discussed in greater depth.

Notes

1 Fatimah Zahara and R. Deddy Harryanto, 'Implementasi Akad Tawarruq dalam Perbankan Syari'ah Indonesia [The Implementation of Akad Tawarruq in Indonesian Islamic Banking]' (2019) 35(2) *Ijtihad Jurnal Hukum Islam dan Pranata Sosial* 53.

2 OIC (Organisation of Islamic Conference), *Al-Qaraarat wa al-Tausiyat: Al-Dawra al-tasi'a 'Ashara li-Majma' al-fiqh al-Islami al-Duwali* (Majma' al-Fiqh al-Islami Al-Duwali, 2009).

3 Zeti Akhtar Aziz, 'Governor's Special Address at GIFF Investors & Issuers Forum: "Islamic Finance: The New Silk Road"' (Pt Bank Negara Malaysia) (2007), www.bnm.gov.my/-/governor-s-special-address-at-giff-investors-issuers-forum-islamic-finance-the-new-silk-road-.

4 Michael Chui, 'Derivatives Markets, Products and Participants: An Overview' Bank for International Settlements, 3, www.bis.org/ifc/publ/ifcb35a.pdf; T.V. Somanathan and V. Anantha Nageswaran, 'The Role of Derivatives in the Global Financial Crisis of 2008', *The Economics of Derivatives* (Cambridge University Press, 2015) 107–121.

5 Juerg M. Syz, *Property Derivatives: Pricing, Hedging and Applications* (John Wiley & Sons, 2008).

6 Chui, above n 4,3.

7 A futures contract refers to an agreement between two parties to buy or sell the commodity at a specific time in the future for an agreed-upon price. Forward contracts can be agreements between buyers and sellers, where the buyer agrees to purchase the asset for a future date at a predetermined price and at a predetermined date. Options are agreements between two parties that gives the purchaser of the option to buy or sell a particular asset at a later date at a predetermined price. Swaps refers to contracts between two parties that involves the exchange of pre-agreed cash flows of two financial instruments for a set period of time; usually the series of cash flows is determined by an uncertain variable, such as an interest rate, foreign exchange, or commodity price. Keith Redhead, *Financial Derivatives: An Introduction to Futures, Forwards, Options and Swaps* (Prentice Hall, 1st edition, 1996).; Chui, above n 4,4.

8 Satyajit Das, *Derivatives Product and Pricing* (John Wiley and Sons, 3rd edition, 2006) 4.

9 Fitri Irka Wahyu Niansyah, Putri Indriana and Amrie Firmansyah, 'The Use of Derivative Instruments in Indonesia and the Comparative Study on Accountant Standards in Derivatives/*Pemanfaatan instrument derivatif di Indonesia dan perbandingan standar akuntansi terkait derivatif*' (August 2018) (2018) 6(2) *Jurnal Ilmiah Akuntansi Kesatuan* 140, 142; Chui, above n 4,4.

10 Although, there have been scholars from a number of institutions such as IIFA and AAOIFI that have urged the prohibition of derivatives. However, these judgements are still openly discussed by Muslim academicians and unresolved, and the issue on permissibility of derivatives is still debatable. See Akhter Md Uddin and Abu Umar Faruq Ahmad, 'Conventional Futures: Derivatives from Islamic Law of Contract' (2020) 62(4) *International Journal of Law and Management* 315, 316.

11 Muhammad Hasan Abdul Ghafar, 'Kitab Al-qawa'id Al-fiqhiyyah bayna Al-asyaalah wa At-tawjiih [Book of Jurisprudence Rules between Authenticity and Guidance]'

(Ar-riqaaq wa al-adab wa al-azkar [Kindness, Etiquette and Remembrance] Al-Maktabah As-shaamilah Al-haditsah, [tr author] https://al-maktaba.org/book/32391/181.

12 Andreas A Jobst, 'Derivatives in Islamic Finance: There is No Right Way to Do the Wrong Thing: Opportunities for Investors' (2013) 22(1) *Journal of Investing* 7, 7.

13 Mohammad Hashim Kamali, 'Prospects for an Islamic Derivative Market in Malaysia' (1999) 4 *Thenderbird Int'l Business Rev*, 523; Muhammad Rizky Prima Sakti et al., 'Shari'ah Issues, Challenges, and Prospects for Islamic Derivatives: Qualitative Study' (2016) 8(2) *Journal of Qualitative Research in Financial Markets* 168, 169; Obiyathulla Ismath Bacha, *Financial Derivatives Markets and Application in Malaysia* (McGraw-Hill, 2001).

14 Modernist Islamic scholars such as M. Fahim Khan, who is a researcher at the Islamic Research and Training Institute, see the alternative derivatives in Islamic finance a chance for modernising the Islamic finance industry. See Muhammad Fahim Khan, *Islamic Futures and Their Markets* (Islamic Research and Training Institute, 1997).

15 Shahih Muslim, Chapter 46: of Salam Sale, Book No 10, Hadith No 3906, www.islamv.com/Quran_And_Hadith/Sahih_Muslim_Hadith/Sahih_Muslim_Hadith_Book_10.htm.

16 Humayon Dar, *Global Islamic Finance Report 2010* (Cambridge Institute of Islamic Finance, 2010) 132.

17 IRTI, *Resolutions and Recommendations of the Council of the Islamic Fiqh Academy 1985–2000*, Islamic Research and Training Institute, Jeddah, 2000; European Council for Fatwa and Research, Final Statement of the Twelfth Ordinary 6–10 of Dhulqi'dah, 1423 AH (2003), www.e-cfr.org/blog/2014/01/31/2-12-البيان- الختامى; Sherin Kunhibava and Balachandran Shanmugam, 'Sharī'ah and Conventional Law Objections to Derivatives: A Comparison' (2010) 24(4) *Arab Law Quarterly* 319, 322.

18 IRTI (2000), *Resolutions and Recommendations of the Council of the Islamic Fiqh Academy 1985–2000*, Islamic Research and Training Institute, Jeddah.

19 Muhammad Taqi Usmani, *An Introduction to Islamic Finance* (Idaratul Ma'arif, 1998) 61.

20 Muhammad Taqi Usmani is among the Islamic scholars who oppose the use of derivatives, and his works and opinions have been highly influential in the Islamic finance industry. This scholar is an adherent of *Hanafi madhab* and has been actively criticising the financial industries that are commonplace in Islamic finance, such as the issue of *sukuk* using LIBOR as a benchmark and the derivatives instruments, namely futures contracts, options, FX swaps, and equities. See ibid.

21 Uddin and Ahmad, above n 10.

22 Ibid., 10, 333; Kamali, above n 13; M El-Gamal, 'Discussion Forum: Islamic Financial Derivatives' (1999) 1(1) *IJIFS*.

23 Zaheer Anwer and Farrukh Habib, 'Re-Visiting Current Debate on Shari'ah Position of Derivatives' (2019) 9(1) *Journal of Islamic Business and Management* 64, 79. On the greater fool theory, see Nassim Nicholas Taleb, *Dynamic Hedging: Managing Vanilla and Exotic Options* (Wiley, 2007) 62.

24 On the Black Wednesday case, see Devansh Lathia, 'How Soros Broke the British Pound', *The Economics Review* (New York), https://theeconreview.com/2018/10/16/how-soros-broke-the-british-pound/. On the global financial crisis, see Donald Johnston, Bubbles in our future? Certainly! (8 September 2018) *The OECD Observer*.

25 Buerhan Saiti and Adam Abdullah, 'The Legal Maxims of Islamic Law (Excluding Five Leading Legal Maxims) and Their Applications in Islamic Finance' (1 November 2017) (2016) 29(2) *Journal of King Abdulaziz University: Islamic Economics*; Abu Umar Faruq Ahmad et al., 'Shari'ah Maxims and Their Implication on Modern Financial Transactions' (2010) 6(3) *Journal of Islamic Economics, Banking and Finance* 75, 79.

26 Anwer and Habib, above n 23.

27 Ibid., 74.

28 No share transactions are entered into in relation to the borrowed shares. But securities regulations require that the seller must always be in the position to deliver shares at the

due date and so must have some rights in relation to shares before any sale can occur. Current practice may be to take an option to purchase in relation to those shares.

29 Zamir Iqbal and Abbas Mirakhor, *An Introduction to Islamic Finance: Theory and Practice* (John Wiley & Sons, 2011) 183.

30 Ibid.

31 Anwer and Habib, above n 23.

32 Corporate Finance Institute, *Long and Short Positions*, Corporate Finance Institute, https://corporatefinanceinstitute.com/resources/knowledge/trading-investing/long-and-short-positions/.

33 Chui, above n 4,3.

34 Sami Al Suwailem, 'Financial Engineering: An Islamic Perspective' (2007) 9(1) *Jurnal Fakultas Hukum UII* 87, 89.

35 Keputusan Direktur Bursa Efek Indonesia No No. Kep-00023/BEI/02–2017 tentang Perubahan Nomor II-H tentang Persyaratan dan Perdagangan Efek dalam Transaksi Marjin dan Transaksi Short Selling [*Decree of the board of directors of Indonesian stock exchange, No. Kep-00023/BEI/02–2017* on the amendment of regulation number II-H on the requirement for securities trading in margin transaction and short selling transaction], https://idx.co.id/media/1361/10.pdf, [tr author].

36 U.S. Securities and Exchange Commission, Short Sales, www.sec.gov/answers/shortsale.htm.

37 Asyraf Wajdi Dusuki and Edib Smolo, 'Islamic Hedging: Rationale, Necessity, and Challenges' (Paper presented at the International Seminar on Muamalat, Islamic Economics and Finance (SMEKI 09), Kuala Lumpur, 20–21 October 2009); Ehab M. Injadat, 'Futures and Forwards Contracts from Perspective of Islamic Law' (2014) 1(2) *Journal of Economics and Political Economy* 241; ibid.

38 Jobst, above n 12, 11.

39 Nicholas C. Dau-Schmidt, 'Forward Contracts: Prohibitions on Risk and Speculation under Islamic Law' (2012) 19(2) *Indiana Journal of Global Legal Studies* 533.

40 Uddin and Ahmad, above n 10, 316.

41 Yudi Ahmad Faisal, 'Islamic Derivatives in Indonesia: A Study on Indonesian Ulama Council (MUI)'s Fatwa on Tahawwut (Hedging)' (2016) 2 *Islam Ekonomisi Ve Finansi Dergisi* 35; Uddin and Ahmad, above n 10; Niansyah, Indriana and Firmansyah, above n 9.

42 Islamic Banking Working Group contains four elements which are Financial Service Authority, the NSB-MUI, Indonesian Accountant Association, and Supreme Court. See Hukum Online, MUI Keluarkan Fatwa Transaksi Hedging Syariah [MUI Issues Fatwa on Islamic Hedging Transaction], (Hukum Online) (2017) [tr author] www.hukumonline.com/berita/baca/lt551d2d0e8585d/mui-keluarkan-fatwa-transaksi-hedging-syariah/.

43 Muhammad Syamsuddin, 'Dilema Transaksi Tawarruq Pada Lembaga Keuangan Syariah [Dilemma in Tawarruq Transaction in Islamic Financial Institutions]' (Pt NU Online) (2017), [tr author] https://islam.nu.or.id/post/read/84388/dilema-transaksi-tawarruq-pada-lembaga-keuangan-syariah.

44 'Guiding Principles of Risk Management for Institutions (Other Than Insurance Institutions) Offering only Islamic Financial Services', *(Kuala Lumpur)* [2005] Islamic Financial Services Board, 16.

45 Obiyathulla Ismath Bacha, 'Dual Banking Systems and Interest Rate Risk for Islamic Banks' (2004) 8(1) *The Journal of Accounting, Commerce and Finance – Islamic Perspective* 1, 7.

46 Ibid., 14.

47 Ibid.

48 Nadhirah Nordin et al., 'Contracting with Gharar (Uncertainty) in Forward Contract: What Does Islam Says?' (2014) 10(15) *Asian Social Science Journal* 37, 37.

49 Ibid.

50 Tariqullah Khan and Habib Ahmed, 'Risk Management, an Analysis of Issues in Islamic Financial Industry' (Pt Islamic Development Bank) (2001) 91(9) *Islamic Research and Training Institute (IRTI)* 183.

51 Mohamad Yazid, M.N Asmadi and H Mohd Liki, 'The Practices of Islamic Finance in Upholding the Islamic Values and the Maqasid Shariah' (2015) 4(1) *International Review of Management and Business Research* 286, 288.
52 Abu Ishaq Ibrahim Musa al-Gharnati al-Maliki Al-Syatibi, *al-Muwafaqat fi Usul al*-Syari'ah [Reconciliation of the Fundamentals of Islamic Law] (Dar al-Kutub al-'Ilmiyyah, 1991) vol. 2, 3.
53 Mohammad Hashim Kamali, '"Maqasid Al-Shari'ah": The Objectives of Islamic Law' (Pt Islamic Research Institute, International Islamic University, Islamabad) (1999) 38(2) *Islamic Studies* 193.
54 Yazid, Asmadi and Mohd Liki, above n 51, 289; Rusdiana Priatna Wijaya and Nurizal Ismail, 'Sharia Credit Card in the View of Maqasid al-Sharia' (2020) 4(1) *Al-Iktisab: Journal of Islamic Economic Law*, 8.
55 National Sharia Board of Indonesian Council of Ulama, Fatwa No. 5/DSN-MUI/IV/2000 on Salam Transaction, Indonesian Council of Ulama.
56 National Sharia Board of Indonesian Council of Ulama *Fatwa MUI No 110/DSN-MUI/IX/2017 on contract in transaction*, Indonesian Council of Ulama.
57 National Sharia Board of Indonesian Council of Ulama, *Fatwa No. 06/DSN-MUI/IV/2000 on Istishna' transaction | fatwa MUI No 22/DSN-MUI/III/2002 on Istinshna' Paralel*, Indonesian Council of Ulama.
58 National Sharia Board of Indonesian Council of Ulama, *Fatwa MUI No 85/DSN-MUI/XII/2012 on Promise (wa'ad) in Shariah Financial and Business Transactions,* Indonesian Council of Ulama.
59 Nadirsyah Hosen, 'Behind the Scenes: Fatwas of Majelis Ulama Indonesia (1975–1998)' (2004) 15(2) *Journal of Islamic Studies* 147.
60 National Sharia Board of Indonesian Council of Ulama, *Fatwa No. 5/DSN-MUI/IV/2000 on Salam Transaction*, Indonesian Council of Ulama.
61 National Sharia Board of Indonesian Council of Ulama, *Fatwa No. 06/DSN-MUI/IV/2000 on Istishna' transaction | fatwa MUI No 22/DSN-MUI/III/2002 on Istinshna' Paralel*, Indonesian Council of Ulama.
62 National Sharia Board of Indonesian Council of Ulama *Fatwa MUI No 110/DSN-MUI/IX/2017 on contract in transaction*, Indonesian Council of Ulama.
63 National Sharia Board of Indonesian Council of Ulama, *Fatwa MUI No13/DSN-MUI/2000 tentang uang muka dalam murabahah [Fatwa MUI No 13/DSN-MUI/2000 on Down payment in Murabahah]*, Indonesian Council of Ulama.
64 National Sharia Board of Indonesian Council of Ulama, *Fatwa MUI No 85/DSN-MUI/XII/2012 on Promise (wa'ad) in Shariah Financial and Business Transactions*, Indonesian Council of Ulama.
65 National Sharia Board of Indonesian Council of Ulama, *Fatwa MUI No 96/MUI/III/2015 on Islamic Version of Hedging Contract (tahawwut) based on wa'ad (unilateral promise),* Indonesian Council of Ulama.
66 National Sharia Board of Indonesian Council of Ulama, *Fatwa MUI No 28/DSN-MUI/III/2002 on foreign exchange currency (bay al-sharf),* Indonesian Council of Ulama.
67 National Sharia Board of Indonesian Council of Ulama, Fatwa MUI No. 82/DSN-MUI/VIII/ 2011 commodity trading based on *sharia* principles in the commodity exchange, Indonesian Council of Ulama.
68 *Tawarruq* in Arabic comes from the word *wariq* that is the character of symbol for silver. Later, the word *tawarruq* came to have a wider meaning, which is seeking cash by various ways, or seeking silver, gold, or the like. See Ibrahim Fadel Aldabo, *At-Tawarruq Haqiqatuhu, Anwa'uhu (Al-Fiqhu Al-Ma'ruf wa Al-Mashrafi Al-munazzam)* [Tawarruq, Its Reality, Its Types (The Well-known Jurisprudence and Organized Banking)], https://ketabonline.com/ar/books/92555/read, 9 [tr author].
69 Zahara and Harryanto, above n 1, 54.
70 Salman H. Khan, 'Organised Tawarruq in Practice: A Shariah Non-Compliant and Unjustified Transaction', *New Horizon* (Kuala Lumpur), 16–21, www.islamic-finance.com/library/Khan_tawarruq.pdf.

71 Zahara and Harryanto, above n 1, 57.
72 Ibid., 57.
73 OIC (Organisation of Islamic Conference), *Al-Qaraarat wa al-Tausiyat: Al-Dawra al-tasi'a 'Ashara li-Majma' al-fiqh al-Islami al-Duwali* (Majma' al-Fiqh al-Islami Al-Duwali, 2009).
74 Ibid., 59. See also Muhamad Nadratuzzaman Hosen and Amirah Ahmad Nahrawi, 'Comparative Analysis of Islamic Banking Products between Malaysia and Indonesia' (2012) 1(2) *International Journal of Academic Research in Economics and Management Sciences* 120, 138.
75 Syamsuddin, above n 43.
76 In terms of *ba'i inah*, the NSB-MUI tend to be careful (*ihtiyaat*) and decided it was *haram* on account that it may cause fraud in society. While in Malaysia, the progress of practising this contract is showing no return, and about 80% of the house financing in Bank Muamalat Malaysia Berhad are based on *ba'i inah* contracts. See Bagya Agung Prabowo, 'The Practice of Murabahah Syariah in Syariah Banking (Critical Analysis towards the Application of Murabahah Scheme in Indonesia and Malaysia' (2009) 16(1) *Jurnal Hukum IUS QUIA IUSTUM.*
77 Shahruddin Amir, 'Is Bay Al-Tawarruq Better Alternative in Fulfilling Islamic Finance Objectives?', in *Celebrating 30 Years of Islamic Banking and Finance Institutions in Malaysia* (Unit Penerbitan USIM, 2013) 1983–2013; Mastura Mohd Shafie, Mat Noor Mat Zain and Nik Abdul Rahim Nik Abdul Ghani, 'Commodity Murabahah Deposits in Islamic Banking: An Easy Way Out' (2020) 42(1) *Islamiyyat* 15, 18; Obiyathulla Ismath Bacha, Abbas Mirakhor and Noureddine Krichene, *Islamic Capital Markets: A Comparative Approach* (John Wiley & Sons, 2013).
78 AAOIFI, *Accounting and Auditing Organisation for Islamic Financial Institutions Sharia Standard No. 30* (AAOIFI, 2008), art 4.
79 Fathullah Asni and Jasni Sulong, 'Non-Ethical Elements in Tawarruq Munazzam Product for Islamic Housing Financing in Malaysia' (2018) 8(12) *International Journal of Academic Research in Business and Social Sciences* 1013, 1017; Shafie, Zain and Ghani, above n 77; Salman H. Khan, 'Why Tawarruq Needs To Go? AOIFI and the OIC Fiqh Academy: Divergence or Agreement?', *New Horizon Islamic Banking*, www.newhorizonislamicbanking.com/index.cfm.
80 Asyraf Wajdi Dusuki, 'Commodity Murabahah Program (CMP): An Innovative Approach to Liquidity Management' (Paper presented at the 5th International Islamic Finance Conference, Kuala Lumpur).
81 Rafiq Yunus Al-Misri, *Al-Riba wa al-Hasm al-Zamani fi al-Iqtisad al-*Islami [Riba and Time Decisive in the Islamic Economy] (Dar al-Maktabi, 2000) 321.
82 Mahmoud A. El-Gamal, 'Interest and the Paradox of Contemporary Islamic Law and Finance' (2003) 27 *Fordham International Law Journal* 108, 128.
83 Jusuf Wanandi, 'Islam in Indonesia: Its History, Development and Future Challenges' (Pt Routledge) (2002) 9(2) *Asia-Pacific Review* 104.
84 Din Wahid, 'Nurturing Salafi Manhaj: A Study of Salafi Pesantren in Contemporary Indonesia' (2014) 15(2) *Wacana* 367, 368; Martin Van Bruinessen, 'Wahhabi Influences in Indonesia, Real and Imagined', *Journée d'Etudes Wahhabisme* (Leiden), www.archivesaudiovisuelles.msh-paris.fr/11/163/Martin_Van_Bruinessen-7.pdf.
85 Ibrahim El-Houdaiby, 'The Identity of Al-Azhar and Its Doctrine', *Ahram Online* (Egypt), https://english.ahram.org.eg/NewsContentPrint/4/0/48668/Opinion/0/The-identity-of-AlAzhar-and-itsdoctrine.aspx; H.A. Hellyer, *The Once and Future Azhar: On the Credibility of Sunni Islam's Preeminent Institution* (5 October 2017), www.abc.net.au/religion/the-once-and-future-azhar-on-the-credibility-of-sunni-islams-pre/10095336
86 See Chapter 2, Section 2.4.
87 J. Burhanudin, *Ulama dan Kekuasaan: Pergumulan Elite Politik Muslim Dalam Sejarah Indonesia* [Ulama and Power: The Struggle of Muslim Political Elite in Indonesian History] (Mizan, 2012).
88 Ibid. Also see Abdullah Saeed, 'Ijtihad and Innovation in Neo-Modernist Islamic thought in Indonesia' (Pt Routledge) (1997) 8(3) *Islam and Christian-Muslim Relations* 279.

89 Prabowo, above n 76, 13.
90 Ibid.
91 See Chapter 4. Also see *Central Bank of Malaysia Act 2009* (Malaysia) pt. VII.
92 Undang-Undang Republik Indonesia No 21 Tahun 2008 Tentang Perbankan Syariah [*Law No. 21 of 2008 on Islamic Banking*] ch 4 s 26.
93 Rohmad, Muhammad Iman Sastra Mihajat and Aznan Hasan, 'Tawarruq Practice for Liquidity Management in Islamic Money Market in Indonesia and Malaysia' (2013) 1(2) *Equilibrium, Jurnal IAIN Kudus* 2017, 223.
94 National Sharia Board of Indonesian Council of Ulama, *Fatwa DSN MUI No.82/DSN-MUI/VIII/2011 Tentang Perdagangan Komoditi Berdasarkan Prinsip Syariah di Bursa Komoditi* [Fatwa DSN MUI No.82/DSN-MUI/VIII/2011 on Commodity Trading Based on Sharia Principles on the Commodity Exchange] (Indonesian Council of Ulama).
95 Syamsuddin, above n 43.
96 Ali Samsuri, 'Membincang Konsep *Tawarruq* Dalam Dunia Perbankan Dewasa ini [Discussing the Concept of Tawarruq in the Banking World Today]' (2015) 9(1) *Jurnal IAIN Kediri* 29, 29 [tr author].
97 International Islamic Financial Market is a global standard-setting body for Islamic Finance which focuses on standardisation of Islamic financial contracts. See International Islamic Financial Market, *IIFM Members*, www.iifm.net/membership/iifm-members/.
98 Faisal, above n 41,58.
99 Jonathan Ercanbrack, 'The Standardization of Islamic Financial Law: Lawmaking in Modern Financial Markets' (2019) 67(4) *The American Journal of Comparative Law* 825, 835.
100 Ibid.; Ghazala Ghalib Khan and Zafar Atiq uz, 'Fatwa Institution and Product Development for Islamic Finance in Pakistan' (Pt Pluto Journals) (2019) 16(2) *Policy Perspectives* 107.
101 Adiwarman Karim is a renowned scholar of Islamic finance in Indonesia and is also a member of MUI. See Andika Aldi and Dimas 'Dinamika Tawarruq Sebagai Inovasi Produk Perbankan Syariah [The Dynamic of Tawarruq as an Innovative Islamic Banking Product]', *Komite Nasional Ekonomi dan Keuangan Syariah* (Jakarta), [tr author], https://knks.go.id/berita/298/dinamika-tawarruq-sebagai-inovasi-produk-perbankan-syariah?category=1.
102 Faisal, above n 41, 57.
103 Chaidir Iswanaji, 'Challenges Inhibiting Islamic Banking Growth in Indonesia Using the Analytical Hierarchy Process' (2018) 4(2) *Journal of Islamic Economics Lariba* 97, 102.
104 *Bank BNI Syariah (Appellant) vs Darman Sugianto (Appealed)* (2019) 13/Pdt.G/2019/PTA.MU, 1–14 (Religious High Court of North Moluccas). [tr author].
105 Ibid. [tr author].
106 *Darman Sugianto (Plaintiff) vs Bank BNI Syariah (Defendant)* (2019) 303/Pdt.G/2018/PA.Lbh, 1–67 (Religious Court of Labuha) [tr author].
107 *Bank BNI Syariah (Appellant) vs Darman Sugianto (Appealed)* (2019) 13/Pdt.G/2019/PTA.MU, 1–14 (Religious High Court of North Moluccas). [tr author].
108 Ibid.
109 Ibid.
110 Undang-Undang Republik Indonesia No 04 Tahun 1996 Tentang Hak Tanggungan Atas Tanah Beserta Benda-Benda Yang Berkaitan Dengan Tanah [*Law No. 04 of 1996 on Mortgage Right to Land and Objects Related to Land] (Indonesia)]* ch 2 s 6.
111 *Bank BNI Syariah (Appellant) vs Darman Sugianto (Appealed)* (2019) 13/Pdt.G/2019/PTA.MU, 1–14 (Religious High Court of North Moluccas) [tr author].
112 Ibid.
113 Ibid.

7 Implementation of Basel Accords and Implications for Islamic Banking

7.1 Introduction

The previous chapter analysed the issues of conflict in dual banking systems in the context of incorporating *sharia*-compliant products into regulations and the issues of inconsistency arising from *fatwa* bodies. This chapter will examine the application of the Basel Accords and their adoption with respect to the regulation and supervision of Islamic banking in Indonesia. It is argued that although conventional bank regulation cannot be wholly applied to Islamic banks due to the latter's distinctive *sharia*-specific risks, the Basel Accords, by contrast, are imperative for both Islamic and conventional banks due to their promotion of prudential regulation, transparency, and their opposition to destabilising speculation.

Despite the changes that have been made by the Indonesian financial authorities through issuing and adopting several regulations relating to some aspects of Islamic law to meet *sharia* compatibility, the challenges to Islamic banks being recognised as global players remain. One of these challenges is for Islamic banks to apply the Basel Core Principles, which may entail difficult institutional and Islamic legal reforms. In countries with a dual banking system, implementing the Basel Accords is not an easy matter, with key areas being how these international standards can apply or be adapted in a dual banking system and to what extent this standard measurement could assist the growth of Islamic banking. Thus, this chapter first outlines the establishment of the Basel Accords and then details the changes to the Basel Accords over time. It then discusses the significance of implementing the Basel Accords in Indonesia. Finally, the chapter critically examines the implication of the Basel Accords in the dual banking system of Indonesia.

7.2 Background to the Basel Accords

In the aftermath of the global financial crisis in 2008, discussion surged over regulation and supervision of banking capital requirements and credit risk in every country. The Basel Accords[1] are a set of principles to measure the risk level with respect to unforeseen events, like a customer's default. The Basel Committee on Banking Supervision (BCBS) has played a leading role in determining the capital requirement or the amount of money required by a bank to cover monetary losses due to

DOI: 10.4324/9781003393986-7

unexpected bad events. In other words, to hedge the contract, each bank has various amounts of money, and the question of how a bank should calculate this amount to estimate the capital allocation arises. The Basel Committee considered these issues and proposed the Basel Accords, which undertook a detailed study to set the capital requirements for financial companies and to ensure the safe and sound operation of banks worldwide.

Most banking systems in the world have implemented the Basel Accords, although the global banking industry still faces difficulties in adjusting to this international standardisation. In Muslim-majority countries with Islamic financial institutions and rules, the complications of adapting global regulatory norms are compounded by the additional and often conflicting demands of religion.[2] The Basel Committee has no authority to legally bind member countries to utilize its standard; however, the committees are working together to formulate the best guidelines to overcome financial problems and maintain economic stability.[3] Basel realises the importance of maintaining the commitment of managing risk, and the banks' responsibility to secure the shareholders' funds and increase public confidence.[4] Banks are exposed to dynamic risk, and a lack of management may ultimately result in bank failure. To continue to grow and prosper, banks need appropriate management and to recognise the need for cushions of capital. Any country that adopts the Basel Accords must implement them through their national regulations. In addition, to ensure the compatibility of Basel rules across countries, the Basel Committee has established open and constructive dialogue among banking supervisors and established the Accords Implementation Group,[5] which comprises senior line supervisors. Their aim is to facilitate the sharing of knowledge about the practice of the Basel Accords in their countries.[6] Implementing the Basel Accords and ensuring that banks comply with them incurs extra costs, as the banks need to hold adequate amounts of money in reserve to hedge their contracts and this security amount must be settled as collateral in case an undesirable event occurs (such as defaults by borrowers).[7]

The global application of the Basel Accords varies across countries depending on the agreement of the national monetary authority. To date, each country, whether members or non-members of BCBS, has implemented, to some extent, different regulations; some are more stringent while others are lenient, depending upon the national condition of the banking industry and if the economy is facing a financial crisis.[8] In Indonesia, the implementation of the Basel Accords has sought the cooperation of the FSA. Indonesia is one of the strategic members of the Basel Committee, and the application of the Basel Accords has been adopted in a manner suitable to the Indonesian jurisdiction, requiring all active banks operating in Indonesia to adhere to the FSA's rules.[9] Since the financial activities in most countries are now rated by international ratings agencies such as Standard & Poor's and Moody's, the refusal to implement these international standards would likely result in being discredited in international markets.[10]

The Basel Committee on Banking Supervision (BCBS) was created within the Bank for International Settlements (BIS) and is often referred to as 'the central bank of central banks', which was established on 17 May 1930 in Basel, Switzerland.[11] Although the recommendations of the Basel Committee do not have the force of law,

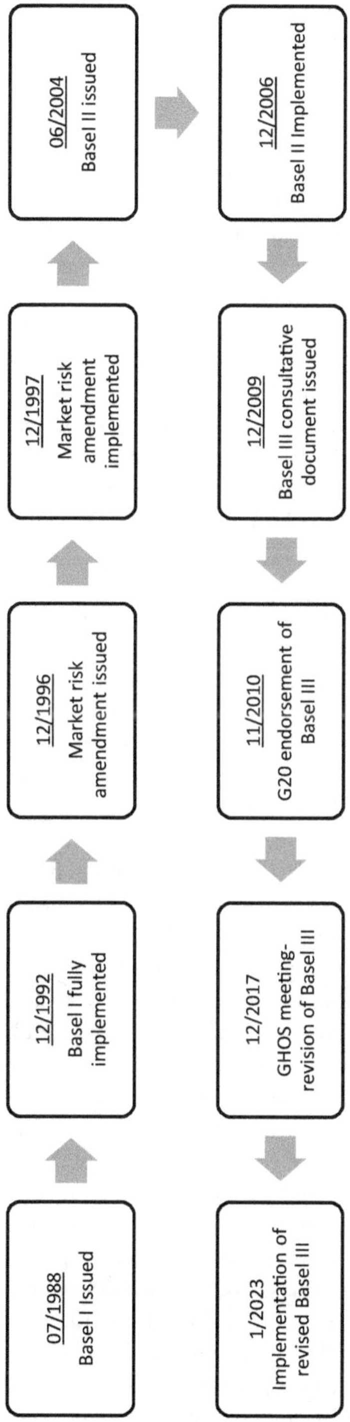

Figure 7.1 Basel Accords Reforms From 1988 up to the Projected 2023 Reforms

Source: Author, the information is extracted from the history of the Basel Committee[12]

such is its authority and standing that most regulators consider its recommendations essential for bank stability. The principles of Basel are updated and readjusted according to the need of banks and the condition of the world economy. The membership of the Basel Committee grows as countries adopt the various Basel Accords.[13] This growth in membership is largely due to the realisation of the importance of making banks more resilient and increasing confidence in the banking system.

Three Basel Accords have been released by the Basel Committee on Banking Supervision (BCBS): Basel I in 1988, Basel II in 2004, and Basel III, originally planned to be fully effective for 2019 but then deferred to 1 January 2023, after revisions were made at the meeting of the Group of Central Bank Governor and Heads of Supervision meeting in December 2017.[14] 'Basel IV' is an unofficial term used by the banking practitioners to refer to revisions to Basel III in 2010–2011.[15] It includes updated methods of calculating capital requirements and a requirement that individual banks' loss histories be retained. The Group of Central Bank Governors and Heads of Supervision (GHOS) – an oversight body of Basel Committee – announced the Basel III reforms and the revised minimum capital requirements for market risk in late 2017.[16]

7.3 Basel Accords – the Three Pillars

The history of bankruptcy of major international banks was incurred from the lack of risk management and low amounts of security; in response to this, the professional bankers of the central banks around the world gathered at the Basel Committee meeting and set standardised minimum capital requirements for banks as a security for the back up to reduce the risk of losses.[17] The Basel principles, in standardising risk sensitivity, evolve from time to time, following the dynamic conditions of an economy.

Basel I (1988) was a milestone in finance and banking history. It dealt with credit risk (default risk) and the risk of counterparty failure and provided guidelines for capital requirements and risk weighting for banks. Indeed, before this standard there was no single definition of bank capital. This was the initial step to define this capital requirement. However, there were other types of risks not yet covered by these rules, primarily related to the risk of a bank run.[18] The US subprime financial crisis during the 1980s motivated the Basel Committee to revise Concordat and re-issued improved principles for the supervision of banks learning from the past risks.[19]

The basic problem of Basel I was that it focused on the costs of credit and overlooked considerations of customer risk and financial stability. The required Total Capital Adequacy Ratio (CAR) under Basel I was set at 8% of a bank's risk-weighted asset, and it also set out the basic structure of the capital requirement calculation but ignored different types of risk and risk exposure. Realising that various types of risks had not been incorporated into the CAR, the BCBS began work on a new capital accord which refined the framework to address these risks.

Basel II (2004) paved the way as a result of deficiencies in Basel I due to its oversimplified calculations and classifications. Basel II provided further guidelines for the capital adequacy calculations for risk-weighted assets (RWA). Basel II also dealt with operational risk and market risk. The Basel II Accord also introduced the 'three pillars' approach: (1) minimum capital requirements, (2) supervisory review by a central bank to monitor banks' capital adequacy and internal assessment process, and (3) market discipline through disclosure requirements and encouragement of sound banking practices.[20] The disclosure of bank information includes compliance with the Basel Accords, capital adequacy, and risk exposure and assessment considered essential to support the objective of facilitating market discipline and systemic stability. These three pillars are detailed in Table 7.1.

The downfall of Lehman Brothers, which led to the global financial crisis of 2007–2008, revealed that despite the implementation of Basel II, many financial institutions were operating with inadequate liquidity buffers and excessive leverage,

Table 7.1 The Three Pillars of Basel II

Pillar 1	Minimum capital requirements	Banks should maintain a minimum capital adequacy requirement of 8% of risk-weighted assets.
Pillar 2	Supervisory review process	• Supervisors should review and evaluate banks' capital adequacy assessment and strategy and monitor their ability to fulfil capital requirements according to regulations, and supervisors should also take action if the bank fails to do so. • Supervisors should expect the bank to hold more capital than the minimum capital adequacy ratio required in the regulation, and supervisors should have the ability to ensure that the bank is able to hold capital in excess of the regulated capital requirement. • Supervisors should intervene at an early stage before the bank falls below the minimum capital required and support that particular bank and undertake remedial action if the bank is unable to meet the minimum requirements.

Pillar 3	Disclosure and market discipline	• Capital
		  • Banks should disclose their capital structure and component, terms, and condition of capital instrument.
		  • Banks should disclose the information on their liabilities and assets provisioning and income recognition.
		• Risk exposure
		  • Banks should disclose their exposure to risk and strategies in managing the risk.
		• Capital adequacy
		  • Banks should disclose their CAR and information on their calculating mechanism based on the Basel Accords.
		  • Banks should disclose information of analysis on capital conversion factor, such as a change in capital structure and its impact on capital ratio, or a change in capital management strategy and its impact on future capital plans.
		  • Banks should disclose the structure and process of their capital allocation in business activities.

Source: Author, information obtained from the Bank for International Settlements (2001)[21]

The table shows the three pillars of Basel II.

along with a lack of risk management.[22] In response to this financial crisis, the Basel Committee issued a further package of rules to strengthen banking regulation and supervision.

Basel III (2010) responded to the shortcomings in Basel II with regard to the quality and quantity of regulatory capital, leverage ratios, and liquidity requirements. Basel III introduced two fundamental revisions: (1) micro-prudential supervision, which is firm-specific, and (2) macro-prudential supervision, which is financial system-wide.[23] These revisions included additional capital buffers and tightened leverage ratios and liquidity coverage ratios (LCR).

Under the micro-prudential revisions, Basel III reformed capital regulations with each bank's Tier 1 and Tier 2 minimum capital requirements being set at 8% of its risk-weighted assets.[24] The total CAR requirement (including the capital conservation buffer) increased to 10.5%. Under Tier 1, the minimum capital ratio is 6%, but the bank is required to hold a minimum Tier 1 capital ratio plus 2.5% capital conservation buffer, making up the total required Tier 1 capital to 8.5%.[25] Basel III also required banks to have a total of 7% under the total common equity ratio, with the minimum of 4.5% of risk-weighted assets in tangible common equity, and a mandatory conservation buffer of 2.5%.[26]

Basel III introduced three additional capital requirements to ensure that banks built up a capital buffer to provide further protection against risks in times of financial stress. These are:

- *Conservation buffer*, which is mandatory and is 2.5% from common equity of RWA.
- *Countercyclical buffer*, which is imposed by the central bank where there are high credit risks or difficult macroeconomic conditions. These range from 0% to 2.5% of common equity of RWA.
- *Capital surcharge*, which is imposed on the bank to provide a buffer against systemic risk.[27] This ranges from 1% to 2.5% from common equity of RWA.

Besides capital requirements, under macro-prudential revisions, Basel III introduced a leverage ratio and a liquidity coverage ratio (LCR).[28] These tools were introduced based on the past financial crisis, where the financial companies had insufficient equity to back up debts. In 2017, Basel III was again revised. A higher CAR, stricter RWA requirements, and higher capital floors compared to the previous Basel Accords was set.[29] It also included revisions to the calculation of the leverage ratio buffer and the treatment of sovereign debt. However, this revision of Basel III will be phased in after 2027 to help banks mitigate the impact of the tighter capital requirements.[30]

7.4 Significance of Basel Implementation

The Basel Accords are significant for the future growth of the banking industry worldwide, as they promote safety and security in financial systems and accurately add the amount of capital required to the degree of risks in a bank. As a global market player, the Islamic financial industry has to accept the conditions imposed by the changes in the global market because capital adequacy is going to remain a core issue for risk management in both conventional and Islamic banks. In line with this, Akkizidis and Khandelwal state:

> The overall impact of a failure in either a conventional bank or an Islamic bank will be felt by the entire financial market and thus risk management needs to be integrated. The common concept of having sufficient capital cannot be refuted in Islamic finance.[31]

Bouslama and Lahrichi further said that, "In the Islamic context, separating risk from transactions would create more risk and would lead to greater instability in the economy".[32]

The importance of the Basel Consultative Papers is evident in the tightening of banks' capital adequacy and leverage positions. In the past, before the establishment of the Basel Committee, capital requirements were not clearly defined, and banks did not consider an adequate capital framework to secure their borrower in the time of default. The introduction of the Basel Accords brought into view the importance of a bank's regulatory capital and its calculation methods to maintain the prescribed amount of capital reserved for the bank to be secured.

The Basel Committee maintains its standards and concerns for strengthening the banking system and the quality of capital in order to prevent banks from unexpected losses. It does this by improving banks' ability to resist financial stress by recommending stricter capital and liquidity requirements. Banks are also expected to understand the importance of maintaining short- and long-term liquidity conditions to cover net cash outflow, while ensuring a leverage ratio of greater than 3%.[33] By restricting banks from taking on excessive leverage positions, it is expected that the capital structure of banks will be more stable.[34] Thus, the Basel Accords are essential for the banking system, as they define capital regulatory requirements and provide a package to maintain the leverage position of the banks. They also provide valuable universal guidelines for regulatory bodies to minimize impacts of economic stress during times of financial burden.

7.5 Impact of Basel Implementation

In Indonesia, with its dual banking system, the application of the three pillars of Basel (minimum capital requirement, supervisory review, and market discipline) focuses attention most on the role of banking supervisors in overall risk management by ensuring the bank's minimum capital requirements and enhancing transparency and accountability in the market.[35] The role of banking supervisors is all the more critical in Islamic banking, due to its evolving nature, where the activities should be *sharia* compliant, and where the profits generated from business activities should not be based on profit maximisation alone, but must also avoid uncertainty and ensure customers are protected. The third pillar of the Basel Accords is of great importance for Islamic banking as it strives to gain recognition and legitimacy in the wider banking industry as well as in the eyes of the Indonesian public.

In what follows, it will be argued that Indonesian Islamic banks should embrace the three pillars of the Basel Accord. This is because, first, these pillars broadly align with basic Islamic principles of avoiding reckless high-risk behaviour and foreseeable harm (due, for example, to financial crises). Second, Islamic banks will be able to adjust to a more restrictive risk management regime because of the risk-sharing nature of most Islamic bank products (such as *mudharabah* and *musharakah*). In other words, the Basel Accords could help create a more level playing field for Indonesian Islamic banks in a world dominated by conventional banks. As will be shown in what follows, although following the Basel Accords recommendations would be desirable overall, the implementation would nonetheless require some institutional reforms to Islamic banking practices – especially when it comes to Pillar 2 relating to supervisory structures, both at the micro and macro levels.

7.5.1 Pillar 1 – Application in Islamic Finance

In Pillar 1, the implementation of the Basel Accords under Tier 1 would favour the Islamic banking industry. Tier 1 relates to a bank's core capital – the core measure of a bank's financial strength – which primarily consists of common stock, retained earnings, and intangible assets. As discussed in Chapter 5, Islamic banking investments should be based on 'real' transactions (i.e. the exchange of actually produced goods/services) and should avoid any 'toxic' transactions involving uncertainty (*gharar*) and speculative gambles (*maysir*).[36] This also applies to the Islamic bank's Tier 1 core capital. The prohibition of interest being charged favours Islamic banks, as some portion of loan losses could be absorbed by partnership (*mudharabah*) deposits. Islamic banks are also prohibited from using perpetual debt instruments under Tier 2 capital and those debt-based derivatives transactions because these instruments are considered to not be *sharia* compliant. This situation also favours Islamic banks because, as per the Basel rules, the minimum capital ratio reserve requirement is set at 8%. An Islamic bank is set to provide 6% under Tier 1 capital and the rest for Tier 2 capital and capital conservation buffer, which should not exceed Tier 1 capital.[37] Tier 2 capital is considered less reliable than Tier 1 capital because the Tier 2 components consist of assets that are more difficult to liquidate and accurately calculate.

Islamic banks generally do not rely on Tier 2 capital to fulfil the capital requirement, since they are able to fulfil the regulatory Basel Capital requirement under Tier 1 (above 8%) and their Tier 1 core capital ratio is more resilient than that of risky assets in Tier 2.[38] Under loss-loan reserves in Tier 2 capital, the risk-sharing approach in Islamic banking allows the bank to share the profit or loss with the partnership (*mudharabah*) in credit contracts. In this position, Islamic banks are able to transfer the losses to their customers, and if a bank fails to cover the expected decline in real economic value of credit, losses are then absorbed by both partnership (*mudharabah*) customers and the bank.[39] Therefore, a bank should have a general provision setting out what would constitute an adequate percentage of partnership (*mudharabah*) funds should be invested in the bank's project. This percentage should be calculated based on the degree of riskiness of the project.[40] So, this provision should ensure that a bank has adequate reserve capital to meet future risks and maintain a healthy turnover for

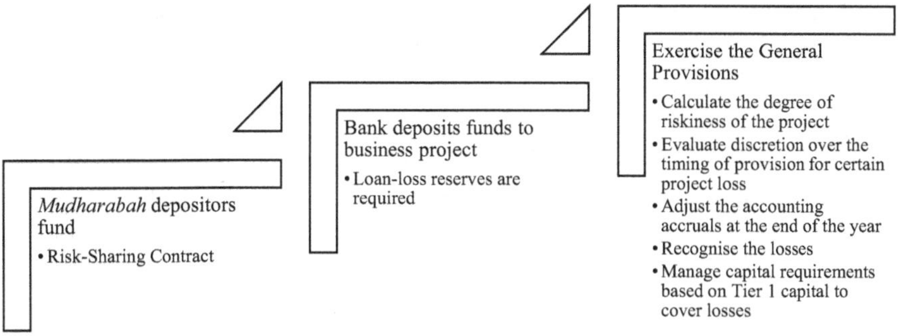

Figure 7.2 General Provisions of Tier 2 in the Risk-sharing Principle Approach

Source: Author, based on information extracted from Ismail and Shahimi (2010)[41]

the partnership (*mudharabah*) business projects. Figure 7.2 shows the process of general provision in measuring the use of the *mudharabah* deposit fund under risk-sharing business projects.

Since 2013, the FSA has issued the standard regulatory capital requirement for all banks, and as an active member of BCBS, Indonesia is set to adopt the full set of Basel III in the phase period. This can be seen from *FSA Regulation POJK No. 34/ POJK.03/2016 on The Standard Minimum of Capital Requirement for Commercial Banking*, where the CAR in both conventional and Islamic banks must be in line with the Basel III Accords.[42] In 2020, the national CAR for conventional banks was 23.52% and for Islamic banks it was 20.41%, which is double the standard minimum Basel III requirement, including the capital conservation buffer (10.5 %).[43]

Despite this strong CAR position, Islamic banking in Indonesia is facing problems with equity injections.[44] In other words, while the majority of Islamic banks in Indonesia have fulfilled the requirements of Basel III and are regularly audited by national and international auditors, a lack of ability to get funding still inhibits their business and still impedes their growth. Islamic banks in Indonesia mostly rely on the business of 'conservative' (low-risk) loans to the real economy and tend to be wary of using contemporary derivatives and investment instruments. This wariness is due to *sharia* constraints, which prohibit such transactions as prohibited by the NSB-MUI. But it is also due to significant scale constraints on these relatively small banks. (For example, in 2020 only four of Indonesia's 13 Islamic banks were listed on the Indonesian Stock Exchange.[45]) This makes Islamic banks less attractive to investors and less competitive, and this position has led them to depend on current equity to grow their business. As the Indonesian Islamic finance practitioner Farouk Alwyni put it: "Islamic banks in Indonesia require more money from investors beyond normal deposit transactions to expand their business nationally and internationally".[46] It is likely for these reasons that in February 2021 the government facilitated the creation of Indonesia's largest Islamic bank, and Indonesia's seventh-largest bank overall, by integrating three state Islamic banks (with the total assets amounting to Rp 240 trillion [AUD 24.6 billion]).[47]

7.5.2 Pillar 2 – Supervisory Review Process and Its Application in Indonesia

Under Pillar 2, BCBS issued the core principles for effective banking supervision, which include independence, accountability, resourcing, and legal protection for banking supervisors. In Indonesia, the main shortcomings in the regulatory and supervisory issues are the crisis management decisions and the potential for delays in decision-making that can undermine timely actions. Breuer, Guajardo, and Kinda note that

> the test for legal protection is 'misuse of authority' rather than 'good faith,' that it applies only to actions taken in situations of near crisis or crisis, and that it does not extend to the institution itself and persons acting on its behalf.[48]

The Executive Board of the International Monetary Fund (IMF) in the forum of the Financial System Stability Assessment (FSSA) has also noted that "although legal protection for staff and agencies involved in oversight and crisis management has been strengthened with recent reforms, it is not in line with best international practice and risks causing inaction bias".[49]

The challenge to effective supervision stems from the complex structure in the internal regulatory and supervisory bodies, and an insufficiently intrusive supervisory approach across sectors.[50] There are four dominant regulatory and supervisory bodies involved in financial industries: BI as the national central bank, the FSA as the leading regulatory institution for entire financial institutions, the Ministry of Finance, and the Indonesian Deposit Insurance Corporation. As for Islamic banking, there is also the NSB of the MUI, as a 'private' regulatory entity, overseeing *sharia* compliance. Although the government has taken action by approving the *Prevention and Resolution of Financial System Crisis Law, No. 9 of 2016* ('PPKSK Law') which clarifies the responsibilities of the agencies involved in crisis management and resolution, challenges remain in designing a dispute resolution strategy and coherently guiding all these supervisory bodies in the implementation of strategy.[51] In response to this challenge, the Financial System Stability Committee (or KSSK) was established to determine and coordinate the response to distress or failure of the banking system in a crisis as laid down in PPKSK Law.[52]

However, there is potential for highly deleterious delays in decision-making, as this coordination would dilute the responsibility and accountability of each of the supervisory agencies in situations of near crisis or crisis. This can clearly be evident from the PPKSK Law Chapter 4, Art 32, para 2 where it is said that action and coordination will only be carried out if the committee has received a report pertaining to a crisis in financial system stability.[53] It appears that the financial regulatory authority does not have clear primacy to stabilise financial conditions in a crisis situation. Breuer, Guajardo, and Kinda commented on this and proposed that, "It would also be desirable to set out more detailed guidance on the role of the KSSK and each agency in a decree, as the authorities have proposed".[54]

To this end, it would be highly desirable if each agency's mandate more clearly specified its strategies for achieving financial stability objectives. Clarity of these mandates also would help reduce redundancies and foster collaboration across agencies. This is also in line with the core principle of the Basel Accords in Pillar 2, which says:

> The supervisor has effective internal governance and communication process that enable supervisory decisions to be taken at a level appropriate to the significance of the issue and timely decisions to be taken in the case of an emergency. The governing body is structured to avoid any real or perceived conflicts of interest.[55]

This is of paramount concern in Indonesia, not just because of the devastating experience of the financial crisis in the late 1990s, but also because its dual financial system is more administratively complex than others. As noted, the supervisory structure and processes are rendered complex because of the mix of multiple state and private agencies (particularly relating to *sharia*-specific products and risks). As discussed in Chapter 4, neither the FSA nor BI currently play any supervisory or auditing role in the oversight or assessment of risks related to *sharia* compliance – rather, the SSBs, answerable to the NSB of the MUI, are the principal sources of essential information on Islamic banks' *sharia* compliance.[56] As argued in Chapter 4, Section 4.4, this supervisory structure is highly problematic for a number of reasons. First, SSB personnel are paid by the banks which they supervise, thereby undermining their independence. Second, SSB members are often members of the NSB-MUI, which oversees them, thereby undermining accountability. Third, there is nothing in the current legal framework that protects SSB members from being sued for making decisions that prove to be against the financial interests of bank clients or the banks themselves. The need for protection of supervisors while performing their duty is also stated in Pillar 2 of the Basel Accords: "the supervisor and its staff are should be adequately protected against the cost of defending their actions and/or omissions made while discharging their duties in good faith".[57] Given that the NSB-MUI is a private body and that the SSBs act under the auspices of the NSB-MUI, there are no laws that would protect these supervisory bodies in carrying out their duties in good faith. And fourth, SSBs operate at arm's length from BI and the FSA, thereby undermining transparency and control of the Indonesian financial system overall. All of these problems clearly conflict with Basel's Pillar 2 on independence, accountability, resourcing, and legal protection for supervisors.[58]

7.5.3 Pillar 3 – Market Discipline

This section argues that Islamic banks would benefit from disclosures (by both themselves and conventional banks), as it may put them in a better competitive position and may increase the public legitimacy for Islamic banking, thereby increasing deposits and investment contracts.

Under Pillar 3 of the Basel Accords, banks are required to publicly disclose information relating to their risks, capital adequacy, and policies for managing risk in order to complement the operation of minimum capital requirements (Pillar 1) and the supervisory review process (Pillar 2).[59] This is also in line with the virtues of Islamic law and the *sharia* principles in Islamic finance, where Islamic banks are encouraged to be transparent and free from all forms of fraud. Honesty and transparency also can be found in the Qur'an (among others in Surah Al-Mutaffifin verses 1–3, and Surah An-Nisa' verse 135), all forms of concealment, fraud, or attempts at misrepresentation violate the principles of justice and fairness in *sharia*.[60] At the level of international Islamic standard-setting organisations, the IFSB-4 standard has been issued, which outlines new requirements for institutions offering Islamic financial services to follow in preparing disclosures and promote transparency and market discipline.[61]

In Indonesia, the requirement of Islamic banks to disclose their risks has been regulated under the *FSA Regulation No 65/POJK.03/2016 on Risk Management Practice for Islamic Bank and Islamic Business Units*, whereby Islamic banks are required to disclose ten risks and provide information in their annual reports.[62] However, Bischof, Ernst & Young, and Price Waterhouse Coopers suggest that increasing risk-based regulation does not necessarily improve the quality of risk disclosure.[63] Similarly, Radwan and Oliveira et al. also note that even with restricted regulations and *sharia* principles there is no assurance that customers are protected or that Islamic banks strictly follow consumer protection directives for providing fair and just transactions; in fact, the banks tend to comply with the minimum required and do not present a reliable and transparent report depicting their risk profile.[64] For example, in profit sharing–based contracts, due to the private-equity nature of some Islamic instruments, the interest rate risk in Islamic banks is exposed with the returns on their investment activities, and when there is an increase in benchmark rates it will give rise to investor expectations of higher rates of return.

In practice, Islamic banks can benefit from applying PLS principles to depositors by using profit-smoothing reserves, which enable Islamic banks to channel retained earnings from these reserves to remunerate depositors and avoid any possible withdrawals in order to compete with conventional banks.[65] Yet, the use of profit smoothing is not appreciated by many scholars, such as Archer and Karim, Affandi, Al-Zumai and Al-Wasmi, who say these reserved account activities promote accounting manipulation and lack of transparency in Islamic finance. Furthermore, Islamic banks need to adjust their equity base and maintain higher capital ratios to avoid any solvency problems, especially when their reserves are no longer capable of providing profits.[66] Regrettably, as Abdullah et al., and supported by Hameed, stressed, there is still lack of transparency in the practice of financial reporting among Islamic banks, and this is due to lack of financial reporting standards to ensure transparency.[67] Thus, it is another reason why there is a need for reform by the financial authorities.

Since Islamic banking principles encourage disclosure, these principles can decrease uncertainty and ambiguity for customers; therefore, it is imperative to all parties to have full access of banking information covered by the agreement.[68] A refusal to provide such information will put the banks at systemic risk, as failure to do so may lead to lack of investor confidence and even withdrawal of funds. The GFC 2008 financial crisis was the real result of irresponsibility and ethical failure of market discipline and risk disclosure, where the crisis stems from unethical subprime lending that led to a global economic collapse with US banks suffering US$2.5 trillion in loan losses and with eight million Americans losing their homes.[69] Given that, the main factor behind the growth of Islamic finance over the last few decades is the brand of 'Islamic banking' and the trust that has come along with it, the brand reflecting the values that are perceived to be inherent in Islamic banking and their financial activities.[70] Therefore, it is a key element for banks to ensure the transparency on financial literacy and provide customers with effective disclosure of necessary information needed to make informed decisions, as it deepens customer relationships and encourages customer loyalty.

7.6 Concluding Remarks

This chapter noted the urgency of international standardisation of maintaining capital requirement against global systemic risk and analysed the implementation of the Basel Accords in a dual banking system. It also examined the problem that Indonesia's dual banking system, with its mix of public and private (religious) supervisory agencies, may be inconsistent with international best practices. It was argued that aside from consistently maintaining healthy capital adequacy ratios, Indonesian Islamic banks should embrace the three pillars of the Basel Accords, as these pillars are broadly compatible with Islamic principles and help avoid high-risk behaviour. If fully applied, it can make Islamic banks be more competitive in a world dominated by conventional banks.

In the context of disclosure of risks and market discipline in Islamic banks, this chapter also recommended the use of average profit smoothing against interest rates in Islamic banking prices, implementing Pillar 3 of the Basel Accords. The use of conventional interest rates as benchmarks in Islamic finance is critically important in determining their interest rate risk and profit-sharing ratios, including for term deposits. Without this benchmark, interest rate risk management would be unduly complex for Islamic banks. However, issues of transparency and disclosure in profit smoothing will still intermittently occur in Islamic banks, which may reduce public legitimacy for Islamic banks, thus requiring, as discussed, reform by the financial authorities.

This chapter also argued that Pillar 2 of the Basel Accords should be taken into account by the Indonesian financial authorities to overcome deficiencies in the current regulatory and supervisory arrangements, particularly in relation to the complexity of the existing structures and the potential delays in decision-making at the time of dynamic financial stress. Further reforms should be developed in terms of clarity of the roles of each agency in a decree so that each agency has clear financial stability objectives, and it will also be more authoritative for supervisors to take appropriate decisions in case of emergencies, rather than relying on the KSSK coordination between agencies in the time of a crisis.

In terms of a *sharia* model or guideline of supervision in Indonesia, the FSA should develop more streamlined and centralised procedures and regulations for *sharia*-compliant risk management so that the problems of independence and accountability of SSBs are addressed. Furthermore, to ensure the protection of the SSBs from legal liability and retribution for making impartial religious-legal decisions, they should be provided with legal protection as per the Basel Accords' requirement that supervisors be financed in a manner which permits them to conduct effective supervision and to carry out their duties in good faith. The only way to guarantee this is if the *sharia*-compliant supervision is incorporated into a government supervisory agency. These reforms will increase the transparency of the regulatory and supervisory process in line with best international practices. As will be discussed in the next chapter, risk does exist in Islamic banks and is even greater than in conventional banks, because their business practices must be based on *sharia* principles.

Notes

1 Basel Accords means the Basel documents containing sets of rules for banking regulation and supervisory formed by the professional bankers of central banks across the globe. The focus is particularly on formalizing the capital adequacy standards obliged for financial companies to take adequate hedging actions. The Basel Accords dynamically changes over time according to economic conditions and has been revised from the Basel I Accords to Basel II to Basel III; Basel IV Accords have also been proposed.

2 Ibrahim Warde, *Islamic Finance in the Global Economy* (Edinburgh University Press, 2010) 199.

3 Hal S. Scott and Philip A. Wellons, *International Finance: Transactions, Policy, and Regulation* (Foundation Press, 1995) 236.

4 The basics of the three pillars in Basel III remain unchanged from Basel II, with certain modification. The three mutually reinforcing pillars are: (1) *minimum capital requirement regulation* based on risk-weighted assets (RWA), maintaining capital through the calculation of credit and market and operational risk; (2) *the process of supervisory review*, through regulation and frameworks for dealing with risk that a bank is exposed to; and (3) *market discipline*, in which the bank has to ensure transparency and disclosure information. See Basel Committee on Banking Supervision, 'Basel III' Bank for International Settlement, www.bis.org/bcbs/basel3/b3summarytable.pdf.

5 The members of the Basel Committee are central banks and supervisory authorities from the members of the largest financial sector; the committee created Governors and Heads of Supervision (GHoS), which consist of central banks' governors and heads of supervision of member countries. For further discussion, see the Basel Committee on Banking Supervision, 'Group of Governors and Heads of Supervision Announces Higher Global Minimum Capital Standards' Bank for International Settlements, www.bis.org/press/p100912.htm.

6 William J. McDonough, 'Implementing the New Basel Accord' Bank For International Settlement, www.bis.org/review/r030217a.pdf.

7 Basel Committee on Banking Supervision, 'Consultative Document: Capital Requirements for Banks' Equity Investments in Funds' Bank for International Settlements, www.bis.org/publ/bcbs257.pdf.

8 Stefan Hohl et al., *The Basel Framework in 100 Jurisdictions: Implementation Status and Proportionality Practices* (Financial Stability Institute, 2018) vol. 11; Matthew R. Barnes, *Banking Regulation and the Basel III Accord: An Examination of the Risks and Shortcomings Posed By Basel III* (University of Wolverhampton, 2019).

9 Global Custodian, 'The Basel Committee Invites New Members from G20', *Global Custodian* (London), 11 June 2009, www.globalcustodian.com/the-basel-committee-invites-new-members-from-g20/.

10 Warde, above n 2, 199.

11 Basel Committee on Banking Supervision, 'History of the Basel Committee' Bank for International Settlements, www.bis.org/bcbs/history.htm. David Levi-Faur and Ilana Blumsack, *Mapping Global Financial Institutions* (Global Governance and the European Union 2020) 25.

12 Basel Committee on Banking Supervision, 'History of the Basel Committee', above n 11.

13 Basel Committee on Banking Supervision, 'History of the Basel Committee', above n 11.

14 Basel Committee on Banking Supervision, 'Governors and Heads of Supervision finalise Basel III reforms' Bank for International Settlements, www.bis.org/press/p171207.htm.

15 It is important to note to avoid confusion of terminology, Basel IV is not an official term used by BCBS, and the term is not mentioned in the document, being known as the completion of the Basel III Accords. In this chapter, the term Basel IV will be used to differentiate between the unrevised Basel III and the newly revised Basel III in 2017.

16 Basel Committee on Banking Supervision, 'Governors and Heads of Supervision Finalise Basel III Reforms', above n 13.

17 Ibid.

18 A bank run occurs as a result of the bank panicking when most of the customers suddenly withdraw funds in huge amounts; this panic may cause a tendency into a true default situation without proper solvency. See Rajkamal Iyer and Manju Puri, *Understanding Bank Runs: The Importance of Depositor-Bank Relationships and Networks* (American Economic Review, 2012) vol. 102, 2.

19 During this era, banks were lending extensively while countries' external indebtedness was also growing enormously. See, Francesco Cannata and Mario Quagliariello, 'The Role of Basel II in the Subprime Financial Crisis: Guilty or Not Guilty?' (2009). CAREFIN Research Paper No. 3/09, https://ssrn.com/abstract=1330417.

20 Basel Committee on Banking Supervision, 'Basel II: International Convergence of Capital Measurement and Capital Standards: A Revised Framework – Comprehensive Version' Bank for International Settlements, www.bis.org/publ/bcbs128.htm.

21 Basel Committee on Banking Supervision, 'Consultative Document: The New Basel Capital Accord' Bank for International Settlements, www.bis.org/publ/bcbsca02.htm.

22 Basel Committee on Banking Supervision, 'History of the Basel Committee', above n 11.

23 Hervé Hannoun, 'The Basel III Capital Framework: A Decisive Breakthrough' Bank for International Settlements, www.bis.org/speeches/sp101125a.pdf.

24 Tier 1 capital is the core capital. For example, paid-up capital, statutory reserves, disclosed free reserves, and capital reserves representing surplus arising out of sale proceeds of assets. Tier 2 capital is supplementary capital. For example, undisclosed reserve and cumulative perpetual preference shares, revaluation reserves, and general provision and loss reserves. See Basel Committee on Banking Supervision, 'International Convergence of Capital Measurement and Capital Standards' Bank for International Settlements, www.bis.org/publ/bcbs04a.htm.

25 Bank Committee on Banking Supervision, 'RBC Risk-based Capital Requirements RBC20 Calculation of Minimum Risk-based Capital Requirements' Bank for International Settlements, 3 www.bis.org/basel_framework/chapter/RBC/20.htm?inforce=20191215.

26 Ibid.

27 Systemic risk is also known as undiversifiable risk; in finance it is the risk that collapses the entire financial system or affects the overall market. This type of risk is unpredictable and unavoidable. See Jaime Caruana, 'Systemic Risk: How to Deal With It?' Bank for International Settlements, www.bis.org/publ/othp08.htm.

28 LCR has two components: (1) HQLA and (2) total expected net cash outflow. The formula for calculation of LCR is: , where *S* stands for the stock of HQLA and *N* stands for the total expected net cash outflows over 30 calendar days.

29 PricewaterhouseCoopers (PwC), *Basel IV: The Output Floor* (January 2018), 2 www.pwc.co.uk/financial-services/assets/pdf/hot-topic-basel-iv-the-output-floor.pdf.

30 Basel Committee on Banking Supervision, 'High-Level Summary of Basel III Reforms' Bank for International Settlements, 12, www.bis.org/bcbs/publ/d424_hlsummary.pdf.
31 Loannis Akkizidis and Sunil Kumar Khandelwal, *Financial Risk Management for Islamic Banking and Finance* (Palgrave Macmillan, 2008) 84.
32 Ghassen Bouslama and Younes Lahrichi, 'Uncertainty and Risk Management from Islamic Perspective' (2017) 39 *Research in International Business and Finance* 718, 721.
33 Arindan Banyopadhyay, *Managing Portfolio Credit Risk in Banks: An Indian Perspective* (Cambridge University Press, 2016) 346–348.
34 Ibid.
35 Akkizidis and Khandelwal, above n 32, 84.
36 Mike Kennedy, *Basel III and Islamic Finance: What Lies Ahead?* (February 2012) Eurekahedge, www.eurekahedge.com/Research/News/96/February_2012_alternative_investment_IFN_Basel_III_and_Islamic_Finance_What_Lies_Ahead.
37 Bank for International Settlements, *Basel III Monitoring Report* (October 2018), 15 www.bis.org/bcbs/publ/d449.pdf.
38 Abdul Ghafar Ismail and Shahida Shahimi, 'Do Risk-Based Capital Requirements Allocate Financing and Cause a "Bigger" Loan Loss Provisoin for Islamic Banks?' (2002) 4(1) *IQTISAD Journal of Islamic Economics* 1, 17.
39 Ibid., 10.
40 General provisions are defined under Basel III; it is referred to as provisions for loan loss reserves held against futures. This is categorised under Tier 2 capital whose gain or losses are unidentified. See Basel Committee on Banking Supervision, 'Regulatory Treatment of Accounting Provisions' Bank for International Settlements, www.bis.org/bcbs/publ/d385.pdf.
41 Ismail and Shahimi, above n 39.
42 Financial Service Authority of Indonesia, 'Booklet of Indonesian Banking-2018' Otoritas Jasa Keuangan, 55, www.ojk.go.id/id/kanal/perbankan/data-dan-statistik/booklet-perbankan-indonesia/Documents/Pages/Booklet-Perbankan-Indonesia-2018/Booklet%20Perbankan%20Indonesia%202018.pdf.
43 Financial Service Authority of Indonesia, *Laporan Profil Industri Perbankan Triwulan III 2020* [The Report of the Profile of Banking Industry Quarter III 2020], www.ojk.go.id/id/kanal/perbankan/data-dan-statistik/laporan-profil-industri-perbankan/Documents/Laporan%20Profil%20Industri%20Perbankan%20-%20Triwulan%20III%202020.pdf, 27–32.
44 Yogie Respati, 'Basel III belum jadi prioritas bank syariah', Keuangan Syariah, 1 February 2016, http://keuangansyariah.mysharing.co/basel-iii-belum-jadi-prioritas-bank-syariah/.
45 Agustina Permatasari, 'Kenapa Banyak Bank Syariah Belum 'Go Public'? [Why There Aren't Many Islamic Banks Go Public?]', *Sharia News* (Jakarta), 10 July 2018, https://sharianews.com/posts/kenapa-banyak-bank-syariah-belum-go-public.
46 Ibid.
47 Tabita Diela, 'Indonesia's Largest Islamic Bank Starts Operations', *Nasdaq* (Jakarta), 1 February 2021, www.nasdaq.com/articles/indonesias-largest-islamic-bank-starts-operations-2021-02-01. 1.
48 Luis Breuer, Jaime Guajardo, and Tidiane Kinda, 'Realizing Indonesia's Economic Potential', *Chapter 13: Reinforcing Financial Stability* (International Monetary Fund, 2018), 294.
49 The Financial, 'IMF Executive Board Approves Indonesia's 2017 Financial System Stability Assessment', *The Financial* (Georgia), www.finchannel.com/business/65624-imf-executive-board-approves-indonesia-s-2017-financial-system-stability-assessmen.
50 Ibid., 47.
51 Breuer, Guajardo and Kinda, above n 49, 294.
52 Undang-Undang Nomor 9 Tahun 2016 Tentang Pencegahan dan Penanganan Krisis Sistem Keuangan [*Law No. 9 of 2016 on Prevention and Resolution of Financial System Crisis*] (Indonesia) Ch 4, Art 32(2).

53 Ibid.
54 Breuer, Guajardo and Kinda, above n 49.
55 Basel Committee on Banking Supervision, 'Core Principles for Effective Banking Supervision' Bank for International Settlements, 23, www.bis.org/publ/bcbs213.pdf.
56 See Chapters 4 and 5.
57 Basel Committee on Banking Supervision, 'Core Principles for Effective Banking Supervision', above n 56, 24.
58 Ibid., 23.
59 Basel Committee on Banking Supervision, 'The Basel Framework' Bank for International Settlements, 1234, www.bis.org/basel_framework/.
60 Qur'an 4:135; Qur'an 83:1–3.
61 Islamic Financial Services Board, 'IFSB-4: Disclosure to Promote Transparency and Market Discipline for Institutions Offering Islamic Financial Services (Excluding Islamic Insurance (Takaful) Institutions and Islamic Mutual Funds), www.ifsb.org/published.php.
62 Peraturan Otoritas Jasa Keuangan No 65/POJK.03/2016 Tentang Penerapan Manajemen Resiko Bagi Bank Umum Syariah dan Unit Usaha Syariah [*The Regulation of Financial Service Authority of Indonesia* No 65/POJK.03 of 2016 on Risk Management Practice for Islamic Bank and Islamic Business Units] (Indonesia) Art 5.
63 Jannis Bischof, 'The Effects of IFRS 7 Adoption on Bank Disclosure in Europe' (2009) 6(2) *Accounting in Europe* 167; PricewaerhouseCoopers, *Weathering the Rise in Credit Risk: What's Next for Banks in Indonesia?*, PricewaterhouseCoopers GmbH PwC No (2017); Erbst & Young, 'Strategic Business Risk: Insurance' Ernst & Youg Report, www.ey.com/Global/assets.nsf/International/Industry_Insurance_StrategicBusinessRisk_2008/$file/Industry_Insurance_StrategicBusinessRisk_2008.pdf.
64 Saba Radwan, 'Islamic Banking: Why Transparency Matters', *Global Halal Investing Journal* (Malaysia), https://journal.wahedinvest.com/islamic-banking-why-transparency-matters/; Oliveira Jonas, Lúcia Lima Rodrigues and Russell Craig, *Risk Reporting: A Literature Review*, Working Paper, iMARKE: Documentos de Trabalho (2013), http://hdl.handle.net/1822/23683.
65 See Chapter 5. Also see Mohammad Bitar et al., 'The Performance of Islamic Vs. Conventional Banks: Evidence on the Suitability of the Basel Capital Ratios' (2018) 29 *Open Economies Review* 1003.
66 Simon Archer and Rifaat Ahmed Abdel Karim, 'Profit-Sharing Investment Accounts in Islamic Banks: Regulatory Problems and Possible Solutions' (9 September 2009) 10(4) *Journal of Banking Regulation* 300, 303; Muchammad Taufiq Affandi, 'Profit Equalization Reserve and Investment Risk Reserve: Issues and Its Application' (2019) 5(2) *Islamic Economics Journal* 295; Fahad Al-Zumali and Mohammed Al-Wasmi, '2008 Financial Crisis and Islamic Finance: An Unrealized Opportunity' (2016) 29 *International Journal for the Semiotics of Law-Revue Internationale de Semiotique Juridique* 455.
67 Wan Amalina Wan Abdullah, Majella Percy and Jenny D. Stewart, 'Sharia Disclosures in Malaysian and Indonesian Islamic Banks: The Shari'ah Governance System' (2013) 4(2) *Journal of Islamic Accounting and Business Research* 100, 111; Shahul Mohamed Ibrahim Hameed, *IE 2002: Reporting of Islamic Financial Transactions* (International Centre for Education Islamic Finance, 2012) 38.
68 Samir Srairi, 'Transparency and Bank Risk-Taking in GCC Islamic Banking' (2019) 19 *Borsa Istanbul Review* S64.
69 Al-Zumali and Al-Wasmi, above n 67, 467.
70 Radwan, above n 65.

8 Risk and Risk Management in Islamic Banking

8.1 Introduction

This chapter provides an account of the risks associated with banking enterprises and devotes considerable attention to the risks faced by Islamic banks in Indonesia's dual banking system. Risk is an inescapable characteristic of all modern financial systems, and prudent risk management can help banks increase profits because they incur fewer losses on loans and investments. It is argued that Islamic banking faces greater risks compared to conventional banks, especially in the Indonesian context. This chapter also argues that since Islamic banks have unique characteristics (because their business transactions should, by definition, be based on *sharia* rules and principles), they are exposed to greater risks than conventional banking.[1] This claim is a contentious one because a number of advocates of Islamic banking have asserted that one of the chief attractions of Islamic banking is that it entails less risk and greater stability than conventional banking.[2] The reasons for this and how risk is managed in the Islamic financial system are explored in Section 8.3.

To elucidate this argument, this chapter is structured as follows. First, the standard kinds of risks faced by conventional banking are enumerated and briefly explained. Second, it is demonstrated that Indonesian Islamic banks, in their efforts to comply with Islamic law, confront not only greater risks than conventional banks, but unique risks as well. Third, after summing up the major risk factors facing Islamic banking institutions, there is some reflection on risk policy and management of these banks, and the possibility of regulatory reform to better take account of the risks faced by Indonesian Islamic banks.

8.2 Risk and the Mitigation Thereof in Conventional Banking

Risk is defined by the US Securities and Exchange Commission as "the degree of uncertainty and/or potential financial loss inherent in an investment decision".[3] The success of a banking business depends upon its ability to manage risks; it is central to the core business operations of a bank. Poor financial risk management can lead to substantial losses and *in extremis* bank insolvency.[4] Risk management requires a bank to deploy a series of methodologies and procedures in identifying, measuring, monitoring, and controlling risks arising from banking activities.[5]

DOI: 10.4324/9781003393986-8

The overall performance of a bank – normally disclosed in financial statements – is determined by its effectiveness in analysing exposure to risks that can jeopardise its activities.[6] Conventional banks are exposed to a multitude of events that generate risks in their banking activities. These events include customers defaulting on loan or interest payments, a sudden or early withdrawal of money by depositors in long-term deposit accounts, significant changes in the market interest rates, human error, fraud, regulatory changes, system collapse, and less bureaucratic organisations or poor execution of business decisions.[7] Simply focusing on internal bank risk management alone to ensure the effective bank level of risks is not enough. The Basel Committee asserts that the safety and soundness of today's dynamic and complex financial system can only be attained by combining effective supervision, market discipline, and bank-level management, which is vital in reducing the risk of bank insolvency and the potential cost of a bank's failure for depositors.[8] Consequently, the Indonesian FSA and the Basel Committee are in basic agreement about the sources of risk to banks – viz. credit risk, market risk, liquidity risk, operational risk, reputational risk, and strategic risk. However, they do differ in some respects; for example, the FSA lists compliance risk and legal risk which the Basel Committee does not identify;[9] and the Basel Committee lists concentration risk and interest rate risk, which the FSA does not.[10] These differences, however, are not really substantial. The unique risks identified by the FSA are likely to reflect Indonesia's historical challenge of institutional corruption – a risk that could nonetheless be incorporated within the Basel Committee's 'other risks' category.[11] Building on this, this section will explore the risks faced by conventional banks as have been addressed by the Basel Committee, which provides guidance on international best practices.[12] These risk factors, which are discussed next, provide a benchmark to enable a comparison with Islamic banks.

8.2.1 Credit Risk

Credit risk is defined as the risk which occurs due to the failure of any counterparty to fulfil its payment obligations to a bank. This includes the credit risk due to the failure of debtors to pay, counterparty credit risk, and settlement risk.[13] Credit risk may occur through bank activities both in the banking book as well as in trading books.[14] The exposure of a bank to counterparty credit risk exists not only in loan agreements but also in other financial instruments, such as acceptances, interbank transactions, trade financing, foreign exchange transactions, financial futures, swaps, bonds, equities, options, guarantees, and letters of credit, and the settlement of transactions.[15] In the case of foreign exchange currency, the bank is exposed to credit risk due to the movement of exchange rates, as the currencies are not exchanged simultaneously with the risk of losses due to rate fluctuations.[16]

There are four preferred strategies in mitigating credit risk. (1) Banks can hedge credit risk by transferring risks through insurance or by seeking collateral from borrowers' assets or a guarantee from a third party. (2) Banks may also engage in risk reduction by tightening lending products. (3) A further strategy is risk retention, where banks retain a reserve fund for unexpected large financial claims. (4) Banks may also take measures to avoid risk, such as not taking on particular risks in the first place – for example, banks might decide not to lend funds to property speculators to avoid default risks arising out of the collapse of a housing bubble.[17]

8.2.2 Market Risk

Market risk is the risk that arises from unexpected price movements in markets.[18] Banks are exposed to market risk due to endogenous changes in market conditions, such as changes in commodity prices, interest rates, foreign exchange rates, market equity prices, or as a consequence of some exogenous market shock.[19]

The fluctuations in foreign exchange rates will expose banks to foreign exchange or currency risks, and the adverse fluctuation of the currencies in the foreign exchange market can affect the foreign exchange positions of a bank on its own account or on behalf of its customers.[20] Interest rate risk arises due to discrepancies in interest rates when banks engage in asset transformation and when the liabilities and assets differ in maturity and volume.[21] In conventional banking, a bank's asset-liability management committee/group will manage interest rate risk, including the off-balance sheet items.[22]

In Indonesia, banking market competition mimics a landscape of monopolistic competition; even concentration of the five largest banks is quite high, in the range of 50–60% based on the level of banking competition of all commercial banks from 2003 to 2013.[23] Each of these banks (Bank BCA, Bank Mandiri, Bank BRI, Bank Danamon, and Bank Permata) has enough market power to set prices, due to their strong position in the market segment, through their products, service superiority, and location advantage.[24] However, as suggested by Wibowo, the high levels of banking monopolistic competition also encourage banks to take higher risks by charging higher interest that can cause increased failure in the entire financial system.[25]

Having said from the aforementioned market risk case, Basel Committees have set market risk mitigation in several ways. These include: (1) separating the trading book and the banking book, making it easier to identify when it is necessary to hedge banking book credit risk exposure by transferring its internal risk to the trading books;[26] (2) looking at the internal model approach in managing market risk to determine whether it is too expensive to hedge a risk using the current model;[27] and (3) a bank also can retain the Basel "standardised approach for market risk, which relies chiefly on the sensitivities based method where a bank estimates how much the values of its financial instruments change when the value of a prescribed list of underlying risk factor changes".[28]

8.2.3 Strategic Risk

Strategic risk occurs when banks fail to anticipate and respond to industry changes and the financial environment.[29] The goal of strategic risk management is to minimise the risk of loss due to new competitors entering the market or from changes in customer demand.[30] In contrast to market risk, strategic risk is specific to the failure of a bank to anticipate or adequately respond to foreseeable changes in market structures that could undermine its stability and profitability.[31] In order to decide what strategic decision should be undertaken in banking business activities, the proposed strategic decisions should not be made unless senior management understands the risks involved. The financial institutions should fully assess the possible risks that likely confront them, and it is essential to avoid potentially hazardous decisions being made.[32]

8.2.4 Liquidity Risk

Liquidity risk arises where "revenues and outlays are not synchronised".[33] A sudden run on a bank (where depositors seek to withdraw funds at short notice) can cause a liquidity crisis for the bank and could cascade into a systemic collapse.[34] This can occur when a financial institution's assets or commodities that can only be quickly converted into cash at 'fire sale' prices.[35] In this situation, the financial institution is unable to meet short-term debt obligations and ends up with negative working capital.[36] Banks face liquidity risks in meeting withdrawals, paying cheques, regulatory payments, and credit payments.[37] In order to diminish liquidity risks, central banks require commercial banks to have a certain percentage of liquid assets available to meet demands either within the banks' accounts or in the reserve at the central bank.[38]

Liquidity risk can also arise through a decline in earnings as a consequence of falling on net interest income.[39] When a bank is unable to compete in the market, it may attempt to lower the cost of its product and offer services at a cheaper rate. As a result, there may be an increase in non-performing assets, which reduces a bank's cash flow.[40] A further cause of liquidity risk can be high deposit concentration in large corporate entities, households, or governments, where the liquidity can be affected if there is a run on a bank due to a rating agency downgrading the bank's credit rating.[41] Liquidity issues may also arise when a bank is aiming to expand its business, leading to a greater demand for reserve funds by the bank in order to compete on scope and scale in a growing economy.[42]

In response to the global financial crisis of 2007, and the resultant liquidity crisis faced by many internationally active banks, the Basel Committee published *Principles for Sound Liquidity Risk Management and Supervision* in 2008 in order to provide detailed guidance on the risk management and supervision of funding liquidity risk and to help promote better risk management.[43] In the case of an Indonesian conventional bank, Bank Central Asia Tbk in 2017 suffered from an extreme liquidity gap with a value of 18,9837, which implies a bad or low liquidity that can inflict the bank to take high or excessive risk-taking.[44] As also suggested by Arif and Anees, liquidity gap reflects poor asset and liability management, it also indicates that the bank is not handling risk well.[45] Since the liquidity gap will affect liquidity risk, the higher the liquidity gap, the higher the liquidity risk, which makes the bank more risky overall.[46]

In Indonesia, the FSA has been responsible for establishing a sound and robust liquidity risk management framework. This entails three elements:[47] (1) a board of directors responsible for controlling, monitoring, and developing strategies for liquidity risk management; (2) an internal liquidity risk management unit; and (3) a public disclosure policy, in which banks regularly disclose information about their liquidity positions and risk management strategies to the stakeholders and the market in general.

8.2.5 Operational Risk

Operational risk is "the risk of loss resulting from inadequate or failed internal processes, people and systems or from external events".[48] The definition includes fraud and malice, failures of information, human error, commercial disputes, accidents, and other failures in internal processes. It also includes legal risk but excludes strategic and reputational risks.[49] Measuring operational risk is difficult and requires proven methodologies for the qualitative management of its operational and other non-financial risks for all entities (granting of credits and loans, capital investments, insurance, etc.) of a bank; essentially, the mitigation of operational risk can be achieved by adherence to qualitative and quantitative standards for each approach. In line with the measurement of these standards, the Basel Committee has introduced three approaches to the capital assessment of operational risk: (1) the Basic Indicator Approach: this approach calculates operational risk capital uses the bank's total gross income as a risk indicator for the bank's operational risk exposure and sets the required level of capital (for operational risk) equal to the average over the previous three years of a fixed percentage of positive annual gross income.[50] The fixed percentage for alpha is set at around 30% of gross income. (2) The Standardized Approach: by this approach, the bank's activities are divided into eight business lines – viz. corporate finance, trading, and sales, retail banking, commercial banking, payment and settlement, agency services, asset management, and retail brokerage. Each of these business lines must be standardised using a capital charge in order to collect internal loss data in a consistent manner.[51] (3) The Internal Measurement Approach: this approach provides discretion to individual banks on the use of internal loss data. The method is calculated uniformly by the supervisors using quantitative and qualitative standards to ensure the adequacy of the data quality and internal control of the environment.[52]

8.2.6 Reputational Risk

According to the 2020 version of the Basel III framework, reputational risk is

> the risk arising from negative perception on the part of customers, counterparties, shareholders, investors, debt-holders, market analysts, other relevant parties or regulators that can adversely affect a bank's ability to maintain existing, or establish new, business relationships and continued access to sources of funding.[53]

Reputational risk may affect a bank's liabilities since market confidence and the bank's success are positively related to its reputation. Reputational loss can result in loss of business and income where the banks are perceived as being dishonest, callous, or incompetent.[54] The primary methods of dealing with reputational risk are to the development of a well-defined and enforced code of ethics, transparent auditing, and the establishment of rules governing employees' personal conduct, as well as the development of robust policies and procedures to uphold reputation.[55]

8.2.7 Compliance Risk

Compliance risk is

> the risk of legal or regulatory sanctions, material financial loss, or loss to reputation a bank may suffer as a result of its failure to comply with laws, regulations, rules, related self-regulatory organisation standards, and codes of conduct applicable to its banking activities.[56]

This category can also include conflicts of interest, breaches of privacy and data protection, money-laundering, and terrorist financing.[57]

To counter compliance risk, the 2005 paper of the Basel Committee on Banking Supervision provides guidance on three aspects of compliance risk management. (1) A bank's board of directors is responsible for overseeing the management of compliance risk. (2) A bank's senior management is responsible for the effective management of its compliance risk, including ensuring that it is observed and reported to the board of directors. (3) A bank's senior management is responsible for establishing a permanent and effective compliance function. (4) A bank's compliance function should be independent. (5) A bank's compliance function should have the resources to carry out its responsibilities. (6) A bank's compliance function should assist senior management in effectively managing the compliance risk faced by the bank. (7) A bank should comply with applicable laws and regulation in all jurisdictions in which they conduct business and with the local legal and regulatory requirements.[58] Figure 8.1 is the summary of details on how the Basel Accords suggests how banks manage their compliance risk.

8.2.8 Legal Risk

The Basel Accords also refer to legal risk, such as the possibility of fines, penalties, or punitive damages resulting from supervisory actions and private settlements.[59] Banks' ignorance of changing laws can result in a misalignment of a bank's practices and what is legally permissible or obligatory.[60] This legal risk extends to product innovations which might not be legally recognised or which may violate extant financial laws.[61] Just as ignorance of the law can be a source of legal risk, so too can a lack of legal monitoring or expertise with respect to extant and changing legal boundaries.[62]

According to the Basel Committee in 2004 and as supported by Wurtz, the Basel Accords delineated a clear strategy to establish sound practices to manage legal risk relevant to all banks.[63] They comprise three components. First, the bank has to identify the legal risk that can occur and then assess how it may impact on bank stability through qualitative or quantitative methods (such as by measuring the risk of

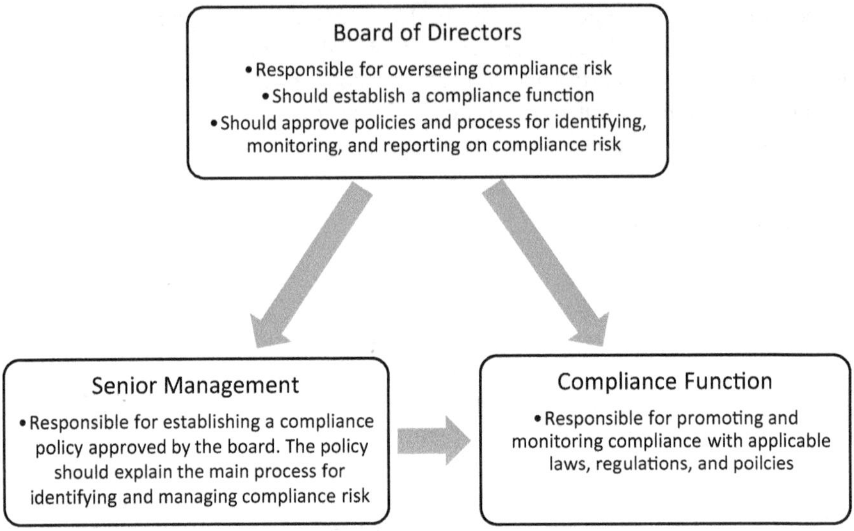

Figure 8.1 Responsibilities of Directors, Senior Management and the Compliance Function

Source: Author, the information is extracted from BIS on *Compliance and the Compliance Function in Banks*.[64] The arrows indicate the direction of oversight and management responsibility.

losses from litigation suits and potential changes of law which render certain banking products unlawful).[65] Finally, a bank should have a legal department which regularly reviews legal documentation to ensure that the existing or newly developed banking products comply with the law.[66]

8.3 Risk in Islamic Banking – the Concept and Practice in Indonesia

It has been argued by some scholars that Islamic banking is a less risky, more stable enterprise than conventional banking. For example, Haron and Azmi express the widely held view that:

> Theoretically, if the internalisation of Islamic values is high among the users of Islamic banking services, the risks involved would naturally be lower compared to conventional banking since the debtor is obligated by religion to pay back all of his debt and thus effectively reducing credit risk. Furthermore, there would not be any risk related to deposit withdrawal as customers would have deposited with the bank for religious reasons and hence would not be motivated by high returns on deposits. Operational risk . . . should very rarely arise because Islamic work ethics would guide the bank workers to be trustworthy, efficient and meticulous in performing their duties.[67]

These assertions may well be true of an idealised conception of Islamic banking, but it is contended in what follows that real-world Islamic banking, especially in Indonesia, faces greater risks than conventional banking. This is for two basic reasons. First, real-world Islamic banks absorb similar risks to conventional banks because the former's activities resemble the latter's in many ways. For example, Islamic banks usually use conventional bank interest rates as a benchmark in product pricing and often adopt conventional products.[68] Second, there are some aspects of Islamic banking which give rise to unique risks not faced in conventional banking. For example, Islamic banks are prohibited from engaging in certain hedging instruments in Indonesia, such as in the use of commodity *murabahah* or *tawarruq*. As discussed in Chapter 6, the NSB of the MUI prohibits the use of so-called Islamic derivatives on the grounds that they involve fictitious trading and *gharar* (uncertainty/ambiguity).[69] This unique risk occurs because Indonesian Islamic banks must follow the MUI's *fatwas* for all their financial products in order to retain their status as *sharia* compliant. Another aspect is the restriction relates to the prohibition of contracts that incur interest payments (*riba*) and the concomitant requirement that bank transactions should be based on real economic activities and share of risks and returns. This entails unique risks in real-world Islamic banks when they enter into non-interest-based financial products (chiefly *murabahah*, *salam*, *istisna*, and *ijarah*) and investing activities (chiefly *mudharabah* and *musharakah*) which expose Islamic banks to new risks not faced by conventional banks.

To understand the unique characteristics of risk management in Islamic banks in comparison to conventional banks, it is necessary to identify the Islamic banking risks and how these risks are mitigated. As noted in Chapter 7, most guidelines and principles in managing risks of Islamic banks are laid down by the IFSB. In relation to Basel principles, the IFSB works cooperatively with Basel in order to articulate the relevant practices of Islamic financial institutions and at the same time harmonise the Islamic banking requirements with the Basel Accords' international standards.[70]

8.3.1 Credit Risk

Islamic banks are exposed to credit risk arising out of Islamic financing. Credit risks arise from the receivable payments from customers' accounts in *murabahah* contracts, counterparty risk in *salam* contracts, receivable accounts from *istisna* contracts and *ijarah* contracts. Credit risk also arises out of investment activities by means of *musharakah* or *mudharabah* contracts in assets in the banking book.[71]

In a *murabahah* transaction, Islamic banks are exposed to credit risks when the bank delivers the asset to the customer but does not receive payment on time or payments cease altogether.[72] In theory, an Islamic bank would be at a higher risk on a non-binding *Murabahah* for the Purchase Order (MPO), where the client has the right to refuse delivery of the product purchased by the bank as cancellation of product purchased would expose the bank to price and market risks.[73] However, in practice the *murabahah* contract has been followed by *wakalah* (the selling party gives their representative his purchasing of things that they bought for the customer) in executing MPO by having the customer, rather than the bank, choosing and agreeing to buy the product.[74] By means of this procedure, the banks greatly diminish the chances of a customer refusing to take possession of a purchased asset due to a change of preference. Nonetheless, Islamic banks still face a risk associated with refusal of the customer to accept goods at the last moment.[75] So this type of contract, in practice, still exposes Islamic banks to higher credit risks than conventional banks because it would be legally possible (even if highly unlikely) that a customer could refuse a deal at the last moment.

In *salam* and *istisna* contracts, the Islamic bank is exposed to the risk of a third-party failure to supply on time (or at all) or a failure to supply the contractually specified quality of goods to the second party (a bank's customer).[76] This could result in a delay in payments, or payments not being secured by the sale of the traded commodities, thereby exposing the bank to financial losses of income and capital.[77] For example, say a customer asks a bank to finance the construction of a house on behalf of the customer. The bank engages a third party – a builder – and uses other depositors' funds to finance the construction of the house. Upon the completion of construction, the bank transfers ownership of the property to the customer through a cash sale. It is at this last stage that the bank is at risk of making a loss if the customer is, for some reason, unable to afford the property, or if the customer refuses to purchase the property because the quality of construction is less than that specified in the contract between the customer and the bank. This type of risk is less likely to be faced by a conventional bank in Indonesia, even if both Islamic and conventional banks can sell their relevant assets (e.g. houses) and keep the revenue.[78] The case would be far more complex and risky for an Islamic bank particularly in the problem of the quality of the asset, wherein the bank faces a dispute between the customer and the builder.

In an *ijarah* contract and/or *ijarah muntahia bittamleek* (IMB),[79] the Islamic bank, as the lessor, retains ownership of a leased asset for an agreed period of time.[80] All liabilities and risks pertaining to the leased asset (including natural disasters and damage done by normal use-depreciation by the lessee) are thus borne by the Islamic bank.[81] Thus, under both *ijarah* and IMB, the Islamic bank is exposed to credit risk on the estimated value of the lease payments while it is in the possession of the bank-as-lessor, prior to the transfer of the leased asset to the customer.[82]

In the case of *mudharabah* investment contracts, the bank is exposed to the risk of losing invested capital or 'capital impairment risk' upon making payment of the capital to the customer when the funds are solely managed by the customer.[83] The risk even becomes higher when the bank does not have appropriate rights to control the manager of a business (*mudharib*) and is not able to participate in the management of the business project, or the bank is not in a position to monitor accurately the activities of *mudharib*, especially when the losses are claimed.[84] In this kind of contract, although the profits generated by the business activity are shared according to the terms and conditions provided in the contract, any losses in the investment are borne solely by the Islamic bank (unless the losses are due to the negligence or misconduct by the customer or breaching the term in the contract).[85] If the losses incurred are due to a customer's negligence, the bank's share of capital is transformed into a debt liability as applied by the contract agreement.[86]

It is well known that in practice, Islamic banks, especially in Indonesia, do not practice real *mudharabah* partnership in the traditional sense.[87] The customer has to repay the capital from a bank plus the profit in every month – the margin of profit being calculated based on the prediction of the profit earned from the activity of the customer in the past.[88] The bank also requires that the collateral and the value should be at least equal to the amount invested in the project, and retains this until the full payment had been made.[89] However, as criticised by Saeed, even though banks have tightened monitoring of *mudharabah* financing and minimised the risk of default by predicting the amount of profit from customer activities, there is always a possibility that the customer will claim that the project business is bankrupt through no fault of its own.[90]

In the case of *musharakah* investment contracts, the Islamic bank is exposed to credit risk in the form of capital impairment risk due to the fact that this is a profit-loss-sharing model for earning investment returns from medium to long-term financing, rather than for trading or liquidity purposes.[91] As a partner to a *musharakah* contract, the bank is exposed to credit risk because it is not entitled to a fixed rate of return and thus receives variable profits generated by the partnership based on a contracted profit-sharing agreement; concomitantly, losses are borne by both the Islamic bank and the business partners according to their respective ratio of invested capital.[92] The invested capital is redeemable at the end of the contract, which has a fixed tenure or is based on mutual agreement, or by the liquidation of the *musharakah* assets.[93] In extreme cases, the bank is exposed to the risk of losing the entire amount of capital invested in an enterprise or asset.[94]

In most cases of Islamic banks, the mitigation of credit risk resembles (but is not identical to) the strategies of conventional banks discussed earlier. Islamic banking mitigation techniques include the following.

First, *Hamish Jiddiyah* (security deposit held as collateral) is a sum paid by the customer (promisor) upon the request from the bank (promisee) to secure the promise to purchase or lease the product/item under an MPO contract.[95] The security deposit serves to indicate the customer's commitment to the purchase, and it is refunded if the customer purchases or leases the product/item from the bank.[96] If, however, the customer fails to honour a binding promise to purchase the product or purchase during the lease period, the Islamic bank can take the security deposit to compensate for the actual loss suffered, with the excess being returned to the customer.[97] In the event that the security deposit is insufficient to cover the losses, the bank has the right of recourse to the clients.[98]

Second, *urbun* (earnest money) is where the customer pays a deposit to the bank on the agreement that the deposit is part of the purchase price when the buyer agrees to complete the contract and purchase the product.[99] Since *urbun* is considered as the part of the price of the item sold, the bank will forfeit the deposit (even if it is more than the actual damage suffered) if the sale does not go ahead or the customer decides to withdraw from the contract.[100] A customer using *urbun* enjoys the right over the item and has effectively fixed the price of the item, having the option of deciding whether to proceed with the sale or not.[101]

Third, guarantee from a third party (recourse or non-recourse guarantee).[102] In this case, "The guarantor may or may not have recourse to the debtor (i.e. purchaser or lessee) and the guarantee can be for a fixed period and for a limited amount, without any consideration being received by the guarantor".[103] The bank here acts as the third party in the contract and has no affiliation to both contract traders. However, "a claim should first be made against the debtor, and then against the guarantor, unless an option is provided to make the claim against either the debtor or the guarantor".[104]

Fourth, pledge of assets as collateral. The pledged asset should be of an agreed-upon quality and can be in the form of an underlying asset or some other form of financial collateral owned by the customer; if the asset is owned by a third party, it is subject to the owner's consent to the pledge.[105] The customer as pledger allows the bank as pledgee to sell the asset without recourse to the courts against the debt of the customer if the latter fails to complete payment.[106] Any surplus from the sale proceeds are to be returned to the pledger, and any shortfall must be treated as unsecured exposure that ranks *pari passu* with other unsecured creditors if the debtor is declared insolvent.[107] The pledged asset here is used by an Islamic bank as security in order to recover the amount due, and the asset must be *sharia* compliant, such as cash-on-deposit, *sukuk*, or *sharia*-compliant equities listed in the main index of a capital market (listed on the stock exchange), *sharia*-compliant guarantees issued by third parties, and other physical assets fulfilling the function of collateral.[108]

As a result of the utilisation of the aforementioned mitigation techniques by Islamic banks in their practice, it is arguable that Islamic banks in fact face a similar level of credit risk to conventional banks. This is also criticised by Mamiza Haq, who argues "Islamic banks have fewer instruments to mitigate risks due to the prohibition of trading associated with uncertainty".[109] Accordingly, Idris found that there is a need for optimisation in strengthening risk management in Islamic banking as the current *sharia* risk techniques still yet to have a comprehensive risk concept.[110] This is because, as noted by several scholars, including Al Rahahleh, Bhatti, Misman, Chong, Liu, and Yousef, that these techniques have been adapted to resemble practices in conventional banking systems, which make Islamic banks effectively or somewhat likely to be involved in interest-bearing transactions when they enter into *murabahah* and/or *mudaharabah* financing; as a result of this, they also behave similarly to conventional banks.[111] If, however, Islamic banks were to forgo these innovations and adhere strictly to the classical conceptions (and 'spirit') of Islamic financial contracts, then they would face substantially greater credit risks compared to conventional banks. This is because they remain too risky (relative to rival conventional bank loans) even when the aforementioned risk-mitigation techniques are available. Accordingly, Sufyati and Yeni also argue that *mudharabah* contracts are still a riskier type of contract than conventional loan contracts.[112]

8.3.2 Market Risk and Equity Investment Risk

In Islamic banks, market risk arises in the following situations: Equity position risk (including *sukuk* held for trading), foreign exchange risk, commodities, and inventory risk. All of these would fall under the category of 'systemic' risk.[113]

In relation to equity position risk, Islamic banks offer instruments based on equity investments in *mudharabah* (partnership) and *musharakah* (joint venture partnership) contracts. The equity position risk arises because of a potential decline in the fair value of the equity position held by the Islamic banks, when the bank enters into equity investment such as in the form of direct investment in projects or joint venture businesses to indirect investments (e.g., stocks and *sukuk*).[114] An Islamic bank can potentially lose its equity position due to the decline in market value, which can trigger additional problems such as credit risk and liquidity risk due to losses in capital investment.[115] Thus, to reduce equity risk, a prudential evaluation must be conducted before a bank's execution of equity participation, such as understanding the background and business plan and analysis of legal and economic environment in which the project will take place.[116]

For example, in the case between *PT Bank Muamalat Indonesia vs CV Benua Engineering Consultants*,[117] Bank Muamalat was required to bear the losses of its equity position due to the failure of the joint-venture business project. Both parties agreed on the *musharakah* contract, but it transpired that the losses incurred by the company resulted in it failing to pay the monthly profit return to the bank, which in turn caused the bank to retain the collateral.[118] However, CV Benua Engineering Consultants argued that this procedure is not in accordance with the contract agreement, since *musharakah* is a partnership contract where both company and bank contribute their capital in the joint venture, and the profit resulted from this project should be shared based on the agreed contract and where the customer can have a choice whether to go to court or to solve the dispute through arbitration institutions.[119] In this court, Dr Muhammad Syafii Antonio was presented as the witness from the Islamic scholars and stated that, in *musharakah* contracts, both parties must agree to the risk-sharing (the potential of profit and loss) resulting from the project and must have an agreed-upon profit-sharing ratio.[120] He further clarified that the Islamic bank is permitted to ask collateral in this contract, but it can only be retained by the bank in case the customer subsequently defaulted due to the customer's negligence.[121] The court accepted the customer's contention in this case on the grounds that there is legal uncertainty in adjudicating the case. The court noted that Art 2 of *Islamic Banking Law No. 21 of 2008* stated that there is a choice of forum for the dispute resolution due to the authority of two courts (religious court and state court) to resolve *sharia* banking disputes.[122] With the issuance of this decision, the Supreme Court noted that the only judicial institution authorised to resolve *sharia* banking disputes is the court within the religious court and can also be carried out outside of the judiciary, such as arbitration institutions.[123] This interpretation gives rise to uncertainty in the risk management of Islamic banking, as the bank enters into a *musharakah* contract but would not be fully aware of the functioning of the business because it will rely primarily on the entrepreneur/customer's report of the business. In this case, Islamic banks may be disadvantaged by the uncertainty of business project activities, in the event where the bank has to clarify whether it is true the project is bankrupt due to natural loss, or it is just a trick from the customer to avoid the collateral being executed in the court.

All banks face equity risks due to the potential loss of equity arising out of a fall in the value of company shares owned by banks.[124] For Islamic banks, however, not only can they hold shares in publicly listed companies on stock exchanges and face equity risk due to stock fluctuations and company declines; they can also face equity risk with unlisted companies into which they have entered into profit-loss sharing *mudharaba* and *musharaka* contracts.[125] Since an Islamic bank is effectively a contracted shareholder in a given business, a fall in the value of the equity of that business would constitute a realised equity risk.[126] In the extreme case of business failure, the bank would lose, without recourse, its invested capital altogether.[127] It is thus important for Islamic banks to consider methods of mitigating this kind of risk; the background and the business plan of the project, the legal entity of the project, and its impact on the economic situation need to be carefully assessed. Unfortunately, the risk for Islamic banks is exacerbated when they are unable to oversee or play a management role in the running of the businesses in which they are invested to guard against poor decision-making by the entrepreneur, as seen in the aforementioned court example. Such risk mitigation is practically impossible because detailed monitoring of such partnerships would prohibitively increase their transaction and enforcement costs relative to conventional banks with which they compete.

In the case of foreign exchange risk, Islamic banks are exposed to a risk due to the currency fluctuations and the volatility of day-to-day foreign exchange rates involving the conversion of one currency into another currency at an agreed market rate.[128] This fluctuation either directly or indirectly affects the cash flow, revenue, expenses, and overall financial positions of companies.[129] In the case of commodities and inventory risk, when an Islamic bank holds or takes long positions in commodities with a view to resale or lease, a bank is exposed to the day-to-day fluctuation of market prices in secondary markets for those commodities.[130] Although one may argue that Islamic banks have a limited range of commodities due to restrictions of uncertainty in trade as compared to conventional banks which made them able to spread risk through commodity diversification, in fact, as Fitch analyses there are still constraints on Islamic banks to evolve their risk-management practices, including the proper oversight management of their bank's capital/solvency positions and future profits.[131]

Certainly, market instability affects both Islamic and conventional banks. Boumediene and Caby, supported by Chakroun, Sebai, and Gallali, have empirically demonstrated that when, for example, the global financial crisis occurred in 2008, both conventional and Islamic banks experienced increases in their systemic risks, and the study also finds that that systemic risk and share price volatility was lower for Islamic banks.[132] However, the mitigation of market risk occurs in a different way for Islamic banks as compared to their conventional counterparts. These findings can be explained by the fact that although both types of banks are significant participants in real estate markets, so were exposed to the collapse in property price bubble collapses, the Islamic banks were not exposed to the concomitant risks associated with mortgage-backed securities that conventional banks heavily engaged in up to 2007.[133] The Islamic banks were not exposed to the risks associated with securitisation because such products are religiously prohibited to them.[134] On the other hand, unlike their conventional counterparts, Islamic banks are prohibited from engaging in hedging using standard futures contracts and other derivatives as a method of mitigating risks arising out of day-to-day market volatility.[135] Thus, one may conclude that although Islamic banks are shielded to some extent from large financial crisis events associated with certain 'synthetic' financial instruments, they are less shielded from daily market volatility risk for precisely the same reason – the prohibition on risk-affecting financial innovations.

8.3.3 Liquidity Risk

Besides having to maintain sufficient capital reserves to cover liquidity risk by holding tradeable high-quality liquid assets, Islamic banks also must ensure that their available funding products are *sharia* compliant on an interest-free basis. This, however, presents something of a challenge to Islamic banks because they can be exposed to liquidity risks when or if they are unable to satisfy sudden increases in depositors' short-term demand for cash, or their inability to convert securities or high-quality assets to cash without affecting income and banking operational activities.[136] In theory, this problem arises out of the fact that Islamic banks' funds are provided by 'on call' *mudharabah* current accounts held by depositors who may make withdrawals at any time without notice, while their *mudharabah* investments with entrepreneurs are made on a more long-term basis.[137] It might be argued the Islamic banks do not bear the whole credit risk because current account holders (depositors) participate in profit-loss-sharing investments with the bank and so bear some of the risk themselves.[138] This, however, does not actually happen in practice in all cases. Chong and Liu claim that in the case of the Malaysian Islamic Bank, the *mudharabah* depositors do not really enter profit-loss-sharing investment, and says:

> anecdotal evidence shows that, contrary to the asset-liability matching explanation, the Islamic bank depositors in practice do not fully share in the financing losses incurred by Islamic banks. The Bank Islam Malaysia Berhad's depositors, for example, continued to receive 'market' investment rate of returns despite the bank's reported loss of RM480 million (US$127 million) as at June 30, 2005 due to non-performing loans.[139]

This claim also points out that the Governor of the Central Bank of Malaysia, Dr Zeti Akhtar Aziz, said much the same thing on 15 February 2006.[140]

Similarly, in the case of Indonesian Islamic banks, Pratiwi and Suprayogi found that the investment rate of return for depositors was not affected even though the bank's amount of liquidity increased, which implies that Indonesian Islamic banks do not fully match this rate of return with their asset liabilities despite the increase in the number of depositors entering into equity investments.[141] This is also supported by Kasri and Kassim, who find that when deposit return rates in Islamic banks do in fact fall below those of the deposit interest rates offered by conventional banks, Islamic banks' depositors do indeed shift to conventional banks.[142] For this reason, it can be argued that in practice Indonesian Islamic banks are avoiding liquidity risk (associated with losing depositors in economic downturns) by contravening the classical 'spirit' of Islamic law associated with *mudharabah* deposit accounts. They do this because if they do not, they would face substantially higher liquidity risk due to more volatile deposit-returns (which are not preferred by depositors) than conventional banks.

8.3.4 Legal Risk and Sharia *Compliance Risk*

Like all banks, Islamic banks are also exposed to legal risk. However, it is arguable that, in addition to the 'normal' legal risks faced by any bank due to failures of internal monitoring and enforcement of legal obligations as stated in the Basel Accords (see Section 8.2.8), there is a major unique source of legal risk for Islamic banks derived from the nature of being *sharia* compliant in all its financial instruments. This unique risk is even more difficult to quantify than 'normal' legal risks because of the inconsistencies in the rulings of *fatwa* bodies – whether it is the MUI, influential local organisations such as NU or Muhammadiyah, or an international body like the Organisation of Islamic Cooperation, etc. Because of the diversity of nation-state jurisdictions in which Islamic banks can operate, a particular Islamic financial instrument may be permitted by one *fatwa* body in one jurisdiction but prohibited by others in different jurisdictions.[143] This can be highly problematic for Islamic banks that operate across national jurisdictions, as is increasingly the case as financial markets become ever more globally interconnected. If Islamic banks are not able to act quickly in accordance with new rulings within their 'home' jurisdictions as well as 'foreign' jurisdictions that may impact on their assets and liabilities, this then generates greater legal risk for Islamic banks. Examples of this include the case of a ruling that resulted in the collapse in the value of *sukuk*. In 2008, the chair of the Sharia Board of AAOIFI unexpectedly handed down a *fatwa* stating that *sukuk* transactions were not *sharia* compliant because they substantively resembled conventional bonds. This had a detrimental effect on the value of approximately 80% of the US$80 billion of *sukuk* in the market at the time.[144] Islamic banks are thus exposed to unique legal and compliance risks, where they have to comply with both the government regulations as well as *sharia* regulations (*sharia* compliance). If an Islamic bank is found to have breached the *sharia* rules in their transactions, the income generated from said transactions will not be recognised as being *sharia* compliant and will be considered religiously illegitimate; indeed, in religious terms, the very contracts themselves could be rendered 'invalid'.[145] As such, the challenge of legal risk for Islamic banks becomes higher with the additional *sharia*-compliant risk. This kind of specific risk simply does not arise for conventional banks.

8.3.5 Reputational Risk

Sharia compliance is of particular concern to Islamic banks because their identity and *raison d'être* rests on it. Thus, an added reputational risk for Islamic banks is if there is a perception that the Islamic bank's dealings are not *sharia* compliant.[146] This could have an impact upon an Islamic bank's market position, profitability, and liquidity.[147]

In order to be Islamically and commercially successful, Indonesian Islamic banks have to balance between *sharia* compliance of financial instruments and the attractiveness of their financial products to all customers (whether Muslim or non-Muslim) in their existing dual banking system, in a way that they would be competitive with their conventional bank rivals.[148] However, as opined by Shinsuke,

> most practices of Islamic finance do not necessarily satisfy both the conditions. Many controversies regarding this matter – for example, determining which condition must or should be considered more important by Islamic finance – have been observed throughout the history of this field, as shown in the case of *murabaha* and *mudaraba*. The situation of Islamic finance in the 2000s stimulated this controversy because the new products mentioned above were developed giving high priority to marketability.[149]

It is not unreasonable to suggest that if there is not 'centralisation' and stability of *fatwa* determination, then as the number of financial *fatwa*-giving scholars grows with industry demand, the number of divergent opinions will similarly grow. This can create greater uncertainty on the part about the 'authenticity' and reputation of *any* given Islamic bank. In Indonesia, the question of whether Islamic banks are really 'Islamic' is perhaps the most important risk they face as the religiosity has a significant effect on customer intention to adopt Islamic banking services in Indonesia.[150] The costs to Islamic banks if they fail to control this risk would be enormous.

This risk is not merely a notional one. The practices of Islamic banks have been severely criticised by several Islamic economists, such as Al-Amine, Malik and Mustafa, and Shinsuke. Such critics actively foster controversy over whether Islamic banks are really 'Islamic' at all by raising doubts about some innovations sanctioned by various national and international Islamic *fatwa*-issuing bodies.[151] There is now a perception among at least some Indonesian consumers that the Islamic banks are imitating conventional banks, and that Islamic banks often use *hilah* (a legal trick or stratagem) to design their 'un-Islamic' products to look more 'Islamic'.[152] In line with this, a study conducted by BI, and also supported by Fianto et al., and Karim and Affif, reveal that, based on the survey from 11 provinces in Indonesia from 2000 to 2004, *sharia*-compliant service quality (in addition to safe banking products and service) is one of the dominant indicators of consumers' choice of Islamic banks. The study also suggests that the products offered by Islamic banks should not be a duplicate of existing conventional bank activities. In areas where consumers are more realistic and religious, Islamic banks should maintain good reputations and distinguish themselves as unique for their *sharia* compliance.[153] However, this finding also indicates that reputational risk is higher for Islamic banks compared to their conventional rivals, because their attractiveness is premised upon an ethico-religious reputation.

There is another reason for concern about the reputational risk for Islamic banks in Indonesia: the current mode of operation of the SSBs may well render them less than optimal in ensuring *sharia* compliance of individual banks.[154] At present, the SSBs of Islamic banks essentially serve as *sharia* advisory and supervisory bodies; the senior management of banks are required to report and to consult SSBs and request *fatwa* from them to ensure that the contracts, products, and services the banks engage are *sharia* compliant.[155] In practice, Baehaqi finds that the SSB obtain information about the post-transaction of Islamic banking activities normally through regular meetings and annual reports provided by the bank.[156] This can cause SSBs to be misinformed about post-transaction data, since they only observe through regular reports from senior bank management, which may not be entirely accountable and transparent to the SSBs, especially when it comes to ex-post transaction in the banking activities. An SSB can ask, for example, about the pre-transaction mechanisms relating to deposits and financing ventures, but it has no right to information about post-transaction activities. It is also claimed by Baehaqi and is also supported by Sadhila, Adnan, and Alfarizy, that Islamic banks have sometimes issued new products without the vetting of their SSBs and even without a supporting *fatwa*.[157] In other words, although the SSBs have the obligation to advise and give direction on *sharia*-permissible transactions, they have no right to oversee whether this advice and direction is actually followed by bank officers on an ex-post basis. This specific kind of reputational risk is not a problem for conventional banks, and thus is a source of higher risk unique to Islamic banks.

8.4 A Summing-up of Risks in Islamic and Conventional Banking and the Possibility of Regulatory Reforms

8.4.1 Summing-up of the Risk Factors in Islamic and Conventional Banks

As has been indicated throughout this chapter, there are certain similarities and differences relating to risks faced by Islamic and conventional banks. It has been argued that due to the nature of Islamic banks, being guided as they are by the *sharia* and bound by its prohibitions, there are certain kinds of risks which are unique to them; furthermore, where the risks are of the same kind as those faced by conventional banks, they can nonetheless be greater for their Islamic counterparts. For conventional banks, interest-bearing loans and other instruments such as insurance and derivatives are utilised to transfer the risk to borrowers, to ensure loans and interest (the main source of profit) are paid, and to protect against the risk of capital loss. By contrast, the basic principles that differentiate Islamic and conventional banking are risk-sharing, the prohibition of interest, and the special *sharia* limits placed on the kinds of assets they can trade in. These prohibitions mean that Islamic banks do not have access to the full range of risk-mitigating instruments available to conventional banks, such as insurance and all manner of new kinds of derivatives. Islamic banks also face unequal legal and compliance risks because they have to be cognisant of and meet additional *sharia* requirements over and above those of conventional banks. Due to the liquidity risk inherent in *mudharabah* deposit accounts and *musharakah* investment accounts, Islamic banks have sought to use various stratagems to mitigate these special risks. However, these stratagems carry with them their own risks unique to Islamic banks – viz. reputational risk due to public perception that an Islamic bank may be betraying its own professed religious mission and identity.

The argument that Islamic banks face higher risks than conventional banks is a serious issue for the Islamic finance industry. It is because the *sharia* prohibits the giving or taking of interest on loans that Islamic banks face the special categories of rate of return risks and equity investment risks. The difficulty faced by Indonesian Islamic banks in following *sharia* requirements whilst at the same time meeting their business needs in a competitive banking industry means that, in practice, the pressure of *sharia* non-compliance in order to survive is a genuine concern.

8.4.2 Possible Regulatory Reforms in Islamic Banking Risk Management

As discussed previously, under Indonesia's dual banking system, Islamic banks face the serious challenge of harmonising the *sharia* principles in all their financial transactions whilst at the same time providing competitive financial services in a market dominated by conventional banks. These two goals require an extensive risk-management framework in the system which should be provided by the proficient *sharia* scholars. Ansari proposes that the central *sharia* advisory board should provide rulings pertaining to the impact of international regulations on Islamic financial standards and should oversee the practice of Islamic financial institutions in each jurisdiction to reduce management costs and enhance future research for product innovations.[158] As also discussed in Chapter 4, the integration of Islamic banks into the general risk-management frameworks for Indonesian banking will serve to mitigate some risks confronted by Islamic banks especially in conjunction with legal and compliance risks.

Up to 2011, Islamic banks in Indonesia were supervised by BI and had to adjust their risk-management strategies to the general risks faced by conventional banks[159] (the eight risk categories discussed in Section 8.2). However, after 2011, the responsibility for bank supervision was transferred to the FSA, which laid down the fundamental policies regarding risk management for Islamic banking.[160] The regulator has worked cooperatively with the MUI and the international Islamic banking standards of the IFSB in an effort to ensure compliance with *sharia* principles. Based on the *FSA regulation on The Implementation of Risk Management for Islamic Commercial Banks and Islamic Business Units No 65/POJK.03/2016*, the FSA has asserted that the risk-management regulations applied to conventional banks should also apply to Islamic banks as long as there is no contradiction between the regulations governing the two types of banks.[161] However, even though some financial risk management can be readily adopted from conventional finance, a careful review is always required at the time of accepting any new type of conventional risk procedure. In line with this, Hasan et al., and as also supported by Shafii and Abdul Rahman, indicate that there is a possibility of an inaccurate valuation of assets and liabilities that constitute other interest elements by applying conventional risk procedures in Islamic banks, which can lead to mismanagement of financial procedures, deception, and manipulation of financial statements.[162] For example, there may be some financial assets based on partnerships or profit-sharing (e.g., *murabahah* and *musharakah*), and when the conventional risks procedure is applied they would not reflect cash flows that have fitted to the approximation repayment of principal and interest, as these types of financing typically are based on an approximation of the customer's profit share throughout the partnership and also include a supplementary contract that stipulate the terms of revision to the repayment of principal and interest.[163]

It was also acknowledged by the FSA that additional risks faced by Islamic banks – namely, *sharia* compliance risk, rate of return risk, and equity investment risk – had to be added to the eight pre-existing general risk categories. That said, there is little doubt that this reform has not just been a matter of accommodating the unique nature of Islamic banks in Indonesia; it has also been a matter of Islamic banks conforming to some conventional banking norms. So apart from *sharia* principles, Islamic banks have been required to adjust to modern risk management techniques (integrated management and risk-based supervision) so that they can achieve robust innovative risk management without breaking Islamic law.

8.5 Concluding Remarks

This chapter has categorised and critically examined the risks faced by conventional and Islamic banks. Islamic finance literature generally argues that Islamic banking is superior to conventional banking because it entails less risk and greater stability. However, it was argued that Islamic banks are exposed to some higher common risks and additional unique risks compared to conventional banks. These higher and additional risks are not mere accidents: they are first and foremost a function of the nature of Islamic banking itself, which is grounded in an Islamic reputational legitimacy and also because the *sharia* uncompromisingly requires that banks *share* risk rather than *shift* it onto customers. Yet at the same time, Islamic banks are becoming more complex and face the pressing need to meet competitive banking industry standards and practices to survive in 'real-world' markets.

Certainly, these risks can be managed and mitigated by different risk-management strategies tailored to the various categories of risk, but as argued earlier, some of the techniques developed for Islamic banking have been adapted to resemble practices in conventional banking systems. As a result, by adopting modern *mudharabah* and *musharakah* financing to compete with conventional banks, Islamic banks expose themselves to liquidity and credit risks associated with fragile depositor confidence, asset price collapses, and investment project failures tied to the real economy. Since they share in the risks, they face greater exposure – including legal risk exposure, as was demonstrated in case of *PT Bank Muamalat Indonesia vs CV Benua Engineering*. Even if Islamic banks strictly adhered to the classical conceptions of Islamic financial contracts, they still remain risky, because in practice Islamic banks are unable to oversee or play a management role in the running of the business in which they are invested, which limits their monitoring of partnership projects.

The nature of the risks faced by Islamic banks as identified in this chapter has potential implications for regulatory reform in the banking sector in Indonesia. A clear risk-management standard requires a strong commitment on the part of policymakers to institutional and industry-level standards, but if monitoring and enforcement of the standards is in some way deficient with respect to transparency and accountability, then risk can be heightened rather than mitigated. This is of particular importance in Indonesia where, as discussed earlier, there are issues with the FSA regulation that limits SSB access to Islamic banks' post-transaction data, thereby limiting the transparency of the banks with respect to their very *raison d'etre*.

Furthermore, even though conventional financial risk-management techniques have been allowed to be adopted by Islamic banks, the bank should be vigilant when accepting any treatment procedure, as scholars suggest that there is the possibility of inaccurate valuation in assets and liability when these risk procedures are applied. In line with the suggestion made in Chapter 4, it is possible that legal, compliance, and ultimately reputational risks currently faced by Indonesian Islamic banks could be further mitigated by institutional reform to the supervisory arrangements that govern Islamic banks in Indonesia's dual financial system. This point shall be returned to in the final chapter.

Notes

1 Hameeda Abu Hussain and Jasim Al-Ajmi, 'Risk Management Practices of Conventional and Islamic Banks in Bahrain' (2012) 13(3) *The Journal of Risk Finance* 215.

2 Muhammad Umer Chapra, *Towards a Just Monetary System* (International Institute of Islamic Thought, 1985) vol. 8; Umer Chapra, 'The Case against Riba: Is It Compelling?' in Salman Syed Ali and Ausaf Ahmad (eds), *Islamic Banking and Finance: Fundamentals and Contemporary Issues* (Islamic Research and Training Institute, 2007); Muhammad Nejatullah Siddiqi, *Issues in Islamic Banking* (The Islamic Foundation, 1983); Edib Smolo and Abbas Mirakhor, 'The Global Financial Crisis and Its Implications for the Islamic Financial Industry' (2010) 3(4) *International Journal of Islamic and Middle Eastern Finance and Management* 372; Wazir Jahan Karim, 'The Economic Crisis, Capitalism and Islam: The Making of a New Economic Order?' (2010) 7(1–2) *Globalizations* 105.

3 US Securities and Exchange Commission, 'What Is Risk?' (Pt U.S. Securities and Exchange Commission), www.investor.gov/introduction-investing/investing-basics/what-risk.

4 Basel Committee on Banking Supervision, 'Principles for the Sound Management of Operational Risk' Bank For International Settlements, 3, www.bis.org/publ/bcbs195.pdf.

5 Razeen Sappideen, 'The Regulation of Credit, Market and Operational Risk Management Under the Basel Accords' (2004) *Journal of Business Law* 59.

6 Adina Apătăchioae, 'The Performance, Banking Risks and Their Regulation' (2015) 20 *Procedia Economics and Finance* 35, 37.

7 Arun Chockalingam, Shaunak Dabadghao and Rene Soetekouw, 'Strategic Risk, Banks and Basel III: Estimating Economic Capital Requirements' (2018) 19(3) *Journal of Risk Finance* 225.

8 Secretariat of the Basel Committee on Banking Supervision, 'The New Basel Capital Accord: An Explanatory Note' Bank for International Settlements, 1, www.bis.org/publ/bcbsca01.pdf.

9 Peraturan Otoritas Jasa Keuangan No 18/POJK.03/2016 Tentang Penerapan Manajemen Risiko Bagi Bank Umum [*Financial Service Authority Regulation No 18/POJK.03/2016 on the Risk Management Implementation for Commercial Bank*].

10 Basel Committee on Banking Supervision, 'The Basel Framework' Bank for International Settlements, 1053, www.bis.org/basel_framework/.

11 Septiana Dwiputrianti, 'Memahami Strategi Pemberantasan Korupsi di Indonesia [Understanding the Strategy for Eradicating Corruption in the Case of Indonesia]' (2009) 6(3) *Jurnal Ilmu Administrasi* 256, [tr author]. Apătăchioae, above n 6.

12 The financial risk is divided into many categories that could cover whole chapters; the researcher narrowed this down to the objective of the banks and in the context of Indonesian commercial banks based on the *Financial Service Authority of Indonesia Regulation of 2016* Reg. 18/POJK.03 on Implementation of Risk Management for Commercial Banks.
13 *Concentration risk* is a banking term which shows the overall spread of the bank's outstanding accounts over the number or variety of debtors to whom the bank has lent money; it is the percentage that each bank loan represents, while *counterparty credit risk* is the risk arising from the possibility that the counterparty may default on amounts owed on a derivative transaction. *Settlement risk* is also known as 'Herstatt risk', named after failure of German Bank Herstatt; it is the risk arising from the loss "when a bank in a foreign exchange transaction pays the currency it sold but does not receive the currency it bought". See Basel Committee on Banking Supervision, 'Principle of the Management of Credit Risk: Consultative Document' Bank for International Settlements, www.bis.org/publ/bcbs54.htm.
14 *Trading book* is a term used in accounting which refers to assets held by a bank that are regularly traded, while a banking book in accounting is the balance per book, and it is the amount shown in the company's records which is held to prevent risks such as a default. PricewaterhouseCoopers, 'Basel IV: Revised Trading and Banking Book Boundary for Market Risk' PricewaterhouseCoopers GmbH PwC, 6–15, www.pwc.com/gx/en/advisory-services/basel-iv/toobox-booklet-basel-iv.pdf.
15 Muhammad Kabir Hassan and Mehmet Dicle, 'Basel II and Capital Requirements for Islamic Banks' (Paper presented at the Sixth International Conference on Islamic Economics, Banking and Finance, Jakarta, 22–24 November 2005) 249.
16 Basel Committee on Banking Supervision, 'MAR 11 Definitions and Application of Market Risk' Bank for International Settlements, 3, www.bis.org/basel_framework/chapter/MAR/11.htm?tldate=20220125&inforce=20220101&published=20191215.
17 Basel Committee on Banking Supervision, 'Principle for the Management of Credit Risk' 10–13, www.bis.org/publ/bcbsc125.pdf.
18 Shelagh A. Heffernan, *Modern Banking* (John Wiley & Sons, 2005).
19 Ibid.
20 Basel Committee on Banking Supervision, 'MAR 11 Definitions and Application of Market Risk', above n 16, 3.
21 Basel Committee on Banking Supervision, 'Interest Rate Risk in the Banking Book' Bank for International Settlements, 3, www.bis.org/bcbs/publ/d319.htm.
22 Although it is not listed into the balance sheet of the bank, off–balance sheet items are still assets and liabilities of the bank. They are indirectly owned or an obligation of the company. For example, when a bank sells it loans through securitisation, the secured debt is wiped from the banking book. See ibid.
23 I.G.B. Erri Wibowo and Buddi Wibowo, 'The Effect of Competition Levels and Banking Concentration on Systemic Risks: Indonesia's Case' (2017) 9 *Indonesian Capital Market Review* 85, 98.
24 Ibid.
25 Ibid., 98.
26 Basel Committee on Banking Supervision, 'The Basel Framework', above n 10, 145.
27 Ibid., 675.
28 For example, when there is an increase in interest rates, the bank is required to change the value of their financial instruments and to match it to the current amount of interest rate; this is to protect the bank from the risk of rising interest rates. See ibid., 630.
29 Basel Committee on Banking Supervision, 'Risk Management Principles for Electronic Banking' Bank for International Settlements, 6, www.bis.org/publ/bcbs82.pdf.
30 Ibid.
31 Vishal Kapoor, 'Strategic Risk Management and Balance Sheet Management under the New Regulatory Environment' (Pt Moody's Analytic, Inc) (2012), 18, www.

moodysanalytics.com/-/media/presentation/2012/2012-18-09-strategic-risk-management-for-distribution-online.pdf.

32 Randall S. Kroszner, 'Strategic Risk Management in an Interconnected World' (Paper presented at the Risk Management Association Annual Risk Management Conference, Baltimore, Maryland, 20 October 2008) 3, www.bis.org/review/r081023b.pdf.

33 Basel Committee on Banking Supervision, *Funding Liquidity Risk: Definition and Measurement* (July 2010), 8, www.bis.org/publ/work316.pdf.

34 Ibid.

35 Basel Committee on Banking Supervision, 'International Framework for Liquidity Risk Measurement, Standards and Monitoring' Bank for International Settlements, 4, www.bis.org/publ/bcbs165.htm.

36 Ibid.

37 Ibid.

38 Basel Committee on Banking Supervision, *Basel III, the Liquidity Coverage Ratio and Liquidity Risk Monitoring Tools* (January 2013), 14, www.bis.org/publ/bcbs238.pdf.

39 Basel Committee on Banking Supervision, above n 35.

40 K. Subramoniam, 'Basel III Framework on Liquidity Standards: The Challenges Before the Indian Banks on Liquidity Risk Management' (Pt IUP Publications) (2015) 14(3) *IUP Journal of Bank Management* 40, 43.

41 Ibid.

42 Ibid.

43 Basel Committee on Banking Supervision, 'Principles for Sound Liquidity Risk Management and Supervision' Bank for International Settlements, www.bis.org/publ/bcbs144.htm.

44 Dhaneswworo Arsojotegto Yuwonoputro and Muhamad Syaichu, 'Indonesian Banks Risk-Taking: The Effect of Liquidity Risk, Capital Buffer and BOPO: Z-Score Measure Approach' (2019) 8(3) *Diponegoro Journal of Management* 149.

45 Ahmed Arif and Ahmed Nauman Anees, 'Liquidity Risk and Performance of Banking System' (Pt Emerald Group Publishing Limited) (2012) 20(2) *Journal of Financial Regulation and Compliance* 182.

46 Yuwonoputro and Syaichu, above n 44, 152.

47 Peraturan Otoritas Jasa Keuangan No 18/POJK.03/2016 Tentang Penerapan Manajemen Risiko Bagi Bank Umum [*Financial Service Authority Regulation No 18/POJK.03/2016 on the Risk Management Implementation for Commercial Bank*].

48 Basel Committee on Banking Supervision, 'The Basel Framework', above n 10, 762.

49 Operational risk could be triggered by one or more failures in internal processes. For example, if a bank staff member mistakenly writes the wrong amount in the banking book, for example, the correct amount should be written IDR 10 million, but if the staff member wrote IDR 100 million instead, this would ultimately cause a loss to the bank. In another case, the operational risk could come from accidents such as natural disasters, fires, power supply failure, and failure of internet access, which all affect company operations, but the risk could be worse for the company's stability.

50 Basel Committee on Banking Supervision, 'Operational Risk: Revisions to the Simpler Approaches' Bank for International Settlements, 5 www.bis.org/publ/bcbs291.pdf.

51 Ibid.

52 Ibid.

53 Basel Committee on Banking Supervision, 'The Basel Framework', above n 10, 1072.

54 For example, the Australian Banking Royal Commission inquiry on the failure of the banks to do any of these things; the breakdown in trust of banks, the exploitation of vulnerable consumers, the promotion of the bank's interests over that of the customers to the extent of charging dead customers fees; charging customers fees for services that were not delivered and so on. For further reading, see Australian Banking Royal Commission, *Final Report on Royal Commission into Misconduct in the Banking, Superannuation*

and Financial Services Industry (2019), www.royalcommission.gov.au/sites/default/files/2019-02/fsrc-volume-1-final-report.pdf.

55 Basel Committee on Banking Supervision, *Management of Non-Financial Risks*, 158, www.bis.org/publ/othp04_8.pdf.

56 Basel Committee on Banking Supervision, *Compliance and the Compliance Function in Banks* (April 2005), 7, www.bis.org/publ/bcbs113.pdf.

57 Ibid. An example compliance risk can be seen when the Commonwealth Bank of Australia (CBA) agreed to pay a $700 million fine plus costs (without challenging it through the courts) for breaches of anti-money laundering and terror-financing laws, after being accused by the Australian federal financial intelligence agency AUSTRACT in 2017 of systemic failure to report suspicious transfers and accounts. See Matthew Doran and Michael Janda, 'Commonwealth Bank to Pay $700 m Fine for Anti-Money Laundering, Terror Financing Law Breaches', *ABC News* (Sydney), 4 June 2018, www.abc.net.au/news/2018-06-04/commonwealth-bank-pay-$700-million-fine-money-laundering-breach/9831064.

58 Basel Committee on Banking Supervision, *above n* 56, 9.

59 Basel Committee on Banking Supervision, *International Convergence of Capital Measurement and Capital Standards, a Revised Framework* (June 2004), www.bis.org/publ/bcbs107.htm.

60 For example, in the United States, the bank is not permitted to operate leasing, insurance, or brokerage house activities. On the other hand, in Indonesia, for example, a bank can offer insurance product by way of collaboration with an insurance company to bank customers (known as *bancassurance*). So, each country has different types of restrictions on banking business activities. See *US Code of Federal Regulations (List of permissible nonbanking activities) 2005, Banks and Banking*. Regulations. Subpart C – Nonbanking Activities and Acquisitions by Bank Holding Companies, www.gpo.gov/fdsys/pkg/CFR-2005-title12-vol3/xml/CFR-2005-title12-vol3-sec225-28.xml. See *Circular Letter of Financial Service Authority of Indonesia No. 33/SEOJK.03/2016* on Risk Management Implementation on the Bank who operate the *Bancassurance*.

61 Katja Julie Wurtz, 'The Definition of Legal Risk and Its Management by Central Banks' (2007) 1(1) *International In-house Counsel Journal* 43.

62 Basel Committee on Banking Supervision, 'International Convergence of Capital Measurement and Capital Standards, a Revised Framework', June 2004.

63 Wurtz, above n 62,47.

64 Basel Committee on Banking Supervision, *Compliance and the Compliance Function in Banks* (April 2005), www.bis.org/publ/bcbs113.pdf.

65 Roger McCormick, *Legal Risk in the Financial Markets* (Oxford University Press, 2006).

66 Basel Committee on Banking Supervision, 'Sound Practices for the Management and Supervision of Operational Risk' Bank for International Settlements, www.bis.org/publ/bcbs96.htm.

67 Sudin Haron, *Islamic Finance and Banking System: Philosophies, Principles & Practices* (McGraw Hill, 2009) 355.

68 See Chapter 5, Section 5.4.

69 See Chapter 6.

70 Islamic Financial Services Board, *About IFSB* (Accessed on 27 October 2017), www.ifsb.org/background.php.

71 Islamic Financial Services Board, 'IFSB 2 Capital Adequacy Standard for Institutions (Other Than Insurance Institutions) Offerings Only Islamic Financial Services' Islamic Financial Service Board, 4, www.ifsb.org/standard/ifsb2.pdf.

72 Ibid.

73 An MPO contract refers to an agreement whereby the Islamic bank sells the purchased product by the bank to the customer after inclusion of profit margin and other costs into the real price of the asset/product purchased; the contract can be binding or non-binding. See ibid., 21.

74 Novea Elysa Wardhani, Masruchin Ruba'i and Thohir Luth, 'The Contract of Murabahah Bil Wakalah on the Saving-Loan Cooperative and Syariah FInancing (KSPPS) Reviewed from Justice and Benefit Perspective' (2017) 64 *Journal of Law, Policy and Globalisation*.

75 Bagya Agung Probowo, 'Reputation Oversight by the Sharia Supervisory Board toward Wakalah Contract Application on Murabahah Financing' (2019) 436 *Advances in Social Science, Education and Humanities Research* 775.

76 Global Islamic Finance Report, *Global Islamic Finance Report 2015* (Cambridge Institute of Islamic Finance, 2015) 165.

77 Ibid.

78 For the Indonesian regulation on how a bank can sell the customer's collateral, see Peraturan Otoritas Jasa Keuangan Republik Indonesia No 11/POJK.03/2019 tentang Prinsip Kehati-hatian dalam Aktivitas Sekuritisasi Aset Bagi Bank Umum [The Regulation of Financial Service Authority of Indonesia No 11/POJK.03/2019 on Prudential Principles in Asset Securitisation Activities for Commercial Banks].

79 An IMB contract is also known as *Ijarah wa Iqtina*; in this transaction the bank (lessor) promises to transfer the right of ownership in the leased asset to the lessee at the end of the contract as a sale or a gift, based on the agreement that the promise is separately mentioned and upon the fulfilment of the *ijarah* obligation. See Islamic Financial Services Board, above n 71, 33.

80 Ibid.

81 Faten Ben Bouheni, Chantal Ammi and Aldo Levy, *Banking Governance, Performance and Risk-Taking: Conventional Banks vs Islamic Banks* (John Wiley & Sons, 2016).

82 Islamic Financial Services Board, above n 71, 33.

83 Riduwan et al., 'The Problems of Mudarabah Financing Collateral in Islamic Rural Banks', *TEST, Engineering and Management* (Oakland), 14706–14712. www.researchgate.net/publication/342623464_The_Problems_of_Mudarabah_Financing_Collateral_in_Islamic_Rural_Banks.

84 Ibid.

85 Financial Services Authority of Indonesia, *Buku Standar produk Mudharabah seri standar produk perbankan syariah* 5 [The Standard Book for Mudharabah Instrument for Islamic Banking 5] (Financial Services Authority of Indonesia, 2019).

86 Ibid., 38.

87 See Chapter 5, Section 5.4.1 for further discussion of the practice of *mudharabah* in Indonesian Islamic banks.

88 Ibid.

89 See Chapter 5, Section 5.4.1. Also see Moh Nurul Qomar, 'Mudharabah as the Islamic Financing Product from the Perspective of Abdullah Saeed/*Mudharabah Sebagai Produk Pembiayaan Perbankan Syariah Perspektif Abdullah Saeed*' (2018) 2(2), *Journal of Islamic Banking and Finance* 10, 201.

90 Ibid.

91 Islamic Financial Services Board, above n 71, 6.

92 Ibid., 38.

93 Ibid.

94 Ibid.

95 Habib Ahmed, Mehmet Asutay and Rodney Wilson, *Islamic Banking and Financial Crisis: Reputation, Stability and Risks* (Edinburgh University Press, 2013) 118.

96 Ibid.

97 Islamic Financial Services Board, above n 71, 7.

98 Ibid.

99 Abdul Rahim Abdul Rahman, 'Islamic Microfinance: A Missing Component in Islamic Banking' (2007) 1(2) *Kyoto Bulletin of Islamic Area Studies* 38, 49.

100 Ibid., 50.

101 Hussain author Kureshi, *Contracts and Deals in Islamic Finance: A User's Guide to Cash Flows, Balance Sheets, and Capital Structures* (Wiley, 2015) ch 11.
102 A recourse loan is one that is personally guaranteed by the borrower(s), and a non-recourse loan means that, if something goes awry in the property, its furniture, fixtures, and equipment, the leases, etc, the only recourse a lender has is to seize the collateral specified in the loan agreement, even if its value does not cover the entire debt. Non-recourse loans are generally made to what is known as a limited partnership or special purpose entity that is structured for the sole purpose of that real estate deal which becomes a shield for the borrowers in the event the business project fails. See Abdullah Haron and John Lee Hin Hock, 'Inherent Risk: Credit and Market Risks' in Simon Archer and Rifaat Ahmed Abdel Karim (eds), *Islamic Finance: The Regulatory Challenge* (Wiley, 2012).
103 Ibid.
104 Islamic Financial Services Board, above n 71, 7.
105 Ibid.
106 Ibid.
107 Ibid.
108 Ibid.
109 Mamiza Haq, 'Is Islamic Banking More Risky Compared to Conventional Banking?', *The Conversation* (Queensland), https://theconversation.com/is-islamic-banking-more-risky-compared-to-conventional-banking-62993.
110 Miftah Idris, 'Strengthening Risk Management of Sharia Banking in Indonesia' (2019) 3(1) *Madani Legal Review* 1, 5.
111 Naseem Al Rahahleh, Ishaq Bhatti and Faridah Najuna Misman, 'Developments in Risk Management in Islamic Finance: A Review' (2019) 12(37) *Journal of Risk and Financial Management* 1, 18.; Beng Soon Chong and Ming-Hua Liu, 'Islamic Banking: Interest-Free or Interest-Based?' (2009) 17(1) *Pacific-Basin Finance Journal* 125.; Tarik M. Yousef, 'The Murabaha Syndrome in Islamic Finance: Laws, Institutions and Politics' in Clement Henry and Rodney Wilson (eds), *The Politics of Islamic Finance* (Edinburgh University Press, 2004).
112 H.S. Sofyati and Oktaviani Yeni, *Risk Mitigation of Moral Hazard on Mudharabah Financing (Case Study: An Islamic Bank)* (2nd International Conference on Indonesian Economy and Development (ICIED 2017), 14–15 August 2017) (Jakarta).
113 Islamic Financial Services Board, above n 71, 13.
114 Mahfod Aldoseri and Andrew Worthington, 'Risk Management in Islamic Banking: An Emerging Market Imperative' in Sabri Boubaker, Bonnie G. Buchanan and Duc Khuong Nguyen (eds), *Risk Management in Emerging Markets: Issues, Framework, and Modeling* (Emerald, 2016), 10.
115 Ibid.
116 Habib Ahmed and Tariqullah Khan, 'Risk Management in Islamic Banking', *Handbook of Islamic Banking* (Edward Elgar Publishing, 2007), 149.
117 *CV Benua Engineering Consultants VS PT Bank Muamalat Syariah* (2012) 93/PUU-X/2012 1 (Constitutional Court of Indonesia).
118 Ibid., 28.
119 Ibid.
120 Ibid., 19.
121 Ibid., 20.
122 Ibid., 39.
123 Hermansyah, 'Lima Peristiwa Penting di Akhir Agustus 2013 Mengenai Peradilan Agama dan Ekonomi Syariah [Five Important Events in Late August 2013 on Religious Court and Islamic Economics]' (Pt Mahakamah Agung) (2013), [tr author], https://badilag.mahkamahagung.go.id/seputar-ditjen-badilag/seputar-ditjen-badilag/lima-peristiwa-penting-di-akhir-agustus-2013-mengenai-peradilan-agama-dan-ekonomi-syariah-59.

124 PricewaterhouseCoopers, above n 14.
125 Aldoseri and Worthington, above n 114.
126 Peraturan Otoritas Jasa Keuangan No 65/POJK.03/2016 Tentang Penerapan Manajemen Resiko Bagi Bank Umum Syariah dan Unit Usaha Syariah [The Regulation of Financial Service Authority of Indonesia No 65/POJK.03 of 2016 on Risk Management Practice for Islamic Bank and Islamic Business Units] (Indonesia) Ch 1.
127 Islamic Financial Services Board, above n 71, 29.
128 Mohamed Helmy, *Risk Management in Islamic Banks*, Thesis for Master of International Business Administration (ESLSCA Business School 2012), 20, https://mpra.ub.uni-muenchen.de/38706/1/MPRA_paper_38706.pdf.
129 Islamic Financial Services Board, above n 71, 14.
130 Ibid., 15.
131 Al Natoor-Basharand Saif Shawqi, 'Islamic Derivatives Increasingly Necessary, But Constraints Remain', *Fitch Ratings* (London), www.fitchratings.com/research/islamic-finance/islamic-derivatives-increasingly-necessary-constraints-remain-17-06-2020.
132 Mohamed Amin Chakroun, Saber Sebai and Mohamed Imen Gallali, 'Market Risk in Islamic and Conventional Banks' (2016) 5 *International Journal of Business and Commerce* 66; Aniss Boumediene and Jerome Caby, 'The Stability of Islamic Banks During the Subprime Crisis' (Pt SSRN) (2009), https://papers.ssrn.com/sol3/papers.cfm?abstract_id=1524775.
133 Boumediene and Caby, above n 132, 3.
134 Ibid., 6.
135 Ibid., 2.
136 Peraturan Otoritas Jasa Keuangan No 65/POJK.03/2016 Tentang Penerapan Manajemen Resiko Bagi Bank Umum Syariah dan Unit Usaha Syariah [The Regulation of Financial Service Authority of Indonesia No 65/POJK.03 of 2016 on Risk Management Practice for Islamic Bank and Islamic Business Units] (Indonesia) Ch 1, s 4.
137 Islamic Financial Services Board, above n 71, 20.
138 Ibid.
139 Chong and Liu, above n 111, 142.
140 Ibid.
141 Aprilia Pratiwi and Noven Suprayogi, 'Bank Syariah di Indonesia: Analisis Pengaruh Rata-Rata Tingkat Bagi Hasil Deposito dan Rata-Rata Tingkat Suku Bunga Deposito Terhadap Jumlah Deposito dan Jumlah Nasabah Deposito Periode 2009–2014 [Islamic Banks in Indonesia: Analysis of the Effect of the Average Deposit Profit Sharing Rate and the Average Deposit Interest Rate on the Total Time Deposit and the Number of Time Deposit Customers from 2009–2014]' (2017) 4(2) *Jurnal ekonomi Syariah Teori dan Terapan* 89, 96 [tr author].
142 Rahmatina A. Kasri and Salina H. Kassim, 'Empirical Determinants of Saving in the Islamic Banks: Evidence from Indonesia' (2009) 22(2) *Journal of King Abdulaziz University: Islamic Economics* 3.
143 See Chapter 6 for the discussion about inconsistency in *fatwa* bodies.
144 David Oakley, 'Sukuk Market: Clarification of Rules Does Market a Favour', *Financial Times*, www.ft.com/content/57504a52-3c0f-11dd-9cb2-0000779fd2ac; Naim Asmadi Mohamed, Isa Mohamad Yazid and Mohd Liki Hamid, 'The Effects of New AAOIFI Standards on Sukuk in Choosing the Most Authentic Islamic Principles' (Pt Emerald Group Publishing Limited) (2013) 4(1) *Journal of Islamic Accounting and Business Research* 77.
145 Islamic Financial Services Board, above n 71, 27.
146 Peraturan Otoritas Jasa Keuangan No 65/POJK.03/2016 Tentang Penerapan Manajemen Resiko Bagi Bank Umum Syariah dan Unit Usaha Syariah [The Regulation of Financial Service Authority of Indonesia No 65/POJK.03 of 2016 on Risk Management Practice for Islamic Bank and Islamic Business Units] (Indonesia) Ch. 2.
147 Islamic Financial Services Board, above n 71, 4.

148 Nagaoka Shinsuke, 'Critical Overview of the History of Islamic Economics: Formation, Transformation, and New Horizons' (2012) 11(2) *Asian and African Area Studies Journal* 114, 126.

149 Ibid., 116.

150 Heri Sudarsono, Yunice Karima Tumewang and Muamar Nur Kholid, 'Customer Adoption of Islamic Banking Services: Empirical Evidence from Indonesia' (2021) 8(3) *Journal of Asian Finance, Economics and Business* 1193, 1200.; H. Cisse et al., *The World Bank Legal Review, Volume 5: Fostering Development through Opportunity, Inclusion, and Equity* (World Bank Publications, 2013) 131.

151 Muhammad Shaukat Malik, Ali Malik and Waqas Mustafa, 'Controversies That Make Islamic Banking Controversial: An Analysis of Issues and Challenges' (2011) 2(1) *American Journal of Social and Management Sciences* 41; Muhammad Al-Amine and Muhammad Al-Bashir, 'Sukuk Market: Innovations and Challenges' (2008) 15 *Islamic Economic Studies* 1; Shinsuke, above n 148.

152 Ust. Ahmad Sarwat, Lc., MA is an Indonesian scholar in the field of *fiqh*, including *fiqh mu'amalah*; he owned Rumah Fiqih Indonesia (House of *Fiqh* Indonesia) and actively published books and social media. See Ahmad Sarwat, 'Bank Syariah Sama Saja Dengan Bank Konvensional, Benarkah? [Islamic Bank Is the Same as Conventional Bank, Really?]' on *Konsultasi Fiqih*, https://rumahfiqih.com/konsultasi-1937-bank-syariah-sama-saja-dengan-bank-konvensional-benarkah.html.

153 Bank Indonesia, *Pemetaan Hasil Penelitian Potensi, Preferensi, dan Perilaku Masyarakat Terhadap Bank Syariah di Indonesia* [Potency, Preference, and People's Behaviour toward Islamic Bank in Indonesia: A Compilation] (Bank Indonesia, 2005); Bayu Arie Fianto et al., 'Customer Loyalty to Islamic Banks: Evidence from Indonesia' (2020) 7(1) *Cogent Business & Management* 1; Adiwarman Karim and Adi Zakaria Affif, 'Islamic Banking Consumer Behaviour in Indonesia: A Qualitative Approach' (Paper presented at the 7th International Conference on Islamic Economics, Jakarta), www.academia.edu/download/34809212/27_Adiwarman_and_Adi_Zakaria_Islamic_Banking_Consumer.pdf.

154 Ahmad Baehaqi, 'Usulan Model Sistem Pengawasan Syariah Pada Perbankan Syariah di Indonesia [Proposed Model of Sharia Supervision System in Islamic Banking in Indonesia]' (2014) 1(2) *Jurnal Dinamika Akuntasi dan Bisnis* 119, 126 [tr author].

155 Peraturan Otoritas Jasa Keuangan No 30/POJK.05/2014 Tentang Tata Kelola Perusahaan yang Baik Bagi Perusahaan Pembiayaan [Regulation of Financial Service Authority of Indonesia No 30/POJK.05/2014 on Good Corporate Governance for Financing Companies] art 38 [tr author].

156 Baehaqi, above n 154.

157 Ibid., 126; Sadhila and Muhammad Akhyar Adnan, 'Analisis Kepatuhan Dewan Pengawas Syariah (DPS) Terhadap Ketentuan Otoritas Jasa Keuangan (OJK) (Studi Kasus Pada BPRS di Yogyakarta) [Analaysis of Sharia Supervisory Board Compliance on the Regulation of Financial Service Authority (Case Study at BPRS Yogyakarta)]' (2017) 1(2) *Reviu Akuntasi dan Bisnis Indonesia* 152; Shallman Al Farizy, 'Pengawasan Baitul Maal Wat-Tamwil (BMT) Berbadan Hukum [Supervision of Baitul Maal Wat-Tamwil (BMT) Incorporated Financial Institution', *Shallman*, https://shallmanalfarizy.com/2017/12/pengawasan-baitul-maal-wat-tamwil-bmt-berbadan-hukum/.

158 Omar Mustafa Ansari, 'Central Shari'ah Board' (Paper presented at the World Bank 11th Annual Conference on Islamic Banking and Finance, Bahrain, http://aaoifi.com/wp-content/uploads/2016/11/Mr.-Omar-Ansari-Central-Shariah-Board-for-AAOIFI-WB-conference-November-2016-v4.pdf.

159 Peraturan Bank Indonesia No 5/8/PBI/2003 Tentang Penerapan Manajemen Risiko Bagi Bank Umum [Regulation of Bank Indonesia No 5/8/PBI/2003 on the Implementation of Risk Management for Commercial Banks].

160 See Chapter 3.

161 Peraturan Otoritas Jasa Keuangan No 65/POJK.03/2016 Tentang Penerapan Manajemen Resiko Bagi Bank Umum Syariah dan Unit Usaha Syariah [The Regulation of Financial Service Authority of Indonesia No 65/POJK.03 of 2016 on Risk Management Practice for Islamic Bank and Islamic Business Units] (Indonesia).

162 M. Kabir Hassan et al., 'A Survey on Islamic Finance and Accounting Standards' (2019) 19 *Borsa Istanbul Review* S1, S10; Zurina Shafii and Abdul Rahim Abdul Rahman, 'Issues on the Application of IFRS9 and Fair Value Measurement for Islamic Financial Instruments' (Pt Emerald Group Publishing Limited) (2016) 7(3) *Journal of Islamic Accounting and Business Research* 202.

163 Shafii and Abdul Rahman, above n 162, 204.

9 Reform Proposals, Further Research and Conclusion

9.1 The Overarching Themes

This book has been motivated by the now undeniable fact that Islamic banking is here to stay. As Errico and Farahbaksh assert, "Islamic banking is no longer an interesting experiment, but growing reality which is expanding outside the traditional borders of Muslim countries into western economies where conventional banking is followed".[1] The question that now exercises the minds of both scholars and banking practitioners is how Islamic banks will be integrated into a world dominated by conventional finance. Will Islamic banking abandon the substance of its *sharia* principles? Will it become ghettoised by adherence to out-of-time pre-modern practices? Or is there a middle way?

This book has argued that a middle way is possible for Indonesia. It has argued for the development of effective regulation and supervision of Indonesian Islamic banks to encourage prudent risk management whilst simultaneously compromising *sharia* compliance. There are certain essential features of Islamic banking that are its *raison d'etre* and that unambiguously distinguish it from conventional banking: the *sharia* demands the prohibition of *riba*, *maysir*, *gharar*, and harmful investments, and propounds profit-loss sharing in 'real' transactions. These features are non-negotiable and must be maintained if Islamic banking is to retain its distinctive identity. However, the book has shown that *sharia* is not a singular codified law; rather, it is open to multiple interpretations due to its jurisprudential pluralism, which provides the basis for innovation and modernisation in Islamic finance. This insight can be applied specially to bank regulation and supervision. As Alam, Zainuddin, and Rizvi state, "Regulatory frameworks and supervision are vital to ensure the performance of any financial institution, including its ability to enhance financial institutions' credibility, directly impacting depositors or investor's faith in the financial institutions".[2]

It is therefore important that the idea of modernising Islamic finance, which is evolving from the source of *ijtihad*, is comprehensively used in this study in carrying out its objective. Islamic economists and scholars such as Habib Ahmed, Nadri, Venardos, Antonio, and Hakim argue that the harmonisation of the *sharia* interpretations with a consistent and efficient regulatory framework is the single biggest challenge for any Islamic financial system.[3] Indeed, as noted in Chapters 3 and 6, complex *sharia*-related issues can create inequality in the regulatory framework

DOI: 10.4324/9781003393986-9

governing Islamic banks because state financial authorities likely view them through the lens of conventional financial systems. For all these reasons, Islamic financial institutions need to be standardised or harmonised by *sharia* rulings in a manner that is comprehensible in terms of the dominant system.

On this basis, it has been argued that further reforms are required in the regulatory and supervisory framework which is consistent with *sharia* precepts but at the same time is pragmatic and flexible enough to meet internationally accepted regulatory and prudential supervision requirements. This would both better integrate Islamic banking into the wider finance system and render it more competitive in an industry dominated by conventional banks. In general terms, there should be greater centralisation of Indonesian Islamic bank regulation and supervision by integrating these functions into the existing state monetary authorities' structures and by Islamic banks conforming to international best practice as exemplified by the Pillars of the Basel Accords.

The great challenge in accommodating Islamic banks to the 'real world' of global market competition, as expressed by Mariyani-Squire, is that "in order to have a viable Islamic banking sector, it has been necessary to respond to the realities of the market place – that the idealized account of Islamic banking simply cannot exist in the real world".[4] For some scholars, the modernising of Islamic banking and finance, as claimed by Dusuki and Abozaid contains the great danger of religious dilution:

> the restricted view of understanding the *shari'ah* by only focusing on the legal forms of a contract needs to be changed. Instead, the 'substance' of the *shari'ah*, that has greater implications for the realisation of *maqasid al-shari'ah*, should be equally looked into especially in structuring a financial product. Otherwise, Islamic banks are just an exercise in semantics; their functions and operations are no different from conventional banks, except in their use of euphemisms to disguise interest and circumvent the many *shari'ah* prohibitions.[5]

Indeed, some Islamic economists also take the view that the *sharia* precepts in Islamic banking are fundamentally incompatible with the integration of Islamic banking into the world of conventional global finances. Hakim sceptically contends that "regulating different *sharia* regimes will be ineffective, cumbersome and costly".[6] On the other hand, as argued by Antonio and supported by Shaharuddin, the current standardisation strategies in Islamic finance are often only formalities, and in any case do not aim to cover each and every aspect of financial practice comprehensively.[7] Meanwhile, Ercanbrack argues:

> the processes that determine the composition of Islamic financial law (IFL) highlight the starkly reduced role of jurists in developing law in accordance with the traditional methodology (*usul al-fiqh*). Such analyses have failed to consider the standardisation effort as a lawmaking project driven by market forces, which must be realized if authentic *sharia* principles are to be given effect. Therefore, examination of these market-led processes and their contribution to the creation of Islamic standards is essential for understanding what

standardisation means in relation to the fulfillment of Islamic principles and whether a high degree of standardisation is desirable.[8]

Other scholars, such as Khan, Shinsuke, Al-Amine, and Al-Bashir and Malik and Mustafa, go further by arguing that there is a potential of '*fatwa* shopping' related to financial matters which can cause scholars to be 'bribed'; moreover, there is sometimes inconsistency in *fatwas* or even the reversal of *fatwas* on various matters relating to Islamic banking.[9] For these latter scholars, the pressures to integrate 'true' Islamic banking into the conventional financial system has resulted in the corruption of the very mechanisms by which *fiqh* operates. This is a serious issue because, as argued in Chapters 2 and 8, unique legal and reputational risks arise out of perceived doubts over whether Islamic financial law in Indonesia is a mere legal 'veneer', which is itself due in large part to sceptical scholarly opinions about *sharia* banking products.

In essence, this book rejects the kind of scepticism just expressed. As Alam, Zainuddin, and Rizvi argue, "Islamic banking operations are riskier in nature when compared to conventional banking which is why . . . Islamic banking operations demands an equally strong regulatory framework to control for its underperformance and bring it on level playing field of conventional banks".[10] The book thus tentatively makes the case for some broad reforms to Islamic banking (especially in Indonesia) that aspire towards standardisation and harmonisation of regulation and *sharia* interpretation on matters of banking and finance. One of the reasons these reforms are proposed is that it is the author's conviction that they can indeed facilitate the industry's growth, financial stability, time and cost savings, and transparency and consistency in financial reporting through standardisation in line with international best practice. It is through integration that Islamic banking will be better able to compete and flourish in a competitive global market, rather than remaining a ghettoised fringe in the world of finance.

There has been wide discussion about international financial standards in conventional banks; however, standardisation with *sharia* is rarely recognised or addressed in detail. As argued in Chapters 7 and 8, in order to assess how banking regulations could be better established according to a Basel Accords global regulatory framework, this book has explored the implications of this international best practice for Islamic banks and whether this can be rendered compatible with the demands of the *sharia* in Indonesia's dual banking system. The position taken in this book is that no inherent contradiction exists between Basel standards and the overarching imperatives of the *sharia*.

9.1.1 Recapitulation of the Book Structure

As discussed in Chapter 1, one of the main questions posed in this research is to what extent the risk management of Islamic banks in Indonesia's dual banking system follows the international financial standards developed by the Basel Committee on Banking Supervision which were developed to strengthen the regulation, supervision, and risk management of banks.

The *sharia*-related issues still persist and pertain to the use of interest (*riba*) in modern Indonesian Islamic banking, as highlighted in Chapter 2 that the theology-based interpretation is the major challenge faced by Indonesian Islamic banking. Notwithstanding, the regulatory framework is another big challenge of Indonesia's dual banking system, and as discussed in Chapter 3, the government policies to expand the market share of Islamic banking is one of the priorities which should be done soon.

The unresolved tensions in the current dual banking system have been explored in the remaining chapters. In Chapter 4, it was argued that the implementation of multiple regulatory and supervisory strategies has given rise to potential conflicts of interest being built into *fatwa* production and bank supervision institutional arrangements. An example of this is *ulama* being granted the role of doctrinal supervision through the internal SSB system and NSB, which incurred questions over their effectiveness, independency, and subjectivity. The nature of the conflict of interest exists in this set of arrangements where actually SSB members can have a concurrent post in NSB, and where they do not have an independent source of funds to monitor the supervision of their client bank, which can result in the mis-selling of Islamic financial products by those who have interest in giving the *fatwas*.

Chapters 5 and 6 analysed the gaps between Islamic principles governing contracts in the classical period and the modern needs of business and the community. It argues that in order to be viable, Islamic banks require further reforms that largely depend on innovations in Islamic financial instruments so as to meet market demand and customers' preferences, stability and risk management while also ensuring the spirit of the *sharia*. Furthermore, to create a more effective and prudent regulatory and supervisory system, these reforms need to be consistent with international financial guidelines. As summarised in Chapters 7 and 8, contrary to the opinion of some scholars, it is argued that Islamic banking faces greater risks than conventional banks in Indonesian dual banking systems because their unique characteristics should, by definition, be based on *sharia* rules and principles. Again, the reforms proposed in this book address the question of how *sharia* precepts can be upheld so that Islamic finance can be sustainable, meet the needs of the modern financial industry, and manage financial risks while also effectively conforming to internationally accepted regulatory and prudential supervision requirements.

The findings of this book thus provide insights for Indonesian Islamic banks in ensuring standardisation, regulation, and supervision, and risk management that can enhance their competitiveness at home and at the international level.

9.2 Recommendations for Institutional Reform

One of the main purposes of this research is to provide pragmatic grounds for greater flexibility of *sharia* interpretation as well as standardisation of Islamic financial regulatory and supervisory frameworks in keeping with international financial standards. For example, this research proposes reform to develop more streamlined and centralised procedures and regulations for *sharia*-compliant risk management as opposed to a manifold regulatory and supervisory approach, because the former provides a more risk-efficient framework and upholds accountability and independence, whereas the latter contains a mix of multiple state and private agencies (particularly relating to the *sharia* supervisory or auditing role by the SSBs under the auspice of the NSB-MUI) and the standard is vague and cumbersome. The following sections summarise and outline recommendations for institutional reforms made based on the preceding chapters, with special attention to regulation and supervision of Islamic banks that would be beneficial to the financial system as a whole in Indonesia.

9.2.1 Proposal 1: Removing Sectarianism in Fatwa *Rulings*

As discussed in Chapters 2 and 6, the sectarianism in *ijtihad* can cause unconsolidated Indonesian Islamic *fatwa* councils (viz. the MUI, *Lajnah Batsul Masail* NU, and *Lajnah Tarjih* Muhammadiyah) to promulgate sometimes conflicting legal opinions about financial contracts and products, which can (and does) lead to religious-legal uncertainty both for Islamic banks and their potential customers. If modern Islamic financial notions of efficiency, stability, and sustainability are viewed in terms of *maslahah* and *maqasid sharia*, then in many cases it is possible to avoid prohibitive *fatwas* (grounded on charges of *riba*, *maysir*, or *gharar*) over a range of banking financial instruments (including the controversial *tawarruq* product). Further, this recommendation is in line with the four Sunni schools of jurisprudence (*al-mazahib al-arba'ah*) where such methodological pluralism offers more comprehensive legal rules to cope with an ever-changing world and serve the public interest (*maslahah*). As for Indonesia in particular, this recommendation can also reduce tensions between civil society Islamic organisations, and thereby avoid confusion and sectarian conflict in society.

9.2.2 Proposal 2: Comprehensive Legal Framework for Effective Regulation

Chapter 3 argues that flexibility in the legal system enables the development of the financial institutions in Indonesia's dual system of the regulatory framework. This is preferable to a situation in which the state hegemonically imposes a conventional finance regulatory framework on Islamic banks without regard for their religious requirement to be *sharia* compliant. The recommended approach is applying legal pluralism instead of exclusive secularism. The former allows both secular and religious laws to be reconciled within the same regulatory institutional framework, while the latter approach ignores other legal systems such as religious law and other types of self-regulation which exist in society. The latter, by contrast, is also liable to be seen as a curtailing of religious freedom in the face of a national ideology that purports to protect said freedom.

Chapter 3 also critically examines the secular state, which is confronted by the harmonisation of Islamic principles within the secular state framework, where the growth of Islamic financial institutions cannot be separated from the supporting rules that accommodate their financial transactions, and these rules (recognised *sharia* rules) should be endogenously adjusted to economic reality. It proposes the development of legal systems and discusses the dynamic and fluid institution with the ability to adapt to societal changes as well as flexibility to meet the needs of the marketplace at home and internationally. This is because the need for Islamic banking originated with Indonesian Muslims who wanted financial institutions that better suited the precepts of their faith. This chapter argues that a more level playing field for Islamic banks should be strived for by harmonising Indonesian state law with existing Islamic legal rulings. In this way, legal clarity and certainty will be provided to both financial institutions and the regulatory and supervisory authorities.

9.2.3 Proposal 3: Transparency and Clarity for **Sharia** *Supervisory Institutional Arrangements*

In terms of *sharia*-compliant supervision, the state has endorsed the internal SSBs under the auspices of the NSB-MUI to oversee religious supervision of Islamic banks. This is mandated by *Regulation of Bank Indonesia No 11/15/PBI/2009 on Converting the Conventional Bank into Islamic Bank*. However, as discussed in Chapters 4 and 7, this regulation separates private and state agencies into multiple regulatory and supervisory frameworks which embeds a conflict of interest in the supervisory agencies since SSB members can also be concurrent members of the NSB-MUI at the state level. Further, as discussed in Chapter 4, SSB members can hold multiple positions in other financial institutions, including positions on the NSB-MUI at the national level. The conflict of interest becomes obvious when it is realised that the NSB-MUI is responsible for the approval of the proposal of new financial products whilst also acting as the state authoritative body responsible for the appointment and dismissal of SSB members. Due to this, conflicts of interest in the production of *fatwas* at the industry level and compliance judgements at the individual bank level are inevitable.

The separated *sharia*-compliant supervisory system (such as the separation between the NSB-MUI and FSA) also may lead to the disputes of coordination with governmental supervisory bodies. The supervisory functions of the NSB-MUI and its SSBs can be reformed by incorporating these functions into the FSA's own structure to provide authoritative, independent state supervision of Islamic banking practices. In this way, the parameters for all Islamic financial operations (including supervision, auditing, reporting, and regulation) should be handled by the FSA, and that the SSB functions of the *sharia*-compliant supervision must be transferred to the FSA sub-committees. While the SSBs retained their functions as advisors, who are responsible for giving *sharia* advice and who also act as Islamic financial consultants for their bank clients.

Furthermore, at present the NSB-MUI and its SSBs do not have independent remuneration; they are paid by their client banks. Therefore, incorporating them to the FSA is the most comprehensive approach to greatly reducing conflict of interest, particularly with respect to the lucrative '*fatwa* market'. As discussed in Chapter 4, if such institutional regulatory reform is applied, this will also provide greater assurance of *sharia* compliance of Islamic financial activities and promote *fatwa* consistency, because the FSA has authority for the enforcement of standardised regulation for Islamic financial products-contracts. Moreover, this proposal encourages banking stability because Islamic banks do not have high costs for *sharia*-compliant risk and pay for the SSBs; since the FSA has independent remuneration, the banks can use this resource as their revenue, which can place Islamic banks at a level on a par with conventional banks. By managing the overall supervisory of *sharia*-compliance risk in the hands of the FSA and BI, such a supervisory system can provide transparency and also streamline the currently more cumbersome process of producing, implementing, and monitoring *sharia* compliance, thereby enabling Indonesian central financial authorities (BI and the FSA) to better ensure the stable functioning of the overall Indonesian financial system.

9.2.4 Proposal 4: Clarifying the Permissibility of Modern Islamic Financial Instruments

As discussed in Chapter 5, an important controversial question that has arisen is whether Islamic finance is currently violating the pure intent (or 'substance') of Islamic prohibitions of *riba*. The claim has been based on the assertion that Islamic financial scholars sanction financial instruments that are almost identical to conventional finance and sometimes use the same interest rate benchmark as do conventional bank products. It is true that modern Islamic scholars have extended the laws of contracts in ways that are not necessarily the same as the laws of contracts prevailing in the classical (pre-colonial) Islamic period. However, as argued in this chapter, despite various personal views the question of the legal validity of financial products and banking practices in all respects is, in fact, ultimately determined according to the supporting evidence from the Qur'an, the *hadith*, and *ijma* by scholars trained in classical *fiqh*. Although several scholars argue that modern Islamic banking products are not Islamically compatible or do not completely eradicate the seeming similarity to bank interest, these Islamic products do *de jure* technically comply with *sharia* as judged by qualified *ulama* and still clearly retain some distinctively Islamic features not found in conventional bank products. This modern version of the traditional approach can thus be said to bridge the gap between today's financial practice and the real transactions in classical *muamalah fiqh*.

With respect to the issue of '*riba*-like' contracts in modern Islamic banking, most Indonesian scholars, like their Malaysian counterparts, have used this as *hilah* (legal stratagem) to circumvent *riba* prohibitions, including any forms of interest.[11] Although this situation is not ideal, if Islamic banks were to attempt to follow the strictures of the *sharia* from before the period of modern banking, they would face the paradox of being relegated to a minor curiosum in an industry dominated by more competitive conventional banks. The realisation of using *hilah* can be seen in the practice of PLS products, where under classical *mudharabah* financial contract predetermined fixed amount is prohibited, as realised profit will not be known *ex ante*. However, *ulama* has applied *hilah* through *istihsan* and *maslahah* to determine the use of Profit Equalisation Reserve (PER) or income smoothing to maintain the loyalty of customers of Islamic banks especially to customers who are sensitive to interest rates. In this way, the actual profit for PLS depositors can either be increased or minimised following the interest rate conditions.

It is for these reasons that this book has consistently advocated a middle-ground approach that accommodates feasibility and practicality of modern Islamic banking transactions, as opposed to perfect adherence of an idealised version of the classical Islamic commercial contracts. This approach allows Islamic finance to maintain the sustainability and efficiency to meet the needs of the modern Islamic financial industry in the real world of a competitive financial system dominated by conventional banking. Furthermore, although to have 'pure' financial products that are unrelated to interest rates would be highly desirable, Islamic banks are 'forced' by the secular monetary authority (BI) to use interest rates to regulate the transmission of monetary policy. If Islamic banks did not use this benchmark, it would be exceedingly difficult for BI as the central monetary authority to regulate the Indonesian macro-economy – and such regulation is of vital importance to the nation since internationally comparable interest rates have a significant impact on both domestic productive investment and capital inflows to Indonesia.

9.2.5 Proposal 5: Clarifying the Regulation of Islamic Derivatives

Similar to the issue of legal uncertainty, Chapter 6 notes there is a lack of legal clarity about whether 'Islamic' derivatives (not all derivatives) are permissible in Islamic finance. It is an important issue for Islamic banks because derivatives, if allowable, would provide a valuable means of hedging risk in an industry where conventional banks can already do so. The controversy stems first from conflicting scholarly opinions about whether some derivatives are permissible in *sharia* terms, and second, from the fact that the construction and trade in these complex hedging instruments occurs in some Muslim jurisdictions but is prohibited in others. As discussed in Chapter 6, Indonesian scholars at the MUI do not accept certain kinds of derivative transactions, such as the *tawarruq* derivative, due to its close resemblance to interest-bearing assets. *Tawarruq* derivatives are also prohibited by the IIFA. On the other hand, the IIFM organisation has declared it permissible to use such derivatives on the grounds that they are an essential element of sound risk management in the Islamic financial market and thus are of net benefit to the Muslim community (*maslahah*). The author thus takes the view that the MUI should further reflect upon the vitally important role that derivatives play in hedging against price fluctuations and possible market failures, and rather than prohibiting them outright, consider better regulation.

Chapter 6 argues that there is a middle way between the extremes: if derivatives are utilised prudently in the financial market, it would result in substantial economic benefits for Islamic banks and can improve their management of market and investment risk, because it would enable Islamic banks to ensure the sufficiency of internal funds by minimising the impact of unexpected fluctuations in cash flows while simultaneously increasing their competitiveness in the global market. This, however, must be premised on internationally recognised *sharia* guidelines, such as that of the IFSB where the central banks of each jurisdiction are agreed to a set of agreements clarifying how financial derivatives should be used and whether such derivative activities met the conditions set down in the *sharia*. Settling on international *sharia* guidelines for Islamic financial products would be a significant step forward, especially for trades across national borders with their own regulatory and supervisory authorities, because it would provide predictability and consistency to the matter of trading in Islamic derivatives and would also greatly reduce excessive speculative behaviour in derivatives trading.

Finally, such guidelines could also reduce the challenge of public perception and legitimacy that the general public (including private investors) have towards Islamic finance in Indonesia and elsewhere due to legal uncertainty, as this uncertainty is particularly related to the lack of coherent *fatwas* and secular laws relating to the use of Islamic financial products. In sum, it is suggested here that in the long run, the MUI should think about the choice between a fragile Islamic banking industry (without *tawarruq* hedging) that could easily disappear or a robust and a stable industry (with *tawarruq* hedging) – or in other words, a choice between an ideal that disappears in an economic crisis or an imperfect reality that provides distinctive religious benefits to the majority of co-religionists.

9.2.6 Proposal 6: Instituting International Best Practice

As indicated in Chapter 4, while reforms on *sharia* guidelines is important, it is not sufficient. The dual regulatory and supervisory system also needs to be re-considered. Without an efficient institutional mechanism for implementing correct *sharia* legal rules, this reform is moot and may not be enforceable. As noted in Chapter 7, one of the major challenges for Islamic banks is to apply the international standards set down in the Basel Accords, which may entail difficult institutional and Islamic legal reforms.

Chapter 7 critically analyses the implementation and implications of embracing the three pillars of the Basel Accords for Indonesian Islamic banks. It proposes the modification of the existing financial regulatory and supervisory system in line with the best international practice and risks, which provide more comprehensive guidelines for prudential regulation, transparency, and stable trading guided by market fundamentals. This chapter also notes that, although conventional bank regulations cannot wholly apply to Islamic banks due to the latter's *sharia*-specific risks, the three pillars of the Basel Accords, by contrast, are imperative and should be followed by Islamic banks. This is because, first, these pillars are broadly aligned with the *sharia* principles of avoiding excessive high-risk behaviour and foreseeable harm due to financial crisis. Second, Islamic banks can adjust to a more stringent risk-management regime due to their risk-sharing nature in financial instruments (such as *mudharabah* and *musharakah*).

This book proposes that one possible solution to the problem of porous boundaries between the regularity bodies of BI and the FSA is if each authority be provided with clearly delineated mandates for meeting their statutory responsibilities. For example, the FSA and BI should have a clear mandate for managing a systemic bank crisis when confronted with the inevitable exposure to market risk due to losses arising from movement in market prices. In this situation, the BI should have a systemic solution to monetary crisis to increase resilience of the monetary system, and the FSA should focus on reducing the impacts of the financial crisis on systemic banks in the 'real' economy when they do occur and if their viability is threatened. This would increase the collaboration across agencies in line with Pillar 2 of the Basel Accords. However, setting out more detailed guidance on the role of financial supervisors alone is not sufficient. To achieve the objective of financial stability, institutional reform of the entire structure of Islamic banking supervision to meet international standards is also required. As discussed in Chapter 4, the Islamic banking supervisory structure in Indonesia is exceedingly complex due to the mix of multiple state and private agencies overseeing Islamic banks. This supervisory structure is confronted with several problematic issues. First, the SSBs are paid by the banks, which undermine their independency. Second, SSB members are often members of the NSB-MUI, which oversees SSBs and thereby undermines their accountability. Third, there is no legal framework that protects SSB members from having to defend their actions in civil suits if they issue judgements that are not in the financial interest of their bank clients. Fourth, SSBs operate at arm's length from the FSA and thereby undermine transparency and supervisory control of the overall Indonesian financial system. All these issues are clearly not in line with the Basel Accords' Pillar 2 on independence, accountability, resourcing, and legal protection for supervisors.

Further, this chapter suggests that Islamic financial services should embrace Pillar 3 of the Basel Accords in preparing disclosures and promoting transparency in financial reporting standards. Pillar 3 of the Basel Accords provides general guidance to banking supervisors and regulators to formulate and improve regulatory frameworks for public disclosure where the banking industry should disclose their financial reports and other disclosures to the public, which enables market participants to have access to timely and reliable information to assess a bank's activities and the risks inherent in those activities. This is also consistent with *sharia* principles, where Islamic banks are encouraged to be transparent and free from all forms of fraud. As noted in Chapter 7, Pillar 3 also needs to be taken into account by Indonesian financial authorities to overcome deficiencies of transparency on financial literacy and to ensure banks provide customers with effective disclosure of the necessary information needed to make informed decisions, as this would improve customer relationships and therefore assist in achieving the goal of mutual respect and recognition between customers and banks.

9.2.7 Proposal 7: Reform of Risk Management Procedures

The final reform focuses on prudent risk management that can help banks mitigate risks faced by Islamic banks in Indonesia's dual banking system. As argued in Chapter 8, Islamic banks are exposed to greater risks than conventional banking for two reasons. First, Islamic banks absorb many of the same kinds of risks, such as liquidity and capital risk, that conventional banks do simply because they are financial intermediaries between those with surplus capital and those with shortages. Second, Islamic banks are also exposed to unique risks due to their professed efforts to comply with the imperatives of the *sharia*.

In order to be Islamically and commercially successful, Indonesian Islamic banks have to balance between *sharia* compliance and providing competitive financial services in an industry dominated by conventional bank rivals. To establish these two goals requires a clear risk-management standard of authority and responsibility for managing, monitoring, and reporting risks for all banks, and a strong commitment on the part of the proficient *sharia* scholars and the policymaker to institutional and industry-level standards.

However, as discussed in Chapters 4 and 7, if monitoring and enforcement of the standards is in some way cumbersome with respect to transparency and accountability, then risks could be heightened rather than mitigated. This is of particular importance in Indonesia, where FSA regulations limit SSBs access to Islamic banks' post-transaction data, thereby undermining the transparency of the banks' operations.

Therefore, this book proposes that an extensive institutional reform to the supervisory arrangements in the Indonesian dual banking system should be made by centralising the whole risks supervision (which includes risks in financial matters and risk of *sharia* compliance) to the hand of the FSA. This could be done by reforming the current multiple state and private Indonesian supervisory institutions (FSA and SSB), where all the monitoring, managing, and risk reporting of Islamic banking should be incorporated in the FSA and its sub-committees. As discussed under proposal 6, this reform would greatly reduce the deficiencies in risk management. Such clarity of structure in the financial system will also result in harmonisation with the best international practice of the Basel Accords and facilitate the recognition of Islamic banks as global players in international financial markets.

9.3 Future Research

This book has sought to highlight the numerous practical issues faced by Islamic banks in Indonesia, ranging from uncertainty about competing *fatwas*, to unique reputational risks, and to the regulatory framework governing its dual banking system. It is recognised that the book has been limited to an analysis of Indonesia's Islamic banking systems, as well as to practical reforms relevant to its dual legal and regulatory framework. As such, many significant issues remain to be fully explored with respect to the development of regulation and supervision of Islamic banking in other jurisdictions. Comparative work in other jurisdictions would further clarify the way in which the modern Islamic financial systems are evolving and whether there are national idiosyncrasies or common characteristics that are ascertainable across jurisdictions. Certainly, other jurisdictions that have also adopted a dual banking system (such as Malaysia and several MENA countries) should be given special attention because, as they too evolve, they may offer models that can provide invaluable insights and innovative developments that prove valuable to Indonesia and other countries.

Further research on empirical studies and tests relating to the dual regulatory and supervisory frameworks, such as the relationship between bank risk indicators and the financial stability of the banking system and the different approaches to banking supervision in Islamic finance adopted around the world followed by comparative research, may attract greater scholarly attention and will be imperative for visualising the standardisation of this dual legal and regulatory framework that surpasses the distinctions from one country to another.

9.4 Final Remarks

This book argues that the standardisation of Islamic financial regulatory and supervisory frameworks that accord with *sharia* need not be confined to a single interpretation; multiple interpretations and applications should be understood and explored if modernisation of Islamic law and finance is to be achieved (Chapter 2). This method should be recognised and applied by a secular, but religiously informed, country such as Indonesia (Chapter 3). This can be done by developing comprehensive procedural rules and institutional reforms within the existing dual legal and regulatory frameworks so as to facilitate modern Islamic financial products and services (Chapter 4). Furthermore, in order to ensure the sustainability and efficiency of a modern Islamic financial industry in the real world of competitive financial systems, a modern interpretation of the *sharia* based on traditional texts should be deployed by Islamic scholars regardless of their disciplinary background (Chapter 5). In this way, legal uncertainty can be reduced in Indonesian Islamic banking, thereby making the overall financial system more stable over time (Chapter 6). However, setting out more detailed guidelines and rulings alone is not sufficient to achieve financial stability. Institutional reform that meets contemporary international standards, as exemplified by the Basel Accords, is also required (Chapter 7). Finally, Indonesia's central financial authorities (the FSA and BI) should institutionally reform the regulatory and supervisory agencies that oversee the Islamic banks' financial risk supervision, including risks related to *sharia* compliance (Chapter 8).

Thus, this book contributes to a viable Islamic banking sector, secured by international best practice, in Indonesia's modern financial system. The reforms suggested in this book provide important insights into the problems, challenges, and successes associated with developing an improved model of an Islamic banking system. The reforms proposed in this study may be utilised in further research to broaden the horizons of researchers and regulators alike. It is further hoped that this knowledge can be used to build a flourishing and ultimately more just financial system for future generations of Muslims, both in Indonesia and around the world.

Notes

1 Luca Errico and Mitra Farahbaksh, *Islamic Banking: Issues in Prudential Regulations and Supervision*, IMF Working Paper No 98/30, International Monetary Fund (1998) 31.

2 Nafis Alam, Sara Sophia Binti Zainuddin and Syed Aun R. Rizvi, 'Ramifications of Varying Banking Regulations on Performance of Islamic Banks' (2019) 19(1) *Borsa Istanbul Review* 46, 50.

3 Habib Ahmed, 'Islamic Law, Adaptability and Financial Development' (2006) 13(2) *Islamic Economic Studies* 79; Kamran Nadri, 'A Critique of Islamic Banking and Finance:Harmonization of Fatawa (Islamic Opinions) and the Nature of Modern

Economic' (Paper presented at the IIUM Internationational Conference on Islamic Banking Finance (IICiBF), Kuala Lumpur, Muhammad Syafii Antonio and Aam Slamet Rusydiana, 'What Is the Future Outlook of Shariah Harmonization' (2010) 33(70) *Jurnal Dialog Balitbang, Kementerian Agama RI* 1; Angelo M. Venardos, *Islamic Banking and Finance in South East Asia: Its Development and Future* (World Scientific Publishing, 2nd edition, 2006); Rahmat Hakim, 'Harmonization of Shariah Rulings in Islamic Finance: An Analysis' (2013) 7(2) *Ijtihad Journal of Law and Islamic Economics* 267.

4 Edward Mariyani-Squire, 'Tensions in Islamic Economics' (2013) 12(1) *Trikonomika* 1, 8.

5 Asyraf Wajdi Dusuki and Abdulazeem Abozaid, 'A Critical Appraisal on the Challenges of Realizing Maqasid al-Shari'ah in Islamic Banking and Finance' (2007) 15(2) *IIUM Journal of Economics and Management* 143, 144.

6 Hakim, above n 3, 268.

7 Antonio and Rusydiana, above n 3; Amir Shaharuddin, 'The Bay' al-Inah Controversy in Malaysian Islamic Banking' (2012) 26(4) *Journal of Arab Law Quarterly* 499.

8 Jonathan Ercanbrack, 'The Standardization of Islamic Financial Law: Lawmaking in Modern Financial Markets' (2019) 67(4) *The American Journal of Comparative Law* 825, 825.

9 Feisal Khan, 'How 'Islamic' Is Islamic Banking?' (2010) 76(3) *Journal of Economic Behaviour & Organization* 805; Nagaoka Shinsuke, 'Critical Overview of the History of Islamic Economics: Formation, Transformation, and New Horizons' (2012) 11(2) *Asian and African Area Studies Journal* 114; Muhammad Al-Amine and Muhammad Al-Bashir, 'Sukuk Market: Innovations and Challenges' (2008) 15 *Islamic Economic Studies* 1; Muhammad Shaukat Malik, Ali Malik and Waqas Mustafa, 'Controversies That Make Islamic Banking Controversial: An Analysis of Issues and Challenges' (2011) 2(1) *American Journal of Social and Management Sciences* 41.

10 Alam, Zainuddin and Rizvi, above n 2, 50.

11 Muhammad Maksum, 'The Sharia Compliance of Islamic Multi Contract in Islamic Banking' (2017) 162 *Social Science, Education and Humanities Research*, 154.

Bibliography

Al-Qur'an

The Qur'an: A New Translation by M.A.S. Abdel Haleem (Oxford University Press, 2004).

Cases

Indonesia

Bank BNI Syariah vs Darman Sugianto (2019) 13/Pdt.G/2019/PTA.MU, 1–14 (Religious High Court of North Moluccas)

CV Benua Engineering Consultant vs PT Bank Muamalat Syariah (2012) 93/PUU-X/2012 1 (Constitutional Court of Indonesia)

PT. Elnusa, Tbk Vs PT. Bank Mega, Tbk (2011) 284/Pdt.G/2011/PN.Jak.Sel (South Jakarta District Court)

Rudi Purwanto (2017) No. 16/PID.SUS-TPK/2017/PT.MDN (High Court Medan)

Syarifuddin Arsyad Temenggung (2019) 1555K/Pid.Sus/2019 (The Supreme Court of the Republic of Indonesia)

United Kingdom

Shamil Bank of Bahrain vs Beximco Pharm. Ltd. (2004) EWCA Civ 19

Legislation and regulation

Indonesia

Legislation

Undang-Undang Dasar Republik Indonesia 1945 [*Constitution of the Republic of Indonesia 1945*]

Undang-Undang Nomor 9 Tahun 2016 Tentang Pencegahan dan Penanganan Krisis Sistem Keuangan [*Law No 9 of 2016 on the Prevention and Resolution of Financial System Crisis*] (Indonesia)

Undang-Undang Republik Indonesia No 04 Tahun 1996 Tentang Hak Tanggungan Atas Tanah Beserta Benda-Benda Yang Berkaitan Dengan Tanah [*Law No 04 of 1996 on the Mortgage Right to Land and Objects Related to Land*] (Indonesia)

Undang-Undang Republik Indonesia No 21 Tahun 2008 Tentang Perbankan Syariah [*Law No 21 of 2008 on Islamic Banking*]

Undang-Undang Republik Indonesia Nomor 7 Tahun 1992 Tentang Perbankan [*Law No 7 of 1992 on Banking*] (Indonesia)

Undang-Undang Republik Indonesia Nomor 10 Tahun 1998 Tentang Perbankan *[Law No 10 of 1998 on Banking*] (Indonesia)

Undang-Undang Republik Indonesia Nomor 21 Tahun 2011 Tentang Otoritas Jasa Keuangan [*Law No 21 of 2011 on Financial Services Authority*] (Indonesia)

Regulation

Financial Service Authority of Indonesia, *Buku Standar produk Mudharabah seri standar produk perbankan syariah 5* [*The Standard Book for Mudharabah Instrument for Islamic Banking 5*] (Financial Services Authority of Indonesia, 2019)

Peraturan Bank Indonesia No 5/8/PBI/2003 Tentang Penerapan Manajemen Risiko Bagi Bank Umum [*The Regulation of Bank Indonesia* No 5/8/PBI/2003 on The Implementation of Risk Management for Commercial Banks]

Peraturan Bank Indonesia No 6/24/PBI/2004 Tentang Bank Umum yang Melaksanakan Kegiatan Usaha Berdasarkan Prinsip Syariah [*The Regulation of Bank Indonesia* No 6/24/PBI/2004 on Banks Applying Islamic Principles]

Peraturan Bank Indonesia No 11/3/PBI/2009 Tentang Bank Syariah [*The Regulation of Bank Indonesia*, No. 11/3/PBI/2009 on Islamic Bank]

Peraturan Bank Indonesia No 11/15/PBI/2009 Tentang Perubahan Kegiatan Usaha Bank Konvensional Menjadi Bank Syariah [*The Regulation of Bank Indonesia* No 11/15/PBI/2009 on Converting the Conventional Bank into an Islamic Bank]

Peraturan Bank Indonesia Nomor 7/46/PBI/2005 Tentang Akad Penghimpunan dan Penyaluran Dana Bagi Bank yang Melaksanakan Kegiatan Usaha Berdasarkan Prinsip Syariah [*The Regulation of Bank Indonesia* No 7/46/PBI/2005 on the Deposit and Financing of Funds for Banks Conducting Business Based on Sharia Principles] (Indonesia)

Peraturan Kementerian Keuangan No 92/PMK.01/2017 Tentang Organisasi dan Tata Kerja Sekretariat Komite Stabilitas Sistem Keuangan [*Ministry of Finance Regulation No 92/PMK.01/2017 on the Organisation and Working Instructions of the Secretariat for the Financial System Stability Committee*] (Indonesia)

Peraturan Otoritas Jasa Keuangan No 18/POJK.03/2016 Tentang Penerapan Manajemen Resiko Bagi Bank Umum [*The Regulation of Financial Service Authority of Indonesia* No 18/POJK.03 of 2016 on Risk Management Practices for Commercial Banks]

Peraturan Otoritas Jasa Keuangan No 21/POJK.03/2014 Tentang Kewajiban Penyediaan Modal Minimum Bank Umum Syariah [*The Regulation of the Financial Service Authority* No 21/POJK.03/2014 on Minimum Capital Requirement for Islamic Commercial Banks] (Indonesia)

Peraturan Otoritas Jasa Keuangan No 24/POJK.03/2015 Tentang Produk dan Aktivitas Bank Syariah dan Unit Usaha Syariah [*The Regulation of Financial Service Authority of Indonesia* No 24/POJK.03/2015 on the Products and Services of Islamic Banks and Islamic Business Units]

Peraturan Otoritas Jasa Keuangan No 30/POJK.05/2014 Tentang Tata Kelola Perusahaan yang Baik Bagi Perusahaan Pembiayaan [*The Regulation of the Financial Service Authority of Indonesia* No 30/POJK.05/2014 on Good Corporate Governance for Financing Companies]

Peraturan Otoritas Jasa Keuangan No 65/POJK.03/2016 Tentang Penerapan Manajemen Resiko Bagi Bank Umum Syariah dan Unit Usaha Syariah [*The Regulation of Financial Service Authority of Indonesia* No 65/POJK.03 of 2016 on Risk Management Practice for Islamic Bank and Islamic Business Units] (Indonesia)

Peraturan Otoritas Jasa Keuangan Republik Indonesia No 11/POJK.03/2019 Tentang Prinsip Kehati-Hatian Dalam Aktivitas Sekuritisasi Aset Bagi Bank Umum [*The Regulation of the Financial Service Authority of Indonesia* No 11/POJK.03/2019 on Prudential Principles in Asset Securitisation Activities for Commercial Banks]

Peraturan Pemerintah No 72 Tahun 1992 Tentang Bank Berdasarkan Prinsip Bagi Hasil [*Government Regulation No 72 of 1992 on Banks Applying Profit Sharing Principles*]

'Pernyataan Standard Akuntansi Keuangan [Statement of Financial Accounting Standards]', *Akuntansi Mudharabah (Jakarta)* (2007) Ikatan Akuntan Indonesia, 105, 1–42.

Surat Edaran Bank Indonesia No 12/13/DPbS tentang Pelaksanaan Good Corporate Governance bagi Bank Umum Syariah dan Unit Usaha Syariah [*Circular of the Bank Indonesia* No. 12/13/DPbS on the Implementation of Good Corporate Governance for Islamic Commercial Banks and Islamic Business Units]

Malaysia

Central Bank of Malaysia Act 1958 (Act 519)

Central Bank of Malaysia Act 2009 (Act 701)

'Guidance Note on Issuance of Sukuk Wakala bi Al-Istithmar in Labuan International Business and Financial Centre', *Characteristics of Sukuk Wakala Bi Al-istithmar in Labuan IBFC (Labuan)* (2017) Labuan Financial Service Authority No 1, 6

Fatwas (Islamic legal verdicts)

European Council for Fatwa and Research, Final Statement of the Twelfth Ordinary 6–10 of Dhulqi'dah, 1423 AH (2003) www.e-cfr.org/blog/2014/01/31/2-12-البيان-الختامي

National Sharia Board of Indonesian Council of Ulama, *Fatwa No. 5/DSN-MUI/IV/2000 on Salam Transactions*, Indonesian Council of Ulama

National Sharia Board of Indonesian Council of Ulama, *Fatwa No. 6/DSN-MUI/IV/2000 on Istishna' Transaction*, Indonesian Council of Ulama

Nasional Sharia Board of Indonesian Council of Ulama, *Fatwa MUI No. 7/DSN-MUI/IV/2000 on Mudharabah Financing*, Indonesian Council of Ulama

National Sharia Board of Indonesian Council of Ulama, *Fatwa MUI No 13/DSN-MUI/2000 on Downpayment in Murabahah]*, Indonesian Council of Ulama

National Sharia Board of Indonesian Council of Ulama, *Fatwa MUI No 22/DSN-MUI/III/2002 on Istinshna' Paralel*, Indonesian Council of Ulama

National Sharia Board of Indonesian Council of Ulama, *Fatwa MUI No 28/DSN-MUI/III/2002 on Foreign Exchange Currency (Bay al-Sharf)*, Indonesian Council of Ulama.

National Sharia Board of Indonesian Council of Ulama, *Fatwa MUI No. 82/DSN-MUI/VIII/2011 Commodity Trading Based on Sharia Principles in the Commodity Exchange*, Indonesian Council of Ulama

National Sharia Board of Indonesian Council of Ulama, *Fatwa MUI No 85/DSN-MUI/XII/2012 on Promise (wa'ad) in Shariah Financial and Business Transactions*, Indonesian Council of Ulama

National Sharia Board of Indonesian Council of Ulama, *Fatwa MUI No 96/MUI/III/2015 on Islamic Version of Hedging Contract (tahawwut) Based on wa'ad (Unilateral Promise)*, Indonesian Council of Ulama

National Sharia Board of Indonesian Council of Ulama, *Fatwa MUI No 110/DSN-MUI/IX/2017 on Contracts in Transactions*, Indonesian Council of Ulama

OIC (Organisation of Islamic Conference), *Al-Qaraarat wa al-Tausiyat: Al-Dawra al-tasi'a 'Ashara li-Majma' al-fiqh al-Islami al-Duwali*, Majma' al-Fiqh al-Islami Al-Duwali, Jidda (2009)

International instruments

International agreements

Basel Committee on Banking Supervision, 'The Basel Framework' Bank for International Settlements, www.bis.org/basel_framework/

Basel Committee on Banking Supervision, 'Basel II: International Convergence of Capital Measurement and Capital Standards: A Revised Framework-Comprehensive Version' Bank for International Settlements, www.bis.org/publ/bcbs128.htm

Basel Committee on Banking Supervision, 'Basel III' Bank for International Settlement, www.bis.org/bcbs/basel3/b3summarytable.pdf

Basel Committee on Banking Supervision, 'Basel III: Finalising Post-Crisis Reforms' Bank for International Settlements, www.bis.org/bcbs/publ/d424.htm

Basel Committee on Banking Supervision, 'Consultative Document: Capital Requirements for Banks' Equity Investments in Funds' Bank for International Settlements, www.bis.org/publ/bcbs257.pdf

Basel Committee on Banking Supervision, 'Consultative Document: The New Basel Capital Accord' Bank for International Settlements, www.bis.org/publ/bcbsca02.htm

Basel Committee on Banking Supervision, 'Core Principles for Effective Banking Supervision' Bank for International Settlements, www.bis.org/publ/bcbs213.pdf

Basel Committee on Banking Supervision, 'Governors and Heads of Supervision finalise Basel III reforms' Bank for International Settlements, www.bis.org/press/p171207.htm

Basel Committee on Banking Supervision, 'Group of Governors and Heads of Supervision Announces Higher Global Minimum Capital Standards' Bank for International Settlements, www.bis.org/press/p100912.htm

Basel Committee on Banking Supervision, 'High-Level Summary of Basel III Reforms 'Bank for International Settlements', www.bis.org/bcbs/publ/d424_hlsummary.pdf

Basel Committee on Banking Supervision, 'History of the Basel Committee' Bank for International Settlements, www.bis.org/bcbs/history.htm

Basel Committee on Banking Supervision, 'Interest Rate Risk in the Banking Book' Bank for International Settlements, www.bis.org/bcbs/publ/d319.htm

Basel Committee on Banking Supervision, 'International Convergence of Capital Measurement and Capital Standards' Bank for International Settlements, www.bis.org/publ/bcbs04a.htm

Basel Committee on Banking Supervision, 'International Framework for Liquidity Risk Measurement, Standards and Monitoring' Bank for International Settlements, www.bis.org/publ/bcbs165.htm

Basel Committee on Banking Supervision, 'MAR 11 Definitions and Application of Market Risk' Bank for International Settlements, www.bis.org/basel_framework/chapter/MAR/11.htm?tldate=20220125&inforce=20220101&published=20191215

Basel Committee on Banking Supervision, 'The New Basel Capital Accord: An Explanatory Note' Bank for International Settlements, www.bis.org/publ/bcbsca01.pdf

Basel Committee on Banking Supervision, 'Operational Risk-Revisions to the Simpler Approaches' Bank for International Settlements, www.bis.org/publ/bcbs291.pdf

Basel Committee on Banking Supervision, 'Overview of Pillar 2 Supervisory Review Practices and Approaches' Bank for International Settlements, www.bis.org/bcbs/publ/d465.pdf

Basel Committee on Banking Supervision, 'Pillar 3 (Market Discipline)' Bank for International Settlements, www.bis.org/publ/bcbsca10.pdf

Basel Committee on Banking Supervision, 'Principle for the Management of Credit Risk' www.bis.org/publ/bcbsc125.pdf

Basel Committee on Banking Supervision, 'Principle of the Management of Credit Risk: Consultative Document' Bank for International Settlements, www.bis.org/publ/bcbs54.htm

Basel Committee on Banking Supervision, 'Principles for Sound Liquidity Risk Management and Supervision' Bank for International Settlements, www.bis.org/publ/bcbs144.htm

Basel Committee on Banking Supervision, 'Principles for the Sound Management of Operational Risk' Bank for International Settlements, www.bis.org/publ/bcbs195.pdf

Basel Committee on Banking Supervision, 'RBC Risk-Based Capital Requirements RBC20 Calculation of Minimum Risk-Based Capital Requirements' Bank for International Settlements, www.bis.org/basel_framework/chapter/RBC/20.htm?inforce=20191215

Basel Committee on Banking Supervision, 'Regulatory Treatment of Accounting Provisions' Bank for International Settlements, www.bis.org/bcbs/publ/d385.pdf

Basel Committee on Banking Supervision, 'Risk Management Principles for Electronic Banking' Bank for International Settlements, www.bis.org/publ/bcbs82.pdf

Basel Committee on Banking Supervision, 'Sound Practices for the Management and Supervision of Operational Risk' Bank for International Settlements, www.bis.org/publ/bcbs96.htm

Islamic Financial Services Board, 'Guiding Principles on Conduct of Business for Institutions Offering Islamic Financial Services' [2009] Islamic Financial Services Board

Islamic Financial Services Board, 'Guiding Principles on Corporate Governance for Institutions Offering Only Islamic Financial Services (Excluding Islamic Insurance (Takaful) Institutions and Islamic Mutual Funds)' [2006] Islamic Financial Services Board

Islamic Financial Services Board, 'Guiding Principles on Shari'ah Governance Systems for Institutions Offering Islamic Financial Services' [2009] Islamic Financial Services Board

Islamic Financial Services Board, 'IFSB-1 Guiding Principles of Risk Management for Institutions (Other Than Insurance Institutions) Offering only Islamic Financial Services' [2005] Islamic Financial Services Board

Islamic Financial Services Board, 'IFSB-2 Capital Adequacy Standard for Institutions (Other Than Insurance Institutions) Offerings Only Islamic Financial Services' [2002] Islamic Financial Service Board, www.ifsb.org/standard/ifsb2.pdf

Islamic Financial Services Board, 'IFSB-15 Revised Capital Adequacy Standard for Institutions Offering Islamic Financial Services [Excluding Islamic Insurance (Takaful) Institutions and Islamic Collective Investment Schemes]' [2013] Islamic Financial Services Board

Islamic Financial Services Board, 'IFSB-17 Core Principles for Islamic Finance Regulation (Banking Segment)' [2015] Islamic Financial Services Board

Technical Committee of IOSCO, 'Mitigating Systemic Risk: A Role for Securities Regulators' [2011] International Organization of Securities Commissions No OR01/11

Articles/Books/Reports/Working Papers/Theses

Abdul Ghafar, Ismail, 'Tawarruq Time Deposit with Wakalah Principle: An Option That Triggers New Issues' (2016) 9(3) *International Journal of Islamic and Middle Eastern Finance and Management* 388

Abdul Ghafar, Ismail, and Muhammad Hasan, 'Kitab Al-qawa'id Al-fiqhiyyah bayna Al-asyaalah wa At-tawjiih [Book of Jurisprudence Rules between Authenticity and Guidance]' *Ar-riqaaq wa al-adab wa al-azkar* [Kindness, Etiquette and Remembrance] (Al-Maktabah As-shaamilah Al-haditsah), https://al-maktaba.org/book/32391/181

Abdullah, Burhanuddin, and Wimboh Santoso, 'The Indonesian Banking Industry: Competition, Consolidation and Systemic Stability' (BIS Paper 4, Bank for International Settlements, 2001)

Abdullah, Wan Amalina Wan, Majella Percy, and Jenny D. Stewart, 'Sharia Disclosures in Malaysian and Indonesian Islamic Banks: The Shari'ah Governance System' (2013) 4(2) *Journal of Islamic Accounting and Business Research* 100

Abdullah, Zaitun, Barkah, and Rifkiyati Bachri, 'Hybrid Contract on Sharia Life Insurance in Indonesia' (Paper presented at the IOP Conference, Jakarta) https://iopscience.iop.org/article/10.1088/1755-1315/175/1/012129/pdf

Abu Hussain, Hameeda, and Jasim Al-Ajmi, 'Risk Management Practices of Conventional and Islamic Banks in Bahrain' (2012) 13(3) *The Journal of Risk Finance* 215

Abul, Hassan, and Mollah Sabur, *Islamic Finance: Ethical Underpinnings, Products, and Institutions* (Palgrave Macmillan, 2018)

Adnan, Muhammad Akhyar, and Muhamad Muhamad, 'Agency Problems in Mudarabah Financing: The Case of Sharia (Rural) Banks, Indonesia' (2007) 15(2) *IIUM International Journal of Economics, Management and Accounting* 219.

Affandi, Muchammad Taufiq, 'Profit Equalization Reserve and Investment Risk Reserve: Issues and Its Application' (2019) 5(2) *Islamic Economics Journal* 295

Ahmad, Abdelrahman Yousri, 'Does Islamic Banking Help in Economic Development of Muslim Countries' (2016) 6(2) *Journal of Islamic Business and Management* 19

Ahmad, Abu Umar Faruq, *Developments in Islamic Banking Practice: The Experience of Bangladesh* (Universal Publisher, 2010)

Ahmad, Abu Umar Faruq, and M. Kabir Hassan, 'The Time Value of Money Concept in Islamic Finance' (2006) 23(1) *American Journal of Islamic Social Sciences* 66

Ahmad, Abu Umar Faruq et al., 'Shari'ah Maxims and Their Implication on Modern Financial Transactions' (2010) 6(3) *Journal of Islamic Economics, Banking and Finance* 75

Ahmad, Ausaf, 'Contemporary Practices of Islamic Financing Techniques' (1994) 2(1) *Islamic Economic Studies*

Ahmad, Ellida Fauziah et al., 'The Acceptability of Tawarruq as a Product for Financing within the Islamic Banking System' (2017) 1 *International Journal of Management and Applied Research* 31

Ahmed, Habib, 'Islamic Law, Adaptability and Financial Development' (2006) 13(2) *Islamic Economic Studies* 79

Ahmed, Habib, 'Maqasid al-Shari'ah and Islamic Financial Products: A Framework for Assessment' (2011) 3(1) *ISRA International Journal of Islamic Finance* 149

Ahmed, Habib, 'Islamic Banking and Shari'ah Compliance: A Product Development Perspective' (2014) 3(2) *Journal of Islamic Finance, IIUM Institute of Islamic Banking and Finance* 15

Ahmed, Habib, Mehmet Asutay, and Rodney Wilson, *Islamic Banking and Financial Crisis: Reputation, Stability and Risks* (Edinburgh University Press, 2013)

Ahmed, Habib, and Tariqullah Khan, 'Risk Management in Islamic Banking', *Handbook of Islamic Banking* (Edward Elgar Publishing, 2007)

Ahroum, Rida, Othmane Touri, and Boujemaa Achchab, 'Murabaha and Musharakah Moutanaquissah Pricing: An Interest-Free Approach' (2020) 11(1) *Journal of Islamic Accounting and Business Research* 201

Akkizidis, Loannis, and Sunil Kumar Khandelwal, *Financial Risk Management for Islamic Banking and Finance* (Palgrave Macmillan, 2008)

Al-Ali, Salim, *Raising Capital on Sukuk Markets: Structural, Legal and Regulatory Issues* (Springer, 2019)

Alam, Nafis, 'The Impact of Regulatory and Supervisory Structures on Bank Risk and Efficiency: Evidence from Dual Banking System' (1 June 2012) 4(1) *Asian Journal of Finance & Accounting* 216

Alam, Nafis, Sara Sophia Binti Zainuddin, and Syed Aun R. Rizvi, 'Ramifications of Varying Banking Regulations on Performance of Islamic Banks' (2019) 19(1) *Borsa Istanbul Review* 46

Al-Amine, Muhammad, and Muhammad Al-Bashir, 'Sukuk Market: Innovations and Challenges' (2008) 15 *Islamic Economic Studies* 1

Aldabo, Ibrahim Fadel, *At-Tawarruq Haqiqatuhu, Anwa'uhu (Al-Fiqhu Al-Ma'ruf wa Al-Mashrafi Al-munazzam)* [*Tawarruq, Its Reality, Its Types (The Well-Known Jurisprudence and Organized Banking)*], https://ketabonline.com/ar/books/92555/read

Aldohni, Abdul Karim, *The Legal and Regulatory Aspects of Islamic Banking: A Comparative Look at the United Kingdom and Malaysia* (Routledge, 2011)

Aldoseri, Mahfod, and Andrew Worthington, 'Risk Management in Islamic Banking: An Emerging Market Imperative' in Sabri Boubaker, Bonnie G. Buchanan, and Duc Khuong Nguyen (eds), *Risk Management in Emerging Markets: Issues, Framework, and Modeling* (Emerald, 2016).

Al-hakim, Sofyan, 'Perkembangan regulasi perbankan syariah di Indonesia [The Development of Islamic Banking Regulation in Indonesia]' (2013) 13(1) *Ijtihad, Jurnal Wacana Hukum Islam dan Kemanusiaan* 15, 18

Alhammadi, Salah, Khaled Alotaibi, and Dzikri F. Hakam, 'Analysing Islamic Banking Ethical Performance from Maqasid al-Shari'ah Perspective: Evidence from Indonesia' (2020) *Journal of Sustainable Finance and Investment* 1

Ali, Abdullah bin Hamid, 'Scholarly Consensus: Ijma: Between Use and Misuse' (2010) 12(2) *Journal of Islamic Law & Culture* 92

Alkhamees, Ahmad A, *A Critique of Creative Shari'ah Compliance in the Islamic Finance Industry* (Brill | Nijhoff, 2017)

Al-kharsani, Muhammad Amin Al-husaini, *Taysiir at-Tahriir 'ala Kitaabi at-Tahriir fi Ushul al-Fiqh al-Jaami' bayna Isytilahii al-Hanafiyah wa al-Syafi'iyyah* [Facilitating the Refine of Kitab al-Tahriir That Combine the Hanafi and Shafi'i Terms] (Dar Al Kotob Al Ilmiyah, 2017)

Al-Misri, Rafiq Yunus, *Al-Riba wa al-Hasm al-Zamani fi al-Iqtisad al-Islami* [Riba and Time Decisive in the Islamic Economy] (Dar al-Maktabi, 2000).

Almuqaty, Mohammed Marzouq, *The Impact and Challenges of Basel III Implementation in Saudi Arabia* (PhD Thesis, Brunel University, 2018).

Alqahtani, Faisal, David G. Mayes, and Kym Brown, 'Economic Turmoil and Islamic Banking: Evidence from the Gulf Cooperation Council' (2016) 39 *Pacific-Basin Finance Journal* 44

Al Rahahleh, Naseem, Ishaq Bhatti, and Faridah Najuna Misman, 'Developments in Risk Management in Islamic Finance: A Review' (2019) 12(37) *Journal of Risk and Financial Management* 1

Alrifai, Tariq, *Islamic Finance and the New Financial System: An Ethical Approach to Preventing Future Financial Crises* (Wiley, 2015)

Al-Syatibi, Abu Ishaq Ibrahim Musa al-Gharnati al-Maliki, *al-Muwafaqat fi Usul al-Syari'ah* [Reconciliation of the Fundamentals of Islamic Law] (Dar al-Kutub al-'Ilmiyyah, 1991) vol. 2

Alwazna, Rafat Y., 'Islamic Law: Its Sources, Interpretation and the Translation of It into Laws Written in English' (2016) 29(2) *International Journal for the Semiotics of Law-Revue Internationale de Semiotique Juridique* 251

Al-Zarqa, Mustafa, *Nizam al-Ta'min: haqiqatuh, wa al-ra'y al-shar'i fih* [System of Insurance: Its Nature and the Sharia Perspective] (Mu'assasat Al-Risalah, 1994)

Al-Zuhayli, Wahbah, and M. El-Gamal, 'Financial Transactions in Islamic Jurisprudence: volume 1' (2003) *Islamic Jurisprudence and Its Proofs, Dar Al-Fikr, Damascus*

Al-Zumali, Fahad, and Mohammed Al-Wasmi, '2008 Financial Crisis and Islamic Finance: An Unrealized Opportunity' (2016) 29 *International Journal for the Semiotics of Law-Revue Internationale de Semiotique Juridique* 455

Amal, Alabbad, 'Essays on the Performance, Disclosure, and Corporate Governance of Islamic banks' (2015) https://doi.org/doi:10.7282/T3S46V07

Amaroh, Siti, and Masturin, 'The Determinants of Maqasid Shariah Based Performance of Islamic Banks in Indonesia' (2018) 11(1) *Jurnal Iqtishadia Kajian Ekonomi dan Bisnis Islam* 354

Amin, Ma'ruf, '*Solusi Hukum Islam (Makharij Fiqhiyah) Sebagai Pendorong Arus Baru Ekonomi Syariah di Indonesia* [Islamic Legal Solutions (*Makharij Fiqhiyah*) as a Driving Force for the New Flow of Sharia Economy in Indonesia]' (Scientific Oration State Islamic University of Maulana Malik Ibrahim, 2017)

Amir, Shahruddin, 'Is Bay Al-Tawarruq Better Alternative in Fulfilling Islamic Finance Objectives?', *In Celebrating 30 Years of Islamic Banking and Finance Institutions in Malaysia* (Unit Penerbitan USIM, 2013) 1983–2013

Anas, Malik ibn, *Al-Muwatta' of Imam Malik ibn Anas* (Aisha Abdurrahman Bewley trans, Diwan Press, 2014).

Ansari, Omar Mustafa, 'Central Shari'ah Board' (Paper presented at the World Bank 11th Annual Conference on Islamic Banking and Finance, Bahrain), http://aaoifi.com/wp-content/uploads/2016/11/Mr.-Omar-Ansari-Central-Shariah-Board-for-AAOIFI-WB-conference-November-2016-v4.pdf

Anshori, Abdul Ghofur, *Perbankan Syariah di Indonesia* [Islamic Banking in Indonesia] (Gadjah Mada University Press, 2018)

Antonio, Muhammad Syafii, and Aam Slamet Rusydiana, 'What Is the Future Outlook of Shariah Harmonization?' (2010) 33(70) *Jurnal Dialog Balitbang, Kementerian Agama RI* 1

Antonio, Muhammad Syafii, Yuliar D. Sanrego, and Muhammad Taufiq, 'An Analysis of Islamic Banking Performance: Maqashid Index Implementation in Indonesia and Jordania' (2012) 1(1) *Journal of Islamic Finance*

Anwer, Zaheer, and Farrukh Habib, 'Re-Visiting Current Debate on Shari'ah Position of Derivatives' (2019) 9(1) *Journal of Islamic Business and Management* 64

Apătăchioae, Adina, 'The Performance, Banking Risks and Their Regulation' (2015) 20 *Procedia Economics and Finance* 35

Archer, Simon, *Islamic Capital Markets and Products* (Wiley, 1st edition, 2017).

Archer, Simon, and Rifaat Ahmed Abdel Karim, 'Profit-Sharing Investment Accounts in Islamic Banks: Regulatory Problems and Possible Solutions' (9 September 2009) 10(4) *Journal of Banking Regulation* 300

Arfazadeh, Homayoon, 'A Practitioner's Approach to Interest Claims under Sharia Law in International Arbitration' in Filip De Ly and Laurent Levy (eds), *Interest, Auxiliary and Alternative Remedies in International Arbitration* (International Chamber of Commerce, 2008).

Arif, Ahmed, and Ahmed Nauman Anees, 'Liquidity Risk and Performance of Banking System' (Pt Emerald Group Publishing Limited) (2012) 20(2) *Journal of Financial Regulation and Compliance* 182

Ariffin, Noraini Mohd, and Salina Kassim, 'Risk Management Practices of Selected Islamic Banks in Malaysia' (2014) 3(1) *Aceh International Journal of Social Sciences* 26

Arofa, Aini Silvy, 'Regulasi Terkait Pengawasan Terhadap Penerapan Prinsip-prinsip Syariah pada Lembaga Keuangan Syariah [Regulations on Sharia-Compliant Supervision in Islamic Financial Institutions]' (2014) 6(2) *Jurnal Hukum Islam dan Bisnis* 229

As, Fariz, *Tinjauan Hukum Islam Terhadap Praktik Denda Keterlambatan di Perbankan Syariah (Studi Murabahah di Bank Syariah Mandiri Semarang) [The Practice of Penalty Fee in Islamic Banking Based on Islamic Law (Case Study of Murabahah Business Contract at Bank Syariah Mandiri Semarang)]* (Universitas Negeri Semarang, 2018)

Ascarya, and Diana Yumanita, *Bank Syariah* [Islamic Bank] (Pusat Pendidikan dan Studi Kebanksentralan 2005)

Asmadi Mohamed, Naim, Isa Mohamad Yazid, and Mohd Liki Hamid, 'The Effects of New AAOIFI Standards on Sukuk in Choosing the Most Authentic Islamic Principles' (Pt Emerald Group Publishing Limited) (2013) 4(1) *Journal of Islamic Accounting and Business Research* 77

Asni, Fathullah, and Jasni Sulong, 'Non-Ethical Elements in Tawarruq Munazzam Product for Islamic Housing Financing in Malaysia' (2018) 8(12) *International Journal of Academic Research in Business and Social Sciences* 1013

Asutay, Mehmet, 'Conceptualising and Locating the Social Failure of Islamic Finance: Aspirations of Islamic Moral Economy vs. the Realities of Islamic Finance' (2012) 11(2) *Asian and African Area Studies Journal* 93

Bacha, Obiyathulla Ismath, *Financial Derivatives Markets and Application in Malaysia* (McGraw-Hill, 2001)

Bacha, Obiyathulla Ismath, 'Dual Banking Systems and Interest Rate Risk for Islamic Banks' (2004) 8(1) *The Journal of Accounting, Commerce and Finance: Islamic Perspective* 1

Bacha, Obiyathulla Ismath, Abbas Mirakhor, and Noureddine Krichene, *Islamic Capital Markets: A Comparative Approach* (John Wiley & Sons, 2013).

Badri, Muhammad Arifin, 'Mencari Solusi Bank Syariah [Finding the Solution for Islamic Bank]', *Majalah As-Sunnah* (Surakarta).

Baehaqi, Ahmad, 'Usulan Model Sistem Pengawasan Syariah Pada Perbankan Syariah di Indonesia [Proposed Model of Sharia Supervision System in Islamic Banking in Indonesia]' (2014) 1(2) *Jurnal Dinamika Akuntasi dan Bisnis* 119

Bahari, Zakaria, Zahri Hamat, and Mutiara Dwi Sari, 'History of Islamic Bank in Indonesia: Issues Behind Its Establishment' (2016) 2(5) *International Journal of Finance and Banking Research* 178

Bank Indonesia, *Pemetaan Hasil Penelitian Potensi, Preferensi, dan Perilaku Masyarakat Terhadap Bank Syariah di Indonesia* [Potency, Preference, and People's Behaviour Toward Islamic Bank in Indonesia: A Compilation] (Bank Indonesia, 2005)

Banyopadhyay, Arindan, *Managing Portfolio Credit Risk in Banks: An Indian Perspective* (Cambridge University Press, 2016)

Barnes, Matthew R., *Banking Regulation and the Basel III Accord: An Examination of the Risks and Shortcomings Posed by Basel III* (University of Wolverhampton, 2019)

Bellalah, Mondher, and Omar Masood, *Islamic Banking and Finance* (Cambridge Scholars Publisher, 2013)

Bhatti, Maria, *Islamic Law and International Commercial Arbitration* (Routledge, 2018)

Bhatti, Maria, and Ishaq Bhatti, 'Development in Legal Issues of Corporate Governance in Islamic Finance' (Pt Al-Ain: Emerald Group Publishing Limited) (2009) 25(1) *Journal of Economic and Administrative Sciences* 67

Bischof, Jannis, 'The Effects of IFRS 7 Adoption on Bank Disclosure in Europe' (2009) 6(2) *Accounting in Europe* 167

Bitar, Mohammad et al., 'The Performance of Islamic Vs. Conventional Banks: Evidence on the Suitability of the Basel Capital Ratios' (2018) 29 *Open Economies Review* 1003

Boudjellal, Mohammed, 'Three Decades of Experimentation: Rethinking the Theory of Islamic Banking' (2006) 10(1) *Review of Islamic Economics* 23

Bouheni, Faten Ben, Chantal Ammi, and Aldo Levy, *Banking Governance, Performance and Risk-Taking: Conventional Banks vs Islamic Banks* (John Wiley & Sons, 2016)

Boukhatem, Jamel, and Fatma Ben Moussa, 'The Effect of Islamic Banks on GDP Growth: Some Evidence from Selected MENA Countries' (2018) 18(3) *Borsa Istanbul Review* 231

Boumediene, Aniss, and Jerome Caby, 'The Stability of Islamic Banks during the Subprime Crisis' (Pt SSRN) (2009), https://papers.ssrn.com/sol3/papers.cfm?abstract_id=1524775

Bouslama, Ghassen, and Younes Lahrichi, 'Uncertainty and Risk Management from Islamic Perspective' (2017) 39 *Research in International Business and Finance* 718

Boyd, John H., Gianni De Nicolo, and Smith Bruce D., 'Crises in Competitive versus Monopolistic Banking Systems' (2004) 36(3) *Journal of Money, Credit, and Banking* 487

Breuer, Luis, Jaime Guajardo, and Tidiane Kinda, 'Chapter 13, Reinforcing Financial Stability' in *Realizing Indonesia's Economic Potential* (International Monetary Fund, 2018)

Brito, José Almeida, and Kose John, 'Leverage and Growth Opportunities: Risk-Avoidance Induced by Risky Debt' [1] (2002) *SSRN Electronic Journal* 1

Bruinessen, Martin Van, 'Wahhabi Influences in Indonesia, Real and Imagined', *Journée d'Etudes Wahhabisme* (Leiden), www.archivesaudiovisuelles.msh-paris.fr/11/163/Martin_Van_Bruinessen-7.pdf

Bukhari, Naseem, 'Islamic Banking Theory, Practice and Challenges' (2006) 1(1) *The Journal of Commerce* 85

Burhanudin, J., *Ulama dan Kekuasaan: Pergumulan Elite Politik Muslim Dalam Sejarah Indonesia* [Ulama and Power: The Struggle of Muslim Political Elite in Indonesian History] (Mizan, 2012)

Chakroun, Mohamed Amin, Saber Sebai and Mohamed Imen Gallali, 'Market Risk in Islamic and Conventional Banks' (2016) 5 *International Journal of Business and Commerce* 66

Chapra, Muhammad Umer, *Towards a Just Monetary System* (International Institute of Islamic Thought, 1985) vol. 8

Chapra, Muhammad Umer, 'The Case against Riba: Is It Compelling?' in Salman Syed Ali and Ausaf Ahmad (eds), *Islamic Banking and Finance: Fundamentals and Contemporary Issues* (Islamic Research and Training Institute, 2007)

Chockalingam, Arun, Shaunak Dabadghao, and Rene Soetekouw, 'Strategic Risk, Banks and Basel III: Estimating Economic Capital Requirements' (2018) 19(3) *Journal of Risk Finance* 225

Chong, Beng Soon, and Ming-Hua Liu, 'Islamic Banking: Interest-Free or Interest-Based?' (2009) 17(1) *Pacific-Basin Finance Journal* 125

Choudhury, Masudul Alam, 'Islamic Economics and Finance: A Fiasco' (2008) 20(1) *The Middle East Business and Economic Review* 38

Chowdhury, Mohammad Ashraful, and Rahman Syed, 'The Effect of Conventional Bank's Interest Rate & Islamic Bank's Profit Rate on Investment & Return: An Empirical Investigation in Bangladesh' (2014) 5(1) *Asia-Pacific Journal of Business* 33

Dalimartha, Felix, and Faisal Santiago, 'Banking Legislation Renewal as a Preventive Effort of Banking Corruption Crime' (Proceedings of the 1st International Conference on Law, Social Science, Economics, and Education, ICLSSEE 2021, 6 March 2021, Jakarta, Indonesia.

Damodaran, Aswath, 'Value and Risk: Beyond Betas' (2005) 61(2) *Financial Analysts Journal* 38

Dar, Humayon, *Global Islamic Finance Report 2010* (Cambridge Institute of Islamic Finance, 2010)

Darsono et al., 'Dynamics of Financing Products and Contracts' in Muhammad Syafii Antonio (ed), *Dynamics of Islamic Finance Products and Contracts in Indonesia* (Tazkia Publishing, 2012) 1–477

Das, Satyajit, *Derivatives Product and Pricing* (John Wiley and Sons, 3rd edition, 2006)

Dau-Schmidt, Nicholas C., 'Forward Contracts: Prohibitions on Risk and Speculation under Islamic Law' (2012) 19(2) *Indiana Journal of Global Legal Studies* 533

Djamil, Fathurrahman, *Metode Ijtihad Majlis Tarjih Muhammadiyah* [The Method of Ijtihad of Majlis Tarjih Muhammadiyah] (Logos, 1995)

Dusuki, Asyraf Wajdi, 'Commodity Murabahah Program (CMP): An Innovative Approach to Liquidity Management' (Paper presented at the 5th International Islamic Finance Conference, organized by Monash University-Kuala Lumpur, 3–4 September 2007)

Dusuki, Asyraf Wajdi, and Abdulazeem Abozaid, 'A Critical Appraisal on the Challenges of Realizing Maqasid al-Shari'ah in Islamic Banking and Finance' (2007) 15(2) *IIUM Journal of Economics and Management* 143

Dusuki, Asyraf Wajdi, and Edib Smolo, 'Islamic Hedging: Rationale, Necessity, and Challenges' (Paper presented at the International Seminar on Muamalat, Islamic Economics and Finance (SMEKI 09), Kuala Lumpur, 20–21 October 2009)

Dwiputrianti, Septiana, 'Memahami Strategi Pemberantasan Korupsi di Indonesia [Understanding the Strategy for Eradicating Corruption in the Case of Indonesia]' (2009) 6(3) *Jurnal Ilmu Administrasi* 256

El-Gamal, Mahmoud A., 'Discussion Forum: Islamic Financial Derivatives' (1999) 1(1) *IJIFS*

El-Gamal, Mahmoud A., 'Interest and the Paradox of Contemporary Islamic Law and Finance' (2003) 27 *Fordham International Law Journal* 108

El-Gamal, Mahmoud A., *Islamic Finance: Law, Economics, and Practice* (Cambridge University Press, 2006)

Ercanbrack, Jonathan G., *The Law of Islamic Finance in the United Kingdom: Legal Pluralism and Financial Competition* (PhD Thesis, University of London, 2011)

Ercanbrack, Jonathan, G., 'The Standardization of Islamic Financial Law: Lawmaking in Modern Financial Markets' (2019) 67(4) *The American Journal of Comparative Law* 825

Errico, Luca, and Mitra Farahbaksh, *Islamic Banking: Issues in Prudential Regulations and Supervision*, IMF Working Paper No 98/30, International Monetary Fund (1998)

Esposito, John L., and Natana J. DeLong-Bas, *Shariah: What Everyone Needs to Know* (Oxford University Press, 2018)

Faisal, Yudi Ahmad, 'Islamic Derivatives in Indonesia: A Study on Indonesian Ulama Council (MUI)'s Fatwa on Tahawwut (Hedging)' (2016) 2 *Islam Ekonomisi Ve Finansi Dergisi* 35

Farikhah, Itsna Nur, *Implementasi Peran dan Fungsi Dewan Pengawas Syariah (DPS) pada Koperasi Simpan Pinjam Pembiayaan Syariah (KSPSS) (Study Kasus di Forum Koperasi Syariah Bojonegoro)* [The Implementation of Role and Functions of Sharia Supervisory Board at Islamic

Financial Cooperation, Case Study at Bojonegoro] (Universitas Islam Negeri Walisongo, 2018), http://eprints.walisongo.ac.id/8161/1/132311074.pdf

Fauzia, Amelia, 'Antara Hitam dan Putih: Penghulu pada Masa Kolonial Belanda [Caught between three fires: The Javanese Pengulu Under the Dutch Colonial Administration]' (2003) 10(2) *Indonesian Journal for Islamic Studies* 24, 175

Fealy, Greg, and Robin Bush, 'The Political Decline of Traditional Ulama in Indonesia: The State, Umma and Nahdlatul Ulama' (2014) 42(5) *Asian Journal of Social Science* 536

Fianto, Bayu Arie et al., 'Customer Loyalty to Islamic Banks: Evidence from Indonesia' (2020) 7(1) *Cogent Business & Management* 1

Fuad, Ahmad Masfuful, 'Qiyas Sebagai Salah Satu Metode Istinbat al-Hukm [Qiyas as One of the Way of Inference]' (2016) 15(1) *Jurnal Penelitian Hukum Islam Mazahib* 42

Gayo, Akhyar Ari, *Laporan Akhir Penelitian Hukum tentang Kedudukan Fatwa MUI dalam Upaya Mendorong Pelaksanan Ekonomi Syariah* [The Final Report on the Status of Fatwa MUI in Support of Islamic Financial Activities], Ministry of Law and Human Right Republic of Indonesia No. 4 (2011)

Gayo, Akhyar Ari, '*Dinamika Legislasi Hukum Islam: Analisa Atas Upaya Pembentukan Hukum Perikatan Syariah* [Islamic Law Legislation Dynamic: Analysis on the Means of Forming Sharia Law of Obligations]' [485] (2015) 4(3) *Jurnal Rechtsvinding* 15

Ghafur, W. Muhammad, 'Pengaruh Fatwa MUI Tentang Keharaman Bunga/Interest Terhadap Perkembangan Perbankan Syariah di Indonesia [The Influence of MUI Fatwa on the Prohibition of Banking Interest in the Development of Islamic Banking in Indonesia]' (2008) 17(2) *Jurnal Penelitian Agama* 355

Ghoni, Abdul, *Islamic Wisdom* (Elex Media Komputindo, 2018)

Goodhart, Charles, Philipp Hartmann, David T. Llewellyn, Liliana Rojas-Suarez, and Steven Weisbrod, *Financial Regulation: Why, How, and Where Now?* (Routledge, 1998)

Grassa, Rihab, 'Shariah Supervisory System in Islamic Financial Institutions: New Issues and Challenges: A Comparative Analysis between Southeast Asia Models and GCC Models' (Pt Emerald) (2013) 29(4) *Humanomics* 333

Grassa, Rihab, 'Shariah Supervisory Systems in Islamic Finance Institutions across the OIC Member Countries' (Pt Emerald Group Publishing Limited) (2015) 23(2) *Journal of Financial Regulation and Compliance* 135

Grassa, Rihab, and Kouthar Gazdar, 'Law and Islamic Finance: How Legal Origins Affect Islamic Finance Development?' (2014) 14(3) *Borsa Istanbul Review* 158

Hadi, Ahmad Chairul, '*Problematika Pembiayaan Mudharabah di Perbankan Syariah Indonesia* [The Problems of Mudharabah Contract in Indonesian Islamic Banking]' (2011) 3(2) *Al-Iqtishad: Jurnal Ilmu Ekonomi Syariah* 193

Hakim, Rahmat, 'Harmonization of Shariah Rulings in Islamic Finance: An Analysis' (2013) 7(2) *Ijtihad Journal of Law and Islamic Economics* 267

Hallaq, Wael B., 'Was the Gate of Ijtihad Closed?' (1984) 16(1) *International Journal of Middle East Studies* 3

Hallaq, Wael B., *Shari'a: Theory, Practice, Transformations* (Cambridge University Press, 2009)

Hamdaoui, Mekki, and Samir Maktouf, 'Financial Reforms and Banking System Vulnerability: The Role of Regulatory Frameworks' (2020) 52 *Structural Change and Economic Dynamics* 184

Hameed, Shahul Mohamed Ibrahim, *IE 2002: Reporting of Islamic Financial Transactions* (International Centre for Education Islamic Finance, 2012)

Hamilton, James D., and Charles H. Whiteman, 'The Observable Implications of Self-Fulfilling Expectations' (1985) 16(3) *Journal of Monetary Economics* 353

Hamza, Hichem, 'Sharia Governance in Islamic Banks: Effectiveness and Supervision Model' (2013) 6(3) *International Journal of Islamic and Middle Eastern Finance and Management* 226

Haron, Abdullah, and John Lee Hin Hock, 'Inherent Risk: Credit and Market Risks' in Simon Archer and Rifaat Ahmed Abdel Karim (eds), *Islamic Finance: The Regulatory Challenge* (Wiley, 2012)

Haron, Sudin, *Islamic Finance and Banking System: Philosophies, Principles & Practices* (McGraw Hill, 2009)

Harrison, Tina, and Essam B. Ibrahim, *Islamic Finance: Principles, Performance and Prospects* (Springer International Publishing AG, 2016)

Hasan, Ahmad, 'The Principle of Istihsan in Islamic Jurisprudence' (Pt Islamic Research Institute, International Islamic University, Islamabad) (1977) 16(4) *Islamic Studies* 347

Hassan, Kabir M., and Mehmet F. Dicle, 'Basel II and Regulatory Framework for Islamic Banks' (2005) 1(1) *Journal of Islamic Economics, Banking and Finance* 1, 16

Hasan, Maher, and Jemma Dridi, 'The Effects of the Global Crisis on Islamic and Conventional Banks: A Comparative Study' (2011) 2(2) *Journal of International Commerce, Economics and Policy* 163

Heffernan, Shelagh A., *Modern Banking* (Wiley, 2020)

Hegazy, Walid S., 'Contemporary Islamic Finance: From Socioeconomic Idealism to Pure Legalism. (Symposium: Islamic Business and Commercial Law)' (2007) 7(2) *Chicago Journal of International Law* 581

Hellyer, H.A., *The Once and Future Azhar: On the Credibility of Sunni Islam's Preeminent Institution* (5 October 2017), www.abc.net.au/religion/the-once-and-future-azhar-on-the-credibility-of-sunni-islams-pre/10095336

Helmy, Mohamed, *Risk Management in Islamic Banks* (Thesis for Master of International Business Administration, ESLSCA Business School, 2012), https://mpra.ub.uni-muenchen.de/38706/1/MPRA_paper_38706.pdf

Hidayat, Rachmad, '*Santri, Kyai*, and *Ulama*: Framing Masculinities within Indonesian Religious Elites' (paper presented at the International Workshop on Masculinities in Asia, Singapore), www.researchgate.net/publication/313644523_Santri_Kyaiand_Ulama_Framing_Masculinities_within_Indonesian_Religius_Elites

Hillier, H. Chad, 'Muhammad Iqbal on Al-Fiqh: Towards a Natural Law Jurisprudence' (2010) 12(3) *Journal of Islamic Law and Culture* 258

Hisyam, Muhammad, *Caught between Three Fires: The Javanese Pangulu under the Dutch Colonial Administration, 1882–1942* (Universiteit Leiden, 2001) vol. 37

Hoebel, E. Adamson, *The Law of Primitive Man: A Study in Comparative Legal Dynamics* (Harvard University Press, 2009)

Hohl, Stefan et al., *The Basel Framework in 100 Jurisdictions: Implementation Status and Proportionality Practices* (Financial Stability Institute, 2018) vol. 11

Hooker, M.B., 'Islam and Medical Science: Evidence from Malaysian and Indonesian Fatwas, 1960–1995' (1997) 4(4) *Studia Islamika* 1

Hooker, M.B., *Indonesian Islam: Social Change Through Contemporary Fatwa* (University of Hawaii Press, 2003)

Hoq, Mohammad Ziaul, Nigar Sulatana, and Muslim Amin, 'The Effect of Trust, Customer Satisfaction and Image on Customers' Loyalty in Islamic Banking Sector' (Pt South Asian Journal of Management) (2010) 17(1) *South Asian Journal of Management* 70

Hornick, Robert N., 'Foreign Banking in Indonesia' (1984) 6(3) *Northwestern Journal of International Law & Business* 760

Hosen, Muhamad Nadratuzzaman, and Amirah Ahmad Nahrawi, 'Comparative Analysis of Islamic Banking Products between Malaysia and Indonesia' (2012) 1(2) *International Journal of Academic Research in Economics and Management Sciences* 120

Hosen, Nadirsyah, 'Behind the Scenes: Fatwas of Majelis Ulama Indonesia (1975–1998)' (2004) 15(2) *Journal of Islamic Studies* 147

Hussainey, Khaled, and Sherif El-Halaby, 'Determinants of Compliance with AAOIFI Standards by Islamic Banks' (Pt Emerald) (2016) 9(1) *International Journal of Islamic and Middle Eastern Finance and Management* 143

Ibrahim, Uzaimah, Aishath Muneeza, and Rusni Hassan, 'Conflicts Facing Islamic Banking in Malaysia: Dual Banking System Versus Dual Legal System' (2012) 6(11) *Australian Journal of Basic and Applied Sciences* 246

Idris, Miftah, 'Strengthening Risk Management of Sharia Banking in Indonesia' (2019) 3(1) *Madani Legal Review* 1

Imamah, Iin Fadilatul, 'Penentuan Nisbah Bagi Hasil Pada Pembiayaan Mudharabah dan Perlakuan Akuntansinya (Studi Kasus pada KSPPS BMT NU Cabang Wringin Kabupaten Bondowoso) [The Determinant of Profit Sharing Ratio on Mudharabah Financing and Its Accounting Treatment (Case Study at KSPPS BMT NU Branch Wringin, Bondowoso Regency)]' (2019) 8(2) *E-Jurnal Ekonomi dan Bisnis Universitas Udayana* 199

Injadat, Ehab M., 'Futures and Forwards Contracts from Perspective of Islamic Law' (2014) 1(2) *Journal of Economics and Political Economy* 241

International Monetary Fund, *Indonesia: Financial System Stability Assessment*, International Monetary Fund No IMF Country Report No. 17/152 (2017)

International Monetary Fund, and World Bank, 'Republic of Indonesia Financial Sector Assessment' (World Bank, 2017)

Iqbal, Zamir, and Abbas Mirakhor, *An Introduction to Islamic Finance: Theory and Practice* (John Wiley & Sons, 2011)

IRTI, *Resolutions and Recommendations of the Council of the Islamic Fiqh Academy 1985–2000* (Islamic Research and Training Institute, 2000)

Islahi, Abdul Azim, 'History of Islamic Banking and Finance' (2018) 26(2) *Intellectual Discourse* 403

Ismail, Abdul Ghafar, and Shahida Shahimi, 'Do Risk-Based Capital Requirements Allocate Financing and Cause a "Bigger" Loan Loss Provision for Islamic Banks?' (2002) 4(1) *IQTISAD Journal of Islamic Economics* 1

Ismal, Rifki, *Islamic Banking in Indonesia: New Perspectives on Monetary and Financial Issues* (John Wiley & Sons, 2013)

Iswanaji, Chaidir, 'Challenges Inhibiting Islamic Banking Growth in Indonesia Using the Analytical Hierarchy Process' (2018) 4(2) *Journal of Islamic Economics Lariba* 97

Jamal, Mulyono, and Muhammad Abdul Aziz, 'Metodologi Istinbath Muhammadiyah dan NU: (Kajian Perbandingan Majelis Tarjih dan Lajnah Bahtsul Masail) [Methodology of *Istinbath* in Muhammadiyah and NU: The Comparative Analysis between *Majlis Tarjih* and *Lajnah Bahtsul Masail*]' (2013) 7(2) *Jurnal hukum dan Ekonomi Islam*

James, Christopher, and Joel Houston, 'Evolution or Extinction: Where Are Banks Headed?' (1996) 9(2) *Journal of Applied Corporate Finance* 8

Jobst, Andreas A., 'Derivatives in Islamic Finance: There Is No Right Way to Do the Wrong Thing: Opportunities for Investors' (2013) 22(1) *Journal of Investing* 7

Johnson, Toni, and Lauren Vriens, 'Islam: Governing Under Sharia' (2014) 25 *Council on Foreign Relations*

Johnston, Donald, Bubbles in Our Future? Certainly! (8 September 2018) *The OECD Observer*

Jonas, Oliveira, Lúcia Lima Rodrigues, and Russell Craig, *Risk Reporting: A Literature Review*, Working Paper, iMARKE – Documentos de Trabalho (2013), http://hdl.handle.net/1822/23683

Kabir Hassan, M. et al., 'A Survey on Islamic Finance and Accounting Standards' (2019) 19 *Borsa Istanbul Review* S1

Kamali, Mohammad Hashim, '"Maqasid Al-Shari'ah": The Objectives of Islamic Law' (Pt Islamic Research Institute, International Islamic University, Islamabad) (1999a) 38(2) *Islamic Studies* 193

Kamali, Mohammad Hashim, 'Prospects for an Islamic Derivative Market in Malaysia' (1999b) 4 *Thenderbird International Business Review*

Kamali, Mohammad Hashim, 'Istiḥsān and the Renewal of Islamic Law' (2004) 43(Winter) *Islamic Studies* 561

Kammer, Alfred et al., IMF Staff Discussion Note, *Islamic Finance: Opportunities, Challenges, and Policy Options*, International Monetary Fund No SDN/15/05 (2015)

Karim, Adiwarman, and Adi Zakaria Affif, 'Islamic Banking Consumer Behaviour in Indonesia: A Qualitative Approach' (paper presented at the 7th International Conference on Islamic Economics, Jakarta), www.academia.edu/download/34809212/27_Adiwarman_and_Adi_Zakaria_Islamic_Banking_Consumer.pdf

Karim, Rifaat Ahmed Abdel, and Simon Archer, *Islamic Finance: The Regulatory Challenge* (Wiley, 2011)

Karim, Wazir Jahan, 'The Economic Crisis, Capitalism and Islam: The Making of a New Economic Order?' (2010) 7(1–2) *Globalizations* 105

Kasri, Rahmatina A., and Salina H.J. Kassim, 'Empirical Determinants of Saving in the Islamic Banks: Evidence from Indonesia' (2009) 22(2) *Journal of King Abdulaziz University: Islamic Economics* 3

Kersten, Carool, *History of Islam in Indonesia: Unity in Diversity* (Ediburgh University Press, 2017)

Khan, Asad et al., 'Comparative Analysis of Regulatory and Supervisory System of Islamic Banks: Evidence from Pakistan, Malaysia, Bahrain, and United Kingdom' (2015) 6(6) *Mediterranean Journal of Social Sciences* 32, 629

Khan, Feisal, 'How "Islamic" is Islamic Banking?' (2010) 76(3) *Journal of Economic Behaviour & Organization* 805

Khan, Ghazala Ghalib, and Zafar Atiq uz, 'Fatwa Institution and Product Development for Islamic Finance in Pakistan' (Pt Pluto Journals) (2019) 16(2) *Policy Perspectives* 107

Khan, L. Ali, 'The Qur'an and the Constitution' (2010) 85 *Tulane Law Review*161

Khan, M. Mansoor, and M. Ishaq Bhatti, 'Islamic Banking and Finance: On Its Way to Globalization' (2008) 34(10) *Managerial Finance* 708

Khan, Mubbsher Munawar et al., 'Comparative Analysis of Islamic and Prevailing Insurance Practices' (2011) 2(10) *International Journal of Business and Social Science* 282

Khan, Muhammad Akram, *What Is Wrong with Islamic Economics? Analysing the Present State and Future Agenda* (Edward Elgar Publishing, 2013)

Khan, Muhammad Fahim, *Islamic Futures and Their Markets* (Islamic Research and Training Institute, 1997)

Khan, Tariqullah, and Habib Ahmed, 'Risk Management, an Analysis of Issues in Islamic Financial Industry' (Pt Islamic Development Bank) (2001) 91(9) *Islamic Research and Training Institute (IRTI)* 183

Kroszner, Randall S., 'Strategic Risk Management in an Interconnected World' (Paper presented at the Risk Management Association Annual Risk Management Conference, Baltimore, Maryland, 20 October 2008), www.bis.org/review/r081023b.pdf

Kunhibava, Sherin, and Balachandran Shanmugam, 'Sharī'ah and Conventional Law Objections to Derivatives: A Comparison' (2010) 24(4) *Arab Law Quarterly* 319

Kureshi, Hussain, *Contracts and Deals in Islamic Finance: A User's Guide to Cash Flows, Balance Sheets, and Capital Structures* (Wiley, 2015)

La Porta, Rafael et al., 'Law and Finance' (1998) 106(6) *Journal of Political Economy* 1113

Levi-Faur, David, and Ilana Blumsack, *Mapping Global Financial Institutions* (Global Governance and the European Union 2020)

Lewis, Marvyn K., Muhamed Ariff, and Shamsher Mohamad, *Risk and Regulation of Islamic Banking* (Edward Elgar Publishing, 2014)

Lindsey, Tim, 'Between Piety and Prudence: State Syariah and the Regulation of Islamic Banking in Indonesia' (2012) 34(1) *The Sydney Law Review* 107

Lubis, Aminah, 'Aplikasi Murabahah Dalam Perbankan Syariah [The Application of Murabahah in Islamic Banking]' (2016) 2(2) *Jurnal Kajian Ilmu-ilmu Keislaman* 181

Machiraju, H.R., *Modern Commercial Banking* (New Age International, 2008)

Magnus, M. et al., 'Upgrading the Basel Standards: From Basel III to Basel IV?' (PE 587 Economic Governance Support Unit, European Parliament Briefing Paper, October 2017)

Maimun, Maimun, '*Rekonstruksi Konsep Ijmak dalam Berijtihad di Era Modern* [Reconstructing the Concept of Consensus in Legal Reasoning at the Modern Period]' (2018) 10(2) *Journal of Law and Economics, ASAS* 1, 46

Majelis Ulama Indonesia, *Himpunan Keputusan dan Fatwa Majelis Ulama Indonesia* [The Compilation of Fatwa of Majelis Ulama Indonesia (MUI)] (Sekretariat MUI, Masjid Istiqlal, 1995)

Maksum, Muhammad, 'The Sharia Compliance of Islamic Multi Contract in Islamic Banking' (2017) 162 *Social Science, Education and Humanities Research* 154

Malaka, Mashur, 'Praktek Monopoli dan Persaingan Usaha [The Monopoly Market and Business Competition]' (July 2014) 7(2) *Jurnal Al-'Adl* 14, 39

Malik, Muhammad Shaukat, Ali Malik, and Waqas Mustafa, 'Controversies That Make Islamic Banking Controversial: An Analysis of Issues and Challenges' (2011) 2(1) *American Journal of Social and Management Sciences* 41

Malim, Moinuddin, 'Innovation in *Sukuk* Structures' in Sohail Jaffer (ed), *Islamic Investment Banking: Emerging Trends, Developments and Opportunities* (Euromoney Institutional Investor PLC, 2010)

Mansyur, H.M. Ali, 'Aspek Hukum Perbankan Syariah dan Implementasinya di Indonesia [Legal Aspect of Islamic Banking and Its Implementation in Indonesia]' (2011) 11 *Jurnal Dinamika Hukum* 67

Mardian, Sepky, 'Tingkat Kepatuhan Syariah di Lembaga Keuangan Syariah [The Level of Sharia Compliance in Islamic Financial Institutions]' (2015) 3(1) *Jurnal Akuntansi dan Keuangan Islam* 57

Mariyani-Squire, Edward, 'Tensions in Islamic Economics' (2013) 12(1) *Trikonomika* 1

Masdar, Hilmy, 'Quo-vadis Islam Moderat Indonesia? Menimbang Kembali Modernisme Nahdlatul Ulama dan Muhammadiyah [Quo-vadis Moderate Islam Indonesia? Reconsidering the NU and Muhammadiyah Modernism]' (2012) 36(2) *Jurnal Miqot*

Masud, Muhammad Khalid, Brinkley Messick, and David S. Powers, *Muftis, Fatwas and Islamic Legal Interpretation* (Harvard University Press, 1996)

McCormick, Roger, *Legal Risk in the Financial Markets* (Oxford University Press, 2006)

McDonald, Larry, and Patrick Robinson, *A Colossal Failure of Common Sense: The Incredible Inside Story of the Collapse of Lehman Brothers* (Random House, 2009)

Mejia, Alejandro Lopez et al., WP/14/219, *Regulation and Supervision of Islamic Banks*, International Monetary Fund No WP/14/219 (2014)

Mohamad, Mohammad Taqiuddin et al., 'The Historical Development of Modern Islamic Banking: A Study in South-East Asia Countries' (2013) 1(1) *African Journal of Business Management* 1

Mollah, Sabur et al., 'The Governance, Risk-Taking, and Performance of Islamic Banks' (Pt Springer Nature) (2017) 51(2) *Journal of Financial Services Research* 195

Mubarok, Jaih, *Metodologi Ijtihad Hukum Islam* [The Methods of Ijtihad in Sharia Law] (UII Press, 2002)

Muhammad, Hanif, 'Differences and Similarities in Islamic and Conventional Banking' (2011) 2(2) *International Journal of Business and Social Science* 166

Mujani, Saiful, and R. William Lidle, 'Politics, Islam, and Public Opinion' (2004) 15(1) *Journal of Democracy* 109

Muslimin, J.M., 'Islamic Law in the Pancasila State' (2012) 12(1) *Journal Ahkam* 15

Nadri, Kamran, 'A Critique of Islamic Banking and Finance: Harmonization of Fatwas (Islamic Opinions) and the Nature of Modern Economic' (Paper presented at the IIUM Internationational Conference on Islamic Banking Finance (IICiBF), Kuala Lumpur)

Najib, Mukhamad, 'Analysis of Brandswitcher Customers in Islamic Banks and Conventional Banks (A Case Study in the Region of Darmaga Bogor)/*Analisis Konsumen Berpindah Merek (Brandswitcher) pada Bank Syariah dan Bank Konvensional (studi kasus pada nasabah di wilayah Darmaga Bogor)*' (July 2009) 4(1) *Islamic Finance and Business Review* 1

Nasirwan and Muhamad Irfan Sukarna, *Laporan Perkembangan Keuangan Syariah Tahun 2013* [The Report on the Development of Islamic Finance Year 2013] (Financial Services Authority of Indonesia, 2013)

Nomran, Naji Mansour, Razali Haron, and Rusni Hassan, 'Bank Performance and Shari'ahSupervisory Board Attributes by Islamic Banks: Does Bank Size Matter?' (2017) 6(Special) *Journal of Islamic Finance* 174

Norazlina, Mamat, and Ahmad Ridzwan, '*Maslahah* Approach Towards Imposition of *Ta'widh* in Islamic Banking' (2019) 39 *Global Journal Al Thaqafah* 39

Nordin, Nadhirah et al., 'Contracting with Gharar (Uncertainty) in Forward Contract: What Does Islam Says?' (2014) 10(15) *Asian Social Science Journal* 37

Nurfaizal, 'Prinsip-Prinsip Muamalah dan Implementasinya Dalam Hukum Perbankan Indonesia [The Foundation of Islamic Commercial Law and Its Implementation in Indonesian Banking]' (2013) 13(1) *Jurnal Hukum Islam* 14, 192

Nurhadi, Nurhadi, '*Bunga Bank Antara Halal dan Haram* [The Bank Interest Rates: Between *Halal* and *Haram*]' (October 2017) 4(2) *Journal of Education and Social Religious Study, Nur El-Islam* 30, 49

Nurhayati, Ratna, and Seno Wibowo Gumbira, 'Countermeasures Criminal Action of Corruption in Banking in the Lending of Credits' (2021) 27(3) *Journal of Contemporary Issues in Business and Government* 1278

Nyazee, Imran Ahsan Khan, *The Concept of Riba and Islamic Banking* (CreateSpace Independent Publishing Platform, 2nd edition, 2016)

Otoritas Jasa Keuangan, *Laporan Perkembangan Keuangan Syariah Indonesia 2017* [The Report on the Development of Islamic Finance in Indonesia 2017] (Financial Service Authority of Indonesia, 2017)

Otto, Jan Michiel, *Sharia and National Law in Muslim Countries* (Leiden University Press, 2008)

Pepinsky, Thomas B., 'Development, Social Change, and Islamic Finance in Contemporary Indonesia, World Development' (2013) 41 *Journal of World Development* 157

Pepinsky, Thomas B., 'Islamic Finance in Multicultural Indonesia' (Paper presented at the Yale Indonesia Forum Internation Conference, Yogyakarta)

Pew Research Center, Mapping the Global Muslim Population (October 2009), www.pewforum.org/2009/10/07/mapping-the-global-muslim-population/

Prabowo, Bagya Agung, 'The Practice of Murabahah Scheme in Syariah Banking: Critical Analysis Towards the Application of Murabahah Scheme in Indonesia and Malaysia' (2009) 16(1) *Jurnal Hukum IUS QUIA IUSTUM*

Pratiwi, Aprilia, and Noven Suprayogi, 'Bank Syariah di Indonesia: Analisis Pengaruh Rata-Rata Tingkat Bagi Hasil Deposito dan Rata-Rata Tingkat Suku Bunga Deposito Terhadap Jumlah Deposito dan Jumlah Nasabah Deposito Periode 2009–2014 [Islamic Banks in Indonesia: Analysis of the Effect of the Average Deposit Profit Sharing Rate and the Average Deposit Interest rate on the Total Time Deposit and the Number of Time Deposit Customers from 2009–2014]' (2017) 4(2) *Jurnal ekonomi Syariah Teori dan Terapan* 89

Prihantono, 'Akad Murabahah dan Permasalahannya dalam Penerapan di Lembaga Keuangan Syariah [Murabahah Conctract and Its Issues in Implementation in Islamic Financial Institutions]' (2018) 14(2) *Jurnal Al-Maslahah Ilmu Syariah* 219

Probowo, Bagya Agung, 'Reputation Oversight by the Sharia Supervisory Board Toward Wakalah Contract Application on Murabahah Financing' (2019) 436 *Advances in Social Science, Education and Humanities Research* 775

Qaed, Issa Qaed Mansour, 'The Concept of Wadiah and Its Application in Islamic Banking' (2014) 2(11) *Journal of Research in Humanities and Social Science* 70

Qomar, Moh Nurul, '*Mudharabah Sebagai Produk Pembiayaan Perbankan Syariah Perspektif Abdullah Saeed* [Mudharabah as the Islamic Financing Product from the Perspective of Abdullah Saeed]' [201] (2018) 2(2) *Journal of Islamic Banking and Finance* 10

Quintyn, Marc, and Michael W. Taylor, *Regulatory and Supervisory Independence and Financial Stability*, IMF Working Paper No WP/02/46, International Monetary Fund (2002)

Rahman, Abdul Rahim Abdul, 'Islamic Microfinance: A Missing Component in Islamic Banking' (2007) 1(2) *Kyoto Bulletin of Islamic Area Studies* 38

Rajafi, Ahmad, 'Ijtihad Eklusif, Telaah atas Pola Ijtihad 3 Ormas Islam di Indonesia [Exclusivism of *Ijtihad*, a Review of Form of *Ijtihad* on Three Large Islamic Organisations in Indonesia]' (2016) *Jurnal Ilmiah Al-Syirah*

Rajan, Raghuram G., 'Do We Still Need Commercial Banks?' The National Bureau of Economic Research, www.nber.org/reporter/fall98/rajan_fall98.html

Rama, Ali, 'Analisis Kerangka Regulasi Model Syariah Governance Lembaga Keuangan Syariah di Indonesia [Analysis of the Concept of Regulation for Islamic Governance Model in Islamic Financial Institution in Indonesia]' (2015) 1(1) *Journal of Islamic Economics LARIBA*

Redhead, Keith, *Financial Derivatives: An Introduction to Futures, Forwards, Options and Swaps* (Prentice Hall, 1st edition, 1996)

Rethel, Lena, 'Whose Legitimacy? Islamic Finance and the Global Financial Order' (Pt Routledge) (2011) 18(1) *Review of International Political Economy* 75

Roger, Orsingher, *Les Banques Dans Le Monde* [Bank of the World] (D.S. Ault trans, Macmillan, 1967)

Rohmad, Muhammad Iman Sastra Mihajat, and Aznan Hasan, 'Tawarruq Practice for Liquidity Management in Islamic Money Market in Indonesia and Malaysia' (2013) 1(2) *Equilibrium, Jurnal IAIN Kudus* 2017

Rosdini, Dini, and Nanda Putri Ghassani Fildzah, 'Comparison of Conservatism in Islamic and Conventional Banks in Indonesia and Malaysia' (2019) 23(2) *Jurnal Manajemen* 239

Sadli, Mohammad, *The Indonesian Crisis* (Institute of Southeast Asian Studies, 1999)

Saeed, Abdullah, 'Ijtihad and Innovation in Neo-Modernist Islamic thought in Indonesia' (Pt Routledge) (1997) 8(3) *Islam and Christian – Muslim Relations* 279

Saeed, Abdullah, 'Idealism and Pragmatism in Islamic Banking: The Application of Sharī'ah Principles and Adjustments.' (1998) 4(2) *Journal of Arabic, Islamic and Middle Eastern Studies* 89

Saeed, Abdullah, 'Indonesian Islamic Banking in Historical and Legal Context' in Tim Lindsey (ed), *Indonesia: Law and Society* (The Federation Press, 1999a) 323–338

Saeed, Abdullah, *Islamic Banking and Interest: A Study of the Prohibition of Riba and Its Contemporary Interpretation* (E.J. Brill, 2nd edition, 1999b)

Saeed, Abdullah, *The Qur'an: An Introduction* (Routledge, 2008)

Saiti, Buerhan, and Adam Abdullah, 'The Legal Maxims of Islamic Law (Excluding Five Leading Legal Maxims) and Their Applications in Islamic Finance' (1 November 2017) (2016) 29(2) *Journal of King Abdulaziz University: Islamic Economics*

Sakirman, 'Epistimologi Ushul Fiqh dalam Konstruk Historis [The Epistomology of Islamic Jurisprudence in Islamic History]' (1 January 2016) 25(1) *Jurnal Emprisima* 1

Sakti, Muhammad Rizky Prima et al., 'Shari'ah Issues, Challenges, and Prospects for Islamic Derivatives: A Qualitative Study' (2016) 8(2) *Journal of Qualitative Research in Financial Markets* 168

Salam, Abdul, 'Bunga Bank Dalam Perspektif Islam (Studi Pendapat Nahdlatul Ulama dan Muhammadiyah) [Interest Rate in Islamic Perspective (Study of the Opinion of Nahdlatul Ulama and Muhammadiyah)]' (2013) 3(1) *Jurnal Ekonomi Syariah Indonesia*

Saleh, Walid, and Ahmad Ajaj, *Unlawful Gain and Legitimate Profit in Islamic Law* (Brill, 1992)

Salim, Arskal, *Contemporary Islamic Law in Indonesia* (Edinburgh University Press, 2015)

Samsuri, Ali, 'Membincang Konsep Tawarruq Dalam Dunia Perbankan Dewasa ini [Discussing the Concept of Tawarruq in the Banking World Today]' (2015) 9(1) *Jurnal IAIN Kediri* 29

Sappideen, Razeen, 'The Regulation of Credit, Market and Operational Risk Management under the Basel Accords' (2004) *Journal of Business Law* 59

Sappideen, Razeen, 'The Regulation of Hedgefunds' (2016)(7) *Journal of Business Law* 1

Sato, Yuri, 'Bank Restructuring and Financial Institution Reform in Indonesia' (2004) 3(1) *The Developing Economies* 91

Scherer, F.M., *The Banking Industry*, Faculty Research Working Paper Series RWP 14-042, Harvard Kennedy School (2014)

Sadhila, and Muhammad Akhyar Adnan, 'Analisis Kepatuhan Dewan Pengawas Syariah (DPS) Terhadap Ketentuan Otoritas Jasa Keuangan (OJK) (Studi Kasus Pada BPRS di Yogyakarta) [Analysis of Sharia Supervisory Board Compliance on the Regulation of Financial Service Authority (Case Study at BPRS Yogyakarta)]' (2017) 1(2) *Reviu Akuntasi dan Bisnis Indonesia* 152

Shafie, Mastura Mohd, Mat Noor Mat Zain, and Nik Abdul Rahim Ghani, 'Commodity Murabahah Deposits in Islamic Banking: An Easy Way Out' (2020) 42(1) *Islamiyyat* 15

Shafii, Zurina, and Abdul Rahim Abdul Rahman, 'Issues on the Application of IFRS9 and Fair Value Measurement for Islamic Financial Instruments' (Pt Emerald Group Publishing Limited) (2016) 7(3) *Journal of Islamic Accounting and Business Research* 202

Shaharuddin, Amir, 'The Bay' al-Inah Controversy in Malaysian Islamic Banking' (2012) 26(4) *Journal of Arab Law Quarterly* 499

Sharawy, Hesham M., 'Understanding the Islamic Prohibition of Interest: A Guide to Aid Economic Cooperation between the Islamic and Western Worlds' (2000) 29 *Georgia Journal of International and Comparative law* 153

Sharbatly, Abdulaziz, *Risk Regulation in Islamic Banking: Does Saudi Arabia Need to Adopt the Risk Regulation Practices of Basel?* (PhD Thesis, University of Westminster, 2016)

Shinsuke, Nagaoka, 'Critical Overview of the History of Islamic Economics: Formation, Transformation, and New Horizons' (2012) 11(2) *Asian and African Area Studies Journal* 114

Shofiyullah, Mz, '*Al-Kutub Al-Mu'tabarah*: Kajian atas Sumber Rujukan dalam Beristinbat Menurut NU, Muhammadiyah, dan Persis [*Al-Kutub Al-Mu'tabarah*: The Analysis of Source of Reference in *Istinbath* according to NU, Muhammadiyah and Persis]' (2008) 42(1) *Jurnal Asy-Syir'ah* 37

Siddiqi, Muhammad Nejatullah, *Issues in Islamic Banking* (The Islamic Foundation, 1983)

Siddiqui, Anjum, 'Financial Contracts, Risk and Performance of Islamic Banking' (2008) 34(10) *Managerial Finance* 680

Sjahdeini, Sutan Remy, *Perbankan Islam dan Kedudukannya dalam Tata Hukum Perbankan Indonesia* [Islamic banking and Its Position in the Indonesian Banking Law System] (Pustaka Utama Grafiti, 1999)

Smolo, Edib, and Abbas Mirakhor, 'The Global Financial Crisis and Its Implications for the Islamic Financial Industry' (2010) 3(4) *International Journal of Islamic and Middle Eastern Finance and Management* 372

Sofiana, Neng Eri, 'Ikrar Jatukrami: Ikrar Pernikahan Konteks Sunda [Jatukrami Pledge: The Wedding Vows in Sudanese Context]' (2019) 4(1) *Jurnal AQLAM-Journal of Islam and Plurality* 80

Sofyati, H.S., and Oktaviani Yeni, 'Risk Mitigation of Moral Hazard on Mudharabah Financing (Case Study: An Islamic Bank)' (2nd International Conference on Indonesian Economy and Development (ICIED, Jakarta, 14–15 August 2017

Sole, Juan, *Introducing Islamic Banks into Coventional Banking Systems (EPub)* (International Monetary Fund, 2007)

Song, Inwon, and Carel Oosthuizen, *Islamic Banking Regulation and Supervision: Survey Results and Challenges*, IMF Working Paper No 14/220, International Monetary Fund (2014)

Srairi, Samir, 'Transparency and Bank Risk-Taking in GCC Islamic Banking' (2019) 19 *Borsa Istanbul Review* S64

Stiglitz, Joseph, *Globalisation and Its Discontents* (W.W. Norton & Company, 2002).

Subramoniam, K., 'Basel III Framework on Liquidity Standards: The Challenges Before the Indian Banks on Liquidity Risk Management' (Pt IUP Publications) (2015) 14(3) *IUP Journal of Bank Management* 40

Sudarsono, Heri, Yunice Karima Tumewang, and Muamar Nur Kholid, 'Customer Adoption of Islamic Banking Services: Empirical Evidence from Indonesia' (2021) 8(3) *Journal of Asian Finance, Economics and Business* 1193

Sudaryo, Yoyo, and Aditya Yudanegara, *Investasi Bank dan Lembaga Keuangan* [Financial Institutions and Banks' Investment] (Penerbit Andi, 2017)

Suma, Muhammad Amin, *Asuransi Syariah dan Asuransi Konvensional: Sistem, Konsep, Aplikasi dan Pemasaran* [Islamic Insurance and Conventional Insurance: System, Concept, Application and Marketing] (Kholam Publishing, 2006)

Suwailem, Sami Al, 'Financial Engineering: An Islamic Perspective' (2007) 9(1) *Jurnal Fakultas Hukum UII* 87

Swandayani, Desi Marilin, and Rohmawati Kusumaningtias, 'Pengaruh Inflasi, Suku Bunga, Nilai Tukar Valas dan Jumlah Uang Beredar Terhadap Profitabilitas pada Perbankan Syariah di Indonesia Periode 2005–2009 [The Effect of Inflation, Interest Rates, Foreign Exchange Rates, and Money Supply to the Profitability of Islamic Banking in Indonesia Period 2005–2009]' (2012) 3(2) *AKRUAL: Jurnal Akuntansi* 147

Syarif, Fazlurrahman, 'Regulatory Framework for Islamic Financial Institutions: Lesson Learnt Between Malaysia and Indonesia' (2019) 2(2) *Journal of Halal Product and Research* 79

Syz, Juerg M., *Property Derivatives: Pricing, Hedging and Applications* (John Wiley & Sons, 2008)

Taleb, Nassim Nicholas, *Dynamic Hedging: Managing Vanilla and Exotic Options* (Wiley, 2007)

Timur, Kuran, 'Islamic Economics and the Islamic Subeconomy' (1995) 9(4) *Journal of Economic and Prespectives* 155

Uddin, Akhter Md, 'Principles of Islamic Finance: Prohibition of Riba, Gharr and Maysir' (Pt University Library of Munich) (2015) (9), https://mpra.ub.uni-muenchen.de/67711/1/MPRA_paper_67711.pdf

Uddin, Akhter Md, and Abu Umar Faruq Ahmad, 'Conventional Futures: Derivatives from Islamic Law of Contract' (2020) 62(4) *International Journal of Law and Management* 315

Ullah, Shakir, and Kun-ho Lee, 'Do Customers Patronize Islamic Banks for Shari'a Compliance?' (Pt Palgrave Macmillan) (2012) 17(3) *Journal of Financial Services Marketing* 206

UNEP, United Nations Environment Programme, *Towards a Sustainable Financial System in Indonesia (Report, February 2015)*

Usmani, Muhammad Taqi, *An Introduction to Islamic Finance* (Idaratul Ma'arif, 1998)

Venardos, Angelo M., *Islamic Banking and Finance in South East Asia: Its Development and Future* (World Scientific Publishing, 2nd edition, 2006)

Venardos, Angelo M., *Current Issues in Islamic Banking and Finance Resilience and Stability in the Present System* (World Scientific, 2010)

Vinals, Jose, and Jonathan Fiechter, *The Making of Good Supervision: Learning to Say 'No'* (International Monetary Fund, 2010)

Visser, Hans, *Islamic Finance: Principles and Practice* (Edward Elgar Publishing, 2013)

Vives, Xavier, 'Competition in the Changing World of Banking' (2001) 17(4) *Oxford Review of Economic Policy* 13, 535

Vogel, Frank E., *Islamic Law and Finance: Religion, Risk, and Return* (Kluwer Law International, 1998)

Wahid, Din, 'Nurturing Salafi Manhaj: A Study of Salafi Pesantren in Contemporary Indonesia' (2014) 15(2) *Wacana* 367

Wanandi, Jusuf, 'Islam in Indonesia: Its History, Development and Future Challenges' (Pt Routledge) (2002) 9(2) *Asia-Pacific Review* 104

Warde, Ibrahim, *Islamic Finance in the Global Economy* (Edinburgh University Press, 2010)

Wardhani, Novea Elysa, Masruchin Ruba'I, and Thohir Luth, 'The Contract of Murabahah Bil Wakalah on the Saving-Loan Cooperative and Syariah FInancing (KSPPS) Reviewed from Justice and Benefit Perspective' (2017) 64 *Journal of Law, Policy and Globalisation*

Wibowo, I.G.B. Erri, and Buddi Wibowo, 'The Effect of Competition Levels and Banking Concentration on Systemic Risks: Indonesia's Case' (2017) 9 *Indonesian Capital Market Review* 85

Wijaya, Krisna, *Analisis Kebijakan Perbankan Nasional* [Analysis of National Banking Policy] (Elex Media Komputindo, 2013)

Wijaya, Rusdiana Priatna, and Nurizal Ismail, 'Sharia Credit Card in the View of Maqasid al-Sharia' (2020) 4(1) *Al-Iktisab: Journal of Islamic Economic Law*

Wilson, Rodney, 'Overview of the Sukuk Market' in *Islamic Bonds: Your Guide to Issuing, Structuring and Investing in Sukuk* (Euromoney Books, 2004) 6

Worthington, Andrew C., and Alsadek H. Gait, *A Primer on Islamic Finance: Definitions, Sources, Principles and Methods* (Discussion Papers in Finance finance: 200909, Griffith University, Department of Accounting, Finance and Economics, 2009).

Wurtz, Katja Julie, 'The Definition of Legal Risk and Its Management by Central Banks' (2007) 1(1) *International In-House Counsel Journal* 43

Yamamah, Ansari, 'The Existence of Al-Urf (Social Tradition) in Islamic Law Theory' (December 2016) 21(12) *IOSR Journal of Humanities and Social Science (IOSR-JHSS)* 43

Yazid, Mohamad, M.N. Asmadi and H. Mohd Liki, 'The Practices of Islamic Finance in Upholding the Islamic Values and the Maqasid Shariah' (2015) 4(1) *International Review of Management and Business Research* 286

Yazid Isa, Mohamad, Asmadi Mohamed Naim, and Mohd Liki Hamid, 'The Effects of New AAOIFI Standards on Sukuk in Choosing the Most Authentic Islamic Principles' (Pt Emerald Group Publishing Limited) (2013) 4(1) *Journal of Islamic Accounting and Business Research* 77

Yousef, Tarik M., 'The Murabaha Syndrome in Islamic Finance: Laws, Institutions and Politics' in Clement Henry and Rodney Wilson (eds), *The Politics of Islamic Finance* (Edinburgh University Press, 2004)

Yusuf, Muhammad Yasir, 'Dinamika Fatwa Bunga Bank di Indonesia: Kajian Terhadap Fatwa MUI, Muhammadiyah dan Nahdlatul Ulama [The Variety of Fatwas on Bank Interest in Indonesia: The Analysis of Fatwa MUI, Muhammadiyah and Nahdlatul Ulama]' 14(2) *Media Syariah* 151

Yusuf, Nasruddin, 'Hadis Sebagai Sumber Hukum Islam [Hadith as the Source of Islamic Law]' (2015) 13(1) *Journal Al-Syir'ah Ilmiah* 21

Yuwonoputro, Dhaneswworo Arsojotegto, and Muhamad Syaichu, 'Indonesian Banks Risk-Taking: The Effect of Liquidity Risk, Capital Buffer and BOPO: Z-Score Measure Approach' (2019) 8(3) *Diponegoro Journal of Management* 149

Zahara, Fatimah, and R. Deddy Harryanto, 'Implementasi Akad Tawarruq dalam Perbankan Syari'ah Indonesia [The Implementation of Akad Tawarruq in Indonesian Islamic Banking]' (2019) 35(2) *Ijtihad Jurnal Hukum Islam dan Pranata Sosial* 53

Zaher, Tarek S., and M. Kabir Hassan, 'A Comparative Literature Survey of Islamic Finance and Banking' (2001) 10(4) *Financial Markets, Institutions & Instruments* 155

Zahra, Siti Fatimah, Ascarya, and Nurul Huda, 'Stability Measurement of Dual Banking System in Indonesia: Markov Switching Approach' (2018) 10(1) *Al-Iqtishad: Jurnal Ilmu Ekonomi Syariah (Journal of Islamic Economics)* 25

Zakariyah, Luqman, 'Custom and Society in Islamic Criminal Law: A Critical Appraisal of the Maxim 'al-ʿĀdah Muḥakkamah' (Custom Is Authoritative) and Its Sisters in Islamic Legal Procedures' (2012) 26(1) *Arab Law Quarterly* 75

Zaman, Asad, 'Crisis in Islamic Economics: Diagnosis and Prescriptions' (2011) 25(1) *Journal of King Abdulaziz University: Islamic Economics* 147–169

Zaman, M. Raquibuz, 'Usury (Riba) and the Place of Bank Interest in Islamic Banking and Finance' (2008) 6(1) *International Journal of Banking and Finance* 1

Zaman, Muhammad Qasim, *The Ulama in Contemporary Islam: Custodians of Change* (Princeton University Press, 2002)

Zaman, Qasim Muhammad, 'Religious Discourse and the Public Sphere in Contemporary Pakistan' (2008) 123 *Revue des mondes musulmans et de la Méditerranée* 55

Zarrouk, Hajer, Khoutem Ben Jedidia, and Mouna Moualhi, 'Is Islamic Bank Profitability Driven by Same Forces as Conventional Banks?' (2016) 9(1) *International Journal of Islamic and Middle Eastern Finance and Management; Bingley* 46

Zuhayli, Wahbah, *Fiqh al-Islami wa-Adilatuhu* [Islamic Jurisprudence and Its Proofs] (Dar al-fikr, Beirut, 2001)

Other soft law instruments

Abdalla, Mohamad, 'Islamic Australia? What Place Is There for Sacred Law in a Secular Land?', *Religion & Ethics, ABC*, www.abc.net.au/religion/islamic-australia-what-place-is-there-for-sacred-law-in-a-secula/10099858

Accounting and Auditing Organization for Islamic Finance AAOIFI, 'Governance and Auditing Standards' (2012), https://ijbssnet.com/journals/Vol_4_No_15_Special_Issue_November_2013/28.pdf

Afonso, Gara, Anna Kovner, and Antoinette Schoar, 'What Happened to US Interbank Lending in the Finacial Crisis?', *VOX CEPR Policy Portal* (London), https://voxeu.org/article/what-happened-us-interbank-lending-financial-crisis

Alawode, Abayomi A., 'Brief Islamic Finance' (Pt World Bank) *Understanding Poverty Financial Sector* (2015), www.worldbank.org/en/topic/financialsector/brief/islamic-finance

Aldi, Andika, and Dimas, 'Dinamika Tawarruq Sebagai Inovasi Produk Perbankan Syariah [The Dynamic of Tawarruq as an Innovative Islamic Banking Product]', *Komite Nasional Ekonomi dan Keuangan Syariah* (Jakarta), https://knks.go.id/berita/298/dinamika-tawarruq-sebagai-inovasi-produk-perbankan-syariah?category=

Al Farizy, Shallman, 'Pengawasan Baitul Maal Wat-Tamwil (BMT) Berbadan Hukum [Supervision of Baitul Maal Wat-Tamwil (BMT) Incorporated Financial Institution]' on *Shallman*, https://shallmanalfarizy.com/2017/12/pengawasan-baitul-maal-wat-tamwil-bmt-berbadan-hukum/

Al-Misriyyah, Dar Al-Ifta, 'Islamic Legal Theory (Ushul al-fiqh)' (Pt Dar al-Iftaa Al-Missriyyah) (2020), www.dar-alifta.org/Foreign/ViewArticle.aspx?ID=110&CategoryID=3

Ardianto, A'an, '*TBC Sebagai Seteru Abadi Muhammadiyah* [TBC as the Eternal Enemy of Muhammadiyah]', *News, UMM Malang* (Malang), 1 February 2020, www.umm.ac.id/id/muhammadiyah/18352.html

Australian Securities and Investments Commission, '20-123MR Court Declares Bendigo and Adelaide Bank Contract Terms Unfair' (Pt ASIC) (2020), https://asic.gov.au/about-asic/news-centre/find-a-media-release/2020-releases/20-123mr-court-declares-bendigo-and-adelaide-bank-contract-terms-unfair/

Azhar, Erwandi Tarmidzi, 'Mudharabah Bank Syariah, Berbagi Riba Berkedok Syariah [Mudharah in Islamic Bank, Sharing *Riba* under the Guise of Sharia]', *Majalah Pengusaha Muslim* (Jakarta), https://pengusahamuslim.com/2780-mudharabah-bank-syariah-1476.html

Azhar, Erwandi Tarmidzi, 'Panduan Murabahah yang Sesuai Syariah [Guidelines for Sharia-Compliant Murabahah]', *Majalah Pengusaha Muslim* (Jakarta), https://pengusahamuslim.com/5473-panduan-murabahah-yang-sesuai-syariah-bagian-1.html

Aziz, Zeti Akhtar, 'Building a Progressive Islamic Banking Sector – Charting the Way Forward' (Pt Bank for International Settlements) (2005) 1 www.bis.org/review/r050629g.pdf

Aziz, Zeti Akhtar, 'Governor's Special Address at GIFF Investors & Issuers Forum: "Islamic Finance: The New Silk Road"' (Pt Bank Negara Malaysia) (2007) www.bnm.gov.my/-/governor-s-special-address-at-giff-investors-issuers-forum-islamic-finance-the-new-silk-road-

Barth, James R., Gerard Caprio, and Ross Levine, 'The Regulation and Supervision of Banks Around the World: A New Database' The World Bank, https://openknowledge.worldbank.org/handle/10986/19664

Beck, Thorsten, Asli Demirguc-Kunt, and Ross Levine, 'Bank Supervision and Corporate Finance' World Bank, http://citeseerx.ist.psu.edu/viewdoc/download?doi=10.1.1.508.2262&rep=rep1&type=pdf

Cambridge Institute of Islamic Finance, 'Overview of the Global Islamic Financial Services Industry', *Global Islamic Finance Report 2020*, www.gifr.net/publications/gifr2020/intro.pdf

Caruana, Jaime, 'Systemic Risk: How to Deal with It?' Bank for International Settlements, www.bis.org/publ/othp08.htm

Chui, Michael, 'Derivatives Markets, Products and Participants: An Overview "Bank for International Settlements"', www.bis.org/ifc/publ/ifcb35a.pdf

Cisse, H. et al., *The World Bank Legal Review, Volume 5: Fostering Development through Opportunity, Inclusion, and Equity* (World Bank Publications, 2013)

Davis, E. Philip, and Ugochi Obasi, *The Effectiveness of Banking Supervision*, Working Paper No. 09-27, Department of Economics and Finance, Brunel University (2009)

Diela, Tabita, 'Indonesia's Largest Islamic Bank Starts Operations', *Nasdaq* (Jakarta), 1 February 2021, www.nasdaq.com/articles/indonesias-largest-islamic-bank-starts-operations-2021-02-01

Difi, Johansyah, 'Bank Indonesia Imposes Sanctions on Bank Mega' (Pt Bank Indonesia) (2011), www.bi.go.id/en/ruang-media/siaran-pers/Pages/sp_131811.aspx

Doran, Matthew, and Michael Janda, 'Commonwealth Bank to Pay $700 m Fine for Anti-Money Laundering, Terror Financing Law Breaches', *ABC News* (Sydney), 4 June 2018, www.abc.net.au/news/2018-06-04/commonwealth-bank-pay-$700-million-fine-money-laundering-breach/9831064

El-Houdaiby, Ibrahim, 'The Identity of Al-Azhar and Its Doctrine', *Ahram Online* (Egypt), https://english.ahram.org.eg/NewsContentPrint/4/0/48668/Opinion/0/The-identity-of-AlAzhar-and-itsdoctrine.aspx

Ernst and Young, 'Strategic Business Risk: Insurance' Ernst & Young Report, www.climate-needs.umd.edu/reports/Ernst%20and%20%20Young-Insurance%20and%20Climate.pdf

The Financial, 'IMF Executive Board Approves Indonesia's 2017 Financial System Stability Assessment', *The Financial* (Georgia), www.finchannel.com/business/65624-imf-executive-board-approves-indonesia-s-2017-financial-system-stability-assessment

Financial Service Authority of Indonesia, 'Booklet of Indonesian Banking-2018' Otoritas Jasa Keuangan, www.ojk.go.id/id/kanal/perbankan/data-dan-statistik/booklet-perbankan-indonesia/Documents/Pages/Booklet-Perbankan-Indonesia-2018/Booklet%20Perbankan%20Indonesia%202018.pdf

Financial Service Authority of Indonesia, 'The Basic Principles of Sharia Capital Market' (2017), www.ojk.go.id/en/kanal/syariah/tentang-syariah/pages/pasar-modal-syariah.aspx

Fitch Ratings, 'Malaysia's Islamic Banking Sector Continues to Expand Despite Pandemic', Fitch Ratings (Singapore), www.fitchratings.com/research/banks/malaysia-islamic-banking-sector-continues-to-expand-despite-pandemic-28-02-2021

Global Custodian, 'The Basel Committee Invites New Members from G20', *Global Custodian* (London), 11 June 2009, www.globalcustodian.com/the-basel-committee-invites-new-members-from-g20/

Hamdani, 'Independensi, Bank Indonesia Harus Bebas dari Tekanan Politik [Bank Indonesia Independence, BI Must Be Free from Political Interference]', *Economics*, *Kompasiana* (Jakarta), 11 May 2018, www.kompasiana.com/cangkoiburong/5af4e3d7ab12ae5cc5443992/independensi-bank-indonesia-harus-bebas-dari-tekanan-politik#

Hannoun, Hervé, 'The Basel III Capital Framework: A Decisive Breakthrough' Bank for International Settlements, www.bis.org/speeches/sp101125a.pdf

Haq, Mamiza, 'Is Islamic Banking More Risky Compared to Conventional Banking?', *The Conversation* (Queensland), https://theconversation.com/is-islamic-banking-more-risky-compared-to-conventional-banking-62993

Hermansyah, 'Lima Peristiwa Penting di Akhir Agustus 2013 Mengenai Peradilan Agama dan Ekonomi Syariah [Five Important Events in Late August 2013 on Religious Court and Islamic Economics]' (Pt Mahakamah Agung) (2013), https://badilag.mahkamahagung.go.id/seputar-ditjen-badilag/seputar-ditjen-badilag/lima-peristiwa-penting-di-akhir-agustus-2013-mengenai-peradilan-agama-dan-ekonomi-syariah-5

Hidayat, Wahyudi, 'Profit Equalisation Reserve (PER) dan Investment Risk Reserve (IRR) dan (Idealisme) Ber Bank Syariah [Profit Equalisation Reserve (PER) and Investment Risk Reserve (IRR) and Idealism in Islamic Banking]', *Kompasiana* (Jakarta), www.kompasiana.com/liwaganteng/550f6a00a33311af35ba7ea5/profit-equalization-reserve-per-dan-investment-risk-reserve-irr-dan-idealisme-ber-bank-syariah

International Organisation of Securities Commissions, *Islamic Capital Market Fact Finding Report* (2004) Islamic Capital Market Task Force of the International Organisation of Securities Commission

Kapoor, Vishal, 'Strategic Risk Management and Balance Sheet Management under the New Regulatory Environment' (Pt Moody's Analytic, Inc) (2012), www.moodysanalytics.com/-/media/presentation/2012/2012-18-09-strategic-risk-management-for-distribution-online.pdf

Kennedy, Mike, 'Basel III and Islamic Finance: What Lies Ahead?', *Islamic Finance News* (London), 11 January 2012, 19–21, www.eurekahedge.com/Research/News/96/February_2012_alternative_investment_IFN_Basel_III_and_Islamic_Finance_What_Lies_Ahead

Kennedy, Simon, 'Fitch: Islamic Finance Standardisation Will Be Slow', *Reuters* (London), www.reuters.com/article/fitch-islamic-finance-standardisation-wi/fitch-islamic-finance-standardisation-will-be-slow-idUSFitb5gH0f

Khan, Salman H., 'Organised Tawarruq in Practice: A Shariah Non-Compliant and Unjustified Transaction', *New Horizon* (Kuala Lumpur), 16–21, www.islamic-finance.com/library/Khan_tawarruq.pdf

Khan, Salman H., 'Why Tawarruq Needs to Go? AOIFI and the OIC Fiqh Academy: Divergence or Agreement?', *New Horizon Islamic Banking*, www.newhorizonislamicbanking.com/index.cfm

Lathia, Devansh, 'How Soros Broke the British Pound', *The Economics Review* (New York), https://theeconreview.com/2018/10/16/how-soros-broke-the-british-pound/

Lavinda, 'S&P Pertahankan Rating Indonesia Tetap BBB- [S&P Maintain the Indonesian Ranking at BBB-]', *Makro News, CNN Indonesia* (Jakarta), www.cnnindonesia.com/ekonomi/20180531200039-532-302651/sp-pertahankan-rating-indonesia-tetap-bbb-

Matanasi, Petrik, 'Majelis Ulama Indonesia: Cara daripada Soeharto Mengatur Islam [Indonesian Ulama Council: How the Soeharto's Regime Managed Islam]', *Politik, Tirto* (Jakarta), https://tirto.id/majelis-ulama-indonesia-cara-daripada-soeharto-mengatur-islam-fQRG

McDonough, William J., 'Implementing the New Basel Accord' Bank for International Settlement, www.bis.org/review/r030217a.pdf

Mulkhan, Abdul Munir, *Masalah-masalah Teologi dan Fiqh dalam Tarjih Muhammadiyah* [Questions about Theology and Fiqh in Tarjih Muhammadiyah] (SIPRESS, 2005) vol. 1

Nahar, Syamsun, 'Pembiayaan Jual-beli *murabahah* [*Murabahah* Based Financing]', *finance, Okezone* (Jakarta), 14 March 2012, https://economy.okezone.com/read/2012/03/14/316/593050/pembiayaan-jual-beli-murabahah

Natoor-Bashar, Al, and Saif Shawqi, 'Islamic Derivatives Increasingly Necessary, But Constraints Remain', *FitchRatings* (London), www.fitchratings.com/research/islamic-finance/islamic-derivatives-increasingly-necessary-constraints-remain-17-06-2020

Oakley, David, 'Sukuk Market: Clarification of Rules Does Market a Favour', *Financial Times*, www.ft.com/content/57504a52-3c0f-11dd-9cb2-0000779fd2ac

Otoritas Jasa Keuangan, 'Bank Umum [Banking]' (2017), www.ojk.go.id/id/kanal/perbankan/Pages/Bank-Umum.aspx#:~:text=Bank%20umum%20adalah%20bank%20yang,jasa%20dalam%20lalu%20lintas%20pembayaran

Otoritas Jasa Keuangan, *Financial System Stability Forum*, Otoritas Jasa Keuangan, www.ojk.go.id/en/kanal/perbankan/stabilitas-sistem-keuangan/Pages/Forum-SSK.aspx

Otoritas Jasa Keuangan, 'Snapshot Perbankan Syariah Desember 2020 [Snapshot of Indonesian Islamic Banking December 2020]' Otoritas Jasa Keuangan, www.ojk.go.id/id/kanal/syariah/berita-dan-kegiatan/publikasi/Pages/-Snapshot-Perbankan-Syariah-Desember-2020.aspx

Permatasari, Agustina, 'Kenapa Banyak Bank Syariah Belum "Go Public"? [Why There Aren't Many Islamic Banks "Go Public"?]', *Sharia News* (Jakarta), 10 July 2018, https://sharianews.com/posts/kenapa-banyak-bank-syariah-belum-go-public

Prabowo, Anto, 'OJK dukung upaya peningkatan adopsi standar IFSB [The FSA Supports the Effort of IFSB Standard Adoption]' (2018), www.ojk.go.id/id/berita-dan-kegiatan/siaran-pers/Pages/Siaran-Pers-OJK-Dukung-Upaya-Peningkatan-Adopsi-Standar-IFSB.aspx

Pricewaterhouse Coopers, 'Basel IV: Revised Trading and Banking Book Boundary for Market Risk' PricewaterhouseCoopers GmbH PwC, www.pwc.com/gx/en/advisory-services/basel-iv/toobox-booklet-basel-iv.pdf

Radwan, Saba, 'Islamic Banking: Why Transparency Matters', *Global Halal Investing Journal* (Malaysia), https://journal.wahedinvest.com/islamic-banking-why-transparency-matters/

Riduwan et al., 'The Problems of Mudarabah Financing Collateral in Islamic Rural Banks', *TEST, Engineering and Management* (Oakland), 14706–14712, www.researchgate.net/publication/342623464_The_Problems_of_Mudarabah_Financing_Collateral_in_Islamic_Rural_Banks

Sarwat, Ahmad, 'Bank Syariah Sama Saja Dengan Bank Konvensional, Benarkah? [Islamic Bank Is the Same as Conventional Bank, Really?]' *Konsultasi Fiqih*, https://rumahfiqih.com/konsultasi-1937-bank-syariah-sama-saja-dengan-bank-konvensional-benarkah.html

Segara, Tirta, 'Bank Indonesia Tuan Rumah IFSB Annual Meeting [Bank Indonesia Hosts the IFSB Annual Meeting]' (Pt Bank Indonesia) (2015) *Siaran Pers*, www.bi.go.id/id/ruang-media/siaran-pers/Pages/sp_172415.aspx

Shabsigh, Ghiath et al., 'Ensuring Financial Stability in Countries with Islamic Banking' (2017) 5 *International Monetary Fund*, www.imf.org/en/Publications/Policy-Papers/Issues/2017/02/21/PP-Ensuring-Financial-Stability-in-Countries-with-Islamic-Banking

Shahih Muslim, Book No.10, on The Book of Transactions, Hadith No 3676, https://sunnah.com/muslim:1534i

Sitepu, Mehulika, 'Yang Perlu Anda Ketahui dari Kasus BLBI Terbaru [What You Need to Know about the Latest BLBI Case]', *BBC Indonesia* (Jakarta), 27 April 2017, www.bbc.com/indonesia/indonesia-39724323

Syamsuddin, Muhammad, 'Dilema Transaksi Tawarruq Pada Lembaga Keuangan Syariah [Dilemma in Tawarruq Transaction in Islamic Financial Institutions]' (Pt NU Online) (2017), https://islam.nu.or.id/post/read/84388/dilema-transaksi-tawarruq-pada-lembaga-keuangan-syariah

US Securities and Exchange Commission, 'What Is Risk?' (Pt U.S. Securities and Exchange Commission), www.investor.gov/introduction-investing/investing-basics/what-risk

Utomo, Budi, 'Perjalanan Kasus BLBI 1998 Hingga 2019 [The Journey of the 1998 BLBI Case to 2019]', *Tagar* (Jakarta), www.tagar.id/perjalanan-kasus-blbi-1998-hingga-2019

Vazza, Agung, 'Indonesia, Country with High Tolerance', *Republika* (Jakarta), 14 June 2017, www.republika.co.id/berita/en/speak-out/17/06/14/orhxaq413-indonesia-country-with-high-tolerance

Index